PRAISE

INSIDEOUT ENNE/

THE GAME-CHANGING GUIDE FOR LEADERS

100% FRESH

By **Wendy Appel**

David Frigstad
Chairman, Frost & Sullivan
www.frost.com
USA

High-functioning teams in a global economy face complex challenges that require diverse skills and varied sources of motivation. To achieve that vital mix, a leader must have an in-depth understanding of behavior and performance in a wide range of industries, countries, and cultures. The Enneagram is an extraordinary system to build team resources uniquely designed to address complexity. Wendy Appel guides leaders to create and manage great teams through use of the Enneagram.

At Frost & Sullivan, a global consulting company helping clients achieve best practices in growth, innovation, and leadership, we thrive in a highly competitive global economy, thanks in no small part to Wendy, who coached us to make masterful use of Enneagram tools. Now she has made the tools available to those who can't work with her directly. This book provides a case study framework to engage the reader, and deep attention to detail to ensure that leaders and teams can learn to use precision tools to achieve a desired result.

I recommend InsideOut Enneagram to all business team leaders. Wendy's work as a coach, grounded in her international business experience, and her carefully structured guidance in this book provide a map for team success that I have not found elsewhere.

Lynne Sedgmore, CBE
CEO of the 157 Group of FE Colleges, UK
http://www.157group.co.uk/
United Kingdom

I have read many books on the Enneagram, and I must say, InsideOut Enneagram is one of the most powerful, useful, practical, and challenging interpretations I have read in a long time. As a practicing chief executive working with the complexities and fast pace of today's organisational life, this is one of the best leadership guides I have found to enable me to improve my leadership and organisational effectiveness. I highly recommend it to every CEO who wishes to maximise their potential and practice.

Eric Nicoli, CBE, chairman, R&R Music

Former chairman, EMI Group,

the Tussauds Group Ltd., and Vue Entertainment

United Kingdom

I am new to the principles of the Enneagram and excited, even at my advanced age, at the potential to up my game. Wendy's book is intriguing and compelling, and I will use it to unleash previously untapped inner resources in my ongoing personal quest to improve my management approach. InsideOut Enneagram is fresh, inviting, and real.

Mario Sikora

Executive leadership coach, consultant

President, International Enneagram Association (IEA)

Coauthor of Awareness to Action: The Enneagram,

Emotional Intelligence, and Change

www.mariosikora.com

USA

Wendy Appel's book brings together three lines of thought—the Enneagram, archetypal psychology, and brain studies—in an engaging and useful way. It is a worthy contribution to the effort of applying the Enneagram in the business world. Though specifically aimed at leaders, her book is chock-full of practical advice and exercises and will be useful for anyone who is seeking to grow from within.

Jane Perdue

Leadership and women's issues consultant,

speaker, and writer

Principal, Braithwaite Innovation Group

www.braithwaiteinnovationgroup.com

USA

Ever traveled to a new city and explored its riches and intricacies with a knowledgeable tour guide? It's totally positive. Wendy Appel offers that same rewarding experience in her new book, InsideOut Enneagram, for anyone on a journey to be a better leader.

Understanding one's self—strengths, weaknesses, blind spots, and shadows—is foundational for effectively leading others. The Enneagram is a beneficial tool for building that self-awareness. Wendy proves herself a master of helping us to use the Enneagram to plumb the heights and depths of our own Types and Triads.

Having trouble relating to or working with a direct report, colleague, or boss? The chapter on "Dynamics and Distinctions" is a not-to-be-missed workplace crystal ball of discovery and insights. Believe you are who you are and can't change? Wendy details the latest in brain science to dispel that myth and encourage you to spread your wings and jump off the cliff of self-discovery.

Years ago I had a boss who wouldn't let me include the Enneagram in a three-day leadership development off-site for the senior team, saying it was too "woo-woo." Too bad I didn't have this book to give him, because it is full of practical workplace examples and case studies. There's plenty of content for those who respond to logic as well as those who relate to emotions.

It requires courage to take that journey within. With Wendy's material and self-reflection exercises, you're in the hands of a very capable guide. Be prepared to think, face the truth, and have an uncomfortable moment or two. The new you that results will be well worth it.

The Enneagram has been a companion and aid in my life for over a decade, and I use it extensively in personal relationships and in a professional capacity. Wendy Appel's book is one of the freshest new contributions I have read on the topic, and provides an invaluable tool for leaders who want to better understand themselves and others. Part overview, part leadership manual, part personal journal, it provides a perfect introduction to this powerful profiling tool. This is more than a book—it is a guide for a journey that will transform your life.

Dr. Graeme Codrington

Author, futurist, speaker

http://www.tomorrowtoday.uk.com

South Africa and United Kingdom

InsideOut Enneagram is an inspirational, insightful, and practical guidebook. It is an invaluable resource for anyone, in any profession, of any age, who wants to be more consciously self-aware of how to become more effective, personally and professionally, in all aspects of one's life. Engaging, relevant, usable, and an excellent synthesis of how human gifts and talents can be used most effectively and creatively!

Angeles Arrien, PhD

Cultural anthropologist

Author of The Four-Fold Way and

The Second Half of Life

www.angelesarrien.com

USA

InsideOut Enneagram is pithy and sharp. Wendy has done a brilliant job of connecting the Enneagram to present-day challenges that leaders face. This book will entice you to embark on a hero's journey of self-discovery to authentic and inspiring leadership. She makes this journey accessible and enjoyable through her skillful, practical use of the Enneagram with helpful tools and exercises to guide and support. InsideOut is a leadership skill. By developing yourself, you'll improve your ability to mobilize others. I am excited to have started my own journey.

Val Harding, PhD

Vice president, Pfizer Inc.

USA

Vincent Schneider
Chief human resource officer, Audemars Piguet SA
Switzerland

Wendy has written an engaging read that taps into veins of gold I hadn't realized were there. InsideOut Enneagram provides wonderful insights into the power and wisdom of the Enneagram. It has the key to unlock the true potential of international teams facing cross-cultural challenges. The Enneagram is a highly intuitive system and adds a comprehensive dimension of understanding to build better teams and better leaders. We live in turbulent times, and I am now better equipped to stay centered in the face of what lies ahead. Be bold, be brave, buy this book, and enjoy what it helps you uncover.

Harriet Moss
Former CEO, Antenna Audio; founder, Stinson/
Bolinas Community Fund and West Marin Fund;
media consultant
USA

InsideOut Enneagram is a fascinating, entertaining read that weaves together the ancient system of the Enneagram with modern knowledge about brain science and psychology. As a student of the Enneagram for the past 25 years, I found InsideOut to be one of the best, most accessible and practical books on the subject I've seen. A must-read!

Judi Neal, PhD
Director, Tyson Center for Spirituality
in the Workplace
Author of Edgewalkers
www.judineal.com
USA

InsideOut Enneagram is a wonderful integration of wisdom and practicality that can guide you on your journey to your true self. Blending science, psychology, myth, and ancient spiritual wisdom, Wendy Appel has provided you with a self-directed workshop in a book. This book is a journey worth taking!

Elisabet Sahtouris, PhD
Evolution biologist and futurist
Author of Earth Dance: Living Systems in Evolution
www.sahtouris.com
Spain

Discovering the unique leader already available within you and polishing that gem through the understanding that this book reveals may be the most valuable, as well as the most enjoyable, journey you've ever taken. In times of great crises, nothing is more needed than good leadership—all we can get! There are countless books reporting it and training it, but I've never seen one more fascinating and fun.

In this astonishing book, Wendy brings the Enneagram's ancient wisdom to leadership and to life. Filled with case studies, exercises, and guidance for each of the Enneagram styles, InsideOut Enneagram is a rich resource sure to draw you in time and again. Wendy's unique Enneagram Typing Cards make it vivid and personal. An extremely practical and engaging approach!

Michael J. Goldberg, JD
Author of The 9 Ways of Working and
Travels with Odysseus
www.9waysofworking.com
USA

This book is a must for leaders, coaches, consultants, or trainers. Indeed, it is the most useful book I have ever read on the Enneagram and its application to leadership; it explains the philosophy behind this centuries-old symbol and takes the new-world Enneagram on a journey that bridges business life and interpersonal relationships. These are explained in the most visual way by many useful examples. And it doesn't stop there. InsideOut Enneagram offers tools for the reader to use and practice.

Sylviane Cannio
Master certified coach, speaker, and former
vice president, International Coach Federation
Author of Communiquer Avec Authenticité et
Rester Vrai (Conscious Communications)
www.canniocoaching.org
Belgium

With many books about the Enneagram on the market, it's important to know what distinguishes InsideOut Enneagram. First, Wendy Appel is a terrific writer—you will be drawn in quickly and compelled to read more. She's also an excellent teacher whose descriptions, graphics, metaphors, case studies, and typing cards give flavor, variety, and depth to her comprehensive treatment of the Enneagram. Most important, you'll have ample opportunity to apply the concepts she covers, for greater understanding and self-awareness. To read InsideOut and follow the exercises is to begin the journey toward transforming yourself. Be prepared for an adventure!

Mary Bast
Coach and mentor
Coauthor of Out of the Box:
Coaching with the Enneagram
www.breakoutofthebox.com
USA

How can I be an effective leader without self-insight and a capacity to inspire and empower others? InsideOut Enneagram provides a comprehensive understanding of how I can use the Enneagram to see myself more clearly—my drivers, tendencies, fears, and strengths—as well as to gain insight into others, all crucial to developing myself as a business leader and fellow human being. I just have to be daring and look inside.

Ellen Johanne Munkvold
Senior country manager, Halliburton
Norway

Wendy Bartlett
Managing Director, Bartlett Mitchell
http://www.bartlettmitchell.co.uk
United Kingdom

At this turbulent time it is important to maximise your main assets; your team, their strengths and what they can deliver. Any tool that gives you an edge is worth your investment. InsideOut Enneagram gets my vote.

Ian Berry
Change master
Author of Changing What's Normal
www.changingwhatsnormal.com
Australia

From the moment I read, "The Enneagram is like the yellow brick road," this book had me hooked! Wendy has taken a leadership development tool that probably originated in 750 BC and made it 21st century. All change is personal first, or inside out, as Wendy describes it. By taking this book to your heart, you will change what's normal in your life, and your world will be the better for it.

Christine Cavanaugh-Simmons
Executive coach and consultant
CCS Consulting, Inc.
USA

Was InsideOut Enneagram worth the read? Absolutely! Wendy has been able to write a book on the Enneagram that is valuable for someone completely new to the Enneagram as well as for the longtime Enneagram practitioner. Her guidance is practical and accessible, and long-time practitioners will discover delightful new insights in every chapter. I can see myself handing this to every new leader I work with, whether for individual coaching or team development.

John Renesch
Futurist
Author of The Great Growing Up and
Getting to the Better Future
www.renesch.com
USA

InsideOut Enneagram is an adventure in self-awareness—learning more about ourselves so we can be better leaders, better coworkers, and better people. This is the kind of book the world needs, for in this fractured world, we need leaders who are self-actualized. This book looks certain to create a shift in those who read and practice.

Leadership is a mysterious and dynamic process. Through the lens of the Enneagram, this book offers a rich and beautifully laid-out approach to the process of understanding behavioral tendencies and inner workings of the complex world of leading and being led.

Wendy Palmer
Author of The Intuitive Body and
The Practice of Freedom
www.consciousembodiment.com
USA

Wendy has creatively integrated the great wisdom the Enneagram provides with her sound and genuine perspectives and expertise in leadership and personal development. There is "a leader in all of us," and this book provides a unique way of exploring this and building capability and confidence as a result.

Gayle Hardie and Malcolm Lazenby
Cofounders, Global Leadership Foundation
www.globalleadershipfoundation.com
Australia

How the mix of personalities blend together to get work done (or not get work done) is of paramount importance when it comes to executing change. Wendy Appel is one of the world's foremost experts on the Enneagram, a solid tool that can help change leaders and change agents understand what makes their people tick. The wisdom found in InsideOut Enneagram will make you more effective in nearly any setting that requires humans to interact.

Steve Chihos
Change leader—theBigRocks, LLC
Blog for change agents: www.theBigRocks.com
USA

It takes courage to actively seek change. It takes clarity to see what change can bring. It takes time, commitment, and wisdom to change from within before speaking out. Wendy shares the power of ancient wisdom for modern times in this valuable, practical companion as you change the way you lead in business and in life! Indeed, this book is helping me re-point my internal compass as I consider my own path Beyond the Summit.

Julie Lewis
Mountaineer, speaker, retreat leader
www.mountainhighme.com
Hong Kong

INSIDE**OUT**
ENNEAGRAM

Copyright © 2011 by Wendy Appel

ISBN 978-0-9848842-0-9

All rights reserved.

Description of 'Basic Centering Practice,' by Wendy Palmer, is included by permission of Wendy Palmer, copyright 2011.

"Carl C. Jung's Process of Individuation" by Dr. Sandra Emma Shelley
is included by permission of Dr. Sandra Emma Shelley, 2011.

No part of this publication may be reproduced in any form or by
any electronic or mechanical means, including information storage
and retrieval systems, without permission in writing from both the
copyright owner and the publisher, except by a reviewer, who may
quote brief passages in a review.

Developmental Editor: Ann Matranga

Copy Editor: Elissa Rabellino

Interior Design and Cover Design: Ceci Sorochin

Palma Publishing
San Rafael, California

Visit www.WendyAppel.com The Enneagram Source for more information about workshops, coaching, and consulting.

InsideOut Enneagram: The Game-Changing Guide for Leaders, is a
companion guidebook to the Enneagram Typing Cards.

Printed in the United States of America
First Printing, February 2012

10 9 8 7 6 5 4 3 2 1

INSIDE**OUT**
ENNEAGRAM

The Game-Changing
Guide for Leaders

100% Fresh

WENDY**APPEL**

TABLE OF **CONTENTS**

FOREWORD

Lynne Sedgmore, CBE
CEO, 157 Group
London, UK

I have been a CEO in three different organisations over the past 13 years. Times have never been more complex or uncertain than today, with ever-growing fiscal requirements to deliver more with fewer resources.

Leadership steeped in good communication is a critical component of success. We need strong relationships based on mutual respect to further our ability to work together on innovative solutions. I believe that to gain a competitive edge, diversity is essential. Leaders who can see the organization through multiple perspectives are more effective and dynamic performers, and at the same time find their own leadership position to be more authentic and satisfying.

I have explored numerous ways to support and develop my staff through the ever-increasing demands placed upon them, and to find ways to assist them in seeing, valuing, and harnessing their diversity. The Enneagram has been the most effective way I have found to accomplish this.

In each of my CEO roles, I have invited staff to work voluntarily with the Enneagram as a tool to understand themselves and their contribution to the organisation. During this time, nearly 100 staff members have engaged and worked with the Enneagram, assisted by external Enneagram facilitators.

Several of my teams have moved from mediocrity to high performance through a process that included seeing and understanding their Type and that of their team members. Their grasp of collective and individual strengths and weaknesses allowed them to move through conflicts and being stuck. Instead of personalising issues that came up, they created synergy.

The Enneagram allowed many individuals to understand their motivations and deep desires. For some, this meant leaving the organisation with the strength to move into new pastures.

Through work with the Enneagram, staff members have been able to grasp differences, and recognise, understand, and accept those differences as positive traits, letting go of judgments and avoidance behaviours. I love nothing more than the moment when someone "gets" their own Type and moves beyond resistance into liberation and power.

As a social Type 8, I have learnt why people feared my strong energy, drive, forthrightness, and speedy action. I understand why my straight talking can be experienced as overly forceful, even rude or aggressive at times.

Over the years, I have learnt to see and let go of "always being right" and my need to find someone to blame. I learnt to see different sides of an issue and allowed my vulnerability to surface and be seen, and to ask questions rather than jump too quickly to gutsy solutions. I am more allowing and more responsive, and have discovered a capacity to listen as well as to talk.

All three of the organisations I led had very high levels of staff satisfaction, outstanding performance, significant financial success, and highly satisfied and successful customers. I attribute a large part of this to our work with the Enneagram in each organisation.

Having studied the Enneagram for nearly 20 years, I did not believe I could find another Enneagram book from which, as a practising leader and CEO, I could learn so much more. Yet, here it is—just what I was looking for.

This exquisite book takes the reader on a rich, multifaceted, and profound Enneagram journey. It is clearly a labour of love—written by a successful leader and coach who has travelled a remarkable inner, and outer, journey.

Wendy enables and encourages readers to take their own leadership journey of inner development using the Enneagram as a powerful guide.

Her invitation is both simple and profound—to undertake the inner journey, with herself and the Enneagram as wise guides, and to discover "your inner solid ground" and apply "your vibrant best" to find true satisfaction while you make the world a better place.

Her understanding of the Enneagram is utterly profound. She writes, unusually, in the first person, providing deep insight into each of the Types.

Her personalised style of writing brings the Types alive as living complex people, rather than theoretical typologies.

Wendy's unique approach illustrates use of the Enneagram in life and in the workplace, including detailed case studies and a structured journaling process.

The journaling process and reflection questions take the reader through nuances and complexities including Wings, Connecting Points, Subtypes and relationships between Types.

Wendy brings new insights from neuroscience, and she integrates the Enneagram with other tools used in business settings, such as the Johari Window, the Myers-Briggs Type Indicator, and emotional intelligence and social intelligence concepts.

Some leaders may feel that the Enneagram is too complex and will take too much time and energy to grasp and implement. However, Wendy provides a clear guide and step-by-step process to walk the journey with solid steppingstones. She simplifies complexity.

I recommend this book and hope you enjoy it and learn from it as much as I have.

....

To bring alive my experience using the Enneagram in a professional context, how I brought it into my organisation, and the results of our investment, I share the following case study.

 CASE STUDY

WHAT WAS THE SITUATION?

Over a period of weeks, an individual member of staff, a senior manager, was struggling to compose herself in meetings and with colleagues. She had walked out of an interview for a promotion and was in conflict with several of her peers and with me, her line manager. Whatever we did, she seemed unable to respond and was in severe danger of being disciplined. Although she could be a prima donna at times, she had never behaved this way before to the extent that her work and role were at risk. Support, challenge, and discussion seemed to be of no avail. She was derailing but was unable to see it herself. It had become apparent at board level, so I knew that I had to intervene.

What was going on in your organization that you wanted to change or transform?

I wanted the senior manager to see that her shadow (her unconscious and habitual reactive patterns) was leaking out in the workplace, affecting her work, her relationships, and perceptions of her, and I wanted to assist her to return to balance, right relationship, and her high performing self. This was not a case of incompetence or the need for skill development.

Why did you choose the Enneagram as part of your intervention?

I felt the Enneagram would give me deep insight into what was going on for her, particularly in working with her shadow. I used Enneagram methods to clarify that she was probably a Type 2 and planned an intervention. Prepared with the knowledge of my own predispositions as a Type 8, I went into her office and approached her in an open and transparent manner, inside her space, not mine, and invited her to work with me, in confidence, to assist her.

My tone was gentle and calm. I explained that I thought she needed space and time to explore a map that could help us both. I listed all the things I had done that may not have helped her, and said that I was at a loss but was open to doing whatever it took to make things better because I valued her so much.

I spent considerable time explaining how valuable she was in the organisation. To my immense relief, she was able to trust me and was prepared to learn about the Enneagram, and she admitted that she was in pain and confusion. It mattered to her that I had come to her, in her space, and not called her into my office.

How did you use the Enneagram?

We read the same book on the Enneagram and shared our Types. She identified as a Type 2. We explored every aspect, and looked at why and how our Types were clashing, along with her fixations and how she could transform. She asked me to give her feedback about her behaviour and she could see the patterns of her Type. She began to talk with other members of the team and opened authentic conversations with them, which instigated a broader awareness and interest in the Enneagram.

What were the results?

To her credit, she began to make improvements within the first three weeks and soon began to reflect skilfully on her behaviours and reactions. The main message she fed back to me was that she stopped feeling "so awful" when she could see herself as a Type in the Enneagram context, and could share who and what she was with others. She was able to see perspectives other than her own. She felt that she had a map to do things differently. Within six weeks she was performing well, beyond her previous performance before all the issues had begun. Her relationships were better than they had ever been.

There was another result. The chairman and board were impressed that she and I had been able to resolve such a "difficult situation," and they agreed to fund me to train and certify in the Enneagram to use it more broadly across the organisation. They said that, "the changes were in the realm of the miraculous."

The whole of my senior management team decided to work with the Enneagram to depersonalise conflicts and difficult issues. We undertook a programme of training in the Enneagram that enabled us to work even more effectively as a senior management team, drawing on the aspects of our Types to "call" difficult behaviours. When we worked with others, they often commented on our "numbers language"—the reference to our different Types—and noticed that it seemed to help us gain clarity when tensions arose.

I brought an external Enneagram facilitator to a two-day session that 30 staff members attended by invitation. Several of them formed a Quality team to understand their Types. They moved from mediocre to high-level performance in six months. They had a large chart of their Types on their staff room wall, and when asked how they had changed so much, they explained that they now understood each other much better.

For example, some of them had been "irritated" by a team member. When they saw a video of her Type, they understood the contribution she could make and reorganised team roles to utilize her positive reflection and her analytical and questioning skills.

The Enneagram allowed us to see the blind spots of the team, composed of two Type 8s, two Type 1s, and one Type 3. We were moving too fast with insufficient reflection. Feedback from our staff of 1,000 let us know that there was too much action, and too many changes emanated from the "top." To change our collective style, we did the following:

→ Introduced a pace and space charter, which encouraged a slower pace and more space for reflection

→ Brought a Type 5 onto the team—someone with reflective, different skills who challenged us

→ Worked together on a management charter to articulate rights and responsibilities—that is, what we offered to staff and what we expected in return

→ Opened dialogue with Types not on our team to understand the impact we were having on others

Our work led to meetings where different perspectives were raised and debated. Staff members who were aware of their Type used them as points of reference and understanding.

When I left and a new CEO came in, he learned the Enneagram because it had become an essential part of the organisation's leadership culture.

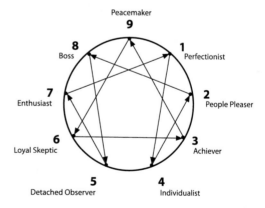

To

Shayna and Bear, my beloved,

devoted, and trusted

companions.

Thank you for teaching me

the power of love and commitment.

🖤

PREFACE

Life is a journey, not a destination. As young people, we set out with an eye on the horizon, looking forward to all that's ahead. At some point, we find ourselves in the middle of our lives, in the middle of a career. We wonder, "Is this it? Is this a life I chose, or did I sleepwalk into it? Am I happy? Is there more to do? Why am I bored? Why do I feel unsettled? Why do I continue to have the same issues with different people?" Or "My life is a mess—how did this happen? My career just fell apart—where did I go wrong? Am I a good enough leader, wife, husband, father, mother, writer, plumber, friend, boss, worker, sculptor, actor, teacher … ?"

Be kind, for everyone you meet is fighting a great battle.

—Philo of Alexandria

If you are asking yourself similar questions, this book was written for you. Perhaps you are called to the threshold of an unexplored world. Instead, you may jump away and get busy to avoid vexing questions, but the voice will get louder and the tug will be stronger. Until, if you're lucky, you run into …

… the adventure of a hero— the adventure of being alive.

—Joseph Campbell and Bill Moyers, *The Power of Myth*[1]

Every year of my childhood, I waited for *The Wizard of Oz* to appear on television. I loved the story and the characters. Perhaps I felt a special bond with Dorothy because she was a young girl from the Midwest like me. She went on a magical adventure and met strange and mysterious folk. Dorothy showed great courage when she found her way through an unknown land to the castle of the Wicked Witch of the West and stole her broom.

Each year, I was surprised by the end of the movie. In my imagination there was another version, where Dorothy's family admitted that they had been to Oz, too. It was obvious to me that the tornado carried the mean woman on a bicycle who captured Toto, as well as all of Dorothy's relatives, to the land of Oz. I could never figure out why, when Dorothy woke up with them standing around her, they wouldn't admit that they had been with her all along.

I loved the music and memorized the lyrics so that I could sing along. "Somewhere over the rainbow … the dreams that you dare to dream really do come true." That song expressed my longing to be somewhere other than where I was. I longed to have an adventure, to explore the world, to meet people from far away, and I was restless at home.

Roll the tape forward to 1993. I was at a retreat center near Prescott, Arizona, going to my first personal development workshop. I had no idea what was in store for me, nor did I know anyone else who was attending. I was the first to arrive.

The retreat center was situated on 40 acres of Anasazi ancestral land with vestiges of ancient tribal structures. Like an animal, I want time to sense my surroundings in a new place. A dog that lived at the center chose to accompany me on my exploration, and I was happy to have her to keep me company. I love dogs to begin with, and beyond that, she brought my grandparents to mind.

As a child, I took long walks with my grandparents when they came to visit or we stayed with them in New Jersey. They had a morning routine—an early wake-up, a two-mile walk, and calisthenics, as working out was then called. At our house, Grandma and Grandpa installed a chin-up bar, a slant board, dumbbells, a device to build chest muscles that had two handgrips and three parallel springs, and something you squeezed with your hands to build muscles in your hands and arms. This replicated the equipment they had in their own home. The slant board was mostly for sit-ups, but we also used it to throw our leg over our head. The day began with all of us doing headstands against the wall and singing "God Bless America." They had a habit of singing while they walked that I adopted as my own and continue to this day. There are two songs they loved that I can recall clearly: "I'm Forever Blowing Bubbles" and Irving Berlin's "It's a Lovely Day Today." My grandparents had a *can-do* attitude that I strive to imitate, along with their walks, calisthenics, and songs. "I can't" wasn't part of their vocabulary.

"Somewhere Over the Rainbow" was on my mind as I wandered the land at the retreat center. I sang it over and over to get the right pitch, and I thought about the meaning. I hoped that the retreat would bring some much-needed clarity and direction in a time of transition. It was not lost on me that Toto was beside me.

At the time, I had a marriage proposal on the table, and I was changing my career. The type of work I had been doing, while remunerative, was no longer satisfying, and I was unwilling to invest my energy in it anymore. I wanted to make the world a better place. But what could I do? Where was the intersection of my ability and my passion? I taped a quote to my computer:

My object in living is to unite My avocation and my vocation

—Robert Frost, "Two Tramps in Mud Time"[2]

Toto and I arrived at Anasazi ruins overlooking the vast high desert landscape, stunning, serene, silent. There was only the sound of the wind and the whoosh of a bird of prey overhead. I took the same walk during our afternoon breaks throughout the course of the retreat, singing all the way.

Up until this point in my life, I had been a *businesswoman*, a *professional*; and personal growth workshops were not part of my experience. This was eye-opening. I was riveted by the magic of what was happening in our group—the connection, openness, revelations. We were strangers to one another, a diverse group. Today, I am still in contact with several of the members from that initiatory retreat.

During the first couple of days, I found myself mostly observing, too frozen with fear to speak out much. Slowly I found my voice and began to engage. Through some wisdom and feedback imparted to us, and time for reflection, I had profound insights. On day four, I popped into the administrator's office and signed up for the next retreat in six months' time, only this would be a 12-day workshop instead of 6! I was hooked.

When the retreat came to an end, we shared one last meal and said our good-byes. I'm great with beginnings but have a hard time with endings. As I was hugging Valerie, whom I had chosen to play the role of my *heart* in one of our activities, I had an epiphany. As she held me, I realized with the force of a lightning bolt that *The Wizard of Oz* was a teaching story—a tale of the heroine's journey.

Until that moment, the archetypal nature of the story had been lost on me. Dorothy went over the rainbow to reclaim and integrate unknown or unacknowledged parts of herself. I finally *got* the metaphor. It was as if everything went from black and white to brilliant color—like the transition in the movie when Dorothy landed in Oz. As the Tin Man journeyed with Dorothy to find his heart, I went to the Arizona high desert and journeyed with Valerie to reconnect with mine. She was the perfect person to give voice to my heart's desire, and the imprint of her warm, soft, engulfing embrace remains with me today.

The Enneagram is like the yellow brick road, a template for an important journey to the inner world. This book can serve as a companion on a *hero's journey*—a journey of individuation to wholeness, and perhaps the adventure of a lifetime.

INTRODUCTION

In a verdant valley rich with orchards and layered with olive terraces, watched over by the Traumuntana Mountains, I sat still for months while I wrote this book. I was caught by the muse and at the same time touched, disturbed, and inspired by an unfolding multitude of world events that often had catastrophic consequences. As I sat cradled in the Sóller Valley, *InsideOut* took shape.

The book has been a labor of love, passion, and purpose. Walking through the olive terraces, I wondered, "Where is the intersection of my experience, gifts, and passion—the thread or theme that brings together work I've done, my special abilities, and the things I love to do most?" One word surfaced: *leadership*.

People say we have "a crisis of leadership," but I believe it is a world spiritual crisis and a crisis of courage.

It takes courage to act decisively in the face of the ambiguous and the unknown; to go against prevailing group-think, cultural conditioning; to transform systems that are broken; and to look within and ask, "How do I contribute to and perpetuate problems we face?" It takes courage to examine deeply held beliefs.

The lemon on the cover, while not obvious at first, is a metaphor for inner alchemy. Like making lemonade out of lemons, you will transform what may seem like inner obstacles into gifts that you offer to the world. We need leaders who bring out the juice, tart though it may be. Most of us recognize people who are juicy in the way that lemons are. We describe them as vibrant, awake, aware, full of life. People pucker their lips, blink in surprise, feel their energy.

This book is an invitation to squeeze that lemon with courage and bring out your tart, vibrant best in the interest of your family, your organization, and your society.

THE CHALLENGES THAT LEADERS FACE TODAY

We live in a complex and fast-changing world. The globalization of markets and people, bound together by social networking, 24/7 news, low-cost air travel, and speedy Internet connectivity, has accelerated in recent years. Our global interdependence means we share concerns about financial markets, leaking nuclear plants in Japan, volcanoes that erupt in Iceland, floods in Australia, earthquakes in Haiti, revolutions in the Middle East, and disappearing polar icecaps.

Globalization has made us financially and ethically interdependent, and culture clash is on the rise. When a global company based in the United States does business in Russia, China, Brazil, and Indonesia, whose ethics and business standards prevail? Can Germany and France impose their culture on Greece? When a product is deemed unsafe in the home country, is it ethical to sell it in another country without safety standards? How do we find our inner compass—the courage and the will to speak and act with integrity?

Many of us work on cross-cultural and international teams, get to know team members rapidly in a virtual online environment, and work collaboratively without ever physically being in the same room. Relationships span time zones, generations, and cultures.

Leadership values and behavior affect large numbers of people who need to align with one another. Organizations today maintain extensive, interconnected employee networks. A leader's success depends on developing, managing, and maintaining relationships inside and outside of the organization.

Those who were once trusted public figures—government leaders, sports stars, corporate CEOs—have lost public confidence in recent years. Cynicism escalates with every ethical breach, war, economic crisis, and environmental crisis. When trust is gone, what is left?

Each of us has to look to ourselves. Although we may have little control over events, this is no time to say "I can't"—as my grandparents would have asserted. We can take control of our own behavior and the way we lead our organizations and our lives.

HOW CAN *INSIDEOUT* HELP YOU TO SUCCESSFULLY LEAD IN TODAY'S WORLD?

Faced with ambiguity, rapid shifts, and unpredictable occurrences, do you ever ask yourself, "Where is my solid ground?" *InsideOut* suggests that it is *inside* of you. The more solid you are, the more confidence you'll have in your ability to weather storms and adapt to change with agility.

Most of us focus our attention outward and neglect our inner life. We think that change is *out there*. Instead of tuning in to the language of our head, heart, and gut, we are busy looking outside, ahead, and down.

We rearrange our organization's structures—shift from centralized to decentralized, hierarchical to matrix, business units to in-country organizations. We downsize and rightsize. We think other people need fixing. "If they would just [fill in the blank], we'd be able to successfully execute the strategy."

> **Solving problems is important. But if learning is to persist, managers and employees must also look inward. They need to reflect critically on their own behavior, identify the ways they often inadvertently contribute to the organization's problems, and then change how they act.**[3]

If you didn't have the power and authority of your position, would people want to work with you or follow you? Do you engage others in your vision and mobilize them to implement a strategy? Do you bring out the best in others and inspire them to high levels of achievement? These are some of the questions that the best leaders ask.

In order to engage and mobilize others, we need *engaged leadership*. There is a call for more thoughtful, empathic, sophisticated, and wise leadership—leaders who are willing to think differently. They ask different questions of themselves, of their colleagues, and of their organizations. They listen deeply to answers and explore multiple perspectives.

Robert Cooper conveyed it best when he wrote:

> **Human greatness cannot be bought or controlled. It can only be invited. By example and through genuine inspiration and compelling influence, exceptional leaders help ordinary people accomplish extraordinary results. To do this, they must develop and apply an energizing, authentic level**

of intelligence and bring it to everything they do, combining the perceptions and impressions of the gut, heart, and mind.[4]

InsideOut uses the Enneagram to shine light on your natural strengths, your challenges, and the mostly subterranean habits of mind and motivations that drive you and others. *InsideOut* turns theory into practice with examples. You won't get a boilerplate set of instructions to build leadership skills. Instead, you'll learn how to find your own instructions and next steps. This book will guide you to change the way you see and think.

Good business is built on a healthy relationship with yourself and stronger relationships with others. When you bring out your best, you evoke that in others. Squeeze that lemon!

 AN INSIDEOUT LEADER'S STORY

Woven throughout this book is the story of a client who used the Enneagram to deal with significant challenges he faced in his new executive role. We'll get to know a character named Lars and learn about his company, New Horizon Health (NHH). We'll follow Lars's leadership journey and learn how the Enneagram helped him to understand how he created his own problems, and how he found his strengths.

Lars's story is not unique. As a consultant and coach, I have worked with numerous leaders in many organizations and witnessed similar stories play out time and again. While the character's name and the name of his organization are fictional, the fundamentals are true.

With each successive chapter, you'll learn more about Lars's challenges, the problems he created for himself and his team, how he managed to resolve some of them, and what he learned.

➔ Lars's story starts on p. 43

CHAPTER 1:

THE LEADERSHIP JOURNEY

Imagine for a moment that you are traveling around the world on a boat, and you have no navigation or sonar system. Often we can see what is immediately in front of us and navigate the exigencies of the moment. If we hit an iceberg or some other object beneath the surface, it's because we didn't see it or anticipate it; we have no way to know what is lurking there. We take on water, bail, and try to patch things up in order to keep moving forward.

This is how most of us live, day to day. The conscious mind deals with the immediate demands of daily life, and the subconscious mind, below the waterline, determines our course. We just do what we do and keep moving forward, or turn off our engines and drift.

What if you could install a navigation and sonar system? You would have to invest time to learn how to use it and to practice navigation skills. What would you gain? Your gains might include insight into where to go and how to get there, the ability to spot and avoid obstacles, and the ability to take passengers on a voyage and give them a feeling of safety. You would know how to chart an expedient route, and you wouldn't be operating in the dark—as much. You could choose your destinations, and—sometimes—you could see trouble ahead, stop drifting, and consciously choose a different route.

I believe she was swept along on a tide, like most of us. There you are, diligently swimming a straight line, minding the form of your strokes, when you look up and see, always a shock, that currents you can't even feel have pulled you off course.

—Julia Glass, *I See You Everywhere*[5]

LEADING FROM THE INSIDEOUT

What lies behind us and what lies before us are tiny matters compared to what lies within us.

—Henry Stanley Haskins, *Meditations in Wall Street* (1940)[6]

The subconscious mind, where our habits, patterns, and beliefs reside, directs the course of our lives, and most of us are unaware that this is happening. To transform as leaders and to transform our organizations require that we examine our core beliefs—both individual and collective. If not, we simply make iterative changes, and that won't be enough to succeed in today's globalized economy.

The Enneagram gives you the possibility to transform the way you show up as a leader. Inner change leads to outer change—when your inner world transforms, an opening is created for extraordinary shifts to occur in your outer world. When you *lead from the InsideOut*, you have the ability to be responsive and flexible enough to act in the moment. Your words and actions are aligned. You take responsibility for creating your life and for leading with integrity and passion.

InsideOut is a reminder that we are not distinct from the outside world. It is part of us and we are part of it. What we enact in our outer world inevitably affects us, and vice versa.

PERHAPS *INSIDEOUT* IS THE BOOK THAT WILL CRACK YOUR WORLD-VIEW WIDE OPEN.

InsideOut will decode the Enneagram for you and open the door to a more intimate relationship with yourself. It will help you to drop your defenses and allow the best of you to emerge—to be the leader that others trust and someone they are inspired to follow. When you work with the Enneagram, it could just give you that extra edge you've been looking for to take your leadership to the next level.

Life is not going back to "normal." Since the economic crisis that began in 2008, many have been waiting. Normal is not coming. It's up to each of us to change—to transform our inner selves and our systems. We have a choice and we have a chance. This is a time for courage. As Gandhi said, "Be the change you want to see." I'll add to that: Be the change you want to *lead*.

EXEMPLAR: RAY C. ANDERSON

I don't know if Ray C. Anderson knew about the Enneagram, but nonetheless he was willing to examine his worldview and make radical changes in his life and his business. Anderson was chairman and chief executive of the world's largest carpet-tile manufacturer when he read a book that described people like him as thieves and plunderers of the planet. He said that reading it was a "spear in the chest experience." He saw the author's point. He even wept. Then he set out to change things. He changed his beliefs, transformed his definition of success, and transformed his business.

According to his obituary in the *New York Times*, "Starting in the early 1970s, Mr. Anderson built a company based in Atlanta, Interface Inc., into a $1.1 billion a year concern manufacturing carpet, fabric and upholstery used in offices and commercial buildings." Anderson "re-invented his worldwide factory operation to reduce its environmental impact and became one of the nation's most effective corporate advocates for environmental sustainability. ... 'What started out as the right thing to do quickly became the smart thing,' he told a business group in Toronto in 2005. 'Cost savings from eliminating waste alone have been $262 million.'"[6]

TO START

Your first step on the path is to find your Enneagram Type. Chapter 6, "The Sorting Process," will walk you through a carefully designed process to identify your Enneagram Type. The *Enneagram Typing Cards,* along with *InsideOut,* will allow you to see all nine Types at once, move the cards around to understand different patterns and constellations, and refer to a condensed description and explanation for each Type. As you become familiar with the Enneagram, you will start to see yourself more clearly. You may notice that you have been drifting—going along with things as they are, rather than making needed change—and you may begin to identify shifts that you want to make.

InsideOut is a hybrid: part reference book, part workbook, part journal. Type-related questions and practices are designed to help you work with the special challenges for your Enneagram Type. In the journal section, you will explore your life thus far and build ideas for new chapters.

The Enneagram is a map and a compass for the most important journey of your life. The journey of each of us includes timing, pace, and destiny. No one can tell you exactly how to get where you're going or how long it will take, but a trusted guide—a coach or another professional—can hold the mirror for you to see yourself clearly. A competent guide will often ask questions you may not think of or may be unwilling to ask yourself.

This book was designed with leaders, managers, coaches, consultants, and counselors in mind. It is also meant for anyone who wants to live more fully, with joy, love, strength, courage, and success.

Approach this book as you would approach a journal or workbook. Tap into it when you need to explore your thoughts and feelings; when you have a question or a revelation, or you need some insight into a situation at work or at home.

Enjoy the learning process, and use the Enneagram as though you were spiraling inward. As you take each turn, a place where you have been before will look and feel different, and you'll feel different. Your connection to self and others will deepen over time as you learn to shift, rather than drift, toward a resourceful and harmonious life, and to lead from your best self. Many good wishes as you embark on your journey.

HOW TO USE THIS GUIDE

InsideOut will help you find your Enneagram Type by guiding you through a process of self-discovery. Discovering your Enneagram Type is an art, not a science. Your ability to make the discovery depends on how well you know *why* you do what you do. It is best to discover your Type by using this guide on your own or with a skilled Enneagram practitioner.

It is important for you to *discover* your Type, and not for someone to tell you "the answer." Why? Because there are many look-alike Types that share common behaviors in the eyes of an outside observer. Beliefs and motivations that drive the person's behavior distinguish one Type from another—and only you know why you do what you do. If you let someone tell you your Type, you miss out on the self-reflection and self-discovery that are key parts of your journey. Equally important, an observer may be wrong about your Type and send you on a time-consuming detour.

Once you claim your Enneagram Type, you will learn more in a section that describes the inner landscape of the nine Types. You will also find Type-specific exercises to use over an extended period of time. The exercises will help you understand how your Type influences the way you live. You'll learn how to put your hands on the controls, take the plane off automatic pilot, and become a navigator.

InsideOut follows a logical sequence, and *guideposts* ✻ help you to move to the next section or jump to a related section, depending on whether you have identified your Type or want more information on some of the Type distinctions.

InsideOut is divided into six parts:

➔ **PART 1: The Framework.** This section demonstrates the value of the Enneagram for you and your organization. The Enneagram system is described and explained.

➔ **PART 2: The Journey.** It takes you on the leader's journey, helping you to identify where you are in your own life story and the journeys of all nine Enneagram Types.

➔ **PART 3: Discover Your Enneagram Type.** You will be guided through a process of self-discovery to find your *best fit* Type. I use the Triad lenses to help you find your Type by understanding distinctions of similar Types. At the same time, you'll learn about the Triads (different groups of three that share common patterns).

➔ **PART 4: Type and Team Interactions.** This section is quite useful for teamwork and understanding others. The focus is on the potential synergies and points of conflict between all the possible Type pairs. It also offers distinguishing characteristics between Types.

➔ **PART 5: How Do We Change from the Inside-Out?** Neuroscience offers explanations of how our brains change and therefore we change. I offer a simple change process to illustrate how you can work with your personal change agenda.

This part also includes *InsideOut—Leaders' Tool Kit*. You'll find several effective practices you can use to gain greater access to your *best self* and loosen the grip of your Type.

➔ **PART 6: Your Journal of Self-Discovery.** This is a personal journal in which you can capture insights and lay the groundwork for your future life story.

AN INSIDEOUT LEADER'S STORY: **THE SITUATION**

Lars is a newly appointed senior director in R&D for a global medical device company called New Horizon Health (NHH). The organization has three business units with multiple product lines. There are 8,500 individual products. NHH has approximately 35,000 employees in offices dispersed throughout North America, Latin America, the Caribbean, Asia Pacific, Europe, MENA (Middle East North Africa), and South Africa. NHH has been in business for 37 years but had a significant growth spurt in the last 12 years, largely due to acquisitions. They have annual revenues of $100 billion.

NHH lost its entrepreneurial spirit many years ago and over time developed almost impenetrable silos. The culture is considered command and control, and the structure is hierarchical. Many other companies moved to a more flexible matrix structure, but NHH was reluctant to change because they associated their operating model with many years of success.

Due to the economic crisis and shrinking profit margins, NHH realized that they needed to streamline operations and reduce redundant positions. They hoped to accomplish this by changing to a matrix model. Although the new structure has been partially implemented, silo behavior continues. People rely on past relationships to get work done, hoping to outlast this latest "restructuring." They believe it is just the flavor of the year. Resistance to any change is high because nothing seems to stick for too long. Why bother?

This company also suffers from over-acquisition and has lost track of its core competency. They now have a highly diversified product line, they have no brand identity, and they have not yet integrated the last four acquisitions into NHH (people, systems, and processes). People play it safe and guard their turf. They are unclear about the unwritten rules of a game in which there is a revolving door of leaders. Leadership development for senior managers is not part of the organization's culture, so they have few internal resources for skill building.

In the face of a changing marketplace, layoffs are imminent. NHH must tackle the following key challenges: global competitors who have more efficient supply chains, budget freezes or delays for capital expenditures, group tenders that tie a client to one vendor for at least three years, downward price pressure on NHH due to group purchasing, purchase decisions now in the hands of business managers rather than the physicians, profits and revenues trending downward, shrinking profit margins.

➔ Lars's story continues on p. 46

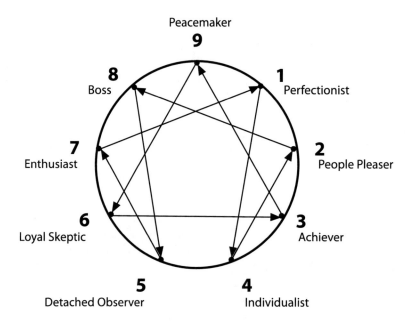

PART 1:

THE FRAMEWORK

The Framework sets the context for your leadership journey. It clarifies the value of the Enneagram for your leadership success. You'll gain an understanding of the system and how and why it works. My wish is that this section entices you to learn about your inner wilderness and how it shapes your worldview and leadership approach—that you realize you can become the captain of your own ship and steer a course to success and satisfaction in work and in life.

Courage is the ability to cultivate a relationship with the unknown; to create a form of friendship with what lies around the corner over the horizon—with those things that have not fully come into being.

—David Whyte, Midlife and the Great Unknown: Finding Courage and Clarity through Poetry, Sounds True, 2003

AN INSIDEOUT LEADER'S STORY: **MEET CAITLIN—LARS'S BOSS**

Catlin is somewhat of an anomaly in the organization. She is known as a maverick, and the CEO at NHH brought her in from the outside to shake things up. She realizes that if NHH doesn't break out of the status quo, they are going to sink like a heavy weight. They have coasted on prior success for too long and lost their innovative edge.

Caitlin promoted Lars into his position as part of her new leadership team to change the culture of NHH. Caitlin challenges Lars to take risks, to break down the silos, and bring change to the organization. Along with this encouragement, she gives Lars a comfortable budget for team development, leadership development, and coaching.

While smart, innovative, and collaborative, Lars does not have "executive presence" in the board meetings, according to Caitlin, and is largely ignored on those rare occasions when he voices his opinion or makes contributions. Lars has yet another big challenge: he is now leading a team made up of a few former peers and different groups distributed among several countries. He has his work cut out for him. Catlin encourages Lars to get some coaching to develop his executive presence.

Lars calls in Chris, a consultant and executive coach, to help him work with his team and deal with some of the gaps in his leadership.

➔ Lars's story continues on p. 53

CHAPTER 2:

WHAT DO WE USE THE ENNEAGRAM FOR?

If you are looking for another four-box model, you've come to the wrong place. The Enneagram is a dynamic system that mirrors the complex, multidimensional nature of human life. There is an energetic flow among the nine Types, and they combine to create a dynamic whole. The inner landscapes of nine distinct personality Types, their worldviews, and their interrelationships are revealed through the Enneagram. Each Type has associated habits and patterns of thinking, feeling, and acting, as well as underlying motivations and beliefs that are largely hidden from conscious awareness. These beliefs and motivations (fears and desires) activate our habits and patterns.

Most other typologies depict Type preferences, skills, and descriptors. The Enneagram offers the possibility for real change and a vision of what change looks like for each Type.

The Enneagram is a map and a compass, but it is by no means the whole story. Each human being is unique, and no system can fully account for the mystery of human nature.

Many consultants and clients are familiar with the DISC system, the Myers-Briggs Type Indicator (MBTI), and a variety of other typologies. Some are fluent in several systems. The Enneagram offers a fresh lens that complements the MBTI and other systems. I use the Enneagram when clients want to understand the underlying motivations and be-

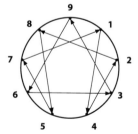

1 PERFECTIONIST
2 PEOPLE PLEASER
3 ACHIEVER
4 INDIVIDUALIST
5 DETACHED OBSERVER
6 LOYAL SKEPTIC
7 ENTHUSIAST
8 BOSS
9 PEACEMAKER

liefs that seem to drive their life script. I also use the Enneagram with teams that are ready to take team development to the next level.

Initially, the major breakthrough that people have when they are exposed to any of the typologies is a realization that people are different—that not everyone thinks the same, processes the same, makes decisions the same way, and so on. While this seems completely logical at first read, having an experience of it with your team adds a whole new dimension of understanding.

I often get asked about the difference between the MBTI and the Enneagram, or whether MBTI Type preferences neatly fit into the Enneagram Types. The most simplistic way to understand how the systems complement each other is that the MBTI describes preferences for how we do things (get our energy, make decisions, gather information, and so on); and the Enneagram describes why and how we behave as we do (beliefs, fears, desires, focus of attention), and how we go about getting our perceived needs met.

The most interesting discussions I have had explore what each system offers and how, together, they reveal a broader and deeper understanding of the person. For instance if you have an INTP/Type 5 and an INFP/Type 5, how does that distinction affect the life script of a Type 5? What does the composite profile reveal, and how can this understanding be of benefit?

ENNEAGRAM TYPES AS ARCHETYPES

Over many years of work, I have come to think of the nine fundamental Enneagram Types as archetypes, and I refer to them as archetypes throughout this book. An archetype is a universal force that is larger than our subjective experience. Archetypes live in our collective unconscious and appear as human themes across many times and places. They include, for example, the Savior Hero, the Great Mother, the Father, the Trickster. Likewise, each of the nine Enneagram Types recurs throughout time and across different cultures. When you work with your Enneagram Type, you are, in essence, taking an archetypal journey.

One of my colleagues talks about "doing a Type." We're "doing our Type" when we react habitually, act compulsively (we know it is not good, but we do it anyway because we can't stop ourselves), and are

THE ENNEAGRAM OFFERS VALUABLE INSIGHTS FOR SELF-TRANSFORMATION.

fixed in our way of seeing the world. We have a box around ourselves that says, "I am like this" or "I am not like that."

Transformation can occur when we decide to stop doing our Type. It happens when we're willing to examine deeply held beliefs about ourselves. Often we aren't aware that we are holding these beliefs or acting on them every day. The Enneagram points to core beliefs for each of the nine Types. This book offers you the chance to stop doing your Type so that you can change your life, literally, from the InsideOut.

LEADERSHIP DEVELOPMENT

In my work as a coach for business leaders, the Enneagram is a highly effective tool. In a relatively short period of time, we're able to identify specific patterns and habits that can derail a career. Likewise, the Enneagram highlights strengths for development. Leaders who are aware of their reactive patterns avoid pitfalls and learn adaptive, flexible behavior to get the results they want. This handbook offers several ways to work with a client to make conscious choices.

WHAT DO WE USE THE ENNEAGRAM FOR?

Whether you are an entrepreneur who started a business or someone who has been promoted into a leadership position, you probably have a success formula. However, your early success formula that got you hard-won gains may very well derail you later on. The skills and abilities you need to effectively lead people may not be the same ones that helped you advance to a leadership position. Flexibility that comes from self-knowledge allows you to match your style with your circumstances. The Enneagram is an entry point to map nine unique and complex worldviews.

CHANGE AND TRANSFORMATION

People may be drawn to the Enneagram simply to understand why they do what they do. Others want to change their lives by shifting old habits and patterns. Sometimes we finally hit a wall and realize that we are the source of our own suffering—or that we can be far more effective in personal and business roles.

TEAM DEVELOPMENT

A great team leader focuses on team members' strengths and capabilities, and seeks creative synergies. We want to have productive meetings, be able to be ourselves without fear of how we will be perceived, and be comfortable with our colleagues. The Enneagram provides a systematic way to understand colleagues, superiors, and subordinates.

✎ CASE STUDY

Pia (Type 6, the Loyal Skeptic) manages Jacques (Type 4, the Individualist). Jacques likes to have a lot of room to do his work in his own unique way, is more of an individual contributor than team focused, and likes to be left alone to do his work with the necessary supports. He is known to be a bit temperamental and moody. Jacques also tends to find ways to draw attention to himself, either through how he dresses, by being provocative in meetings, or through his moody outbursts.

Pia tends to look for what can go wrong and sees worst-case scenarios. It is important to her that people be team players and not lone wolves. She has a hard time trusting others and is known to play the devil's advocate. People can be exhausted by her need to drill down and thoroughly understand until she feels comfortable. She is also very loyal to her company and feels a strong sense of duty.

If Pia learns to appreciate and accept Jacques without trying to make him conform, she will get the best out of him. Although Jacques may want to do things in his own way, he has excellent people skills and a strong work ethic; he invests in what he's doing, is sensitive to others, and has a creative approach to his work. However, when Pia doesn't respect Jacques's need for space and need to have his own unique expression, or she starts to look for what could go wrong, it can create conflict between the two. Pia's need to *know and understand* may be a benefit to her relationship with Jacques. Her tendency to stay with an issue until she feels comfortable may fill Jacques's strong need to feel seen for who he uniquely is and to be understood. Jacques has a need for authentic self-expression, and if Pia appreciates this about him, it will solidify their ability to work together. Jacques's desire for authenticity will help build trust with Pia.

It will be important for Jacques to keep Pia informed about what he is doing and his progress; to participate more fully on the team; and to ask for the support he needs, in order to successfully manage his relationship with Pia.

WE ALL HAVE BLIND SPOTS

Have you ever gotten feedback from several different sources about a specific aspect of your interpersonal style? In the film *Groundhog Day*, an egocentric TV weatherman reluctantly agrees to go to Punxsutawney, Pennsylvania, for the fourth year running, to cover a story about whether the groundhog will see its shadow. In a surreal situation, he finds that it's Groundhog Day again, and again, and again. He has to come to grips with the fact that he is doomed to spend eternity in the same place, repeating the same patterns, seeing the same people, until … he realizes that if he wants things to be different, he himself has to change.

Like the weatherman in the movie, you may find at times that an unpleasant situation feels all too familiar, and you begin to wonder how you got here again. You feel as though you're looking through smudgy glasses; something feels familiar but you can't quite grasp what it is, and you may even feel defensive about it and want to blame others. When this happens, it is quite likely that you have just bumped into one of your blind spots. Yes, spots is plural. Unfortunately, most of us humans have more than one.[7]

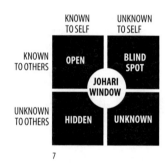

When we operate from our blind spots, it's like being blinded by the sun while driving—we can do real damage to others and ourselves. The Enneagram system sheds light on your blind spots and helps bring them into conscious awareness. You then have the opportunity to modify your behavior and take more control of your interactions.

7

✎ CASE STUDY

Let's take a look at George. He is assertive and enjoys the feeling of power when he takes command of situations. George says he wants people to challenge his ideas and his thinking, but when they do, he's likely to swear and push back hard. He sees this as a natural and normal way to interact. On the receiving end, people experience him as angry, intimidating, and not particularly interested in what they have do say, despite his requests for feedback. George doesn't get it. He wonders why people don't tell him what they think.

This is one of George's blind spots. He is loud, pushy, and comfortable with confrontation and expressing strong opinions.

George assumes that everyone is like him, or ought to be. He has no idea how he comes across to others. He doesn't see the effects of his behavior; the conversations it shuts down; the way people view him as overbearing, insensitive, and angry; and the way they steer clear of him if they can. George is just being George.

THE ENNEAGRAM AND EMOTIONAL INTELLIGENCE

The Enneagram opens the door to a more intimate relationship with yourself. Most of us stay busy with activity and distraction. We can't work out, go for a run, walk, sit on the bus, or train without an electronic device to distract us. What are we running away from? Why don't we like our own company? When we don't like to be with ourselves, do we wonder whether other people like to be with us?

The Enneagram is not an antidote to texting. However, it is a tool to connect to self and quietly listen to an inner voice that can guide you through life.

The chart depicts the dimensions of emotional/social Intelligence. Working with the Enneagram, you can improve your interpersonal awareness and effectiveness, feel better about yourself, decrease your stress level, and adapt more easily to change.

The Enneagram's wisdom can lead to increased emotional intelligence, which is another way to say that you can become more intimate with yourself and begin to shift your style to be more responsive to what life is calling for rather than reacting in habitual ways. This shift will increase your influence with others, as well as your ability to inspire, develop your team, and deal effectively with conflict. You will have the leadership agility of an aikido master.

We're not going on our journey to save the world but to save ourselves.

—Bill Moyers

But in doing that, you save the world. The influence of a vital person vitalizes ...

—Joseph Campbell[8]

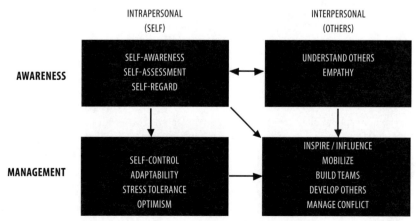

WHY IS THE ENNEAGRAM IMPORTANT?

	INTRAPERSONAL (SELF)	INTERPERSONAL (OTHERS)
AWARENESS	SELF-AWARENESS SELF-ASSESSMENT SELF-REGARD	UNDERSTAND OTHERS EMPATHY
MANAGEMENT	SELF-CONTROL ADAPTABILITY STRESS TOLERANCE OPTIMISM	INSPIRE / INFLUENCE MOBILIZE BUILD TEAMS DEVELOP OTHERS MANAGE CONFLICT

Source: Daniel Goleman (Domains and Competencies) and Reuven Bar-On (Competencies)

AN INSIDEOUT LEADER'S STORY: **MEET LARS**

Lars has been with the company for many years, climbed through the ranks, and finds himself at midlife asking some of the thornier midlife questions. He has a strong urge to learn more about himself, how he gets in his own way, and how to play to his strengths. He wants to step into his new executive role prepared to face the challenges ahead.

This new leadership position forced Lars and his family to move thousands of miles away from a place they loved. Their new home is in an area they would not have chosen, except for the job. The responsibility to forge a new life for his family feels onerous to Lars. The pressure to succeed is great.

Lars's span of control has global reach, and his management team is distributed accordingly. There is a history of competition among his team members and their respective organizations. Their cultures (national and organizational) differ widely. The company has been highly successful but has become big and unwieldy.

NHH's corporate HQ office environment is unpleasant, and it is clear that the company has not progressed. The office buildings are severely outdated and outmoded. People come into work, punch the clock, and leave. Lars wonders, "Where's the esprit de corps?"

He knows it is a matter of time before he'll have to make some hard decisions about cuts in his organization. He also knows that his own job is ultimately at risk.

Caitlin, an outsider who is known as a change maker, hired Lars for his new role. Lars's brand is also change. He is known for his success leading turnaround situations. This new position is a step change for Lars's career. Is he up to the task? How will he build his capabilities as a leader and a newly appointed executive? Will Caitlin give him the support he needs to be successful?

➜ Lars's story continues on p. 78

CHAPTER 3:

HOW DOES THE ENNEAGRAM SYSTEM WORK?

The Enneagram is dynamic, unlike many of the four-box models used in organizations today. It mirrors the complexities of human nature; and its symbol implies movement to depict growth, change, and development.

To make good use of the Enneagram as a tool for change, you will need to understand its composition. This section will serve as a guide to the Enneagram's special language and its presentation as a diagram. You will learn how to make sense of arrows, numbers, and the Enneagram symbol. Like learning a foreign language, it will take an investment of your time and attention, but soon the words you learn will begin to flow and provide you with a foundation for communication and growth.

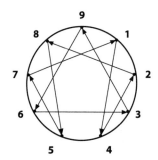

ARROWS

Notice the lines of connection and arrows in the diagram to the right. Each Type has two Connecting Points. The arrows point to *Stress Points*, or what I like to think of as *pressure-relief valves*, for each Type. For example, if you are Type 9, your Stress Point is Type 6, and in a stressful situation your behavior may draw from the less healthy side of Type 6. On the other hand, when you are relaxed, your behavior may reflect healthy aspects of Type 3—your *Integration Point*.

In the diagram, the arrows point in the direction of the Stress Point for each Type. It may seem confusing at first, but in fact you also have access to the healthier qualities of your Stress Point and the more defended qualities of your Integration Point.

Your Stress Point can actually become a resource for you.

As you become familiar with the Enneagram and know yourself more intimately, you will be clear about the systemic ways in which these connections work; you'll then be able to observe how they apply to you and to make them work in your favor.

WINGS

The points on both sides of your Type are called your *Wings*, and they influence the ways you express the characteristics of your Type. Some people relate more to one Wing than another. Others feel that they share qualities with both Wings. You'll hear people say, "I'm a 2 with a 3 wing."

Michael J. Goldberg, author of *The 9 Ways of Working*, theorized that each Type is a blend of both of its Wings. In other words, Type 8 blends Type 9 and Type 7, and displays characteristics of all three Types. The ability to change behavior is linked to recognizing the influence of both wings.

When we don't relate to one of our Wings, it is probably because it lives in our shadow—outside of our conscious awareness. We may not be able to see this in ourselves, may choose not to see it in ourselves, or may want it but don't know how to access that part of ourselves. This is where understanding both of your Wings becomes important.

If you believe you have a dominant wing, you might. What that would mean is that you have integrated aspects of your *dominant* Wing (the healthy and/or unhealthy expression) and that your other wing is a place for more exploration and focus. It will point you to disowned parts of yourself that are important for you to come to know and befriend.

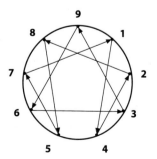

DIFFERENT SIDES OF OUR PERSONALITY

Although you have a core personality Type, you will notice that your reactions can often appear as if you have another one altogether. Your core Enneagram Type is connected to at least four other Types—your two Wings and your two Connection Points. Your parents or primary caregivers also influence how you express your core Type.

These other sides of you will surface in different contexts. As you work with the Enneagram and become an observer of yourself, you will notice how each of these other Types emerges through you as you react to different circumstances—immediate or over time.

The positive sides of these connections offer natural abilities that you can cultivate and develop. It's also important to become aware of how you fall into the traps of the less healthy sides so that you can avoid them.

 CASE STUDY

Leslie identifies as a Type 7, the Enthusiast. After learning about the Enneagram, she felt a strong connection to Type 8, the Boss. She is aware that she doesn't want to be controlled or to take orders from anyone. Over the course of several years, Leslie received direct feedback (invited and uninvited) from family members, friends, colleagues, job reviews, training programs, and 360-degree reviews, saying that she could be pushy, bossy, and demanding, and seemed to want to get her way. She is also known to take charge and make things happen. Working with her coach, she was able to address this feedback by learning to adapt her style to the situation and employ her Type 8 Wing in a conscious way.

Leslie was less aware of being cautious and skeptical of others' agendas, as well as of her lack of trust in her own ability to be decisive and forge ahead with her life—aspects of Type 6, the Loyal Skeptic. Through a process with her coach, she was able to see these aspects of herself as well. This came as a surprise to Leslie, who thought she really knew herself. With this new information and some work, she has been able to become more confident and trusting of herself and others.

These are some of the dynamics at play that make up the internal workings of Type 7.

THE VERTICAL DIMENSION: LEVELS OF DEVELOPMENT

Don Riso and Russ Hudson originated the concept of the Enneagram "Levels of Development,"[9] where they lay out and describe nine levels of emotional health for each of the nine Enneagram Types, including a range of behavior from pathology to undefended and integrated.

Most of us are anchored at one or two average levels of development. When we act in a rigid way, we trigger other people and they also trigger reactions in us. This is the stage where office and family dynamics are often played out.

The less reactive and fixed we are in how we deal with people and situations, the more agile and flexible we become. Over time we anchor at the healthier levels.

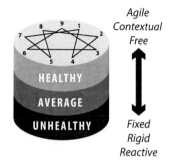

Agile
Contextual
Free

Fixed
Rigid
Reactive

Source: Riso & Hudson

....

✎ CASE STUDY

Francisco is a Type 7 manager (the Enthusiast), and Carmen is a Type 3 employee (the Achiever). Francisco is anchored at an average level of emotional health like most of us. He is visionary, has innovative ideas, and tends to have several number-one priorities at a time. Closing down options, putting a stake in the ground, and saying "Enough" is a challenge for him. Projects seem to grow way beyond their initial scope. He is spread too thin by his own doing, and his team is trying to *do it all*. Carmen's biggest fear is that Francisco will fail and, as a result, she will fail too and won't be seen as a valuable player.

Working for Francisco has her very upset because she doesn't believe she can succeed under his leadership. She is driven and goal oriented, but the priorities are a moving target and the scope of projects is always getting bigger. She doesn't know how to win.

Carmen starts cutting corners, doing the minimum. She even hides or spins data to make it look as if her results are far better than they are. She has started to bad-mouth Francisco behind his back to rally the team against him, thus buffering herself from failure if things go south—hoping that Francisco will be the fall guy and it won't

reflect badly on her. She also tries to position herself as the heir apparent to see if she can edge Francisco out of his job.

Francisco has a hands-off, loose management style. He trusts team members to follow through and ask for help if they need it. Appearing smart, together, and competent is important to him, and he expects the same of others.

Carmen believes that if she asks for help, it will reflect badly on her. Francisco, who gives general directions and thinks people are clear about deadlines, expectations, and priorities, and that they can manage their

When we are in the grip of our Enneagram Type, or *doing our Type*, we react in habitual and patterned ways, and our responses are rigid. As we become more self-aware and begin to shift our reactive patterns, we will find ourselves anchoring at a higher level of emotional health and able to respond with more agility and freedom. We will simply be more present in our world.

If you have ever experienced being the still point in a storm, feeling very contained and quiet and having an inner locus of curiosity about what is unfolding without *knowing*, then you surely have experienced *presence*.

· ·

✏ CASE STUDY

time, is blind to what is going on. He is impatient, involved in his own work, and not very insightful about how his leadership and management style affects his employees. He expects that work will be done well and on time and is often shocked when the output is different than he imagined.

When Carmen's data spin finally comes to light, Francisco turns harsh, judging, blaming, and critical. He doesn't see his role in what is happening. Carmen is now full of shame; her fears of failure have been realized. She lashes out and tries to put the blame on others, hoping they'll take the fall rather than her.

Francisco and Carmen are *doing their Type* and are bringing out unhealthy behaviors in each other. They are, in fact, triggering each other's compulsive behavior.

If Francisco were a healthier Type 7 (higher level), he would be focused, stay the course rather than introduce new projects, close down his options, make a clear action plan, and be available to his team to explain what was going on.

If Carmen were a healthier Type 3, she would ask for help and be less concerned about her image. She would not try to alter data or stab Francisco in the back, but would be clear about what she needed to make her projects a success.

CULTURE AND TYPE

Never doubt the power of culture, and never doubt the force and power of personality. Gurdjieff believed that personality is shaped by culture, and culture is shaped by personality. Senior leaders play a significant role in defining corporate culture. For example, Steve Jobs was a driving force at Apple Computer. When he was ousted by John Scully, Apple took a very different turn until Jobs returned to right the ship. Jobs shaped Apple's business model with his emphasis on design and product choice. *His personality is embedded in Apple's culture.*

When we explore a country's culture, one of the first things we learn is that Enneagram Type transcends national boundaries. All nine Types exist in every culture, worldwide. However, national culture has an effect on the expression of personality, and viewed in a certain light, different cultures represent different archetypes. For instance, if certain behaviors of a particular Type are unacceptable in a culture, an individual may find ways to mute them. On the other hand, behaviors that are rewarded by a culture may be exaggerated.

THE FOLLOWING ARE SOME EXAMPLES OF HOW CULTURE IN-FLUENCES TYPE:

The United States is often seen as a Type 3 culture. This is the archetype of the Achiever: success focused, goal driven, efficient, image conscious, marketing oriented, a promoter of self and products, with a bias for action—*just do it.*

Type 3 behaviors are rewarded in U.S. culture. There is a propensity to take on Achiever behavior whether or not it is germane to your Enneagram Type. On the other hand, non–Type 3 people may have a sense that they don't fit in, and as a result they might rebel or move away.

Sweden is often seen as a Type 1 (the Perfectionist) culture. I know Swedes who spent years in discomfort and left because they couldn't or didn't want to adhere to perfectionist standards.

A French woman who attended one of my workshops approached me afterward and thanked me profusely. She recognized herself as a Type 8, the Boss. Type 8 behaviors are generally not rewarded or accepted among women living in France, and she had to act differently to fit in. For her, it was validating and freeing to find her Type. She no longer felt as though something was wrong with her.

Just as the expression of Enneagram Type is affected by national culture, Type characteristics may be modified or reinforced in a business setting. All companies have a corporate culture. Some may be highly bureaucratic, and others more entrepreneurial. Here are some descriptions of corporate culture: image focused, competitive, stable, risky, risk averse, hierarchical, flat, customer service oriented, fun, open, punitive, empowering, rigid, flexible. A corporate culture may mirror a certain Enneagram Type, and may consciously or unconsciously hire people who reinforce that Type; or the culture may spit people out who don't (they either leave by choice or are fired).

In reaction to a dominant culture, whether national, corporate, or influential at another level, people may *appear* different from their Type. Type-based motivations are still there and will influence choices and behaviors. All nine Types are found in every culture.

PART 2:

THE JOURNEY

Many people are curious about the Enneagram and are satisfied once they identify their Type. At this point, they fold up their map and put it back in the drawer, delighted and surprised to have learned about a system that accurately describes them. Others suddenly realize how much more there is to explore. The door is open.

CHAPTER 4:

THE HERO'S JOURNEY

CARL G. JUNG'S PROCESS OF INDIVIDUATION

By Sandra Emma Shelley, PhD

The Enneagram Journey is linked to the process of individuation. I asked Dr. Sandra Emma Shelley, a Jungian depth psychologist, to describe individuation in Jungian terms as a grounding for readers of this book.

Joseph Campbell wrote, "The privilege of a lifetime is being who you are."[10] As most of us know, this is not such a simple task. Being human, we are made up of a complex interwoven tapestry that includes our psychology, biology, neurology, spirituality, family history, collective histories, and cultural influences.

How do we find the authentic self in light of complex personal and collective stories? Much of Jung's work was devoted to developing an authentic sense of self through the process of individuation. The core of Jung's work is to integrate our unconscious and conscious selves.

The *conscious self* refers to the limited way we know ourselves. It is externally focused and can include habitual patterned behaviors and negative reactions instead of reflection and response to others. Left to our own devices, we will happily fixate and identify with old patterns, worn-out ways of being that lead to a narrowed experience while convincing us that we are on the right path as long as we stay still, be quiet, and don't change.

We all know what it feels like to be stuck at some place in our life, to be trapped in well-worn rigid beliefs and defenses. Most of us can recall a time when we were overwhelmed by life's demands while a deeper inner nudging alerted us to the realization that something was missing. This inner nudge lets us know that it's time to change, time to get to know ourselves better.

An important role of consciousness is to help bring unconscious material to light and integrate it with our personality. This necessary integration is what Jung referred to as the process of *individuation*. Individuation means that we embrace all that we are, and become brave enough to take off our defensive armor and go exploring like the hero of myth and story. Individuation does not lead to perfection, but rather builds the capacity to see ourselves and each other for all our attributes and complex creative gifts as well as the messier, perhaps less preferred character traits—and to accept them all.

In this bridging landscape between conscious and unconscious, we can play, learn, deepen, and individuate. Here we will find the images that arise in dreams, art, literature, film, myth, music, poetry, and our creative work. These images provide information to integrate the fragmented parts of the self in order to become more authentic, deeper, and wiser.

Jung saw individuation as the work of integrating the psyche. He spoke of this as our life task. Toward the end of his life, he wrote:

> **Man's task ... is to become conscious of the contents that press upward from the unconscious. Neither should he persist in his unconsciousness, nor remain identical with the unconscious elements of his being, thus evading his destiny, which is to create more and more consciousness. As far as we can discern, the sole purpose of human existence is to kindle a light in the darkness of mere being.[11]**

THE LEADER'S JOURNEY

We don't receive wisdom; we must discover it for ourselves after a journey that no one can take for us or spare us.

—Marcel Proust

The leader's journey is the hero's journey. This is an opportunity to explore our beliefs and let them go if they have outlived their usefulness; to become intimate with hidden parts of ourselves and harness our gifts; to expand the boundaries of who we believe ourselves to be. It is the process of maturation and transformation, and such growth is a prerequisite for skilled leadership.

When someone ascends to a leadership position, people's expectations of that person rise. Leaders are well paid, are given credit when things go well, and have privileges that come with their position; people look to them for direction, guidance, wisdom, transparency, authenticity, and integrity. By definition, leadership goes beyond what you *know*. Leadership is about how you *show up*.

The leader's journey involves the interior landscape. Who's really there lurking below the surface? What parts of me don't I allow people to see? What parts of me haven't been developed or have been shoved away in a closet? It can be alternately terrifying and exciting to explore the inner self, like a walk on the razor's edge. Notions of *how things are* may be subject to change. Unforeseen possibilities come to the surface.

The leader's journey calls you to uncover the good and true, the monsters, challenges, and tests along the way, and to claim your riches. This is an archetypal journey of self-transformation.

To evolve out of this position of psychological immaturity to the courage of self-responsibility and assurance requires a death and a resurrection. That's the basic motif of the universal hero's journey—leaving one condition and finding the source of life to bring you forth into a richer or mature condition.

—Joseph Campbell with Bill Moyers, *The Power of Myth*[12]

The hero's journey is often described in literature and film, from Odysseus in the *Iliad* to Dorothy in *The Wizard of Oz*, *Siddhartha*, Luke Skywalker in the *Star Wars* trilogy, and Frodo in *The Lord of the Rings*.

Dorothy had to integrate disowned aspects of herself until she realized that she already had what she needed to go home—her ruby slippers. Siddhartha relinquished the comforts of a palace to learn about himself. Odysseus faced demons and temptations, and gained wisdom and confidence at every stop along his travels. Joseph Campbell described Jung's process of individuation as the hero's journey.

The big question is, will you be able to say yes to your adventure? Many people choose to turn away and shut down. They fall asleep or merely exist rather than step into a transformed life. Why? The road is scary, the path is unknown, and it takes a great leap of faith to persist.

The hero's journey may be catalyzed by a precipitating event, or it may be a conscious choice.

The story of the hero's journey has three parts: *departure, initiation,* and *return*. Departure is *giving up* where you are; you let go of what is known and embark on an adventure without a clear destination or detailed map. During our initiation, we enter the unknown realm— our unconscious—to explore the inner landscape, while facing trials, temptations, and detours. The final part is the return to normal life.

There are several stages to the hero's journey, yet you need not go through them all, nor are they necessarily linear.[13] A journey may take place during different times of your life. You may start and not complete it. But with each leg of your journey, you'll go deeper toward the core of yourself.

Every person's life journey is like a labyrinth. We have the possibility to enter, explore, exit, and return, each time developing a more intimate self-relationship. We venture out into the world early in life, slowly leaving our true self behind as we adapt to our circumstances. Over the course of a lifetime, we have many opportunities to venture inward and come back home to ourselves, as did Odysseus when, after a long journey, he finally returned to Ithaca as a more integrated person.

What we call the beginning is often the end. And to make an end is to make a beginning.
The end is where we start from.
—T. S. Eliot, from *Four Quartets*[14]

As you read through each stage of the journey, you may recognize these places. **Mark the checkbox to indicate where you see yourself right now.** At the end of this chapter, there is a place to write reflections and to answer questions about your life journey. In Part 6, "Your Journal of Self-Discovery," you'll have an opportunity to create a new story that has yet to be written.

As the Polynesian saying goes, you are "standing on a whale fishing for minnows." The whale is right under us all the time, yet it is so close and so big that we don't even realize we are standing on it. Our focus is on tiny problems or what is outside of us, like the minnows. We blame other people and situations for problems in our life and don't notice that we are standing on a whale, because we take its presence for granted. The whale is just part of who we are. When we look inside the whale, we are looking inside of ourselves, and we finally come to realize that we are the true source of our own suffering.

It is about the faith, power and courage we all have within us to pursue the intricate path of a personal legend, a path charted by the mysterious magnet of destiny but obscured by distractions.[1]

—Paulo Coelho and Alan R. Clarke, *The Alchemist*[15]

PART I: **THE DEPARTURE**

☐ **THE CALL**

A summons. The adventure can begin with a conscious and informed choice, by a precipitating event (loss of job, relationship, death of someone close, illness, a move, approaching landmark birthday), or by stumbling on an opportunity without conscious intent. There may be early signs that you are about to embark on an adventure— restlessness, discontent, a longing for something unknown. This is the call of your destiny.

The door is round and open. Don't go back to sleep.

—John Moyne and Coleman Barks, *Open Secret: Versions of Rumi*[16]

☐ **REFUSAL OF THE CALL**

You may turn a deaf ear to the call. When the call gets louder, it would be easy just to cover your ears. Even though you know you are stuck, you may not be able to summon the courage to leave your current circumstances to venture into the unknown. Any number of reasons may keep you from answering the call. It could be fear and insecurity, or obligation to family, work, or community; or you may not feel you have what it takes to face the challenges ahead. You might decide that you no longer have to change because you are happy; you have a new romance, job, or financial windfall … and for a while, you might be able to convince yourself that you never heard the call in the first place.

When you refuse the call, you stay stuck. Your life gets smaller and your suffering may increase. You may look successful to the outside world and may be trying to keep up those appearances, even though you feel emptiness inside or that something is missing. By refusing the call, you will create more problems for yourself as you turn away from the juiciness of life and succumb to routine. Never fear, the call is relentless. Often it comes in your dreams. Can you hear it?

☐ SUPERNATURAL AID

When you make a commitment to the quest, the first encounter will be with a guardian figure who represents the protective power of Destiny. He or she affirms that paradise is not lost and assists our hero in crossing the threshold. Throughout your journey, unexpected people will come along just when you need them most, to provide assistance and serve as protectors of your destiny. Ask for them. They will come.

Your guides can show up in the form of friends, trusted advisors, people who happen to cross your path, a place, an animal … and they will be there even if you don't understand their purpose, notice them, or know that they are there to support your dream. Although you face many tests and trials, and find yourself struggling to confront your inner obstacles, your guides will always be there.

… and to know that the Universe is conspiring in our favor, even though we may not understand how.
—Paulo Coelho and Alan R. Clarke, *The Alchemist*[17]

Your unconscious is ever-present, willing you forward on your quest, even when it seems that all is lost, and you are lost.

☐ CROSSING THE THRESHOLD

This is the stage when the hero heeds the call and moves out of the familiar and is no longer stuck in old patterned ways of living. When you cross the threshold, you are moving from the conscious realm into the unconscious realm—onto the path of the unknown. This is the world where dualistic thinking (right/wrong, black/white, good/evil) doesn't apply. You have entered the mystery and left behind what you thought you knew. You venture into the land that lives between two thoughts, between two concepts, and into the realm of the unconscious.

☐ THE BELLY OF THE WHALE

The inward journey takes you into the belly of the whale—the womb—the place of rebirth. You are "swallowed into the unknown and appeared to have died."[18] The person you have known yourself to be disappears.

Different myths speak of dismemberment during this stage. But worry not—as you stay the course, tolerate ambiguity and the unknown, and face yourself, you will remember who you are and come to know yourself again.

The world breaks everyone and afterwards many are strong at the broken places.

—Ernest Hemingway, *A Farewell to Arms*

PART 2: **THE INITIATION**

☐ THE ROAD OF TRIALS

This stage of the journey requires you to let go—let go of who you thought you were, let go of beliefs that are restricting, and let go of whatever is no longer serving you.

Your commitment to the journey will be tested as you face setbacks and challenges. There are a series of tests and trials with increasing levels of difficulty. There will be small victories along the way. If you pay close attention, you will see that there are many signs of hope and people to support you all along the way.

☐ THE ULTIMATE BOON

This stage of the hero's journey is the achievement of the goal of our quest. The veils of reality have been pierced, and you have connected with the source of life within you. You have discovered your true self and expanded your conscious awareness. You see reality as it is and not as you wish it to be. The self you once though you knew is much more grand, capable, wise, and centered. Your transformation has taken place.

"These tests, then, symbolize self-realization, a process of initiation into the mysteries of life."

—Joseph Campbell, *Pathways to Bliss: Mythology and Personal Transformation*[19]

PART 3: **THE RETURN**

You now integrate what you have learned into daily life with compassion and patience. You seek ways to communicate your experience and acquired wisdom to others in terms they can hear and receive. This is a time to bring back your *gold* in service of the renewal of your life, family, community, and organization, and of the planet.

☐ REFUSAL OF THE RETURN

You may not want to go back to the ordinary world. The responsibility may feel too great. "What if people don't want what I have to offer?"

☐ RESCUE FROM WITHOUT

You may need people (friends, allies, family) to coax you back to everyday life. Why leave your blissful state? You may be concerned that your experience, which seemed momentous to you, will appear silly in the light of day. Why attempt to explain your experience to others who are consumed by their own daily dramas? You may discount what seemed so real and precious at the time of your profound insights. Speaking about your journey can make it appear trivial. It can lose its power through explanation.

☐ MASTER OF TWO WORLDS

You have become comfortable and competent in both your inner and outer worlds, and can pass back and forth, one continually informing the other.

☐ FREEDOM TO LIVE

You have given yourself the freedom to live fully. You are simultaneously connected to yourself and to others—you experience the humanity in everyone. You have learned to live without a prescription and to respond effectively to what is called for in the moment. You no longer anticipate the future or regret the past, but live in the present. You take responsibility for creating your life; and you take your acquired wisdom and bring it into form.

WE ALL HAVE A PAIR OF RUBY SLIPPERS. THE TASK AT HAND IS TO LEARN HOW TO USE THEM.

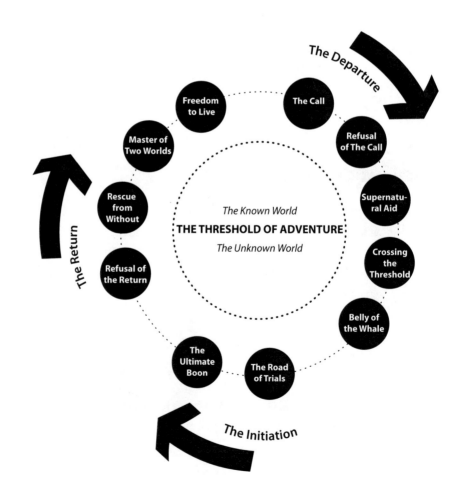

REFLECTIONS ON THE
LEADER'S JOURNEY

STOP AND REFLECT

Do you recognize yourself when reading about the hero's journey? Describe:

Are you firmly on this path now? Where would you locate yourself on the journey?

When the door was wide open, when did you choose to go back to sleep rather than walk through it? What internal obstacle got in your way?

Take time to write about any "aha" moments, thoughts, feelings, or sensations that occurred to you as you read about the hero's journey.

Have you ever started on this path and then stopped? What caused you to stop or pause as you were headed down this road?

PERSONALITY AND TRUE SELF: LEAD FROM YOUR CENTER

Let's take a look at *personality*. What does the term mean, how is it distinct from *true self,* and how do we gain access to *true self*?

We refer to our personality as if we are defined by it and identify our personality as *who we are*. But is that true, or is our personality just a part of our make-up?

There is no one agreed-upon definition of personality, so I will offer the following, which conforms to a general understanding of what is meant by personality:

Personality is a constellation of coping strategies, also known as defenses, to protect us from perceived harm. Personality usually protects parts of us that are in pain, but we don't often recognize the pain. Our actions are unexamined reactive habits and patterns of thought, beliefs, emotions. Our coping strategies help us to navigate life and make the world more understandable. Personality also encapsulates our worldview and how we define ourselves, our self-identity—"I am …"

PERSONALITY: NATURE OR NURTURE? WHERE DO THESE TYPES COME FROM?

THEORY: Personality *emerges* with adaptation to the environment. Our inborn orientation (Type is inborn) largely determines the ways in which we perceive the world around us. Both nature and nurture affect behavior and shape the expression of Type.

Enneagram Type, along with genetics, influences how we adapt to our environment from birth and exerts a significant influence on our personality development. Each of the nine Enneagram Types has unique, innate core needs, drives, and motivations. How each Type gets those needs met is where the personality steps in. Anyone who has children can tell you that differences between siblings emerge very early and are largely inexplicable. By the time children are four or five years old, they have developed a sense of self and a place in the world. Events from birth to age six lay a foundation for emotional health.

✽ Jump to Chapter 9, "Our Brain—the Basics," for more information.

Our personality is invisible to us, much the way culture is invisible—it's just how we are, what we do, how we see the world, and how we distinguish ourselves from others: Graham sees himself as a happy, optimistic person; Kerstin knows herself as a person who takes responsibility. Our personality wants to feel loved, seen, understood, cared for, safe, and secure in a *particular way*.

Our personality is also a comfort seeker—the known is comfortable and familiar; the unknown is not. We tend to cling to our personality (the way we see and define ourselves) for fear of falling into an abyss with no bottom in sight and nothing we can see that will catch our fall. Perhaps we have been so busy putting a mask on each day that we've forgotten who is behind it. If we're not who we think we are, who are we? Answering that question could push us off the edge, so better to keep on doing what we do.

Let's face it—we have become pretty expert at using our coping strategies within their limits, so why mess with a success formula? The more adept we become in our approach to life, the more invested we are in maintaining the status quo.

Personality is a pretty limited and limiting view of how we see ourselves. I imagine that at this moment your thought bubble might be, "Of course my personality is who I am. Who else would I be?" Read on.

The escape is *Nirvana*, which is a state of mind or consciousness, not a place somewhere, like heaven. It is right here, in the midst of the turmoil of life. It is the state you find when you are no longer driven to live by compelling desires, fears, and social commitments, when you have found your center of freedom and can act by choice out of that.

—Jash Raj Subba, *Mythology of the People of Sikkim*[20]

LEAD FROM CENTER: GAIN ACCESS TO YOUR TRUE SELF

Center is a state of being. When we are in our center, we access the undefended, nonreactive part of us—our *true self*. When we relax our defensive structures and are conscious of our predisposed habits and patterns, we can make contact with our center. It is like seeing the world through clean, clear glass—without filters from our past influencing our response in the present moment.

Each Enneagram Type has reactive patterns under pressure. When we recognize our tendency to be defensive, get aggressive, run away, or pull back, we can stop before enacting our pattern. Acting from our center, we have a greater capacity to adjust our approach.

Imagine standing in the center of a sphere, knowing that you can easily and gracefully move in any direction and your awareness of life around you is spherical—that your energy reaches out equally above you, below you, and all around you. You are fully grounded in the present moment and have access to multiple options for responding. This is operating from your center.

When you operate from center, the true self arises and natural strengths take over. *I am* expands to include newly integrated parts of yourself, your *integral self*. Though true self comes and goes, you can learn how to recognize that self, gain access, and return again and again, more often and for longer stretches.

With practice, you can start to recognize when the personality is trying to control the situation and then return to your center. From center you'll manage to have better timing: you'll say the right thing, and take useful action in an appropriate place and at the right time. You'll also notice a calmness forming within you and a more positive response from others when you access and live from this place.

✏ CASE STUDY

Let's look at one of the Peacemakers' defensive patterns: to placate, keep the peace, and not address the difficult issues in service of staying peaceful and comfortable. It takes quite a bit of energy for them to suppress their strong feelings, withhold their opinions, and create a sense of "everything's just fine." Meanwhile, the pressure is building and things are fraying at the edges while they use their will to keep reality at bay.

Shafik is a senior director of a large department of 300 employees in a fairly stable organization. He self-identifies as a Type 9, the Peacemaker. His employees experience him as kind and easy to get along with, and he manages to avoid drawing negative attention from his peers or the higher-ups. There is a certain calm predictability about Shafik that people enjoy.

Shafik's peers and boss don't think they really know him. He rarely offers his opinions or draws attention to himself. He is known to try to quash conflicts on the team when they arise. Some of his peers are aggravated by this, and others appreciate it.

SHAFIK OPERATING FROM PERSONALITY

Everything seemed to be going along smoothly in his job until a restructuring was announced. Shafik's budget was slashed, and he was asked to sever 30 percent of his staff. Change was afoot, and his responsibilities were growing but he had far fewer resources. An ERP (Enterprise Resource Planning) system was purchased, and its installation and implementation were planned to start in six months.

This was an extremely disruptive change, and the staff had to alter the way they coordinated their work with each other and the rest of the organization.

Shafik started feeling intense pressure and stress. He went numb and tried to busy himself with tasks—just treading water. He immersed himself in the comfort of his normal habits and routines, but it wasn't helping. His anxiety and resignation grew. He asked himself, "How will I manage with all this change? How am I going to decide who to sever? How will I be able to face my staff?" Shafik became frozen with indecision. Instead of taking practical action, he withdrew and became lethargic. He slept long hours, got sick, and had to take time off from work. Some might say he was depressed.

This is an example of when Type 9 is under stress and personality takes the reins. His personality wants life to be comfortable, stable, and routine. His personality wants people to see him as kind. The Peacemaker's personality has a subconscious desire to maintain connection with others at all costs.

SHAFIK OPERATING FROM CENTER: AN ALTERNATIVE SCENARIO

He was aware of his natural tendencies to defend against his fears' being realized. He knew that this type of behavior was counterproductive. Rather than stuffing his anger or denying it, Shafik allowed himself to feel angry about being asked to do the dirty work for the decision makers. He then decided to use the power and force of his anger to take action!

In a team meeting with his peers and boss, he let them know what he thought about the decision: aspects he agreed with and others he disagreed with. He requested some time to work within his department and see whether he and his staff could come up with some innovative ideas to generate income and reduce expenses rather than

CASE STUDY

lay off 30 percent of his department. They agreed to give him 30 days.

He used his gifts of seeing others' points of view and gathered together his department to present the larger vision of his organization, the changes that were under way, the business case for the change, and their role in it, and to engage their hearts and minds. Everyone participated in a workshop to look at their *current state*; and then they developed a plan to arrive at the desired *future state* and meet the organization's goals through some creative, innovative approaches.

By acknowledging his anger, taking action, staying engaged, and using his natural gifts and the positive regard he had earned over time, Shafik operated from his center. He didn't act out of fear, but rather he faced reality and took decisive action. Shafik felt a sense of inner calm and demonstrated his passion for his vision and caring for the people in his department.

When Type 9s are in contact with their *true self*, their need for staying peaceful is transformed into an uncanny ability to mediate and see multiple points of view and situations holistically. Most of us expend vast amounts

of energy running our defensive patterns—block and tackle. Our attention is often focused on defending ourselves. What if at least some of that energy were freed up to be deployed for focused action, creativity, collaboration, innovation, and seizing opportunities?

✦ To read more information about personality and center, see "The Vertical Dimension: Levels of Development," in Chapter 3, "How Does the Enneagram System Work?"

THE ROLES WE PLAY: OUR SELF-IDENTITY

Part of what happens as personality develops is that we unwittingly start playing a role: the enthusiastic, fun, happy one; the smart, innovative, odd one; the overachieving, sparkly, accomplished one. What do I mean by *role identity*? Let's take Type 1, the Perfectionist, for instance. Type 1s becomes identified as the one who is *perfect*. While they are often proud of this moniker, they also become trapped by it. Consciously or subconsciously, they feel pressured to keep to a certain standard of perfection, both in how they appear to others and in the quality of what they do. In some way, they actually create a codependency by self-identifying and then becoming identified as the *perfect* one.

It is probably true that people come to expect a certain standard of behavior from them, and they feel the expectation of living up to that standard. What would happen if Type 1s suddenly became disorganized, irresponsible, unreliable; didn't show up on time; turned in work with mistakes; had an affair; did something morally or ethically against what they professed to believe?

When we are living out our role identity, we are *doing our Type.* Our role identity is related to our emotional compulsions and thinking fixations. To continue with the example of Type 1, their thinking fixation is *resentment*, and their emotional compulsion is *anger.* Their role as the Perfectionist is connected with anger, which is their emotional response to self and others when they cannot control their world, and they and others don't live up to their standards. Well, nothing is ever *really perfect enough*, is it?

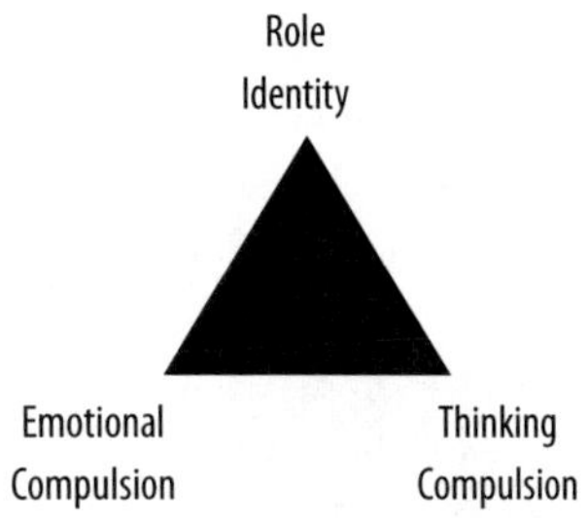

Type 1's fixated thinking revolves around resentment of others who lack enough integrity, aren't principled enough, aren't clean enough, make mistakes, don't live up to their standards, aren't on time, aren't doing what they should be doing, are morally and ethically imperfect / lacking in integrity, are sloughing off ... Again, this is when Type 1, the Perfectionist, is *doing their Type.*

**When I let go of what I am,
I become what I might be.**

—Lao Tzu

At some point, we realize that we have become trapped by our role identity, which we have probably also come to believe is our *success formula.* Fear of the consequences, real or imagined, of not playing our roles is what keeps us trapped. Perhaps the perceived benefits of performing to others' expectations still outweigh the negative. Or perhaps we don't know how to stop ourselves. "Can I allow myself to be different than I think I am or people expect me to be? If I dropped my role, what would replace it? Who would I be? Who am I?" Rather than face these knotty and existential questions, it often feels easier to carry on as is. Until it's not.

Role identity is intimately linked to the compulsive thinking and reactive patterns for each Type. For each of the Types' role identity and how that plays out, jump to the chapter on the Type of your interest.

AN INSIDEOUT LEADER'S STORY: **FIRST MEETING WITH CHRIS**

To get Chris up to speed, Lars shares the following:

"Our vision at NHH is to move to a distributed leadership model—to have networks of leaders in the organization. Conceptually, there is recognition that we have to move from a traditional bureaucratic structure to a flatter, more nimble organization in order to remain competitive. However, I'm not convinced that the leadership here really knows what it will take to make this change a reality and what the new world means for everyone. What they are convinced of, theoretically, is that we have to change in order to deal with a more dynamic and complex world, increased competition, antiquated systems that aren't integrated and shrinking margins."

Lars continues, "One of the key skills required for this model is relationship building both within and outside the organization. While top leaders at NHH know this change is important, Caitlin and I are the only ones actively moving forward with it."

Chris has been taking notes. Now he's ready to learn some specifics. "Lars, can you tell me a little more about the composition of your team? Where are they located?" Lars responds, "My team is made up of several workgroups in five different countries. The largest of them is at the corporate HQ in the U.S. To date, these groups have had minimal contact with one another. The groups that aren't located at HQ are used to being more self-reliant and are accustomed to working together as a team when it makes sense.

"I think the culture change will be most challenging for my largest group, the one at HQ. They have a long history of directive leadership, and based on what I've seen so far, they want to please the boss. They look 'up' rather than 'across.'" He continues, "Some members of my team are predisposed to the direction I'm heading, but most aren't."

The new culture that Lars is charged with developing fits aspects of his leadership style because, as he explained to Chris, he doesn't like being directive. Lars admits that he has a couple of shortcomings—he does not reach out and connect easily, and he tends to be conflict avoidant.

Lars explains, "I would like my group to become a team and act as a leadership team." Chris asks him to elaborate, "How do you see the difference?" Lars shares, "The way I see it, being a team requires them to reach out to one another, work across boundaries, and challenge each other's thinking in meetings. We need to have healthy conflict, otherwise, our ability to innovate and problem-solve together will suffer."

Both Chris and Lars are aware that this kind of skill building is often more difficult and time-consuming than learning a new technical skill. What he is asking of his team is new behavior for most of them, and many are at a loss. Lars reveals to Chris that he became visibly frustrated with his team because even though he communicated what he thought was clear guidance about his expectations, they continued to look to him for direction, and they suppressed any conflict that arose. Silo mentality is entrenched. Lars has to play the hand he was dealt and grow the skills of the team members he inherited when he accepted his position.

Lars admits that he is actually more frustrated with himself than with the team. He feels like he is failing in this new position and instead wants to up-level his game.

How will Lars grow the capacity and capability of his leadership team (LT) to be able to take on the big challenges facing them? Layoffs are on the horizon, and he has to see some progress soon. What will he do?

➔ Lars's story continues on p. 95

CHAPTER 5:

JOURNEY OF THE NINE TYPES

You are now entering into the land of the nine Enneagram Types, where we will journey through each Type's interior landscape. A word to the wise: No one is compelling or *pretty* when in the grip of our habits and patterns or when we are *doing our Type*. It is easier to see the *fixations and compulsions* in others than in ourselves. When you read about your interior landscape, you may not like some of what you read. It takes courage to look in the mirror and acknowledge both our gifts and the ways we act that we don't find particularly appealing. Each of us displays a range of behaviors throughout our lives—sometimes we are at our best and other times we are not.

The following map key describes and defines the various landmarks on the journey. Please take time to read this before you read about the nine Enneagram Types.

One doesn't discover new lands without consenting to lose sight of the shore for a very long time.

—André Gide

MAP KEY TO YOUR JOURNEY HOME

‣ **WORLDVIEW**

This is my map of the world. It is the filter through which I see things. It shapes my response to life and the world around me. Even though

IF YOU CAN'T SEE IT AND ACKNOWLEDGE IT, YOU CAN'T CHANGE IT OR MANAGE IT.

my siblings and I were born into the same family, each one of us sees our family dynamic differently, and the way we respond to this dynamic is shaped by our worldview. My worldview contains my *operating model*: the beliefs I hold that shape how I see the world around me and that drive my patterned way of thinking, feeling, and acting—where I put my energy and attention. I tend to select evidence that confirms my beliefs. I will likely choose friends, relationships, and careers that support and reinforce my beliefs about the world and how I see myself.

▸ COMPULSIONS AND FIXATIONS

This is when I am in the grip of my Type. When I am stuck here, I start running into all sorts of challenges, obstacles, and inexplicable events. Yet I cannot seem to stop myself from doing what I do.

▸ ROLE IDENTITY

This is the role I play on my life journey. This is the way I see myself and probably how others see me. I feel trapped by my role—I don't know who I am without it—and at the same time I attract people and situations that reinforce my role and self-identity. People come to rely on me to be a particular way, and I believe that if I stop playing my role, I will lose my family, friends, and job.

▸ PARADOX

Jump to "The Roles We Play: Our Self-Identity," in Chapter 4, "The Hero's Journey," for more information.

Simply stated, what I try to avoid, I attract by my avoidance behavior. I am motivated by specific fears and desires. When I act on either or both, it keeps my role identity in place, and I continue to reenact my compulsive behavior.

▸ TEMPTATIONS ON THE JOURNEY

These are the temptations I face on my journey. When I succumb to them, I get caught in the grip of my compulsion. Once I am aware of how my compulsions get a grip on me, I can choose to ignore or avoid these temptations.

‣ DETOUR SIGNS

These are the indicator signs along the road pointing to possible detours that take me away from the path to my destination. It's best to stay on the main road, even though the detours will take me to familiar places and the main road is unknown.

‣ COURSE CORRECTION

If I am in the grip of my Type, act on the temptations, and take a detour, this is how I can get back on the main road again.

‣ INTO THE SHADOW

Robert Bly calls the shadow "the long bag we drag behind us."[21] As a child, we got messages to act or not act a particular way, to think or not think a particular way, and to be or not be a particular way. We were scolded, punished, or socially ostracized for not heeding those messages. Ultimately, we tossed all these messages into a bag because the negative repercussions were too great. We sling them over our shoulders and carry them around, but no longer recognize these parts of us. In fact, we carry judgments about these behaviors.

We spend the first part of life stuffing things into the bag and the second part dragging things out. The shadow is the part of us that is unconscious and asleep. Our patterned way of thinking, acting, and feeling lives in the subconscious and has a lot of power to direct the course of our life.

What happens with this shadow material is that some of it leaks out in unhealthy ways. These are repressed and not fully developed parts of us. Our shadow shows up as reactions, projections, and defensive strategies. We unconsciously act out repressed instincts—aggression, anger, rage, sexual instincts, fear, and so on. The behaviors come out as primitive, and "every part of our personality that we do not love will become hostile to us."[22]

Because our shadow contains disowned parts of us, we act without conscious awareness—we don't realize what we are doing and don't recognize these attributes as part of us. These are our blind spots.

▸ WORKING WITH THE SHADOW

Aspects of the descriptions in the "Worldview," "Role Identity," "Temptations on the Journey," and "Detour Signs" sections contain shadow material. The degree of your own self-awareness will determine how much of this is shadow and how much has been integrated.

For purposes of the section "Into the Shadow," I highlight the Wings, because this is a lesser-known part of people's understanding of the Enneagram. While I focus on the less healthy expression of the Wings and the Connecting Points for each Type as the shadow, the *helping allies* are also a part of the shadow. They are the healthy expression of the Wings and Connecting Points, because the shadow is neither good nor bad—just the denied parts of us.

It is likely that you either don't recognize the positive qualities of your *helping allies* because you think these attributes are unattainable, or have glimpsed these things in yourself from time to time but don't know how to gain access.

The value of recognizing and working with your shadow is to learn how to express these parts of you in healthy ways and to integrate them in your self-expression. When you do, you will have much more range of choice for how you respond to life in any given moment.

There's a moment in *Peter Pan* when Wendy's mom comes into the bedroom to catch Peter, and he jumps out the window, leaving his shadow behind. Later he has to get it back. Wendy helps him reattach it to his feet. Let's see if we can reattach our shadow to lessen its power over us.

When I travel to my shadow lands, I find the journey to be very challenging. I am being challenged to examine my life, my deeply held beliefs, my regrets, missed opportunities, undeveloped parts of me that will take work to develop, and my old wounds. I am being challenged to see the world as it is, not as I wish it would be.

Yet, it is by traveling to these unknown lands—and coming to recognize them, know them, and befriend them—that I find the treasures I have been seeking. The challenge in facing the shadow land is also the gift. The shadow is a destination for me to embrace. It takes courage to turn and face my shadow, but unimagined treasures are there that will nourish me for the rest of my life.

‣ HELPING ALLIES

These are other Enneagram Types who have special help to offer me, and actually they are Types I recognize in myself. Two of my travel companions are my Wings. When I connect with the gifts of my Wings, they help me to soar! The other two are the points I am connected to on the Enneagram symbol. I can call on them to join me on my journey, and by the time I reach my destination, they have become an integrated part of how I now know myself.

‣ BURIED TREASURE: TYPE *ALCHEMY*— TRANSFORMING LEAD INTO GOLD

My compulsions are a *distortion* of my true gifts. My compulsions sustain my role identity and worldview, and keep me away from myself. As long as I am playing a role, my true gift is expressed in a fixed and compulsive way. For instance, Type 9, the Peacemaker, tries to quash conflict in order to remain comfortable and stay connected to others. When Type 9s break out of this role, they can use their true gift of mediation to serve in a conscious way.

As I shed my protective layers and courageously look within, I find my buried treasure and become free of the prison I have created for myself—and it is effortless. My true gift emanates from me; there is no striving. However, first I must travel to my shadow land and meet and befriend its inhabitants, or I won't have the ingredients that I need for my own alchemy.

When I take the hero's journey and arrive at my destination—my home away from home; my true, authentic self—this is just the miraculous beginning of the next part of my extraordinary life!

TYPE 1
JOURNEY OF THE PERFECTIONIST

▸ WORLDVIEW

As a young child, I felt something was wrong with me, that I was bad. I felt imperfect and that I needed to do things well—to appear perfect to others and even myself. I took on the role of the *perfect one*. I came to believe that I knew what was right and the right way to do things, and it was important for me to teach others the right way. I believed that of course they wouldn't want to be sloppy, make mistakes, or do things incorrectly, would they?

Social graces are important, and one must adhere to certain standards of behavior. *Should* is a very important word for me. As soon as I hear that voice inside my head, I listen. I have an inner guidance system that charts my course and lets me know immediately when I need to make a course correction. It isn't a very friendly voice, but it has a ring of authority to it, so I listen—even if it is not what I want to do or think or feel.

TYPE 1 - THE PERFECTIONIST
My motto: *Do it right the first time*

Integrity is important to me. I have principles, and it's essential that I live by them. I impose structure in my life in order to get things done. I see things the right way, and I know what is best. I am a good person just trying to make the world a better place (according to my standards of right and wrong). I am responsible for making everything right. I am right, and others should listen to me. I have a hard time seeing the good that exists—either within me or outside of me—because I am too busy focusing on what can be improved.

▸ COMPULSION AND FIXATION:
ANGER AND RESENTMENT

I tend to control and repress my anger. I rationalize and justify my thinking about how I am right and others are wrong. This creates tension and rigidity in my body, tone of voice, and behavior. I start to feel anxious and restless about the world around me and the people in it. As a way to direct this build-up of anxiety and anger, I use its energy to perfect my environment, others, the world, and myself. When I hold on to the anger toward others and let it fester, it takes the form of resentment, and may leak out as sharp-edged criticism, judgments, or angry outbursts.

▸ ROLE IDENTITY

I identify as being the one who strives to be *perfect*. While I am often proud of this quality, I also have become trapped by it. I feel pressure to keep up to a certain standard of perfection, and show modesty and restraint, both in how I appear to others and by the quality of what I do. I realize I have created a codependency by self-identifying and thus become identified as the *perfect* one. It is probably true that people come to expect a high quality from me, and I feel the expectation of living up to this standard.

When you aim for perfection, you discover it's a moving target.
—Geoffrey F. Fisher

I am refined, acceptable, and modest. What would happen if I suddenly became disorganized, irresponsible, and unreliable; was showier in how I dressed and decorated; and drew attention to myself? What if I turned in work with mistakes, had an affair, did something morally or ethically against what I believed? Would I lose my job, family; would friends disappear? What if were to I shed this skin and decide to go for *good enough*, do what I felt like doing, and throw the to-do list out the window?

My thinking compulsion is *resentment* and my emotional compulsion is *anger*. My role as the Perfectionist is connected with anger. This is my emotional response to self and others when I cannot control my world and others don't live up to my standards. Well, nothing is ever *really perfect enough*, is it?

My compulsive thinking, resentment, is to rationalize and justify how I am right, moral, just, and fair, and why others aren't principled enough, aren't clean enough, make mistakes, don't live up to my standards, aren't on time, aren't doing what they should be doing, are morally and ethically imperfect / lacking in integrity, sloughing off … This is when I am *doing my Type* or acting as the authority figure / arbiter of right and wrong / Judge.

Perfectionist

Anger

Resentment ◀┈┈┈┈┈┈▶ Anger

▸ THE PARADOX

I am afraid of being criticized for being wrong, bad, or imperfect in some way. Instead of relaxing, playing, and doing what I really want, I focus on being good and perfect. I become overly perfectionistic, rigid, rule bound, critical, and exacting of my outer world (to include people). This overt focus on what's wrong with the world and avoidance of seeing the good confirms my belief that the world is not the way it should be and needs to be perfected. Thus my role identity is reinforced, and I can become stuck or trapped inside of it.

▸ TEMPTATIONS ON THE JOURNEY

Evaluating, doing things right, being right, continual self-improvement toward some ideal of perfection; continual focus on how to improve people, processes, situations, things.

▸ DETOUR SIGNS

You are your inner critic. You are the final authority; you are the arbiter of right and wrong. Something is not right, and you need to fix it. There is always room for improvement. Enjoy your life later; there is work to be done.

▸ COURSE CORRECTION

Breathe deeply. Slow down; give yourself permission to relax and play. Approach people and situations with curiosity. Seek to understand. You are a human being, not a human doing. Accept "good enough."

▸ INTO THE SHADOW

My Wings carry my shadow, as do my Connecting Points: lands of 9, 2, 4, 7. While the healthy expression of these four Types are companions on my journey, when I turn around to look at the shadow they cast, I see parts of me that I don't want to acknowledge. Sometimes it takes entering the shadow to uncover the gifts that are waiting there.

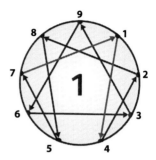

I find unhealthy aspects of my Wings, Types 9 and 2, in my shadow. Type 9 is the part of me that wants to have peace at all costs—to avoid possible conflict and to avoid addressing matters that are important. It is also that part of me that disengages and becomes complacent—the person within who does not want to draw attention, stand out, and express fully who I am.

There are also unhealthy aspects of Type 2 lurking in my shadow: that part of me who believes I need to be needed and wants to make myself indispensable, the person who is waiting and thirsting for approval and appreciation for my good works.

I find unhealthy aspects of the Types I am connected to: Types 4 and 7. Type 4 is where I go when I am feeling underappreciated and overstressed with the myriad of projects, things, and people I am trying to perfect. Suddenly I find myself in a state of melancholy and depression; I become moody and temperamental. Self-pity is a familiar state for me. I long for or envy what others have and I feel that I lack. I may feel the need to draw attention to myself—to be seen as unique and special.

I recognize the following unhealthy Type 7 qualities in myself: being scattered and unfocused, indecisive and gluttonous—wanting to try it all and not restrict myself in any way. I can distract from feelings of emotional pain and anxiety by keeping busy or become an escapist and lead a double life.

Part of my life journey is to make contact with the parts of me that are germane to Types 3, 5, 6, and 8. These may be qualities that I judge in others as being somehow bad or wrong, or that I just don't relate to at all. At some point, it will be important to visit these other lands and see what they have to teach me, what treasures can be found there.

Have no fear of perfection—you'll never reach it.

—Salvador Dali

▸ HELPING ALLIES

When I am stressed and about to succumb to temptation and take a detour, I ask my travel companions for help. Each of them has a gift to offer, something to teach. When I find myself in the land of black and white, it helps to connect with my Type 9 Wing. It is that part of me who is able to see many points of view, feels inner peace, and can mediate and bridge multiple viewpoints.

"I know what's right!" and I am working myself to the bone. This is what happens when I am in the grip of my Type and I am acting as the *father / authority figure*. However, I have a choice. I don't have to be the authority, dictating the right way. When I connect with my Type 2 wing—the *mother / nurturer / inner feminine archetype*—I maintain balance. I put down the whip and find the empathy and compassion for myself that I deserve. I am able to contact my heart and feelings of empathy and compassion for others. My edges soften. I nurture myself and allow myself to be nurtured. I can integrate these other parts of myself.

As I relax, Type 7 becomes accessible to me—the part of me that is spontaneous, playful, adventurous, open, fun-loving, and curious. Suddenly, being exactly on time, structured, and right is not as important as being more flexible, accepting, and encouraging. This is the juicy, vibrant part of me that dresses me up and takes me out!

Sustained periods of rest and reflection can take me to the high side of Type 4, the part of me that makes contact with my feelings, is profoundly sensitive, and opens the door to my unique creative expression and deepest longings.

▸ BURIED TREASURE: TYPE 1 ALCHEMY

Perfection, resentment, and anger transform into serenity and self-acceptance.

No longer do I feel inner agitation, anger, and resentment about controlling and perfecting the world. I become serene. I am accepting of myself and others. I am perfect exactly as I am, and the universe is unfolding exactly as it should be. I am free to be me and no longer feel the need to take responsibility for improving the world!

Out beyond ideas of wrongdoing and rightdoing, there is a field, I'll meet you there.

—Rumi

TYPE 1

POSITIVE CONTRIBUTION	REACTIONS / STRESS
Principled / Ethical / Moral / Integrity	Self--righteous / Certitude Judgmental Critcal Lecture / Preach Black and White Don't allow for own "imperfections" "Shoulds," do what's *right*, superior
Quality High standards Develop policies, procedures, rules Detailed	Don't allow for a creative response Uncompromising / Rigid Need to improve everyone and everything Lack objectivity for "good enough" Miss big picture / Must dot all *i*'s and cross all *t*'s Risk avoidant
Structured / Organized / Orderly / Prioritize / Predictable	Inflexible / Rigid / Controlled Lack spontaneity Boring
Reliable / Responsible / Purposeful / Proper / Honest	Lack tolerance Resentment / Anger / Worry / Anxiety / Moody
"Doers"	Overextend Get exhausted / Difficulty relaxing

TYPE 1 JOURNAL

 STOP AND REFLECT

Look at the Type 1 compulsions: Anger and resentment, and responsible and *should*. As you begin to explore this, you will start seeing your compulsive patterns and their impact on your life.

Think about a time when you felt the need to be *right*. Write about your early memories of this, what triggers this need or compulsion, what your feelings are when this happens. Recount a specific incident and notice the feelings, thoughts, reactions, and body sensations it evokes in you as you tell the story. Write down what you notice.

Think of a time in the recent past when you felt *responsible* for improving a person, a system, an organization, yourself. What precipitated this? What was going on in your internal state when you felt this responsibility? What was your inner dialog; what were your feelings, thoughts? Tell the story.

How does this behavior serve you? How does it hinder you?

How does this pattern play out in your life?

How has this worked for you / benefited you?

See if you can begin to notice your compulsion to show disapproval of others or anger toward them—before you do it. What are the signs—the internal signals that precede your expression of disapproval and anger?

What has been the cost to you?

Recall a time when you felt light and playful, when you were relaxed and had fun, when you allowed yourself to be spontaneous. What was going on? What were the circumstances that enabled you to feel this way? Write about it. Tell the story.

List your *core hurts* (for example, feeling unsupported, accused, unseen, flawed, worthless, unimportant, guilty, devalued, rejected, powerless, inadequate, unlovable).

When you were light and playful, how did you feel both, in the moment and later? Did you notice how others responded to you? Was the response different in some way?

How do your core fears and core hurts relate to each other and reinforce each other?

How can you cultivate more of this in your daily life?

What do your core fears and hurts have to do with your role identity?

Unraveling Your Role Identity (Review the *Role Identity* for Type 1, the Perfectionist)

List your *core fears* (for example, powerlessness, no support, loneliness, rejection, harm, deprivation, shame, exposure, feeling overwhelmed, humiliation, abandonment, pain, inability to fulfill dreams).

How did you come to believe that these fears and hurts were true and real? What is your evidence? How do you know?

What do you believe would happen if you stopped looking for this evidence and chose to look for evidence that negated these fears?

feelings come up for you when you imagine dropping this role?

If you no longer reacted to these fears, how would that affect the role you play?

Describe and list some of the qualities of how you would like to be and be seen. List some descriptive words (warm, playful, powerful …).

If you weren't playing your role of the Perfectionist / the Moralist, who would you be? What

What are the first steps you can take toward embodying these qualities?

▸ **TYPE 1** WORDS

Relax, play, ethics, criticism, idealism, discipline, integrity, perfection, ideals, control, being right, resentment, spontaneity, structure, planning, details, anxiety, melancholy, scheduling, doing, judgment, instincts, sensible, order, morality, fun, joy.

Your Enneagram Type will have a unique relationship with certain words associated with your compulsions and patterns.

Understanding the significance of these words and how they have played out in your life will be telling for you. Being more conscious of your feelings and attitudes toward these words will help you to transform how they live within you, and will help you to create your life story, moving forward.

Resentment is like taking poison and waiting for the other person to die.

—Malachy McCourt

Take your time with this, and find a quiet place where you can reflect. I suggest writing about one word at a time and letting it stew inside of you while you activate your inner observer (the nonjudging observer) and peel back its meaning. You will want to come back to this word again and again.

I suggest picking the first word that calls out to you. Each word has both positive and unhealthy expressions. Write about both. Keep digging deeper. Begin to notice as you go through your day how these words play out in your life.

For instance, *discipline*: what is your association with *discipline*? What does it feel like when you are *in the grip* of needing to be *disciplined*? What are the circumstances that evoke your need for *discipline*? How does it serve you? How does it create challenges and problems for you? Tell stories of times you have experienced *discipline* in yourself and others.

These are just some of the questions you might consider when you begin to explore how each word has shown up on your life journey. Consider how you want to bring these behaviors and qualities forward in a more conscious and intentional way.

▶ WHAT'S IN MY BIG BLACK BAG?
PEERING INTO MY SHADOW

Take a look at your Wings and your Connecting Points (Types 9, 2, 4, 7). What aspects of these Types do you recognize in yourself? What don't you relate to? Write about this. Start to self-observe and notice whether your self-observations are accurate. Inquire within. Ask others for their perceptions.

Go to the sections for your Connecting Points (Types 4 and 7), and Wings (Types 9 and 2), and get to know these parts of yourself. Take time to explore the words for these four Types. It will be quite instructive.

▶ THINGS YOU CAN DO TO MAKE A SHIFT

INTERNAL CRITIC AND THE VOICE OF ANXIETY

One of the big doorways to your own healing will be to tune in to your internal critic and your anxiety. Face your inner critic squarely. See how it is running your life. Write every day—whatever words, pictures, ideas, are there—and put that critical voice on paper without editing so that you can see it for what it is. Write free-form when you wake up in the morning, before you launch into your day.

Go to Chapter 10, "InsideOut—Leaders' Tool Kit," and see the instructions for "Fresh Start."

Engage your anxiety in conversation so that you can better understand what it is covering up that you don't want to see or deal with. Be curious about it, and write without editing about what it has to tell you. Don't run away from it.

CLEAR, QUIET MIND

In addition to Fresh Start, it is important to cultivate objectivity when it comes to your inner critic. Fresh Start will enable you to see it more clearly for what it is. After that, distinguishing the *should* voice from your voice of instinct will be essential. Meditation is an ideal practice for cultivating your quiet mind, even if you start with just five minutes a day.

"InsideOut—Leaders' Tool Kit" contains some basic instructions for meditation.

GROUNDING

Instead of acting on your impulse to be in constant motion, *stop*. Your Instinctual/Gut Center of Intelligence is just following the lead of your inner critic. Connect with your body sensations. What is your body telling you? When you ground your attention in your body, it will help you to hear the clear voice of instinct that is calling you to take grounded action, distinct from the action driven by your compulsive need to be *doing*.

Try the "Centering Basic Practice" in "InsideOut— Leaders' Tool Kit."

Connect with your Instinctual Center. Over time, you will be able to take more grounded action rather than feeling like you are spinning in constant motion.

AN INSIDEOUT LEADER'S STORY: **THE TEAM AND LARS—DIFFERENT REALITIES**

Lars is the fourth leader they have had in five years. Skepticism is high, especially because Lars was brought in from outside this part of the organization. Most of the team members have been with NHH for many years, and some of them for their entire careers. NHH culture is all they know. After years of feeling competent, Lars asks them to step into the unknown and be learners, something they are uncomfortable doing and most of them resist.

Lars's team is used to working in a traditional hierarchical environment. Functional expertise is the coin of the realm, and they have had plenty of resources to work that way. They operate as a workgroup, not as a team. Accountability has been vertical, rather than both vertical and horizontal. They are accustomed to the leader saying, "This is what I want," and their job is to please the leader by delivering it.

This began to frustrate the heck out of Lars. "Why are they looking to me instead of to themselves or each other?"

Lars feels the team members don't get it. He can't understand why they won't just do what he asks. He judges them for resisting. They can see Lars is frustrated with them and note his short temper. They also sense his disappointment and believe he thinks they are slow or incompetent. They wonder, "What does he really want?" They are each, in their own way, trying to figure it out.

Lars continues to try to draw them out and get them to see what he wants by asking leading questions. This is so diametrically opposed to what they are used to that it's hard for them to get it. The team members are starting to feel they are being treated like kids and that Lars is rapping their knuckles for disobedience.

The team perspective: "Why doesn't he just tell us what he wants?" Lars's perspective: "Why don't they get it? They want me to tell them what to do. They are intelligent adults. What is the problem?" This is not a useful dynamic. There is misunderstanding and blame. How will they bridge perspectives?

➜ Lars's story continues on p. 107

TYPE 2
JOURNEY OF THE PEOPLE PLEASER

▸ WORLDVIEW

When I was a young child, I felt that my need for love and attention wasn't getting met. I realized that just because I wanted love and attention didn't mean I would get it. I couldn't seem to make things go the way I wanted them to go. I came to believe that I was not worthy of love and my needs were less important than others'. Since I couldn't make things go the way I wanted by force of will, I learned how to manipulate my outer and inner worlds to have things go my way, to have my needs met, to get love and intimacy.

As I got older, I also began to believe that it was selfish to have my own needs and that I couldn't ask others for help; I had to take care of others first to earn their love. As time went on, I stopped recognizing my own needs, and found myself resenting people who depended on me and then didn't show appreciation for all I did.

My life's focus is on relationships. I see myself as a loving person and always doing for others. I feel that people take me for granted. I hate feeling dependent on others for love, appreciation, and support.

What really sets me off is when I feel obligated to take care of too many people, when people tell me to take care of myself, when people back away from me or create boundaries to keep me from *interfering* in their life—what's that about?

If I am really honest, I use flattery and manipulation to seduce people into caring about me—to get love, appreciation, and approval. I know I do things to get people to like me, and I am attracted to those I perceive to be strong and powerful so that I can make myself indispensable to them and garner their appreciation and power through my association with them. I can use guilt to manipulate, and when all else fails, I can get pretty demanding.

I am a loving, caring, selfless person without needs. I am self-sacrificing, empathic, sensitive, compassionate, well intentioned, and considerate, and I give without limits. If I receive enough appreciation, approval, and love, I will fully be able to love myself.

TYPE 2 - THE PEOPLE PLEASER
My motto: *Where would you be without me?*

▸ COMPULSION AND FIXATION:
PRIDE AND FLATTERY

Pride is a desire to be more important or attractive than others, the unwillingness to acknowledge one's own needs or suffering, the belief that one's intentions are good and virtuous.

I feel self-important when I rescue, please, and help others. Pride is a shield I use to deflect the deeper shame I have about not believing that I am lovable.

Because I so fully identify with being the one who pleases and helps others, I have a hard time receiving the help and support I truly need and desire. I use flattery to get what I want in another way, indirectly, to endear myself to others and eventually make myself indispensable—to get the appreciation and the love I want and need.

▸ ROLE IDENTITY

I identify as the people pleaser, the helper, and the giver. This is my role in life and how I see myself. My seductive powers are strong—I give personalized attention, and in fact I know what you need even before you do! I attract people who seem to need me, and I am attracted to people I think need my help, although I am generally selective about whom I choose. I am happy to orchestrate and run your life or your business for you. My sense of power and control comes from being the one who gives and runs the show, and my value and self-worth are based on the positive response I get from you. On some level, I realize this is a zero-sum game and I'm trapped by this role. Can I let go of control?

I have needs, too, but I don't want to admit it, sometimes even to myself. The paradox is that people see me as needy because I become demanding or can play the martyr when they don't meet the unspoken expectations I have of them. I give hints about what I want, assuming my needs will be met. But when people try to do something for me, I have a hard time receiving—I mean, I am the people pleaser, not the other way around!

‣ THE PARADOX

My belief is that I am selfish and undeserving of love, so I must earn it and focus on the needs of others. People can feel smothered and intruded upon by me. This leads to my eventual abandonment instead of eliciting what I desire most: to feel loved and build a stronger bond. When they run away from me, it serves to confirm my belief that I am unlovable and unlikely to ever get my needs met.

Conversely, I resent it when people depend on me and don't appreciate me; and I resent being dependent on them for love, appreciation, and support. *They are limiting my freedom.* I don't know how to get out of this bind I have created. What if I stopped playing this role? Would I be abandoned and left by my family and friends, by my employer? What would they do without me? Who would I be? What would I do?

As described above, my thinking compulsion is *flattery*, and my emotional compulsion is *pride*. My role as the people pleaser is connected with pride—my emotional response to self and others to maintain my role. I'm the one who helps, and my needs are subordinate to others'—the people pleaser to the rescue!

It's my pride that gets in the way and keeps my role or mask in place. I compulsively think about ways to flatter people to reel them in because of my strong need to be liked—to gain others' appreciation, approval, and love. Flattery is the lure, taking care of and anticipating others' needs is the role, and pride is what holds the codependent dynamic firmly in place. This is when I am *doing* my Type.

‣ TEMPTATIONS ON THE JOURNEY

Doing for others to get love, appreciation, and approval, and ultimately to prove to yourself that you are lovable. Manipulation. Seduction. Demand. Don't take care of yourself. React to situations you have created: when you feel obligated to take care of too many people; when people back away from you; when people tell you to take care of yourself; when you don't respect others' boundaries; when you need others to like you; when you don't accept help.

‣ DETOUR SIGNS

Help and please others to get approval. Believe that you are always loving! Others take you for granted. Self-sacrifice. Seduce people into caring about you. Manipulate to have things go your way. Don't recognize your own needs. Become emotive, dramatic, and directive. Play the martyr. Induce guilt. Intrude. Seek attention and approval. Become possessive. Make yourself indispensable. Become sick and hope to be rescued.

‣ COURSE CORRECTION

See that your power and value do not come from making yourself indispensable to others. Humility is the antidote to your pride. Accept your limits—you cannot do it all to save others. Turn your attention inward and notice how you compare yourself with your idealized self-image. Fill your own well with self-care and self-love, and appreciate yourself for the wonderful person you are, not for what you do for others. See yourself objectively and not as you want to see yourself.

‣ INTO THE SHADOW

My Wings carry my shadow, as do my Connecting Points: lands of 1, 3, 8, 4. While the healthy expressions of these four Types are companions on my journey, when I turn around to look at the shadow they cast, I see parts of me that I don't want to acknowledge.

There are unhealthy aspects of my Wings, Types 1 and 3, in my shadow. The Type 1 part of me resents others for not caring for me and about me the way I want them to. I have unexpressed anger about not having my needs met and may let 'er rip from time to time. Perhaps I share some of the rigidity of Type 1 as well.

There are also unhealthy aspects of Type 3 lurking in my shadow— that part of me lacking authenticity that can be a bit fake and phony. Perhaps I try to craft an image to be seen in a particular way. Do I strive for success by becoming indispensable to powerful people? Will I step on others to get to my goals?

I am also aware of less healthy aspects in myself of the Types I am connected to: Types 8 and 4. Type 8 is where I go when after all that doing for others, I am not feeling appreciated or cared for in the way I expect. I can become demanding, invasive, and domineering—and sometimes full of rage. I want to take revenge.

Type 4 is where I go when I am feeling underappreciated and un-loved. None of my other strategies are working. Suddenly I find my-self in a state of melancholy and depression, and I can become tem-peramental. I might withdraw into my inner world, where I amplify my feelings and the situation—making them bigger than life. I find myself longing for or envying what others have and I feel that I lack. I may try to draw attention to myself because I want to be seen as unique and special.

Part of my life journey will be to make contact with the parts of me that are germane to Types 5, 6, 7, and 9. These may be qualities that I judge in others as being somehow bad or wrong or I just don't relate to at all. At some point, it will be important to visit these other lands and see what they have to teach me, what treasures can be found there.

‣ HELPING ALLIES

I am surrounded by the gift of loving self-acceptance in both of my Wings, Types 1 and 3. This is already available to me and will be very healing when I can receive these gifts. Type 1 is the part of me that can face adversity and problems objectively and doesn't take things personally; that expresses anger directly; and that is principled and acts on ideals and values.

Type 3 is the authentic and truly heroic part of me that is focused on achieving ideals and isn't derailed by the siren's call. Type 3 knows how to distinguish between authentic and fake, and cuts through the crap with a stiletto. It's that part of me that instinctively seizes on opportunities. Instead of trying to make others look good, I put my energy into personal accomplishments.

When I ask for and receive the help of my two Wings, I can soar! My journey will take me to Type 4, another important companion. There I find my purpose in life, my own unique contribution and creative expression. Then comes the time to visit the highlands of Type 8, where I find my true source of power and strength—my big heart.

I am willing to trust my gut and take action on behalf of those who can't—and there are no strings attached. I do it because I care and I can. I am deeply in contact with my wellspring of love.

‣ **BURIED TREASURE:** TYPE 2 ALCHEMY

Pride and flattery transform into humility, freedom, and unconditional love for self and others.

I pull back the curtain on my life and now see how my pride interferes with my ability to receive what I most desire—support, help, and love. I am more comfortable in my own skin and don't feel the need to be someone special or do for others in order to feel lovable and to be loved. I am free! I am truly humbled by the love and generosity I experience from others. I am genuinely openhearted, generous, self-caring, empathic, and nurturing. I am finally able to have the relationships I long for, and I know in the deepest part of my being that I am lovable. This opens the door for me to freely give and receive without expectation or strings attached. I have stepped into my own power and have found my own creative expression in the world; I am no longer the moon, reflecting the sun's light and power. I shine with the power of my clear and open heart.

Love is always bestowed as a gift—freely, willingly, and without expectation…. We don't love to be loved; we love to love.

—Leo Buscaglia

TYPE 2

POSITIVE CONTRIBUTION	REACTIONS / STRESS
Warm / Caring / Empathic / Anticipate needs / Demonstrative / Optimistic / Likable	Not in touch with own needs and feelings / Intrusive / Lack boundaries / Emotional vampire
Relationship building	Possessive / Jealous / Seducer
People manager / Help people reach their potential People / Client advocate / Client relations Human resources Social Focus on "the group / the team" Focus on values / making work meaningful	Get too involved in people's personal lives Disempowering Lose objectivity Lose neutrality Lose focus on business results / Strategy Err on side of people pleasing when needing to make tough business decisions
Responsive / Artistic / Creative	Demanding / Ambitious / Controlling / Domineering
Caretaker / Helpful / Giving of themselves / Generous / Humble / Altruistic	Become exhausted / Don't take care of themselves / Don't accept help / Martyr / Victim / Expectations (give with a hook) / Manipulative / Angry when unappreciated

TYPE 2 JOURNAL

 STOP AND REFLECT

Look at the Type 2 compulsions: Pride and flattery, with a focus on self-image and feeling shame. As you begin to explore this, you will start seeing your compulsive patterns and their impact on your life.

Recall a time when you felt the compulsion to help or please someone. Look into what was motivating you when you had this urge. What was happening? How were you feeling? What did you do? Write about it. When you help or decide to try to please someone, do you have any expectation of getting something in return?

How does this pattern play out in your life?

How has this been beneficial for you?

Recall a time when someone offered to help or support you in some way without your asking directly or indirectly, and you graciously received the help. What were the circumstances? What were you thinking, feeling, and doing? Tell the story. What were the enabling factors that allowed you to receive? How did it feel? What were the internal obstacles you had to overcome? How did you do it?

What has been the cost to you? How has this hindered you?

Write about a time when you chose to make yourself indispensable to someone. What motivated you to do that? What did you hope to gain? How did it benefit you? What was the cost to you?

What was the outcome in this situation—both short and long term?

Recall a time when you used flattery or manipulation to get what you wanted. Write about how this played out for you. What were you thinking, feeling, and doing? What were the sensations in your body? What triggered this for you? What motivated your actions? What was the outcome in this situation—both short and long term?

How can you cultivate more of this in your life—directly asking for and receiving help and support?

Unraveling Your Role Identity (Review the *Role Identity* for Type 2, the People Pleaser)

🖊 List your *core fears* (for example, powerlessness, no support, loneliness, rejection, harm, deprivation, shame, exposure, feeling overwhelmed, humiliation, abandonment, pain, inability to fulfill dreams).

🖊 List your *core hurts* (for example, feeling unsupported, accused, unseen, flawed, worthless, unimportant, guilty, devalued, rejected, powerless, inadequate, unlovable).

🖊 How do your core fears and core hurts relate to each other and reinforce each other?

🖊 What do your core fears and hurts have to do with your role identity?

🖊 How did you come to believe that these fears and hurts were true and real? What is your evidence that this is true? How do you know?

🖊 What do you believe would happen if you stopped looking for this evidence and chose to look for evidence that negated these fears?

🖊 If you no longer reacted to these fears, how would that affect the role you play?

🖊 If you weren't playing your role of the People Pleaser / the Rescuer / the Helpful One, who would you be? What feelings come up for you when you imagine dropping this role?

List some qualities that describe how you would like to be and be seen. List some descriptive words (warm, playful, powerful ...).

What are the first steps you can take toward embodying these qualities?

▸ TYPE 2 WORDS

Giving, self-love, receiving, empathy, victim, pleasing, self-care, control, appreciation, neediness, pride, self-indulgence, martyr, flattery, demanding, manipulation, acceptance, power, humility, value, image, shame, hedonistic.

Your Enneagram Type will have a unique relationship to certain words associated with your compulsions and patterns.

Understanding the significance of these words and how they have played out in your life will be telling for you. Being more conscious of your feelings and attitudes toward these words will help you to transform how they live within you, and help you to create your life story moving forward.

Take your time with this, and find a quiet place where you can reflect. I suggest writing about one word at a time and letting it stew inside of you while you activate your inner observer (the non-judging observer), noticing how you peel back its meaning. You will want to come back to this word time and again.

I suggest picking the first word that calls to you from your list. Each word has both positive and unhealthy expressions. Write about both. Keep digging deeper. Begin to notice as you go through your day how these words play out in your life.

For instance, *appreciation*: What is your association with appreciation? What does it feel like when you are *in the grip* of seeking appreciation? What are the circumstances that evoke your need for appreciation? How does it serve you? How does it create challenges and problems for you? Tell stories of times you have experienced appreciation.

These are just some of the questions you might consider when you begin to explore how each word has shown up on your life journey. Consider how you want to bring these behaviors and qualities forward in a more conscious and intentional way.

✦ Go to the sections for your Connecting Points (Types 8 and 4) and your Wings (Types 1 and 3), and get to know these parts of yourself. Take time to explore the words for these four Types. It will be quite instructive.

‣ WHAT'S IN MY BIG BLACK BAG?
PEERING INTO MY SHADOW

✐ Take a look at your Wings and your two Connecting Points. What aspects of these Types do you recognize in yourself? What don't you relate to? Write about this. Begin to self-observe and notice whether your observations are accurate. Inquire within. Ask others for their perceptions.

‣ THINGS YOU CAN DO TO MAKE A SHIFT

OBJECTIVITY / CULTIVATING A CLEAR, QUIET MIND

A big temptation for Type 2 is to focus on relationships as primary. Your self-worth is inextricably linked to your relationships—feeling lovable, loved, and worthy. Relationships are critical for everyone, but not to the exclusion of taking care of practical matters—tending to business, health, and so on. When attention and focus are primarily on relationships, life is out of balance, and it is easy to get derailed from whatever direction you may have been heading.

✦ "InsideOut—Leaders' Tool Kit" contains instructions for a basic meditation practice. Also explore the section "The Role of Intuition" therein.

To be aware of how much this is at play for you, develop a meditation practice. This will be extremely helpful, allowing you to notice—without judgment—where your attention goes and to observe your recurring thought patterns.

GROUNDING

Getting more grounded in your body and paying attention to your body sensations is essential—yoga, Pilates, hiking, anything that focuses you on your physicality is helpful.

✴ See the "Centering Basic Practice" in "InsideOut— Leaders' Tool Kit."

Your Instinctual/Gut Center of Intelligence is following the lead of your Heart Center with its attention on relationships. Connecting with your body sensations is important for you. Ground your attention in your body to help you hear the clear voice of instinct that is calling you to take grounded action, distinct from the action driven by your compulsive need to be doing for others. Over time, you will be able to take more grounded action based on what is needed, rather than based on being needed.

 ## AN INSIDEOUT LEADER'S STORY: **THE DYNAMICS ARE SET UP**

Lars wants mutual accountability. He wants them to function as a team by problem-finding and problem-solving together. Unfortunately, they have no frame of reference for functioning in this fashion. What Lars doesn't understand is that they are confused. From their perspective, he might as well have been speaking Swahili.

One of the smaller and more remote sites is used to working together and behaving like a small company, structurally. There is more trust among the team members and a willingness to admit that they don't know—the starting point of innovation. Lars has taken to this sub-team and feels that they understand what he is asking of them. He notices that they don't seem to compete with one another, and each one is willing to speak on behalf of the team to the larger organization.

The people on the team in HQ consider themselves the best in the world and believe that the world beats a path to their door. They believe they have "scientific rightness." Saying, "I don't know," "I need help," or "Let's talk about it together" is foreign to them. Like many organizations, they have the not invented here syndrome. Acting as a mutually accountable team cuts against the grain.

The team at HQ feels judged for not doing it right and believes the sub-teams at the remote sites are in favor. Lars continues to be frustrated: "Why aren't they stepping up? Why aren't they operating across organizational boundaries? Why aren't they giving each other feedback? Why are they looking to me for direction? Why aren't they solving this yet? Why are they coming to me for permission?" Lars observes that the HQ team members can't make decisions on the smallest things and are excessively polite with one another.

Frustration grows. Will there be a breakthrough? How do you think the Enneagram can help?

→ Lars's story continues on p. 119

TYPE 3
JOURNEY OF THE ACHIEVER

▸ **WORLDVIEW**

As a young child, I felt inadequate, incompetent, a failure, and incapable of taking care of myself. I thought I had to be the best in order to be valued and loved. Unfortunately, this led to an early childhood belief that I was loved only for my accomplishments and not for me. I have feelings of shame associated with this belief, and the pain is so great that I put a wall around my heart to protect myself. Protected from this pain, I venture out and focus on success so that I can feel loved, valuable, and worthy.

I see life as a contest to be won, and I find myself constantly striving to be successful—to be the best and to avoid failure at all costs. I want people to think I have it all together. Maybe I am self-promoting, but if I don't promote myself, who will? My feelings of self-worth, value, and lovability are all based on the extent to which I can achieve and succeed. Getting the rewards of status, admiration, and recognition is worth it!

I can become pretty agitated, reactive, and defensive to cover up my feelings of helplessness. I avoid showing vulnerability. I can reinvent myself when the need arises, and adapt my image to suit the situation and to shape others' perceptions of me.

When people want my time and attention for more than just superficial contact, I can become reactive or get annoyed. I have a lot of weight on my shoulders and plenty to do. These demands for intimate connection put stress on me, and I certainly don't want to open myself up and be vulnerable. Over time, expecting myself to be the best at everything I do, and to have all the symbols of status and success, can weigh on me and exhaust me.

Yet there is always another goal to achieve, and I do what is necessary to win. Success is what counts. People see me as driven and ambitious. I see myself as outstanding, efficient, and a successful *individual*.

TYPE 3 - THE ACHIEVER
My motto: *Failure is not an option*

▸ COMPULSION AND FIXATION:
DECEIT AND VANITY

Deceit, in this sense, first and foremost is deceiving my own heart. In an effort to feel worthwhile and valuable, I do *what it takes* to be successful and project an image of success. My vanity is my inflated pride in my accomplishments. This is important for me because I believe that being successful and achieving goals will earn me the admiration of people I want to impress.

To others, I may appear vain and self-involved. However, it all comes at a price; I lose contact with my authentic nature, my passion, and my relationships. I am too busy focusing on success in my hunger for praise, admiration, and recognition.

▸ ROLE IDENTITY

I am the achiever. This is how I see myself, and it's the role I play in life. Others see me that way, too. They know that if they give me a challenge, I'll take it on and do whatever it takes to cross the finish line and win the trophy. This raises my status and makes me feel that I am valuable. In fact, I begin to notice the inefficient attitudes and behaviors in others around me. I believe that without me, things would never be accomplished and success would be unattainable. This serves to inflate my self-importance (vanity) and hold it firmly in place.

Unfortunately, getting admiration and recognition only fuels my desire for more, and I feel trapped by my role. My self-worth is based on my performance and the image I project. If that's how I measure myself as a person, my self-worth is a house of cards. I am so busy being a chameleon to project the right image that I don't even know who I am anymore (deceit). I'm not even sure that people like me. I think they just like attaching themselves to my success. Clearly, what garners the recognition I desire is the persona I project, my status, and my achievements, not the real me. This only serves to confirm my belief about myself—that my value or worth is based on what I do, not who I am. On some level, I am a failure as a person. I don't know how to break this cycle.

I want to be authentic. I don't want to have to wear a mask all the time. If I stay busy enough and focus on success, I don't have to think about it or feel the loss of myself and lack of relationships with others. I am in a bind. I depend on admiration from others to feel my self-worth. There are people who are in my life or say the right things to me because they like to be around success. Who are my true friends? Who would be there if I weren't successful? Do people like me for me? They don't even know who I am.

As described above, my thinking compulsion is *deceit*, and my emotional compulsion is *vanity*. My role as the Achiever is connected with vanity, my emotional response to self and others to maintain my role—*I am important; I have status, and others admire me and want what I have—they want to be around me because important things happen in relationship to me.*

It's my vanity that gets in the way and keeps my role or mask in place. My compulsive thinking (deceit) is the way I lie to myself and others to keep my mask in place. I deceive to create the right image to be successful and win the admiration of others. Deceit opens the door to feelings of self-importance—vanity—and self-promotion that allow me to make my mark in the world and achieve success. This is what holds the codependence dynamic firmly in place. This is when I am *doing my Type*.

‣ THE PARADOX

If I am willing to be brutally honest with myself, I know that I cover up my shame about feeling unworthy and not valuable. I do this by making sure that others know I am successful. Whether I name-drop, surround myself with symbols of success, am seen in the right places with the right people, or have a title worthy of envy, people know I am a winner.

The paradox is that I have been so busy putting on a show, I have deceived myself and others. They don't envy me or think I am valuable, they just envy what I appear to have acquired. Success has been more important than valuing the people around me. They see what I can do, but they don't care about me. People don't know who I am, and I have lost contact with my core values too. I have been so busy creating an image that I forgot myself. This brings up feelings of shame and worthlessness.

‣ TEMPTATIONS ON THE JOURNEY

Competing to be the best in everything. Acquiring status symbols. Needing to make a positive impression based on what others value and idealize. Taking shortcuts to get to the goal. Sacrificing quality for speed. Putting relationships in the backseat and emotionally detaching. Self-promoting. Giving the appearance of having it all together. Being superficial. Running away from requests for intimate connection.

‣ DETOUR SIGNS

You must be the best at everything you do. Acquire symbols of status and success. Hide your insecurities and feelings of vulnerability. Seek recognition and status. Failure is not an option. If you can't be assured of success, don't take on the challenge. Ignore relationships; your goals are more important. Efficiency is what counts. Remember, other people are just there to make you look good.

‣ COURSE CORRECTION

Strive for excellence instead of perfect execution. Remember to be effective, not just efficient. People are looking to you to mentor them. Remember, relationships both at work and at home need tending. Realize that everything is not all up to you. Slow down. Look inward and be curious about who is really in there. Take time to relax, contact your heart, and reconnect with your values and what is *really* important to you.

‣ INTO THE SHADOW

My Wings carry my shadow, as do my Connecting Points: lands of 2, 4, 9, 6. While the healthy expressions of these four Types are companions on my journey, when I turn around to look at the shadow they cast, I see parts of me that I don't want to acknowledge.

My shadow in Type 2 contains my neediness and my manipulative and seductive strategies to get what I want. My strong will to control both my inner and outer experiences can be found here. Type 4 contains my moody and temperamental nature, and the times when I am self-absorbed, envious of others, and busy trying to draw attention to myself.

Type 9 is also one of my shadow lands. I take detours there when I am stressed, and then I withdraw, disengage, and become complacent. I am just trying to find my inner peace and avoid any mess I may have created, and any conflict and upset. I go there to avoid looking at myself in the mirror and honestly assessing who is there.

I find myself in Type 6's shadow after long-term stress and unwillingness to face reality. This is the shadow that contains my anxiety, worry, and fear about what could happen. I can become skeptical and suspicious, not trusting of anyone around me—they all want something from me. I can also find myself being vigilant and paranoid.

Part of my life journey will be to make contact with the parts of me that are germane to Types 1, 5, 7, and 8. These may be qualities that I judge in others as being somehow bad or wrong or that I just don't relate to at all. At some point, it will be important to visit these other lands and see what they have to teach me, what treasures can be found there.

▸ HELPING ALLIES

Type 2 is on my right, Type 4 is on my left, and I stand in the middle of the Heart Center. Yet I repress my feelings in order to stay focused on the goal, so that nothing and no one stands in my way. Type 2 is the perfect companion to help me remember that relationships are key to my life, to connect with my empathic nature, and to tune in to others' needs rather than just focusing on my own needs and using others to meet my own ends. Type 4 is ideal to help me connect with my authenticity. Type 4 is bent on being exactly who they are, without compromise. Type 4 is also the antidote to my looking outside myself. Type 4 helps me focus on my inner landscape, to what is important to me—my dreams, my longings, and what matters most. My connection to Type 4 attunes my sensitivity to my inner world and to others. Type 4 gives the gift of depth as an antidote to my leanings toward superficiality.

When I slow down and connect with my own heart, the path opens to Type 6. Here I can integrate the healthier qualities of Type 6: to act responsibly, to be loyal, to honor my commitments, to see the group as more important than my own individual interests, to become aware of the potential consequences of my decisions. Healthy 6 also teaches about faith and trust—these are forces available to support me. I am not alone and don't have to do it all myself. Healthy Type 9 is along for the journey, too, offering me the gifts of acceptance, inner peace, and harmony, to see things holistically rather than just the goal in front of me. Type 9 helps expand my peripheral vision. Type 9s also show me how to lead from behind—that I don't always have to stand out and be the star, but can step back and let others shine.

▸ **BURIED TREASURE:** TYPE 3 ALCHEMY

Authentic heart, harmony, self-acceptance, love of truth.

I am free of my prison! I finally know who I am and the value of who I am, and I like myself! I no longer need to wear different personas to seek status, feel successful, and be the star. No longer does my sense of self-worth come from what I do, whom I know, or the symbols of status around me.

In the deepest part of my being, I now know that I am a valuable person. I believe in myself and have reclaimed my heart's desire. Deceit and vanity have alchemized into authenticity—I am free to be me. Rather than needing to be the star, I mentor others and help them to shine. I have found my tenderness, patience, and big-hearted warmth. I am adaptable and flexible while maintaining my authenticity, and am still able to accomplish a great deal. Others are inspired and motivated by my authenticity, and I use my energy and gifts to better the world.

And the golden bees were making white combs and sweet honey from my old failures.

—Antonio Machado, from "Commentary," *Times Alone*[23]

TYPE 3

POSITIVE CONTRIBUTION	REACTIONS / STRESS
Marketing / Promoting / Selling / Optimistic / Confident / Charming / Gracious	Self--promoting / Slick / Seek admiration / Not trustworthy
Competitive / Want to win / Focused on success and results / Authentic	Win at all costs / Deceive self and others / Lose track of their heart's desire / Ruthless / Abrupt / Impatient
Goal oriented / Efficient / Set up efficient processes and structures / Adaptable	Driving and striving / People and relationships take a backseat / Do whatever it takes / Cut corners / Being effective not important / Change image to give appearance of success or to suit the situation (chameleon)
Achievers / Make things happen / High energy / Focused	Think success lies on their shoulders / Become exhausted / Don't relax and rest—expect same from others
Mentors / Heart centered	See people as an extension of themselves / Use other people to accomplish their ends / Lose track of their own feelings and disregard others' feelings

TYPE 3 JOURNAL

 STOP AND REFLECT

Look at the Type 3 compulsions: Deceit and vanity combined with feelings of shame and self-image focus. As you begin to explore this, you will start to see your compulsive patterns and their impact on your life.

Think about a time when you felt the need to achieve at all costs. Write about your memory of this. What triggered this need or compulsion? What were the feelings, thoughts, reactions, and body sensations this evoked in you? As you retell the story now, what does it bring up for you?

✐ How does this pattern play out in your life?

✐ How has this worked for you / benefited you?

✐ What has been the cost to you?

✐ Recall a situation when you have been deeply touched. Write about it and what came up for you—feelings, thoughts, and body sensations.

✐ What were the benefits that came from this (short and long term)? What were the internal ob-

stacles you had to overcome to allow this for yourself? What were the circumstances that enabled you to make contact with your heart?

✐ How can you cultivate more of this in your life?

Unraveling Your Role Identity (Review the *Role Identity* for Type 3, the Achiever)

✐ List your *core fears* (for example, powerlessness, no support, loneliness, rejection, harm, deprivation, shame, exposure, feeling overwhelmed, humiliation, abandonment, pain, inability to fulfill dreams).

✐ List your *core hurts* (for example, feeling unsupported, accused, unseen, flawed, worthless, unimportant, guilty, devalued, rejected, powerless, inadequate, unlovable).

How do your core fears and core hurts relate to each other and reinforce each other?

What do your core fears and hurts have to do with your role identity?

How did you come to believe that these fears and hurts were true and real? What is your evidence that your beliefs are true? How do you know?

What do you believe would happen if you stopped looking for this evidence and chose to look for evidence that negated these fears?

If you no longer reacted to these fears, how would that affect the role you play?

If you weren't playing your role of the Achiever / the Successful One, who would you be? What feelings come up for you when you imagine dropping this role?

Describe and list some qualities you would like to include in your self-expression. List some descriptive words (warm, playful, powerful …).

What are the first steps you can take toward embodying these qualities?

▸ **TYPE 3** WORDS

Success, image, achievement, promotion, relationships, self-worth, heart's desire, shame, deception, vanity, efficiency, status, love, mentor, support, heroic, value, responsible, loyal.

✎ Your Enneagram Type will have a unique association with certain words related to your compulsions and patterns.

Understanding the significance of these words and how they have played out in your life will be telling for you. Being more conscious of your feelings and attitudes toward these words will help you to transform how they live within you and help you to create your life story moving forward.

Take your time with this, and find a quiet place where you can reflect. I suggest writing about one word at a time and letting it stew inside of you while you activate your inner observer (the nonjudging observer) and peel back its meaning. You will want to come back to this word again and again.

I suggest picking the first word that calls to you in your own list. Each word has both positive connotations and unhealthy expressions. Write about both. Keep digging deeper. Begin to notice as you go through your day how these words play out in your life.

For instance, *status*: What is your association with status? What does it feel like when you are *in the grip* of seeking status? What are the circumstances that evoke your need for status? How does it serve you? How does it create challenges and problems for you? Tell stories of times you have experienced status.

These are just some of the questions you might consider when you begin to explore how each word has shown up on your life journey. Consider how you want to bring these behaviors and qualities forward in a more conscious and intentional way.

✱ Go to the section for your Connecting Points (Types 9 and 6) and your Wings (Types 2 and 4), and get to know these parts of yourself. Take time to explore the words for these four Types. It will be quite instructive.

‣ WHAT'S IN MY BIG BLACK BAG?
PEERING INTO MY SHADOW

✎ Take a look at your Wings and your two Connecting Points. What aspects of these Types do you recognize in yourself? What don't you relate to? Write about this. Start to self-observe and notice whether your self-observations are accurate. Inquire within. Ask others for their perceptions.

‣ THINGS YOU CAN DO TO MAKE A SHIFT

CONNECT WITH YOUR HEART

The Heart Center is your doorway to integrate your shadow and relax around your Type 3 fixations and compulsions.

SLOW DOWN

Pay attention to the miracle of life all around you. Make contact with your heart. Listen to music that you find touching, watch a movie that moves you, spend time with people who inspire you to be your best, read a book about something or someone meaningful to you. Do volunteer work. Whatever doorways open you to your heart, find them and walk through them.

RECLAIM YOUR HEART'S DESIRE

✱ See "InsideOut—Leaders' Tool Kit." Take time with the practices "Reclaim Your Passion," "Gratitude Alphabet," and "Centering Basic Practice."

See if you can take time in nature—wander and wonder. What did you love to do as a child? What were your dreams for yourself and your life? Are you living your life or someone else's life? Write. Make a painting or collage of things you love to do, of what is meaningful to you. See if you can remember and make contact with those long-forgotten dreams.

AN INSIDEOUT LEADER'S STORY: **CHRIS AND LARS CONTRACT FOR WORK**

Chris is now on board and has a fairly good idea of the dynamics at play and the challenges that Lars and his team are facing. After assessing the situation—shadowing Lars, evaluating his 360-degree reviews, and meeting with HR, Caitlin, and the team, Chris is ready to propose how he can best support Lars. Together they develop goals for their work.

In his role, Chris wears three different hats: coach, consultant, and thought partner.

COACHING

- Develop executive presence, to include increasing Lars's ability to influence and to improve his visibility with senior leaders and peers

- Work to amplify strengths and avoid pitfalls

PREPARE LARS

The organization and industry is in a state of transformation. Lars needs to prepare himself to stay grounded and centered through the turbulent times ahead. He needs to be a steady, solid force for his team and organization while keeping his eye on the vision and forging ahead.

CONSULTING

Break down the silos: Shift thinking and behavior from silo to matrix. Create a collaborative, collegial environment where the team members work together across organizational boundaries.

Strategy: Develop and implement an innovative strategy that speaks to the changing demands of the marketplace.

Their work together will have several components:

- Coach Lars

- Build and develop Lars's team

- Consult: Strategic plan and implementation

- Consult: Develop a change-implementation plan

➜ Lars's story continues on p. 132

TYPE 4
JOURNEY OF THE INDIVIDUALIST

‣ WORLDVIEW

When I was a young child, I felt disconnected from the family, somehow estranged or alienated. I didn't feel seen or understood. Not that I was invisible, just different from the rest, and they didn't *get* me. Perhaps I didn't measure up to some ideal—this was a hunch I had, which I have carried through my life. It is what I came to believe about myself. Somehow I am missing something important, and I need to find it.

I thought that if I spent my life trying to achieve this idealized version of myself, I would be loved and accepted, and perhaps I would come to love myself. I think I abandoned myself in the search for my ideal self. I enter a state of melancholy when I feel hopeless that I will ever realize my ideal. Deep down, I have a lot of shame for not living up to my ideal and for what might have been. I feel that I am a failure as a person.

Because I feel different, I decided to emphasize my uniqueness. I am an intuitive, sensitive, and loving person who is deeply profound. Don't people see that? Don't they know I am suffering? I know I can get stuck focusing on my past traumas and cling to my pain. I just can't seem to let go, and I know this keeps me from moving forward. My world can become gray and hopeless. I have regrets and remorse about the past and can feel powerless to change things. I have been a victim of fate and feel victimized by my past.

In fact, I have never really fit in and have always been on the outside. Well, it's other people's issue if they don't accept me the way I am, not mine. People don't meet my emotional needs or expectations, either. They always disappoint me.

I'm different, and it's important for me to stand out, to be different—*I gotta be me!* Then I will be seen for who I really am. I am authenticity in action, true to myself. I need to express myself, and people just need to deal with me. My life is about finding and being who I really am. I try on different personas in search of my true identity—my ideal version of me.

TYPE 4 - THE INDIVIDUALIST
My motto: *I gotta be me*

I romanticize how I think my life should be, I am known to be emotionally intense and to amplify my feelings—I stir things up and can be pretty dramatic. Nothing mundane or superficial for me.

▸ COMPULSION AND FIXATION:
ENVY AND MELANCHOLY

Envy is first a perception and then resentment I hold that another person has something I believe I lack, and deep down I may wish the other person to be deprived of it.

Envy and melancholy together raise my awareness that something is missing in my life; that something is wrong with the way things are. This is my compulsive way of keeping reality at bay, always longing for things to be different than they are. "If only … ," "Other people have what I don't." I long for my ideal.

▸ ROLE IDENTITY

I identify as a unique, special individualist. There is no one quite like me, and I need to express my true/idealized identity when I find it. I long to find my true self, but I carry the belief that I am tragically flawed and deeply wounded—perhaps beyond repair. Life always seems so easy for other people. I envy them and their happiness. My life is tragic, and something is always missing. I need to go out and find it, and then I'll be able to fully express who I am. People will see me for the unique person I know myself to be, and then I can finally be happy.

My moods shift, and my feelings about myself, and how I see myself, shift with my moods. I am prone to feelings of melancholy. This way of feeling is familiar to me—more familiar than happiness and joy. Intimate relationships seem elusive. I am sure I'll be rejected or abandoned, so I reject first. It is less painful that way. It reinforces my feelings of being different. I trust my feelings more than my instincts or my analytical mind. If I have a feeling about someone or something, I am sure it must be true. I tend to take things very personally and have a hard time being objective—especially when it comes to my identity and how people relate to me. I notice every slight, all the ways I am misunderstood and am not enough, and the inherent perfection in others that I don't seem to have. I am unable to fully receive the love and acceptance that is there for me, so I discount it.

I want to be me, but the question remains—who am I? It is hard for me to take practical action toward my dream when it keeps changing. I feel stuck in this loop of wanting to fully express who I am in the world, regretting what might have been and then envying what I don't have—what's missing in me and my life that others seem to have. This sends me into a state of melancholy, and it is tough for me to move into action when I am feeling badly about myself. I go deeper inward, trying to understand what is going on inside of me, and I build a wall around me. Often I blame other people for my unhappiness. I can wallow in past hurts and upsets. I tend to get temperamental and moody, which then pushes people away from me, reinforcing how I feel about myself.

What if I stopped being dramatic and temperamental? What if I were happy and content with my life, felt positive about my future, and saw the glass as half-full? What if I weren't the *deeply sensitive and profound* one? Who would I be? What would it be like to feel happy and to have calm and steadiness in my life—no turbulence, no longing? Who would I be? Would people still find me mysterious, and would they reject me if I were no longer the *temperamental artist* persona that I have been known to be?

▸ THE PARADOX

If I am willing to be brutally honest with myself, I know that I cover up my shame about feeling flawed and unlovable. I do this by expecting others to treat me differentially, and by acting precious, temperamental, overly sensitive, and easily misunderstood. Of course, this all serves to keep people at a distance, which then reinforces my belief.

As described above, my thinking compulsion is *envy*, and my emotional compulsion is *melancholy*. My role as the Individualist is connected with melancholy—my emotional response to self and others that I use to sustain my role as a deeply profound, sensitive, unique person who must be treated that way. *"Can't you see me—my hurt, pain, grief, sorrow, and deep longing for … ?"*

It's my envy that gets in the way and keeps my role in place. Instead of seeing what I *do* have, it is easier to long for what I *don't have* and be envious of others and blame people for not realizing my potential. States of melancholy are difficult to surmount, because these emotional states can be immobilizing. It is a self-reinforcing loop that becomes a trap for me and keeps me from taking action toward my dreams and seeing reality—being objective about my true gifts.

▸ TEMPTATIONS ON THE JOURNEY

Your uniqueness exempts you from the expectations of others. Clinging to your pain and emotional reactions. Controlling yourself (inner experience) and your environment. Striving to achieve your unattainable idealized image. Lingering in states of melancholy, longing, hopelessness, sadness, and fantasy. Envy. Emotional intensity and amplification. Creating drama to get attention. Stirring things up. Self-pitying. Being self-absorbed and temperamental. Believing you have to be unique, or your work and life have to be special, because an ordinary life is mundane, superficial, and beneath you. Alienating yourself from others. Blaming others. Believing you are a failure as a person.

▸ DETOUR SIGNS

Cling to your emotions to feel alive and in contact with yourself. Others will reject you, so reject first! You have been wronged! Hold on to your remorse and regrets from the past. You are a victim of fate. Happiness is not meant for you. Focus on what is missing. You can't have intimate connections. You don't fit in. Focus on how special and unique you are. Draw attention to yourself. Create drama to get attention. The juice of life is external to you—others have it and you don't. You are an outsider. The ordinary is mundane. It's OK to be temperamental. Withdraw.

▸ COURSE CORRECTION

Approach your experience without reacting to it, clinging to it, or needing it to be right, dramatic, or out of the ordinary. Approach life with equanimity. Find a way to stand on the outside of yourself looking in—to see things objectively, not making them bigger or smaller than they are. Your helping allies can assist with this, and it is good to ask for help so that you see things more clearly. However, you must be willing to listen openly to what they are saying. Don't let your feelings throw you off balance. It is better to notice them and not act on them or make them bigger than they are. Perhaps taking a curious stance and inquiring into your feelings would be beneficial. Stop feeding your if-only monsters with gourmet meals! They get way too much attention and are growing larger and larger.

▸ INTO THE SHADOW

My Wings carry my shadow, as do my Connecting Points: lands of 3, 5, 2, 1. While the healthy expressions of these four Types are companions on my journey, when I turn around to look at the shadow they cast, I see parts of me that I don't want to acknowledge. Sometimes it takes entering the shadow to uncover the gifts that are waiting there.

The shadow of Type 3 is the part of me that wants to show off and be recognized, is image focused, loses connection to my authenticity, takes shortcuts, can be vain and self-centered. Lurking in the shadow of Type 5 is the part of me that emotionally detaches from other people and rejects them with the back of my hand, that can be arrogant and dismissive of others, that walls myself away and disappears.

The shadow of Type 2, my point of Stress, is where I become the victim, seductive and manipulative. I disrespect others' boundaries—give unsolicited help and advice. When I enter the shadow of Type 1, I become rigid, have angry outbursts, see things in black and white, and am self-righteous. I can also do things that seriously violate my own morals and ethics.

Part of my life journey is to make contact with the parts of me that are germane to Types 6, 7, 8, and 9. These may be qualities that I judge in others as being somehow bad or wrong, or that I just don't relate to at all. At some point, it will be important to visit these other lands and see what they have to teach me, what treasures can be found there.

‣ HELPING ALLIES

Type 3 is on my right and Type 5 is on my left. They both have something I need to help me on my journey home. For Type 3s, failure is not an option—they are success oriented and can help me let go of my shame about feeling flawed. I am intent on finding and expressing my true identity, and Type 3s are able to change their image to suit the situation—like a shape shifter. Perhaps there is something to be learned there. Type 3 is the part of me that is able to focus on the goal and take action toward that goal—like a heat-seeking missile. They take care of business—no fuss, no muss, no emotional outbursts. Type 3 is future oriented and on the move. It is just what I need to move forward my dream. Type 5s have a great ability to see situations with objectivity and dispassion by detaching from their emotions. They are innovative, and that plus my creativity is a winning combination. Both of these companions serve me well. I will happily put my arms through theirs and take those steps toward realizing my dreams.

My points of Stress and Integration have gifts for me as well. Type 1 offers me the gifts of integrity, idealism, and the discipline to stay the course. They know how to create structure and order—and this can help bring my creative expression to light. Type 2 offers the gift of relationship—reaching out, connecting to others, and building and sustaining those connections. Type 2 specializes in this and puts others' needs before their own. I know I can be pretty self-absorbed. The healthiest expression of Type 2 is the gift of unconditional love for self and others. Yes, self! Loving myself and letting go of my feelings of shame for feeling like a failure will be one of the greatest gifts I can give myself. It will take my new friends, Types 1, 2, 3, and 5, to help loosen the grip that my compulsions have on me so that I can relax enough to access that yummy unconditional love.

‣ BURIED TREASURE: TYPE 4 ALCHEMY

Envy and melancholy alchemize into states of equanimity, emotional balance, and a love of the truth.

I am free! I am no longer imprisoned by my role as the wounded one! I am emotionally honest, self-revealing, truly supportive, kind, and fully engaged in life. I have found my emotional balance and am no longer tossed about by my changing moods. I have claimed my objectivity, and I am finally able to see myself clearly and accept the person I see. I now realize that I had within me what I was seeking all along. I mistakenly believed that others had what I longed for and it was being denied me.

I use my gift of sensitivity in service of others and myself. I have uncovered my capacity to be empathic and have sourced my unique creative expression. The need to feel special and unique and understood has transformed into a gift I have to make others feel deeply special, emotionally understood, respected, cared for, cared about, and seen. People tell me they are inspired by my depth, sensitivity, and authentic expression. I have found my serenity and my calling, and I no longer look outside myself for happiness.

Individuality is only possible if it unfolds from wholeness.

—David Bohm

TYPE 4

POSITIVE CONTRIBUTION	REACTIONS / STRESS
Sensitive / Warm / Humane / Authentic / Take personal interest in employees	Being overly helpful or compulsively intrusive
Self-aware / Insightful both of self and others / Feeling- based intuition	Inconsistent, moody, and temperamental Envious of others Focus on "what's missing" and on past Melancholy / Withdraw / Isolate / Depression Never feel understood
Profoundly creative / Inspired / Highly imaginative / Unique expression Take creative and uncustomary approach to business	Need to "make a statement" and be "different" Avoid doing things they don't like or see as superficial or mundane Overly complex in communication
Heroic in putting ideas into action	Do what they "feel like doing" / Hard time taking practical action
Quality and style driven	Don't develop or implement strategy Don't provide oversight and explicit direction
Strong personal vision with emphasis on shared vision Create organizations that give meaning and purpose	Wanting to fulfill vision at all costs—unwilling to compromise Lose focus on concrete goals and tasks Challenge articulating their vision to be understood

TYPE 4 JOURNAL

 STOP AND REFLECT

Look at the Type 4 compulsions: Envy and melancholy with feelings of shame and a focus on self-image. As you begin to explore this, you will start to see your compulsive patterns and their impact on your life.

Recall a time when you experienced envy for what you perceived that others had and you didn't— when you longed for your life to be different than it was. Write about your memories of this. What triggered this need or compulsion? See if you can remember what circumstances evoked this state of envy and longing for you. What were your feelings, thoughts, reactions, and body sensations when you experienced this? Tell the story.

How does this pattern play out in your life?

How has this worked for you / benefited you?

What has been the cost to you?

Recall a recent time when you acted temperamental. What triggered that in you; what were the circumstances? Can you sense in your body where you felt your reaction before you expressed it? What were you thinking and feeling? See if you can capture the early warning signs so that you are aware of them before you act on them.

Are you aware that you focus your attention on what is missing in your life? Take a moment to reflect on this and write about it. What triggers you to focus your attention here? Look below those triggers and see what's there.

Recall a time when you were content, happy, and fully satisfied with your life—when you felt happy with how life was unfolding for you. What was going on in your life? Tell the story. What were the circumstances that enabled you to feel happy and satisfied? What internal obstacles did you have to overcome in order to find this within yourself? How did you do it?

🛍 List your *core hurts* (for example, feeling unsupported, accused, unseen, flawed, worthless, unimportant, guilty, devalued, rejected, powerless, inadequate, unlovable).

🛍 What were the short- and long-term benefits to you?

🛍 How do your core fears and core hurts relate to each other and reinforce each other?

🛍 How can you cultivate more of this in your daily life?

🛍 What do your core fears and hurts have to do with your role identity?

Unraveling Your Role Identity (Review the *Role Identity* for Type 4, the Individualist)

🛍 List your *core fears* (for example, powerlessness, no support, loneliness, rejection, harm, deprivation, shame, exposure, feeling overwhelmed, humiliation, abandonment, pain, inability to fulfill dreams).

🛍 How did you come to believe that these fears and hurts were true and real? What is your evidence that they are true? How do you know?

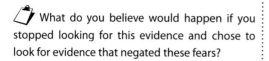 What do you believe would happen if you stopped looking for this evidence and chose to look for evidence that negated these fears?

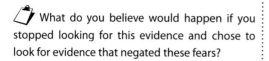 Describe and list some of the qualities you would like to have. List some descriptive words (warm, playful, powerful …).

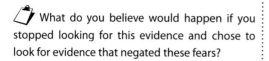 If you no longer reacted to these fears, how would that affect the role you play?

 What are the first steps you can take toward embodying these qualities?

 If you weren't playing your role of the Individualist / the Sensitive One, who would you be? What feelings come up for you when you imagine dropping this role?

‣ **TYPE 4** WORDS

Image, uniqueness, goals, envy, creative expression, sensitivity, melancholy, objectivity, dreams, longing, special, feelings, idealize, understood, shame, unique, acceptance, optimism, gratitude, creativity.

 Your Enneagram Type will have a unique association with certain words related to your compulsions and patterns.

Understanding the significance of these words and how they have played out in your life will be telling for you. Being more conscious of your feelings and attitudes toward these words will help you to transform how they live within you and help you to create your life story moving forward.

Take your time with this, and find a quiet place where you can reflect. I suggest writing about one word at a time and letting it stew inside of you while you activate your inner observer (the nonjudging observer) and peel back its meaning. You will want to come back to this word again and again.

I suggest picking the first word that calls to you from your list. Each word has both positive and unhealthy expressions. Write about both. Keep digging deeper. Begin to notice as you go through your day how these words play out in your life.

For instance, *longing*: What is your association with longing? What does it feel like when you are *in the grip* of longing? What is your reaction to feelings of longing (what do you do or say)? What are the circumstances that evoke longing for you? How does it serve you? How does it create challenges and problems for you? Tell stories of times you have experienced longing.

These are just some of the questions you might consider when you begin to explore how each word has shown up on your life journey. Consider how you want to bring these behaviors and qualities forward in a more conscious and intentional way.

▸ WHAT'S IN MY BIG BLACK BAG?
PEERING INTO MY SHADOW

Take a look at your Wings and your two Connecting Points. What aspects of these Types do you recognize in yourself? What don't you relate to? Write about this. Start to self-observe and notice whether your self-observations are accurate. Inquire within. Ask others for their perceptions.

Go to the sections for your Connecting Points (Types 2 and 1) and your Wings (Types 3 and 5), and get to know these parts of yourself. Taking time to explore the words for these four Types will be quite instructive.

▸ THINGS YOU CAN DO TO MAKE A SHIFT

TAKE ACTION ON YOUR DREAMS

The doorway to integration for Type 4 is through the Gut/Body/ Action (Instinctual) Center. Take action on your dreams. You have dreams, desires, and longings—what are they? Rather than allow your mood state to dictate, set it aside and take action. Let your passion and anger be the fuel for taking purposeful and focused action toward your dreams. You will feel better about yourself, and feel better in general, when you move toward the dreams and goals you set for yourself. Find a coach or someone who can help keep you on track.

Do some daily physical activity—walk, run, hike, play tennis, swim, do yoga … This will be critical to staying grounded in your body.

 Several practices in "InsideOut—Leaders' Tool Kit" will be very useful for you. The sections "Gratitude Alphabet," "Reclaim Your Passion," "Curiosity Is Your Guide," and "Centering Basic Practice" are great places to begin.

SOLICIT INPUT

Ask for feedback from two or three people you trust about what they see as your gifts and where they see you getting stuck. Receive what they have to say—only ask clarifying questions. Don't try to explain yourself; just listen to what they have to say. Write it down. See how closely it matches your own self-perception. Because Type 4 tends to be self-referenced, it is important to get input from others to help you see yourself more clearly.

AN INSIDEOUT LEADER'S STORY: **CHRIS AND LARS DECIDE ON FIRST STEPS**

Lars knows that he is part of the problem and gets in his own way. The challenge for Lars is that he isn't aware of what it is that he is saying, doing, or not doing that creates obstacles for his team and their success. He realizes that it's time to look inside himself and get a better understanding of his own internal workings.

At Chris's suggestion, Lars agrees to work with the Enneagram as part of his coaching arrangement. While Lars has used other personality systems, he is drawn to the dynamic nature of the Enneagram and its ability to get at some of the core issues driving his behavior.

Chris begins with a typing interview using the

Enneagram Typing Cards to help Lars discover his Type. Lars is torn between Type 9 and Type 6. With a little self-reflection and well-formed questions from Chris, Lars is able to see how much his worry, anxiety, self-doubt, concern about what could go wrong, fear, and trust issues have been the focus of his attention throughout his life and continue to this day.

Now that Lars has identified his Enneagram Type (Type 6), Chris has some real data to work with and specific ways to support Lars to see himself more clearly—how his inner obstacles create his outer reality—and to help him to make some needed shifts in his style.

→ Lars's story continues on p. 146

TYPE 5
JOURNEY OF THE DETACHED OBSERVER

▸ WORLDVIEW

As a very young child, I felt small, isolated, empty, alone, and abandoned. I saw myself as separate and came to believe there was no room or support for me. The way I coped with this was to withdraw, separate, and break off contact. I felt safe in my mind and in my world of ideas. I began to turn to the idea that knowledge would bring me recognition and safety, so I looked to develop my expertise in at least one area. This further developed as I came to see myself as highly intelligent, competent, insightful, perceptive, and objective. In fact, secretly I believe I am so smart that others can't understand me.

The way I cope today is to be self-sufficient in an effort to avoid feeling dependent or obligated to fulfill others' expectations, needs, and demands. I do my best to minimize hassles in my life, as well as any physical and emotional needs. I conserve my energy by withdrawing, or by provoking others with sarcastic, cruel, or cutting remarks when I am feeling threatened or intruded upon. Further, I separate my feelings from my memories and thoughts, which allows me to compartmentalize people and different aspects of my life. Then I can observe each part from a distance.

TYPE 5 - THE DETACHED OBSERVER
My motto: *I will figure it out*

Ideas, understanding how things work, mastery, and competence all get my time and attention. I minimize or ignore the needs of my body, and rely on my mind and focus on my ideas. By emotionally detaching, I can live comfortably in my world of ideas and abstractions. I control the amount and quality of interaction that I have with others because I fear being engulfed and intruded upon. I can seal myself off and hide from life, understanding the world through my head but rarely having direct experience, hence becoming a Detached Observer.

‣ COMPULSION AND FIXATION:
STINGINESS AND AVARICE

Avarice is similar to greed but has an element of hoarding, accumulating, collecting—a saving of resources. My greediness can be to hoard energy, love, affection, and time. You can also see my greed manifest through my collections of random things such as books, DVDs, CDs, plates, electronics, or flower bulbs. *Stinginess* combined with *avarice* is both a withholding of and a holding on to.

These compulsions started in my early childhood when I came to believe that there was no support for me and I was on my own. Putting my faith and trust in what I could hoard, and filling up the dry emptiness inside of me with information, gave me the false sense of nourishment and security that I needed to allay my fears enough to forge my way in life.

‣ ROLE IDENTITY

I play the role of the detached observer as a way to protect myself and keep others at bay. Of course, I am also simultaneously detaching from my own feelings and from my heart as a way to hide from myself and from life. This is an attempt to run away from my feelings of inner scarcity, dry emptiness, loneliness, and feelings of inadequacy. If I act as though I don't want or need anything and I don't care, if I show my indifference to the suffering of others and the world, I can keep people at a distance and avoid my own pain. I retreat into my mind and focus on my intellectual pursuits. From this vantage point, other people can become abstractions to me—objects and mental constructs. I confuse my emotional dryness with believing that I am being rational and objective. I can wall myself away.

How do my role and compulsions, avarice and stinginess, work together and reinforce my patterns? By thinking that I understand through detached observation, I replace direct experience and participation in life with concepts and abstractions. My mind is a safe place for me, my escape and my reality. This comes about from my belief that I have no inner reservoir and have to hold on to the little energy, emotions, and attention that I have (avarice and stinginess). I dole out my time, attention, energy, and affection as needed or as I feel that I have the extra capacity to give. I live in my mind and *retain* its ideas.

I am private and resent intrusion or anything that will drain my limited reservoir of energy. I want things my way and can be very self-centered. I avoid feeling obligated to anyone. It serves me to make unilateral decisions so that I maintain control. I distance myself from my feelings; I am secretive—keep my thoughts and activities to myself; and I can be intimidating, intellectually arrogant, aloof, and disdainful of others. I can easily delete people from my life if I feel they demand too much of me.

I maintain the dynamic tension between my role and compulsions by holding on to my belief that I have inner scarcity, that the world is intrusive, that it is withholding of resources and support, that I lack what it takes to deal with the world and have to hold on to the little that I have. I become overly sensitized to others' demands and expectations, feel powerless to negotiate for myself and my needs and wants, and then withdraw or detach to regain control. I compensate for my feelings of inadequacy by becoming an expert.

What if I gave up my role as the expert, the intellectual, the provider of information and wisdom? What if I became less private and more knowable? Would people still find me compelling? What would I have left to stand on for support if I gave up those props? What if I showed that I cared and opened my heart to others? Would I be safe? If I am not the person I think I am, who am I? Who would I be?

I used my mind to understand things, instead of my body to experience them, in service of protecting myself and not getting hurt.

—Wendy Palmer, *Conscious Embodiment: A Practice for Presence,
Confidence and Compassion (2007)*

Detached Observer

Fear

Avarice ←·············→ Stinginess

▸ THE PARADOX

By acting secretive and mysterious, detaching and withdrawing, I invite the intrusions I am trying to avoid. By shutting other people out, I limit the support that is available to me and confirm my belief that no one will ever understand me. How could they when I don't let them in? I am happy to tell people things I know and have learned, but I don't share who I am. By not being emotionally available to myself, I feel dry and empty inside. I am withholding the juice of life from myself by living inside my ivory tower of ideas, and viewing others and myself from a safe distance. Inevitably, I feel powerless if I don't connect with my source of power—my body, instincts, and life force. How can I access that part of me when I am living in the netherworld of my head—in my ideas *about* the world—and I am not in and of the world?

▸ TEMPTATIONS ON THE JOURNEY

Withholding information, time, energy, and attention from others. Being emotionally unavailable to others and myself. Seeing people's actions as intrusions rather than attempts to connect, collaborate, and be intimate. Feeling overwhelmed by others, rather than connecting with my own source of power. Focusing so much on my ideas and thoughts that I am unaware of my surroundings. Spending too much time with my ideas instead of with people.

▸ DETOUR SIGNS

You'll figure it out. Press the delete key. Disappear. Act arrogant. Disconnect. Detach. You're powerless. They are intrusive—withdraw. Your expertise is your true source of power. Your thoughts are reality. Don't show emotion. Don't let people know they affect you. Be secretive. Withdraw from reality into your concepts about reality.

▸ COURSE CORRECTION

Don't try to figure out what you are experiencing and where it might take you before actually having the experience. Let go of needing to know before making contact with your physical and emotional experience. Don't try to think your way across it—you must travel across it. Connect with yourself in an experiential way and let your mind follow your direct experience. Let go of cognitive frames so that you can experience yourself as you are. Engage others. Experience the flow and connections between and among things. Separateness is your illusion. Connection and relationship are what matter.

▸ INTO SHADOW

My Wings carry my shadow, as do as do my Connecting Points: lands of 4, 6, 7, 8. While the healthy expressions of these four Types are companions on my journey, when I turn around to look at the shadow they cast, I see parts of me that I don't want to acknowledge. Sometimes it takes entering the shadow to uncover the gifts that are waiting there.

The shadow of Type 4 is the part of me that wants to be seen as unique and special; that wants to draw attention to myself; and that becomes moody, brooding, and temperamental. Lurking in the shadow of Type 6 is the part of me that becomes suspicious of others, doesn't trust, feels burdened by others' expectations.

I find it very satisfying to visit the shadow lands of Types 4 and 6. They help me confirm how others are at fault for my situation. I don't have to take responsibility for my life. They give me permission to place blame. Here, I can shore up my defenses and put on my suit of armor to defend against being hurt and delay looking within.

When I visit the land of Type 7, it is one place I go to escape from my feelings of insecurity and anxiety. I become distracted, scattered, and unfocused. I have lots of ideas and want to implement them all. Usually I deepen and develop my expertise, but when I am in 7 land, all bets are off. Sustained visits here result in half-baked projects. I take on too much and become overwhelmed by my creation and all I have to handle. My ability to commit to a course of action or to others is severely reduced. I may appear as affable and outgoing, perhaps even charming.

The land of Type 8 brings out a different part of me when I visit its shadow. I become forceful, controlling, dominating, and cutting. The arrogance of my Type 5 shadow, enhanced by the arrogance of my Type 8 shadow, can be quite frightening for others to experience. I act out the rage I have been trying to control for so long and become cruel and punishing. I make people disappear from my life in an instant. My cold and icy stare is enough to keep people away from me—which is just the response I seek.

Part of my life journey will be to make contact with the parts of me that are germane to Types 1, 2, 3, and 9. These may be qualities that I judge in others as being somehow bad or wrong, or that I just don't relate to at all. At some point, it will be important to visit these other lands and see what they have to teach me, what treasures can be found there.

‣ HELPING ALLIES

Type 4 is on my right, and Type 6 is on my left. Each of them offers just the assistance I need on this journey. Type 4s are tuned in to their feelings, and dig deeply inside to truly know and understand themselves. They are profoundly sensitive to those around them and are in contact with their heart. Can I allow myself to connect to this part of me? It helps when I place my attention on my heart and relax around my desire to *think* about how I feel and instead just feel.

Type 6 is at my side to give me the gift of connection to others. Type 6s are social beings, natural networkers. They are engaged in life and naturally collaborate with others. Type 6 offers the gift of loyalty and commitment. I need to strap on these Wings and let them support me on this journey, to help me fly free!

Types 8 and 7 are connected to me as well and are along for the ride. My insecurities begin to fade away when I am connected to my heart and sensitive to others' feelings; when I make a commitment and am loyal to others, and I know that others are loyal and there to support me. I encounter the oasis and life spring of my inner landscape; that once dry, empty place inside me becomes my wellspring of life.

The gifts of Type 8 are now available to me—the gifts of my life force, power, strength, and confidence to go out and fully engage in the world, knowing that I have what it takes within me to meet the world full on. This experience of my strength and power fills up my inner well, and I begin to experience my own juiciness and the juiciness of life. Type 7 is now at my doorstep, offering me the gifts of adventure, play, and spontaneity, of joy and ecstasy—to be in awe of the miracle of life.

It is when you give of yourself that you truly give. For what are your possessions but things you keep and guard for fear you may need them tomorrow?

…

And what is fear of need but need itself?

—Kahlil Gibran, from "On Giving," *The Prophet*[24]

TYPE 5

POSITIVE CONTRIBUTION	REACTIONS / STRESS
Innovative / Inventive / Original / Unconventional	Lost in world of fantasy and ideas Don't take practical action Lack self care / Forget they have a body Try to implement too many ideas at once
Insightful / Visionary / Pioneering	Lack emotionality and empathy / Don't see or care about impact of decisions
Expert / Depth of knowledge / Models and theories / Competent	Absent-minded professor Offer too much information Paralyzed if they think they aren't 100% competent Cruel / Cold / Sarcastic Don't "walk the talk"
Keen observers / Profound / Complex problem solvers	Detached / Ivory tower / Limits access to self / Doesn't trust others
Surround themselves with people who have complementary skills	Uncommunicative / Hoards information / Unavailable / Makes unilateral decisions / Don't give enough direction, guidance, or authority
Take calculated risks	Take bold risks without consulting others
Decisive leader Competitive / Promotes	Avoids confrontation / Don't like losing control by showing anger or strong emotions / Intimidating

‣ **BURIED TREASURE:** TYPE 5 *ALCHEMY*

Detached and separate transforms into omniscience and interconnectedness—I experience myself as an interconnected part of the whole, as no longer separate. I experience gnosis—direct and immediate understanding.

The beliefs that I am alone in the world, without support, and that if I minimize my needs, I don't have to rely on anyone, are no longer relevant. I have come to realize that it was only my illusion that I could detach and compartmentalize, that there was no support for me. The veil has been lifted on my illusion, and I see reality more clearly.

I no longer feel the need to hoard knowledge and information, because it is accessible to me at any moment. Inner knowing and wisdom come through me when I am available to listen and receive. I now see how I thought I *knew* because I consumed information. Now I know that I didn't know. I am fully engaged in life and the world. Before I only knew about life. I now have embodied knowing—I have learned through my own lived experiences. This is also true about love. I feel it in my heart and not from a distance, as an abstract concept or idealization.

I am grounded in my body and feel my own source of power and vitality. I don't have to fear my anger; rather, I can use the energy as a force to take purposeful action in the world. I don't have to withdraw to protect myself. I trust in my ability to stand in my power and stay connected.

I have become curious, playful, whimsical, focused, visionary, pioneering, supportive, and caring. I pay attention to my physical needs; I am emotionally available to others and myself; I am truly joyful and in awe of life and the world. I am of the world, engaged in the world, and fully present in the world.

TYPE 5 JOURNAL

STOP AND REFLECT

Look at the Type 5 compulsions: Combine avarice/greed and stinginess with detachment and withdrawing, and you can see your primary coping strategy: when in fear of _____, you withhold and detach. As you begin to explore this for yourself, you will see your compulsive patterns.

Recall a time in your life when you felt the need to retreat and detach. Write about your memory of this—as many of the circumstances as you can remember. What triggered this need or compulsion? What were your feelings, thoughts, reactions, and body sensations when this happened?

What has been the cost to you?

How does this pattern play out in your life?

Recall a time in the recent past when you felt intruded upon or that your inner sanctum was being invaded. What did the other person say or do that aroused that feeling in you? Where did you feel it in your body? What coping strategy did you use? What were you afraid of? How did this strategy serve you (short term / long term)? What was the cost to you? Write about it. How would your *best self* respond? See if you can imagine responding as your best self. What would that be like? How could you evoke that for yourself?

How has this worked for you / benefited you?

Recall a time when you made contact with your heart. How did it feel? Were you able to express your feelings from your heart? What were the circumstances that enabled this? What internal obstacles did you have to overcome, and how did you do it? Tell the story.

 List your *core hurts* (for example, feeling unsupported, accused, unseen, flawed, worthless, unimportant, guilty, devalued, rejected, powerless, inadequate, unlovable).

What were the short- and long-term results for you and the other person(s), if there was someone else involved?

How do your core fears and core hurts relate to each other and reinforce each other?

How can you cultivate a more open heart and more daily contact with your heart?

What do your core fears and hurts have to do with your role identity?

How did you come to believe that these fears and hurts were true and real? What is your evidence? How do you know?

Unraveling Your Role Identity (Review the *Role Identity* for Type 5, the Detached Observer)

List your *core fears* (for example, powerlessness, no support, loneliness, rejection, harm, deprivation, shame, exposure, feeling overwhelmed, humiliation, abandonment, pain, inability to fulfill dreams).

What do you believe would happen if you stopped looking for this evidence and chose to look for evidence that negated these fears?

Describe and list some of the qualities of how you would like to be and be seen. List some descriptive words (warm, playful, powerful …).

If you no longer reacted to these fears, how would that affect the role you play?

What are the first steps you can take toward embodying these qualities?

If you weren't playing your role of the Detached Observer / the Expert, who would you be? What feelings come up for you when you imagine dropping this role?

▸ **TYPE 5** WORDS

Knowledge, stingy, arrogance, anger, isolation, objectivity, withholding, inner knowing, experience, empathy, problem-solve, control, observe, understand, fear, perceptive, support, joy, power, detach, intrusive, generosity.

Your Enneagram Type will have a unique association with certain words related to your compulsions and patterns.

Understanding the significance of these words and how they have played out in your life will be telling for you. Being more conscious of your feelings and attitudes toward these words will help you to transform how they live within you and help you to create your life story moving forward.

Take your time with this, and find a quiet place where you can reflect. I suggest writing about one word at a time and letting it stew inside of you while you activate your inner observer (the nonjudging observer) and peel back its meaning. You will want to come back to this word again and again.

I suggest picking the first word that calls to you in your list. Each word has both positive connotations and unhealthy expressions. Write about both. Keep digging deeper. Begin to notice as you go through your day how these words play out in your life.

For instance, *fear*: What is your association with fear? What does it feel like when you are *in the grip* of fear? What is your reaction to feelings of fear (what do you do/say)? What are the circumstances that evoke fear for you? How does it serve you? How does it create challenges and problems for you? Tell stories of times when you have experienced fear.

These are just some of the questions you might consider when you begin to explore how each word has shown up on your life journey. Consider how you want to bring these behaviors and qualities forward in a more conscious and intentional way.

Go to the sections for your Connecting Points (Types 7 and 8) and your Wings (Types 4 and 6). Get to know these parts of yourself. Taking time to explore the words for these four Types will be quite instructive.

WHAT'S IN MY BIG BLACK BAG?
PEERING INTO MY SHADOW

Take a look at your Wings and your two Connecting Points. What aspects of these Types do you recognize in yourself? What don't you relate to? Write about this. Start to self-observe, and notice whether your self-observations are accurate. Inquire within. Ask others for their perceptions.

‣ THINGS YOU CAN DO TO MAKE A SHIFT

GROUNDING

It will be very important for you to place your attention in your body. Type 5s tend to forget that they have a body. Throughout the day (several times), notice when your head is swirling with thoughts and ideas. Once you notice, put your attention in your belly. Take a deep breath into your belly. Notice your feet and each part of your body as you work your way up. Put your hand on your heart and keep your attention there. Make contact with your heart. Breathe into your heart. What kinds of body sensations are you having?

✲ In "InsideOut—Leaders' Tool Kit," the "Centering Basic Practice" will be helpful for you to use a few times a day.

CENTERING

Exercise regularly. Find something you enjoy doing, and see if you can exercise every day.

Take time to notice who and what is around you. Take your focus out of your inner world and place it outside of you. See if you can then bring your attention back inside while holding it outside at the same time.

Whenever you can, breathe into your belly and keep your attention there. Feel your feet firmly on the ground. Imagine pulling energy up from the earth, through your feet and into your body. Feel your power in your belly. You can hold your ground.

AN INSIDEOUT LEADER'S STORY: **WHERE'S THE TRUST?**

Lars wants to build trust on his team. There is a disconnect between what he wants and what is happening. Small signs of growing trust are noticeable, but not between the HQ sub-team and Lars.

In a coaching session with Chris, Lars offers, "They still see me as an outsider, and I'm having a hard time integrating at HQ." Chris asks, "How do you know they see you as an outsider? What are you doing to integrate?"

Chris carefully listens to how Lars interprets the team's behavior. He notices that instead of taking what they say and do at face value, he makes inferences from some subtle signs and believes that his interpretation is the truth.

Type 6 (the Loyal Skeptic) is skeptical of others' stated motives and holds belief that people have hidden agendas. The paradox for Type 6s is that they have a hard time trusting others but want people to trust and rely on them. As is revealed later in our story, the HQ team members don't understand what Lars is asking of them, having had no prior experience with a leader like Lars. They think Lars's transmissions are in code.

Chris is able to help Lars see that while he wants his team to act like leaders and make decisions, he hasn't engaged them in defining the change—a critical misstep. He does not demonstrate his trust in them. Further, he is becoming convinced that they don't know how to change. All of this results in a significant trust issue.

What is true is that the team members don't have the mind-set or history that would lead them to the change. However, that is the job of Lars—to help them see themselves in the new world.

Due to the lack of trust, the team is unwilling to raise the hard issues. They continue to make more commitments but don't hold themselves accountable from one meeting to the next. They are unwilling, thus far, to address the systemic issues.

Lars wants them to give feedback to one another, but there isn't buy-in for that kind of communication. They are unwilling to be open and fully authentic in front of their peers. Layoffs are coming, and everyone believes that they need to look good relative to everyone else; that they need to appear competent.

They blame Lars and he blames them. How will they break this logjam?

→ Lars's story continues on p. 175

TYPE 6
JOURNEY OF THE LOYAL SKEPTIC

‣ WORLDVIEW

From an early age, I felt scared, insecure, unsafe, and as if the rug could be pulled out from beneath me at any time. I am like the young child who was afraid of the monsters under the bed and in the closet that could leap out and get me at any time. The world seemed unpredictable and untrustworthy. People became suspect, and I became suspicious and cynical. Life became a matter of endurance.

I came to believe that the world was a threatening and dangerous place, and I have a propensity to imagine the worst. People can't be trusted—they always have ulterior motives, are self-serving, and will run you over if you get in their way. I don't have what it takes (can't trust myself) in the face of this. I am not sure that I will survive. I feel ill-prepared, defenseless, and weak. There is no solid ground to stand on.

I see myself as likable, dependable, and loyal. I secretly believe that I do what I am supposed to do, and others don't. You can't count on other people. The strange thing is that I don't really trust myself either. I doubt my ability to make sound decisions, and when I do decide, I second-guess myself. Often I solicit advice from several others before and after I make decisions. I don't often trust my intuition, because the *should* voice is so strong. I feel a sense of duty and responsibility to others, although I resent having to be the *responsible one*.

Sometimes I act fearful and can become practically paralyzed with fear. At other times you will see me as a big risk taker. I both challenge authority and obey authority—I have an ambivalent relationship to authority figures. At times I appear confident and in charge, and at other times insecure. When conflict arises, I can be pretty aggressive, and then I retreat and withdraw. Often you will experience me as warm—I tend to be pretty social and want to be connected to others. At other times, I am very mistrusting of people and their hidden agendas—what do they really want from me? I get caught between doing things that are selfish and self-centered and being overly responsible.

Of all the liars in the world, sometimes the worst are your own fears.

—Rudyard Kipling

TYPE 6 - THE LOYAL SKEPTIC
My motto: *Be prepared for whatever could go wrong*

▸ COMPULSIONS AND FIXATIONS:
WORRY/ANXIETY AND FEAR/INSECURITY

My thinking compulsion is doubt and worry. To quell my fears and insecurities, I look outside myself to other people, organizations, and beliefs to provide me a sense of safety, and to give me reassurance and guidance.

My emotional compulsion is anticipatory fear and survival anxiety. My focus is on the hidden motives and agendas of others. I feel insecure, which shows up as defensive suspiciousness. I am likely to make preemptive strikes rather than allow myself to be attacked first. I can be apprehensive and guarded, and ultimately I live my life fearing death.

Fear defeats more people than any other one thing in the world.
—Ralph Waldo Emerson

This sets up my focus of attention on how to be safe and secure, so I look for what could go wrong—questions like "What if?" and "I need to know" fuel my need to be prepared. I don't know who or what can be trusted. I don't feel safe, and I become vigilant. I am looking for proof that I am safe. This triggers my need to know and understand, to research. I want tangible proof, but no evidence is good enough; and I don't trust my own instincts, because they are dangerous and animalistic. I doubt what I need, want, feel, experience, or think.

▸ ROLE IDENTITY

I play the role of the loyal and trusted spouse, worker, friend, volunteer, sibling, and so on, and at the same time I resent the role of being the *responsible one*. My idealized self-image is that "I am loyal, I am the glue." I tend to filter out any evidence that does not support the way that I see myself. Not surprisingly, I play a dual role. My other role is the skeptic. I see myself as the one who uncovers potential problems and incongruence in others. I appear to trust others, but I am ever vigilant, looking for what is underneath the surface that could come out and harm me. As you can see, my pattern is to vacillate between two extremes: loyal versus lacking trust.

My role identity is linked closely with my compulsions of fear/worry/anxiety. I am responsible and loyal, but fear causes me to live with the tension between being trusting and nontrusting. I worry about what could happen. I gird myself against potential pitfalls, reprisals, betrayals, disasters, by being vigilant, planning, preparing, being on the defense, and researching things thoroughly. I can also react against my fears by looking outside of myself for something to believe in, and by offering my loyalty and asking for advice.

I maintain my role identity by ignoring evidence (situations, people, life experiences) when and with those whom I have felt safe, accepted, and secure. Instead, I remember and focus on the betrayals, when things went wrong, and when bad things happened.

I am so identified with my role that I don't know if I can let it go. I hear the voice of inner guidance and instinct, but I don't trust it either. If I listen to that voice, what will happen? What if I do that and don't do what I perceive to be the responsible thing? What if people who have counted on me to be this loyal, contingency-planning, prepared, reliable, well-researched, networked person who also has the right resource to recommend—what if I weren't always that way? Who would be in my life if I weren't that way? What about my family? My job? Who would I be?

▸ THE PARADOX

Sometimes my fear and paralysis end up creating the problems I am trying to prevent. I create my own disasters. The economic crisis hits. I hit the panic button. I call my broker and blame him for putting me in the wrong investments. I find other brokers to validate that for me. It's not my fault. I call every financial planner/broker/accountant I can to figure out what to do. Meanwhile, I am paralyzed. I knee-jerk react and rip my money out of the market. Whew, I feel safe again. At least I know what I have. Whoops, I pulled my money out of the market at the bottom. Had I waited, my investments would have rebounded. I don't trust my current broker. I'm in the wrong investments. I need to pull my money out … Meanwhile, the value of my portfolio is a shadow of its former self. See, there is no safety. I can't trust my financial advisors or the market. Where can I place my trust?

▸ TEMPTATIONS ON THE JOURNEY

Seeing conspiracies everywhere. Projecting your shadow onto others—finding your own faults in others rather than looking at yourself in the mirror. Seeing enemies everywhere and going for their soft underbelly with great precision. Falsely accusing people. Making more commitments than you can reasonably deliver. Seeking security outside of yourself. Making things bigger than they are. Worrying about what could go wrong. Letting your feelings of insecurity keep you from taking action in the world. Thinking that other people have the answers. Not trusting your intuition. Focusing on and putting your energy into worrying about what could happen and what could go wrong.

▸ DETOUR SIGNS

Make a preemptive strike. Anticipate what could go wrong. Focus on potential obstacles. You need to know. You need to be certain first. You must earn your security. Be prepared for all contingencies. Doubt yourself. Don't listen to your intuition. Be skeptical and suspicious. Look for people's hidden agendas. Magnify the negative. Hide your insecurities by showing off. Avoid conflict. Blame others. What if … ?

▸ COURSE CORRECTION

Rather than projecting your fears, your concerns, and things you don't like about yourself onto others, have the courage to face yourself. Face your inner reality and your fears. Don't doubt your experience or your intuition—this is your real source of guidance. Access your own inner authority.

Pay attention to experiences that went well, people who have *not* let you down or betrayed you, and people who have been there for you and given to you. See if you can focus your attention on the good in the world. Feel yourself standing on solid ground. Inquire into and be curious about your lack of faith and trust—why you feel inadequate.

Skepticism and worry are the flip side of intuition. See if you can discern between negative thinking and the voice of intuition. Worry will almost always wither under the microscope of interrogation. You can apply your vivid imagination and creative energy to finding possible favorable outcomes. Worry is a choice, and the creative genius you apply to it can be used, also by choice.

Every tomorrow has two handles. We can take hold of it by the handle of anxiety, or by the handle of faith.

—Author unknown

What are the source and intentions of your impulses, your aggressions, and your fears? Develop *discernment* for what is real and what is your projection. What do you *really* need to be afraid of, and what are you seeing that's not really there? Where is your real source of security, your solid ground, and how can you create that for yourself?

Meditate—this is most important so that you can quiet your mind and your anxiety. Through meditation you will be able to observe your habits of thought. You'll be able to cultivate a clear, quiet mind so that you can listen and pay attention to your inner guidance, which has been waiting all of your life to help you.

▸ INTO THE SHADOW

My Wings carry my shadow, as do my Connecting Points: lands of 5, 7, 3, 9. While the healthy expressions of these four Types are companions on my journey, when I turn around to look at the shadow they cast, I see parts of me that I don't want to acknowledge. Sometimes it takes entering the shadow to uncover the gifts that are waiting there.

Type 5 is the more withdrawn and inward part of me, and Type 7 is the more outward part that wants to experience the world. Type 5 is the part of me that detaches emotionally and withdraws. It is the part of me that can stay trapped in my concepts and theories about life, rather than having a lived experience, needing more and more information. It is that greedy and selfish part of me.

Type 7 holds the part of my shadow that is self-centered and can be a bit scattered—trying to do too much. It also holds the more gluttonous part of me, wanting to do it all—more workshops to attend, countries to travel, vacations to take, restaurants to try … It is the part of me that goes into action and seeks change to allay my anxiety and run away from myself—move to a new home, change jobs, and so on.

Type 3 is where I go when I feel most insecure and stressed—simultaneously. It carries the part of me that wants to stand out, be noticed, create the right image—to be the star! This is the more competitive side of my nature and where I can move into self-deception and deceiving others.

When I am operating below conscious awareness, I may be accessing the shadow side of Type 9: when I become conflict avoidant, withdraw inward, disengage, and become complacent. I become comfort seeking and move into avoidance, stuff my anger and vitality, and may become depressed. I am probably attempting to avoid the mess I have created. This is where I go to avoid looking at myself in the mirror and honestly assessing who is there.

Part of my life journey will be to make contact with the parts of me that are germane to Types 1, 2, 4, and 8. These may be qualities that I judge in others as being somehow bad or wrong, or that I just don't relate to at all. At some point, it will be important to visit these other lands and see what they have to teach me, what treasures can be found there.

‣ **HELPING ALLIES**

On my right is Type 5, which I recognize in myself. Type 5's gift to me is objectivity—my ability to step back and pierce the veils to see reality. Type 5 also holds the gift of inner knowing and gnosis—not the acquisition of information but the ability to tap into a wisdom source.

On my left is Type 7, which I also recognize in myself. It is that part of me that can leap into the unknown waters and trust that there will be boat waiting for me, who trusts others until they prove untrustworthy, whose self-confidence and interpersonal comfort I admire, and whose sense of play and spontaneity I desire.

Both of them are at my side. I will put my arms through theirs and take this journey. They can teach me about parts of myself that I may have forgotten or do not trust.

My worry and anxieties will begin to fade away as I learn to be more objective and see reality more clearly, when I begin to trust and hear that inner voice, when I take risks and trust that I will be OK and that I am supported, when I feel less suspicious and more trusting, and when I am more self-confident. The gifts of Types 3 and 9 will be available to me. Type 9 offers me the ability to see multiple viewpoints, to see the world through the eyes of others. This gift will help me to let go of my projections and see people for who they are. What an offering, the gift of self-acceptance. By accepting myself, I open the door to give others the gift of acceptance, too. This leads me to an inner oasis of peace and comfort.

Type 3 is now ready to help me connect with my big heart. As the Tin Man joined Dorothy on her journey, Type 3 is at my side to help me connect with my feelings and deepest longings—to find my inner hero, my courage, and my self-confidence, and to take focused action toward my heart's desire.

▸ BURIED TREASURE: TYPE 6 *ALCHEMY*

Fear, worry, anxiety, doubt, and insecurity are transformed into courage, trust and faith, confidence, and ease.

I have found my courage to face the world and, most important, myself. I see myself more clearly, and as I am honest with myself, I see others more clearly. I become both trusting and trustworthy. I take a stand on behalf of the greater good. I act from my desires and not from what I think I *should* do. I am self-reliant, secure, and decisive, and I have come to believe in the inherent goodness of human nature. I am in contact with my inner guidance and act on it. I know that I am standing on solid ground and, come what may, I can handle it. Meanwhile, I no longer live my life in fear for my survival but fully step into each day with trust, power, and self-confidence.

Doubt is a pain too lonely to know that faith is his twin brother.

—Kahlil Gibran, *Jesus the Son of Man*[25]

TYPE 6

POSITIVE CONTRIBUTION	REACTIONS / STRESS
Respect authority and hierarchy	Challenge authority / Don't trust authority / Devil's advocate
Responsible / Follow-through	Resent being the "responsible one" / Feel pressure / Reluctant to commit
Self-confidence / Self-trust	"Everyone has a hidden agenda; what is it?" "Everyone acts out of self-interest." Suspicious, anxious, worried
Analytical / Planners / Prepared	Analysis paralysis / Risk averse / Indecisive / Self-doubting
Team players	Conflict avoidant / Complaining / What if? / What could go wrong / Negative
Excellent in a crisis	Self-doubting / Over-prepared / Paralyzed by fear
Champion of colleagues, friends, and the underdogs	Projection / Fault finding / Critical and judgmental / Needing to prove themselves and show off
Self-insight	Unwilling to look at self / Skeptical / Suspicious / Paranoid / accusatory / blame
Courageous	Paralyzed by doubt, fear, worry, anxiety

TYPE 6 JOURNAL

 STOP AND REFLECT

Look at the Type 6 compulsions: Combine fear/insecurity with worry/anxiety. As you begin to explore this for yourself, you will start seeing your compulsive patterns.

Recall a time when you felt the need to *know*, to fully understand and prepare in advance. Write about your memory of this. What triggered this need or compulsion? What were your feelings, thoughts, reactions, and body sensations when this was going on? Tell the story.

How does this pattern play out in your life?

How has this worked for you / benefited you?

What has been the cost to you?

Think of a time in the recent past when you were wracked with self-doubt and questioned a decision you made or were paralyzed by indecision. What precipitated this? What was going on in your internal state? Your inner dialog, feelings, thoughts? Tell the story. How does this serve you? How has it hindered you?

See if you can begin to notice your anxiety. Where do you feel it in your body? What are the sensations? Begin to dialog with it. Ask it why it is there. What does it want you to know? See if you can get underneath it to the substrata, to understand the nature of it and what it can teach you. Sit with it; don't run away from it. See if you can tolerate the feelings a little more each time.

What were the short- and long-term results for you?

Recall a time when you had deep and abiding faith and courage; when you trusted yourself completely to handle whatever challenges arose; when you had trust in those around you—you were not alone. A time when you had no worries about what *might* happen, because you had faith in yourself and the unseen world. What was going on? What were the circumstances? Tell the story. How were you able to handle your internal obstacles and get around them? What enabled you to be so courageous?

What can you do to cultivate more of this in your daily life?

Fear is the cheapest room in the house. I'd like to see you in better living conditions.

—Hafiz

Unraveling Your Role Identity (Review the *Role Identity* for Type 6, the Loyal Skeptic)

List your *core fears* (for example, powerlessness, no support, loneliness, rejection, harm, deprivation, shame, exposure, feeling overwhelmed, humiliation, abandonment, pain, inability to fulfill dreams).

List your *core hurts* (for example, feeling unsupported, accused, unseen, flawed, worthless, unimportant, guilty, devalued, rejected, powerless, inadequate, unlovable).

What do you believe would happen if you stopped looking for this evidence and chose to look for evidence that negated these fears?

If you no longer reacted to these fears, how would that affect the role you play?

How do your core fears and core hurts relate to each other and reinforce each other?

If you weren't playing your role of the Loyal Skeptic / the Reliable One, who would you be? What feelings come up for you when you imagine dropping this role?

What do your core fears and hurts have to do with your role identity?

Describe and list some of the qualities you would like to have. List some descriptive words (warm, playful, powerful …).

How did you come to believe that these fears and hurts were true and real? What is your evidence that this is true? How do you know?

What are the first steps you can take toward embodying these qualities?

▸ **TYPE 6** WORDS

Fear and aggression (write about them individually and together). Trust, insecure, loyalty, courage, faith, responsibility, worry, skeptical, prepare, vigilant, doubt, analyze, creativity, confidence, quiet mind, reliable, research, power, promote.

Your Enneagram Type will have a unique association with certain words related to your compulsions and patterns.

Understanding the significance of these words and how they have played out in your life will be telling for you. Being more conscious of your feelings and attitudes toward these words will help you to transform how they live within you and help you to create your life story moving forward.

Take your time with this, and find a quiet place where you can reflect. I suggest writing about one word at a time and letting it stew inside of you while you activate your inner observer (the nonjudging observer) and peel back its meaning. You will want to come back to this word again and again.

I suggest picking the first word that calls to you in your list. Each word has both positive connotations and unhealthy expressions. Write about both. Keep digging deeper. Begin to notice as you go through your day how these words play out in your life.

For instance, *worry*: What is your association with worry? What does it feel like when you are *in the grip* of worry? What are the circumstances that evoke worry for you? How does it serve you? How does it create challenges and problems for you? Tell stories of times when you have experienced worry.

These are just some of the questions you might consider when you begin to explore how each word has shown up on your life journey.

Consider how you want to bring these behaviors and qualities forward in a more conscious and intentional way.

▸ WHAT'S IN MY BIG BLACK BAG?
PEERING INTO MY SHADOW

🗒 Take a look at your Wings and your two Connecting Points (Types 5, 7, 3, 9). What aspects of these Types do you recognize in yourself? What don't you relate to? Write about this. Start to self-observe, and notice whether your self-observations are accurate. Inquire within. Ask others for their perceptions.

✸ Go to the sections for your Stress Point (Type 3) and Integration Point (Type 9) and your Wings (Types 5 and 7). Get to know these parts of yourself. Take time to explore the words for these four Types. It will be quite instructive.

▸ THINGS YOU CAN DO TO MAKE A SHIFT

CULTIVATE YOUR INNER OBSERVER

One of the most important practices to incorporate into your life is meditation. Noticing your thought patterns will be instrumental in helping you to see your compulsive thought patterns so that you can interrupt them.

✸ "InsideOut—Leaders' Tool Kit" contains a basic meditation practice you can follow— even if it is just five minutes a day for starters. This will work wonders for you.

EXPLORE

When you feel pressured to meet others' expectations, breathe deeply into your belly. Relax. Do people really have these expectations of you, or are they self-imposed? Are you really overcommitted, or are you out ahead of yourself worrying about all the things you have to do and feeling overwhelmed? If you are overcommitted, perhaps you have taken on more than you can as a distraction, to stay busy. What are you distracting yourself from?

- If overcommitted, take one thing at a time. Put one foot in front of the other. Either see what you can take off your plate or sequence your tasks. Prioritize. Create a simple project plan for what you need to do.

- If you are distracting, take some quiet time and reflect about this. Is this a pattern? What is it that you don't want to see, feel, or acknowledge?

- If overcommitting is a pattern, this would be good to explore— reflect about how this pattern is serving you in some way and how it is doing you harm.

DEVELOP YOUR INTUITION

✦ "InsideOut—Leaders' Tool Kit" suggests various ways you can tune in to your intuitive voice, and develop and strengthen your intuition.

Practice acting on your intuition. There is a little voice inside you that wants to be heard. When you hear it, see if you can focus in on the voice. Turn up the volume on it; otherwise, the other voices will drown it out. Try acting on it first in low-risk situations. As you have more and more success, try taking bigger risks.

CENTERING

✦ Work with the "Centering Basic Practice" in "InsideOut— Leaders' Tool Kit." This will help you to get more grounded in your body and be able to take focused, practical action.

Type 6s can become paralyzed by feelings of insecurity and can rely heavily on their analytical minds. See if you can breathe deeply into your belly and connect with your power center.

AN INSIDEOUT LEADER'S STORY: **LARS HAS SOME SELF-INSIGHTS**

Chris helps Lars to gain self-insight. He can see himself as a 9ish Type 6, the Loyal Skeptic. His parents significantly influenced how his personality unfolded, so that not only does he appear to others as a Type 9, the Peacemaker, but also he finds himself using many of the Type 9 coping strategies.

Lars shares a bit of his family history to explain why some of his behavior may be out of character with his Type: "I was the first and only member of my family to go to university. Not only that, but I got my PhD." Chris admires Lars: "Your parents must have been so proud of you. That's a huge accomplishment, especially when there is no family history or expectation."

"Actually," Lars says, "there was little, if any, celebration. My parents weren't like that. They never wanted us to think we were special, so they downplayed or ignored significant events." Lars experienced this his entire life. "At some point, I stopped hoping or expecting it to be different, and I learned not to make a big deal about my achievements." In effect, he learned to make himself small. Lars focused on his intellect, analytical abilities, and hard work.

"I don't feel comfortable drawing attention to myself, and I hold back from offering opinions," Lars offers when Chris asks how Lars's history plays out at work. He now understands why Lars seems like a Type 9 yet has the core issues of Type 6.

Chris imagines that the 9ish quality of Lars influences what others experience as his lack of executive presence. Resting at Type 9 is his escape from constant anxiety. His workload and large span of responsibility takes its toll. His team challenges him at every step as he introduces change that is uncomfortable for them. His peers are unsupportive—they wonder, "Why is Lars introducing all this change?" They notice that he gets a lot of support from Caitlin that is not being accorded them. Lars reacts to the pressure and retreats. He second-guesses himself and starts anticipating trouble ahead. "I knew this job was too good to be true," Lars says to himself.

Issues of inclusion and exclusion are at play in several arenas: Lars and his peers, Caitlin and her peers, the different sub-groups on Lars's LT. The potential negative consequences loom large. Chris helps Lars to see how his world-view is shaping his reality. "Lars, do you notice how your focus moves to what could go wrong or what disaster may be around the next corner?"

They talk about trust too. Lars realizes that he has to trust the team and show his own vulnerability. He has to overcome his own fear of conflict if he wants the team members to challenge one another. He knows he needs to model the behavior he asks of his team, and he finds this challenging.

As they end their session, Lars is feeling a bit off-balance. It's a lot to take in, and he is overwhelmed. He searches for ways to explain away the behavior Chris pointed out. His head is spinning.

TYPE 7
JOURNEY OF THE ENTHUSIAST

▸ WORLDVIEW

As a very young child, I felt deprived and frustrated; there was limited nurturing for me. I didn't know what to do or where to go to feel satisfied. I felt disoriented and lost, not knowing where to turn. Deep down, I didn't experience feeling nurtured, loved, or supported. I became scared and didn't trust that I would get my needs met, and I was on my own. I grew up early and felt responsible at a young age.

I had feelings of deprivation, that there would never be enough for me. From time to time, I felt an inner emptiness that was very disturbing. I started looking for ways to fill the emptiness and loneliness I felt inside of me—with food, experiences, ideas, information, activities, friends, plans.

I came to believe that my true source of satisfaction was outside of me, and I had to go find it myself because I didn't trust that anyone was there for me. Believing that I was on my own and there was no support for me, I became independent and self-reliant. I knew that I would have to figure out what would make me feel satisfied—make a plan and have things conform to my plan and go after it. I became confident in my ability to *make* things happen.

One of my most effective ways to cope with life's disappointments was by analyzing—I would try to figure out why people behaved the way they did or why things were happening. This helped me to depersonalize what others were doing and distance myself from my feelings of hurt, sadness, and disappointment.

TYPE 7 - THE ENTHUSIAST
My motto: *Life is an adventure*

I began to inhabit a world of a possible, pleasurable future and took great joy in anticipating and imagining what this new life or next phase would be like and how exciting it would be. My optimism about what was possible became a great strength. I can be your biggest cheerleader and fan! I became idealistic, and my idealism's edges were tinged with naïveté and innocence. Yet no matter what I was doing, I always had an underlying feeling that there was something else I was supposed to be doing, but didn't know what it was, and I despaired of ever finding it.

The way I coped with mistakes, problems, and life's curve balls was to make lemonade out of lemons. I am an expert in the positive reframe. This helps me to disempower my fear. I make sure that I always have options, wonderful things to anticipate, and projects to work on, and I am fascinated by people and intoxicated by ideas. I could be a perpetual scholar, because there are so many exciting things to learn, languages to speak, ideas to contemplate and discuss.

I love seeing the big picture and how everything is interconnected. Boredom will never be a problem for me, because life is way too fascinating. Yet, I do live with the fear that I could become bored—with a job, a relationship, where I live, in a social gathering … I keep lots of balls spinning in the air to avoid becoming bored. That is a *dirty word*.

I see myself as a happy, enthusiastic person—full of life, fun, bubbly, quick-witted, interested and interesting, and a nonconformist. I believe the world is full of possibilities. My focus is anticipating *what's next*. Commitment is tough for me because I like to keep my options open. You never know what opportunities will be presented, and I wouldn't want to miss out! If I'm being honest, I do look for diversions and ways to escape difficult, painful, boring, or uninteresting situations. Best to have an escape hatch; options are good.

▸ COMPULSIONS AND FIXATIONS:
GLUTTONY AND PLANNING/ANTICIPATION

My gluttony is greedy; it is excessive indulgence. I gobble up food and life. I can overindulge and overconsume. I have an appetite for whatever excites or stimulates me, and I want to taste all sorts of different things—the more unusual, novel, and extraordinary, the better. I love the excitement of newness, of change. My challenge is that I don't fully digest what I learn or what I experience before I am thinking about the next. Before the food is going down my throat, I am already taking the next bite. I believe that my fulfillment is somewhere else, in the next thing, the next spoonful. My continual sense of dissatisfaction and fear of boredom keep me anticipating future possibilities and plans, and keeps me on the go.

‣ ROLE IDENTITY

I play the role of the enthusiast. I can get excited and enthusiastic about many things. It is my job to be the *happy one* in the family— to keep things light, fun, and funny. I can charm people out of bad moods. At dinner parties, I manage to keep the conversation going, never leaving those pregnant silences. I can be witty, and there are so many fascinating topics to discuss! I would never want to be boring or bored! Yes, keeping the energy up is something I do and excel at.

My role identity is linked closely with my compulsions of gluttony and anticipating/planning. I am enthusiastic, happy, and upbeat, and I focus on the good times. This, along with my gluttony for and anticipation of experiences, is all to keep up my excitement and happiness. I must continually move from idea to idea, and to the world of possibilities. I attend different events because I am afraid of missing out on something, and being on the go helps to quell my anxiety. This is my gluttony. I don't want to be limited in any way. Anything and everything is possible.

I am so identified with my role that I don't know if I can let it go. My fear of being trapped in pain and of being deprived is so strong that I cannot imagine closing down my options. If I weren't constantly learning and inhaling new information and ideas, what would I talk about? Would people still want to hang out with me or be interested in anything I had to say? What if I weren't *fun* or happy all the time— would people still want to be around me? They count on me to find the silver lining on the cloud, the pot of gold at the end of the rainbow—to be optimistic, see what is possible, offer up options, take them on adventures—don't they? Really, would my friends still be my friends? And if this isn't me, then who am I?

‣ THE PARADOX

Because I only superficially experience what I am doing or sensing in any given moment, I am never able to experience the *satisfaction* that I most desire and am constantly seeking. I miss out on the present moment and the ability to fully digest it, because I am always thinking of the next. Life is passing me by, and I am still feeling dissatisfied.

‣ TEMPTATIONS ON THE JOURNEY

Not sticking with your commitments. Believing there is something better out there than what you have or are doing. Making too many plans, and having too many projects and activities going on at once. 0Not taking one step at a time. Always keeping your options open. Thinking you are missing out on something. Not completing what you have started. Fear of boredom. Being overwhelmed. Not listening. Running away from feelings. Being self-centered.

‣ DETOUR SIGNS

The grass is greener. Keep your options open. Acquire as many experiences as possible. Distract yourself. Stay one step ahead of yourself. Don't worry about the details. Don't worry about completing what you are doing; get on with the next thing. It's OK to be impatient. Don't worry, be happy. Be OK about everything. Overcommit. Be charming and disarming. It's OK to be unreliable. Boredom is not an option. Think about exciting possibilities.

‣ COURSE CORRECTION

Discover what *really* brings you joy—listen to your heart. Be fully anchored in your body, and feel the entire range of your emotions, not just the positive ones. Slow down and spend time alone—get to know yourself. Sense into your body to experience the present moment. Be present—with yourself, others, the world around you—rather than envisioning and imagining what's next or what is possible. Create space in your life. Remember that everything always takes longer than you think it will, so don't try to do it all! Be patient with yourself and others. Trust in the natural unfolding of life. Fully commit, and watch the support you get to move your life forward in a beautiful way.

▸ **INTO THE SHADOW**

My Wings carry my shadow, as do my Connecting Points: lands of 6, 8, 1, 5. While the healthy expressions of these four Types are companions on my journey, when I turn around to look at the shadow they cast, I see parts of me that I don't want to acknowledge. Sometimes it takes entering the shadow to uncover the gifts that are waiting there.

Type 6 holds the shadow of my anxiety, worry, and skepticism. When I begin to get disillusioned (no longer fascinated) and lose trust, I begin to become suspicious and skeptical of other people and their motivations. The bloom has come off the rose for me. This is not a bad thing. It helps bring me more into balance, after a lifetime of wanting to see the best in people and refusing to look at the dark side of people and situations. My tendency to trust first, not have the difficult conversations, and worry about the details later has gotten me in trouble from time to time. Leaping without looking is one of my hallmarks, and Type 6 offers preparation, planning, and healthy skepticism.

I can also take on the worry and anxiety of Type 6 by anticipating what might go wrong. Other things lurking in the shadow of Type 6 are indecision, trying to optimize decisions, and not listening to or being able to hear my inner guidance. I know this part of me, too.

Type 8 holds another part of my shadow. It is the part of me that doesn't want to be controlled or told what to do, or to allow anyone to have power over me. Using more force than necessary, pushing, wanting to get my way, being willful, and wanting to control my outer world are also parts of my shadow residing in Type 8.

Type 1 is where I find myself in moments of stress. This is more in my conscious awareness, because when I react, I know myself to be critical, judgmental, righteous; I get manic about things needing to be just perfect; I don't know when enough is enough; I believe that I know what is right. These behaviors are definitely a part of me that I don't like, and I know that when I am overwhelmed, I have these types of reactions.

Type 5 is less familiar to me. It often lurks below my conscious awareness. When I felt hurt and rejected, I learned to detach emotionally, to close down my heart, and to analyze and compartmentalize. Another aspect of Type 5's shadow that I carry is greed. The greed of Type

5 coupled with the gluttony of my Type can show up as both a with-holding and a holding on to—love, money, information, things—es-pecially when my insecurities and fears have been activated and I feel threatened in some way. Neither Type 7 nor Type 5 has a high tol-erance for people who are emotionally needy of them—their needi-ness taps into our own fears of being needy, which we shut down as children, believing there was no support for us. We judge this in others and ourselves. Our shadows join here.

Part of my life journey will be to make contact with the parts of me that are germane to Types 2, 3, 4, and 9. These may be qualities that I judge in others as being somehow bad or wrong, or just don't re-late to at all. At some point, it will be important to visit these other lands and see what they have to teach me, what treasures can be found there.

▸ HELPING ALLIES

On my right is Type 6, and there is none more reliable. Type 6 can help me access the part of myself that makes commitments, takes re-sponsibility for them, and follows through. Taking care of the group or team is very much a part of what Type 6 models. They do their homework too: they research and plan things thoroughly rather than what I sometimes do—fly by the seat of my pants. Type 6 helps me to look at possible challenges that I could face on the road ahead as a balance to my sometimes-blind optimism.

The healthiest aspects of Type 6s are their faith and trust, and their courage in the face of fear. This too is part of me. I must call forth my courage in the face of my insecurities. My tendency is to be behind the scenes rather than out front. It is important to step up and take responsibility—to step out into the world and risk letting my voice be heard. Type 8 is an essential ally in this area.

On my left is Type 8, and one of the key gifts they offer me is the ability to believe in myself and have the courage of my convictions. That and the faith and responsibility of Type 6 are just the magic in-gredients I need. Type 8 is the part of me that has two feet firmly planted on the ground—that is in contact with my instincts and acts on them. They also are grounded in a certain realism that helps bal-ance my step-off-the-edge-of-the-cliff-type optimism.

Type 8s trust their ability to take on the big challenges, surround themselves with people who support them in moving through these challenges, and own their power. There is solidity to Type 8 that I also possess and need to access. Type 8 is embodied power, not just power of the mind with all of its many ideas—*and* they believe in themselves. It is this belief that gives them the confidence to excel and take on challenges. Type 8s know how to contain energy, and how to focus and channel it toward whatever they are trying to manifest. I know this would serve me well.

When I link my arms with these two, together they give me realism, solidity, courage, and the ability to take responsibility for manifesting my ideas—and to commit wholeheartedly.

From this grounded place, I can quietly reflect and open to true knowing and wisdom like Type 5. Rather than learn a little about a lot, Type 5 gives me the focus and quiet containment to develop my expertise. Type 1 offers the gift of discipline to follow through, and take action on my convictions and my ideals. Together we can move my visions and dreams into tangible form.

▸ BURIED TREASURE: TYPE 7 *ALCHEMY*

Gluttony, fear of deprivation, and enthusiasm is transformed into ecstatic joy, presence, reverence, awe for all of life, sobriety (being firmly grounded in the moment—taking in no more and no less than needed)

Your joy is your sorrow unmasked.

...

The deeper that sorrow carves into your being, the more joy you can contain.

—Kahlil Gibran, from "On Joy and Sorrow," *The Prophet*[26]

When I finally slow down and become profoundly reflective, I may experience feelings of melancholy and depression and a deep well of grief. I have finally run out of steam, and all my running away has caught up with me. If I am willing to stay with it and face my unprocessed sorrow, grief, and lifelong patterns, there will be a wonderful treasure at the end of this journey. I will come out the other side of this black hole with a warm and open heart, clarity, focus, commitment, a renewed raison d'être, creative juice, and joy! It is through the well of sorrow that one truly experiences joy.

Ecstatic joy emanates from my being and comes from an amazing reverence, awe, and gratitude that I derive from being fully engaged in the present moment, at one with myself and my environment. Once I drink from the well of grief and sorrow, I no longer feel the urge to run away from my anxiety and painful feelings, but instead I face them squarely and find that I can survive them. Without effort, my compulsion of gluttony transforms into sobriety. It's as if I wake up and find myself in awe of what is here, now, right in front of me. I don't have to worry anymore about being somewhere else; I am in the eternal here and now. I feel full and satisfied with my life and the world around me, and I have a profound sense of gratitude for my life.

TYPE 7

POSITIVE CONTRIBUTION	REACTIONS / STRESS
Visionaries / Initiators / Inspirational / Motivational / Enthusiastic	Lack follow--through / Missing concrete information / Missing details / Want others to implement
Seize opportunities / See possibilities / Synthesizers / Accomplished achievers / Practical / Productive / Prolific	Scattered / Unfocused / Gluttonous Miss details / Lack of in-depth knowledge / Indecisive / Keep options open
Fun / Playful / Joyous / Expressive / Upbeat / Offer employees freedom to create and produce	Over-disciplined / Critical / Judgmental / Sharp-edged Don't offer enough direction and specificity Want to be liked
Analytical	Lack compassion and empathy
Fast paced	Get bored easily / Impatient / Impulsive
Anticipate the future / Visionary	Not present / Distracted / Incomplete grieving and emotional processing of pain, loss, trauma
Risk takers / Commit / Stay the course	Leap before looking / Always have an escape hatch / Grass is always greener / Leave others to clean up mess
Spontaneous / Resilient / Flexible / Seek change / Positive / Glass is half-full	Don't like structure / Fear of loss of freedom—being trapped / Initiate too much change / Don't want to deal with difficulties or problems /Anxiety

TYPE 7 JOURNAL

 STOP AND REFLECT

Look at the Type 7 compulsions: Gluttony and anticipating/planning. As you begin to explore this for yourself, you will start to see your compulsive patterns and their impact on your life.

Recall a time when you were afraid of being trapped in pain, a job, a relationship, a circumstance … What was going on? What did you do? Write about your memory of this. Tell the story. What triggered this fear? See if you can get underneath the fear. Identify it—what were you afraid would happen? What were your feelings; what were you thinking and doing? What were your body sensations?

How does this pattern play out in your life?

How has this worked for you / benefited you?

What has been the cost to you?

Notice when it is your anxiety talking and not you. Are you filling up the space with words just like you fill up your time with activities? Get into contact with your anxiety. Inquire into it. What is it trying to tell you? Write about it. Where do you feel it in your body when it arises? When have you had that same sensation before? Is there a pattern? The more you try to understand it and listen to it and learn from it, the less hold it will have over you, and it will begin to dissipate over time.

Can you recall a time when you felt your heart harden? Write about it. What were the circumstances that evoked this feeling? What were you trying to protect?

Unraveling Your Role Identity (Review the *Role Identity* for Type 7, the Enthusiast)

List your *core fears* (for example, powerlessness, no support, loneliness, rejection, harm, deprivation, shame, exposure, feeling overwhelmed, humiliation, abandonment, pain, inability to fulfill dreams).

Recall a time when you felt the softening of your heart—when you were able to let down, show your vulnerability, and allow yourself to be supported by others. How did it feel? What was it like for you to allow people to see you *not having it all together*? What were the circumstances? What created enough safety for you to allow this; what were the enablers? What internal obstacles did you have to overcome? Tell the story.

List your *core hurts* (for example, feeling unsupported, accused, unseen, flawed, worthless, unimportant, guilty, devalued, rejected, powerless, inadequate, unlovable).

What were the short- and long-term results?

How do your core fears and core hurts relate to each other and reinforce each other?

How can you cultivate more of this in your life?

What do your core fears and hurts have to do with your role identity?

If you weren't playing your role of the Enthusiast / the Adventurer, who would you be? What feelings come up for you when you imagine dropping this role?

How did you come to believe that these fears and hurts were true and real? What is your evidence that this is true? How do you know?

Describe and list some of the qualities of how you would like to be and be seen. List some descriptive words (warm, playful, powerful …).

What do you believe would happen if you stopped looking for this evidence and chose to look for evidence that negated these fears?

What are the first steps you can take toward embodying these qualities?

If you no longer reacted to these fears, how would that affect the role you play?

‣ **TYPE 7** WORDS

Freedom, joy, gluttony, anticipation, sorrow, completion, pain, vulner-ability, competence, satisfaction, boredom, enthusiastic, present, scat-tered, fear, emptiness, deprivation, desire, alone, fascinating.

Your Enneagram Type will have a unique association with cer-tain words related to your compulsions and patterns.

Understanding the significance of these words and how they have played out in your life will be telling for you. Being more conscious of your feelings and attitudes toward these words will help you to transform how they live within you and help you to create your life story moving forward.

Take your time with this and find a quiet place where you can reflect. I suggest writing about one word at a time and letting it stew inside of you while you activate your inner observer (the nonjudging ob-server) and peel back its meaning. You will want to come back to this word again and again.

I suggest picking the first word that calls to you in your list. Each word has both positive connotations and unhealthy expressions. Write about both. Keep digging deeper. Begin to notice as you go through your day how these words play out in your life.

For instance, *gluttony*: What is your association with gluttony? What does it feel like when you are *in the grip* of gluttony? What are the circumstances that evoke it? How does it serve you? How does it cre-ate challenges and problems for you? Tell stories of times when you have experienced gluttony.

These are just some of the questions you might consider when you begin to explore how each word has shown up on your life journey. Consider how you want to bring these behaviors and qualities for-ward in a more conscious and intentional way.

‣ WHAT'S IN MY BIG BLACK BAG?
PEERING INTO MY SHADOW

✎ Take a look at your Wings and your two Connecting Points (Types 1, 5, 6, and 8). What aspects of these Types do you recognize in yourself? What don't you relate to? Write about this. Start to self-observe and notice. Are your self-observations truly accurate? Inquire within. Ask others for their perceptions.

✦ Go to the sections for your Connecting Points (Types 1 and 5) and your Wings (Types 6 and 8). Take time also to explore the words for these four Types. It will be quite instructive.

‣ **THINGS YOU CAN DO** TO MAKE A SHIFT

BE PRESENT

Slow down. Stop filling every minute of your schedule with people, projects, and plans. Take time to reflect. Spend time alone. Allow your mind to wander and wonder. See if you can continually bring yourself back to the present moment. Notice your body sensations, smells, sights, sounds, and tastes. See if you can take in the *here and now* without planning, wanting to be somewhere else or with someone, or anticipating the next thing. See if you can carve out time daily to just be with yourself and really get to know yourself.

CONNECT WITH YOUR HEART

Give yourself permission to feel sad, lonely, or even sorry for yourself without trying to *snap out of it*. You won't drown in your sorrow; you will come out the other end. The only way out is through. Type 7 is known to move on quickly rather than take the time to grieve fully. Like sampling at the buffet, Type 7s dip into their grief and sorrow but rarely fully go through it. Stay with it. There is gold on the other side.

Notice when you feel hard and impatient with others. Where do you feel this hardness? What evokes it for you? When you experience this hardness, impatience, and judgment, breathe into your belly, put your attention in your heart, and ask yourself, "What if I had a little more generosity in my heart? How would that feel?" See if you feel a softening.

Type 7 can appear quite ungrounded. What do I mean by this? Scattered, unfocused, talking fast, moving from subject to subject, barely taking a breath. Meditating will help with your grounding. Even five minutes a day will help. Yoga is also a great practice for this. When you become aware that you are ungrounded, see if you can take a few deep breaths into your belly. Put your attention in your belly. Feel your lower body. Feel your feet on the ground. Imagine pulling energy up from the earth, through your feet, and up your legs and spine. See the energy coming from the center of the earth, up through you.

✦ "InsideOut—Leaders' Tool Kit" contains simple instructions on meditation.

AN INSIDEOUT LEADER'S STORY: **COACHING LARS**

By the time they have their next coaching session, Lars has sorted out much of what came up at their last meeting. He got some much-needed clarity and found himself feeling less defensive.

As Chris continues to coach Lars, he helps Lars to see how conflicted he feels about claiming his own power and how this shows up in his leadership gaps with the LT and in his perceived lack of executive presence in the boardroom.

Even though Lars has become more trusting, he still feels challenged to take decisive action, and unconsciously waits for permission from some imagined authority, or for this authority figure to make decisions for him. Chris explains, "Lars, Type 6 has a conflicted relationship with authority. Type 6s both respect and challenge authority. Type 6 easily steps into the role of the devil's advocate. Is this familiar to you? Do you recognize this in yourself?"

Lars takes time to reflect and comes up with several examples that support what Chris just said. Chris continues, "Your power is related to your own authority. Rather than abdicate or challenge authority, it is important for you to claim your own." Clunk. Lars hears it, and suddenly some significant pieces of his life puzzle come together.

Chris works with Lars to connect with the high side of Type 3 and feel the power of taking decisive action, as well as connects with the even-handed realism of Type 9 to see the situation from a more objective place rather than through the lens of fear, skepticism, and anxiety about what may go wrong. Additionally, the high side of Type 9 is acceptance of both people and situations. It is a great antidote for some of the blame and frustration that Lars feels right now.

→ Lars's story continues on p. 189

TYPE 8
JOURNEY OF THE BOSS

‣ **WORLDVIEW**

As a young child, I perceived the world as a hostile place. I felt vulnerable, small, and weak. To compensate and deal with these feelings, I decided that I must be strong and not show any vulnerability in order to survive. My childhood innocence was short-lived. Unconsciously, I decided to protect myself from being controlled or dominated.

Feeling weak and vulnerable myself, I chose to project power and strength, and to act out my anger and rage. Imagine me as a gorilla, beating my fists on my chest. I puff myself up to project a dominating presence. This serves to cover up my feelings of vulnerability and powerlessness from others, and sometimes even from myself. While protecting myself from being controlled and dominated, my mission is also to protect others whom I see as vulnerable and seek justice on their behalf.

Over time, my self-image evolved, and I came to know myself as tough, powerful, assertive, honest, and realistic. My communication style is blunt, no-nonsense, and to the point. I don't have time for frivolous talk and social niceties—and forget being PC! I am strong-willed, and I get things done.

I avoid feelings of emptiness by *inhaling and devouring* as much of the world as possible. I like to live large! I came to believe that it is a hard and unjust world, and it is unsafe to be soft or show vulnerability. I see myself as fighting for survival, and if I'm not careful, others will take advantage of me.

TYPE 8- THE BOSS
My motto: *Bring it on!*

To cope with the world, I need to be in control and *impose* my will and truth on others. The more I expand my control, the more protected and less vulnerable I feel. This big, indomitable energy I project and feel inside of me makes me believe that I am capable of taking on big challenges—as if I can move mountains. The power I exude attracts others to follow me on the path I am carving out. I make sure that those in my circle are loyal to me—in fact, I demand it. Loyalty gets them my protection, and together we will make big things happen!

▸ COMPULSIONS AND FIXATIONS:
LUST AND BJECTIFICATION/REVENGE/VENGEANCE

My lust takes the form of unrestrained excess. When I am in the grip of *lust*, it is like a drug—the energy from my belly fuels my actions, my intensity, my expansiveness, and my ability to take command and dominate. I am straightforward and have no pretenses—I say what's on my mind and do what needs doing. I use my force of will and take what I want when I want it—impulsively. I am passionately engaged in life and have a big appetite for all that gives me pleasure.

Ever since I was young, I have worked *against* something or someone in my quest for survival in this world. I push limits and make demands. When I need to, I take the law into my own hands and can see myself as *above the law* or *as* the law. I ask for forgiveness rather than permission.

When I feel threatened, people become objects that I can easily move out of my way, and I feel free to express my anger and rage toward them. They should be able to take it—buck up, be strong. When I seek revenge, it is my way of getting justice—I am righting the wrongs.

The intoxication of anger, like that of the grape, shows us to others, but hides us from ourselves.

—John Dryde

▸ ROLE IDENTITY

I see my role as the boss, the top dog, the protector, the challenger. All of these roles describe me and how others might see me as well. The role I play is a way to demonstrate my power to others, keep them at bay, and keep them in fear of me (or at least intimidated). I project a *you don't want to mess with me* stance. I am a force of nature! Further, my compulsions of lust, revenge, and vengeance fortify my image. My lusty energy makes me look larger than life and overwhelms others.

Expressing anger and rage is something that I feel is my right—and these are not emotions that most people are comfortable expressing or receiving. I am not always aware that my emotional outbursts or big energy scares people off. I know how to speak with confidence—clear and straightforward. This seems to keep people off-balance. I have an animal-like instinct that I use to take bold action and go for the jugular if I need to. Others know that I have no compunction about taking revenge, which further reinforces my dominance and power.

Because I hold the belief that the world is a hostile place and I have to fight for my survival, that others will dominate and control me if they can, I do this to others. Dominate or be dominated. This can elicit either fearful behavior or very aggressive behavior from others. When people are aggressive with me, it just reinforces my belief that the world is hostile, and that I need to maintain my *one-up* position and continue fighting to survive.

What if I were to decide to give up my role as the one who makes things happen, who is dominant—the *alpha*, who is a take-charge, take-control person? What if I were to let people know that I don't feel as strong or as powerful as I act? What if I were to show my vulnerability? What if life really isn't about focusing on survival? What if control is my illusion? What if I allowed myself to show the softer part of me? Would people use my vulnerability to hurt and attack me? Would I still be able to be the leader that people think I am? Would people follow me? What would happen? If I am not the role I have been playing, then who am I? Who would I be?

‣ THE PARADOX

I can appear and act overconfident—*too big to fail*—and this is my Achilles' heel. I can barge in like a bull in a china shop and ignore anyone whom I have hurt or offended, as well as the consequences of my actions. I can leave a path of destruction and dismiss the profound consequences for others.

I am so intent on dealing with the task at hand that I don't tend to the details or give importance to what may be going on under the surface. My focus on the challenge is so willful and single-minded that I can miss subtleties and nuance.

I also forget to listen to and take a look at what is going on inside of me—my connection to my heart, my tenderness, and my own values. The challenge or cause is my top priority. This is my real vulnerability. I can be blindsided and outsmarted, fooled and manipulated, through flattery, deceit, and false loyalty. I become so confident that I start believing my own bloated storyline. I am asleep to my vulnerabilities because I have bullied my way through and gotten away with so much, have forgotten my values, and think I am indomitable. I confront and threaten. Now I am *truly* vulnerable, and my survival is at stake. I don't see it coming, and whoosh!—I have been taken down.

As with each Type, we end up creating what we are trying most to avoid, through our own behavior.

▸ TEMPTATIONS ON THE JOURNEY

Overreliance on my physical strength. Using more power and force than necessary. Avoid showing tenderness, empathy, caring. Avoid situations where I feel out of control or out of my element. Impatience. Avoid peripheral vision. See people as objects. Ignore consequences or impact. Act impulsively. Think that brute force and power of will win the day. Tell instead of ask. Bend the rules for my own purposes. Take things purely for my own pleasure.

▸ DETOUR SIGNS

Aggressive, loud, and boisterous behavior. Zero tolerance for subtlety. Blunt, no-nonsense, and to the point. Demand loyalty. Shoot first, ask questions later. Compromise is a dirty word. Want it, take it. Contempt for rules and the law. Have it your way. Demand! Dominate. Oppose authority. Exaggerate. Confront and intimidate. Take revenge! Direct your rage and anger at others. You are above the law. Forget your heart and your values. Don't worry about the consequences. Justice is what counts.

▸ COURSE CORRECTION

Pause, slow down, cultivate patience. Don't act on impulse based on your fear and reactivity. See if you can notice physical sensations that precede an angry outburst. Breathe deeply, stop, even leave the situation if you need to, so that you don't react. Realize that confrontations threaten your survival. Contact your heart and reconnect with what's really important to you, with your values, with what truly matters. Cultivate empathy—practice seeing the world through others' eyes. It's safe to be tender and to show warmth, feeling, and caring.

In fact, it is the true source of your power—the joining of power and love is unstoppable.

‣ INTO THE SHADOW

My Wings carry my shadow, as do my Connecting Points: lands of 7, 9, 5, 2. While the healthy expressions of these four Types are companions on my journey, when I turn around to look at the shadow they cast, I see parts of me that I don't want to acknowledge. Sometimes it takes entering the shadow to uncover the gifts that are waiting there.

Type 7 is on my right, and Type 9 is on my left. The shadow of Type 7 reinforces my impulsive behavior—my ability to rationalize what I instinctively want to do without regard for the consequences. It is the active and more hyper side of me that is in constant motion. I keep busy to avoid my feelings. I recognize my intolerance for maintenance and the need to be constantly challenged—the aspect of Type 7 that runs away from the specter of boredom and has a hard time with completion.

Type 7 is also the part of me that pseudo-commits—commits until my lust takes over and I feel entitled to have what I want, regardless of the commitments I've made. It is that part of me that wants freedom to choose, to do, and to not be tethered.

Type 9 reinforces my boundaries to keep others and reality at bay. The shadow of Type 9 is the part of me that doesn't want to face and deal with my own issues. When I act from my shadow at Type 9, I can accommodate others to win their acceptance or to get them on my side. When people see me do this, it can be confusing because it looks out of character for me.

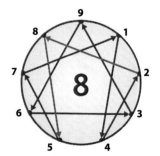

I can also be stubborn, be guarded, disengage, and close up like a clamshell as part of my shadow. Type 9 struggles with lack of self *self-importance*, and my focus on demonstrating my own self-importance by acting larger than life, dominating a conversation, taking over the room, and so on, is a way that I try to overcome this.

Type 5 is my Stress Point and my shadow point. Continually pushing against the world and trying to survive takes its toll on me. Much of what I have been running away from—feelings of inner emptiness, emotional detachment, insecurities—live here in the shadow of Type 5. Counter to how others experience me and I know myself, when I access my Type 5 shadow, I become withdrawn and detached.

Type 2 contains aspects of my shadow, the part of me that is emotionally volatile, needy, seductive, and manipulative, and that can play victim and martyr—what I abhor most. Type 2 also comes through me when I become demanding that my needs be met and when I act possessive. I don't easily see this in myself, but I clearly see it in others, and it enrages me because it brings up my feelings of powerlessness. This shadow looms large for me.

Part of my life journey is to make contact with the parts of me that are germane to Types 1, 3, 4, and 6. These are often qualities I judge in others as somehow bad or wrong or that I just don't relate to at all. At some point, it will be important to visit these other lands and see what they have to teach me and what treasures can be found there.

▸ HELPING ALLIES

Type 7, on my right, offers the gifts of spontaneity, play, adventure, and joy to my Atlas gotta-push-the-boulder-up-the-mountain behavior. Type 7s help me to recapture the childlike innocence that I stuffed into my black bag so long ago. Type 7s also bring a visionary and big-picture-thinking quality to my approach. They see and understand interconnections and systems, and can help me pay attention to potential downstream effects of my decisions and actions. I know that I can rely on Type 7s to help me be more socially adept, charming, and disarming.

Type 9, on my left, offers the gift of seeing others' viewpoints and knows how to mediate rather than dominate. Type 9s bring patience to my otherwise impatient and impulsive approach. They are gifted at seeing situations holistically—the 360-degree picture. Type 9s focus their attention on accommodating others. They can teach me to be kind, which would serve me well.

Type 9s also know how to blend into the background and observe. My place tends to be out in front and *on point*. Adding this to my repertoire could be quite valuable. I don't want to be a one-trick pony. Being out in front makes me more vulnerable. Observing allows me to learn more about the situation, and to see some of the subtleties and distinctions before taking action. Type 9s contain their energy and manage their anger, something I need to do more often. Type 9s are quite important allies and teachers for me.

When I connect with my lighter, more playful, intuitive side and my kinder, gentler, contained, and subtle side with greater peripheral vision, I see a more nuanced and colorful world. With my clearer vision, I open to my helping allies Types 2 and 5. Type 5 shows me how to focus my energy—to detach and get perspective, to develop my expertise rather than act primarily on my impulses. Type 5 helps me to look inward and open to my inner knowing. Type 2 helps me to look inward and connect with my heart, open my heart to others, and peer into others' hearts.

My helping allies have given me the gift of sight, and for this gift I am deeply grateful. I can now move forward with a full and wise heart, clarity, intent, purpose, and greater awareness.

▸ **BURIED TREASURE:** TYPE 8 *ALCHEMY*

Vengeance, revenge, objectification, and lust are transformed into innocence, unity, big-heartedness, and action for the greater good.

The world is clearer and more multifaceted. My blinders are off. I return to a time of childlike innocence where I see that people are inherently good and I don't have to fight for my survival. I allow people to see and experience my inner teddy bear that loves to be tender, sweet, warm, and caring. My focus has shifted to the well-being of others. No longer do people feel coerced and steamrolled by me. Instead, they are inspired to follow me. I realize that I don't have to push so hard, but can allow life to unfold more organically. I have found my playful and fun-loving side, and derive much pleasure from the simple things in life. Opening up myself and my heart to my family and friends is more natural for me, and it has become a source of love, joy, and pleasure.

Self-reverence, self-knowledge, self-control, — These three alone lead life to sovereign power.

—Alfred Lord Tennyson

I no longer see others merely as objects. I have a profound understanding and experience of unity—that we are all part of the same soup and are interconnected. What I do to myself, I am enacting in the world, and what I do to others, I am doing to myself. I realize that staying connected to my heart is most important. I now enlist my energy to take action for the greater good. I derive great joy and satisfaction when I harness my courage and power and align them with my values to make a positive impact on the world.

I care.

TYPE 8

POSITIVE CONTRIBUTION	REACTIONS / STRESS
Like challenges	Bored with *maintenance*
Take charge / Natural leaders / Direct / Expressive	Don't follow or take direction / Tell, don't ask ("just do it") People feel *steamrolled, oppressed, pushed, shut down, intimidated, disempowered, afraid to take risks or speak up*
Protective	Dominating Demand loyalty Don't show vulnerability
Strategic	Not interested in detail
Big risk takers	Prone to big failures and take people with them / Lustful
Expressive / Direct	Confrontational / Act out anger and rage / Controlling / "Get to the point"
Justice / Competitive / Fight the good fight	Seek revenge / Dominate
Engaging / Warm / Caring / Empathic	Lack vulnerability / Bully / Tyrannical / Harsh / Judgmental
Charismatic	Fast / Impatient / "Get to the point!"
Instinctive / Sensitive to people's needs / Generous	Missing empathy and compassion / "Shoot, ready, aim"

TYPE 8 JOURNAL

 STOP AND REFLECT

Look at the Type 8 compulsions: Lust and revenge/vengeance and rage/anger. As you begin to explore this for yourself, you will start to see your compulsive patterns and their impact on your life.

Recall a time when you felt the need to get revenge or to right a wrong. Write about your memory of this. What were the circumstances? Write down as much detail as you can remember. What triggered this need or compulsion? What were your feelings, thoughts, reactions, and body sensations when this was going on? Write about it.

What has been the cost to you?

Think of a time in the recent past when you acted on impulse and then justified why you did what you did. What was going on in your internal state when you did this? Your inner dialog, feelings, thoughts? Tell the story. How does this behavior serve you? How does it hinder you?

How does this pattern play out in your life?

How has this worked for you / benefited you?

See if you can begin to notice your impulse to act, before you take action. What are the signs?

✑ Recall a time when you experienced yourself as big-hearted and open-hearted—when you allowed someone to see your softer side. What was it like for you to reveal this part of yourself? How did it feel? What were the circumstances that invited you to share this part of you? What internal obstacles did you have to overcome? How did you do that? Tell the story.

✑ List your *core fears* (for example, powerlessness, no support, loneliness, rejection, harm, deprivation, shame, exposure, feeling overwhelmed, humiliation, abandonment, pain, inability to fulfill dreams).

✑ List your *core hurts* (for example, feeling unsupported, accused, unseen, flawed, worthless, unimportant, guilty, devalued, rejected, powerless, inadequate, unlovable).

✑ What were the short- and long-term results of this?

✑ How do your core fears and core hurts relate to each other and reinforce each other?

✑ What if you could create more honest, heart-to-heart connections in your life? Imagine what that would be like?

✑ What do your core fears and hurts have to do with your role identity?

Unraveling Your Role Identity (Review the *Role Identity* for Type 8, the Boss)

How did you come to believe that these fears and hurts were true and real? What is your evidence? How do you know?

If you weren't playing your role of the Boss / the Challenger, who would you be? What feelings come up for you when you imagine dropping this role?

What do you believe would happen if you stopped looking for this evidence and chose to look for evidence that negated these fears?

Describe and list some of the qualities you would like to have. List some descriptive words (warm, playful, powerful …).

If you no longer reacted to these fears, how would that affect the role you play?

What are the first steps you can take toward embodying these qualities?

‣ **TYPE 8** WORDS

Power, vulnerability, instincts, childlike, strength, loyalty, rage, action, lust, justice, control, relaxation, love, protection, force, emotions, empathy, boredom, innocence, contain, expertise, peripheral vision.

Your Enneagram Type will have a unique association with certain words related to your compulsions and patterns.

Understanding the significance of these words and how they play out in your life will be telling. Being more conscious of your feelings and attitudes toward these words will help you to transform how they live within you and help you to create your life story moving forward.

Take your time with this, and find a quiet place where you can reflect. I suggest writing about one word at a time and letting it stew inside of you while you activate your inner observer (the nonjudging observer) and peel back its meaning. You will want to come back to this word again and again.

I suggest picking the first word that calls to you in your own list. Each word has both positive connotations and unhealthy expressions. Write about both. Keep digging deeper. Begin to notice as you go through your day how these words play out in your life.

For instance, *lust*: What is your association with lust? What does it feel like when you are *in the grip* of lust? What are the circumstances that evoke lust for you? How does it serve you? How does it create challenges and problems for you? Tell stories of times you have experienced lust.

These are just some of the questions you might consider when you begin to explore how each word has shown up on your life journey. Consider how you want to bring these behaviors and qualities forward in a more conscious and intentional way.

‣ **WHAT'S IN MY BIG BLACK BAG?**
PEERING INTO MY SHADOW

Take a look at your Wings and your two Connecting Points (Types 7, 9, 5, 2). What aspects of these Types do you recognize in

✳ Go to the sections for your Connecting Points (Types 5 and 2) and your Wings (Types 7 and 9), and get to know these parts of yourself. Take time to explore the words for these four Types. It will be quite instructive.

yourself? What don't you relate to? Write about this. Start to self-observe, and notice whether your self-observations are accurate. Inquire within. Ask others for their perceptions.

▶ **THINGS YOU CAN DO** TO MAKE A SHIFT

MANAGE YOUR IMPULSES

You have great instincts, but they shouldn't always be enacted. Rather than move with your impulses, see if you can tune in and listen to what your rational mind has to say—not the rational mind that is about to justify your impulse, but the clearer quiet mind of reason. Pause when you feel the impulse. See if you can breathe into your belly and relax. Engage your mind. Then engage your heart. What does your heart have to say about your impulse? What are some of the potential consequences of your action? When you pause to consider and tune in, you will have the freedom to choose. You'll have more control over your impulses, rather than being a victim of them.

CULTIVATE PATIENCE

Notice your impatience with others. Pause. See if you can tune in to your heart and soften it by asking, "What if there were a little more kindness in my heart? What would that feel like?" Remember that Type 8s tend to push more than needed and use more force than needed. This also takes its toll on you. See if you can push just a little less each time, and then notice the response you get from others. Notice how using less force feels to you.

CULTIVATE CURIOSITY

People tend to be intimidated by your self-confidence, bravado, and confrontational style. You may not know it, but you are missing out on a lot, because others don't feel safe sharing things with you.

People hold back information, opinions, feelings, and recommendations. Create safety for people by being open to what they have to say rather than reacting to it. Instead of reacting, ask a question to clarify, to better understand, to uncover their thinking, to learn more about what they think and feel. It will serve you well.

CONNECT WITH YOUR HEART

Slow down and take time for your heart. Do things you love to do— engage in an artistic pursuit such as painting, photography, or sculpture. You will not only enjoy it, but also find that it brings out a compelling part of you.

 In "InsideOut—Leaders' Tool Kit," see "Curiosity Is Your Guide," "Centering Basic Practice," and "Mindfulness Meditation" for practices that will be useful to incorporate in your daily life.

AN INSIDEOUT LEADER'S STORY: **LARS FEELS THE PRESSURE TO PRODUCE**

Lars can see how his frustration with himself and others doesn't forward his efforts. Willing others to change doesn't work. He needs to slow down a bit and be more realistic about how far and how fast the team can move within a given timeframe.

Chris is aware that the pressure to perform precipitates a stress reaction in Lars. By tracking him on the Enneagram, he observes how Lars acts out some of the less healthy aspects of Types 3, 6, and 9. Chris starts writing on his pad of paper for Lars to see: "If you look at the 3-6-9 triangle, you can see your self-doubt and insecurities cause self-defeating behaviors, like blaming people on the team and lashing out at some of them (Type 6). You then retreat and hide out in your office and make yourself unavailable (Type 9). This triggers a fear of failure (core issue for Type 3), and as you described to me, Lars, you then become very goal oriented and push the team to go faster than they are ready to go. You ignore the need to build relationships and maintain the relationships you've been developing, and instead become task focused and goal focused, and ig-

nore your feelings and theirs. Can you see this happening?"

Through their coaching process, Lars can see how his behavior amplifies the problem. His reactive pattern moves him further away from success rather than toward it.

Lars blames his team for the very things that he is unwilling to face about himself. His defensive behavior and preemptive strikes to ward off criticism from the team are not helping.

Lars's voice drops, and he looks down. "I can see why I am having a hard time building trust with the team." Chris knows he has to pace himself with Lars because Lars can absorb only so much at a time, and it will take courage and a commitment to make needed changes.

Lars leaves their coaching session with a lot to think about. Chris has given Lars some actionable things to do to begin the process of shifting some of his longstanding patterns.

→ Lars's story continues on p. 201

TYPE 9
JOURNEY OF THE PEACEMAKER

‣ WORLDVIEW

When I was quite young, I felt a loss of connection to my parents or caregivers. While I might not have specific memories of this today, I am left with the fear of losing my connection to others—to the people who do love me or are in relationship with me. My self-perception is that I am unimportant and inadequate, and in some way insignificant. As a child, I didn't stir things up too much, although I may have been a bit accident-prone. I was a pretty easygoing kid and spent a lot of time in my own imaginary world.

Because I am afraid to lose my connection to others, I believe I need to disconnect from myself (forget myself). The way I do this is to make sure that I don't make waves, I make sure that other people's needs and desires are accommodated, I go along with others' agendas, I don't voice strong opinions or do or say anything that could provoke conflict, and I avoid drawing attention to myself. If a conflict starts to surface, I do my best to put out any flames. I am resigned to never taking center stage. I have no confidence that I will ever be loved or valued in my own right. How could I be, when people don't really know who I am?

I can easily get swept up in others' agendas and lose track of my own desires and direction in life. I am not particularly passionate or excitable about anything, nor do I long for something else. I am just comfortable and I go along. People envy my apparent comfort and that I appear to be accepting of my lot in life. I am known for my accepting of others and what life brings me. What they don't see is that I am really stuck—stuck in my comforting habits and routines. I make decisions by abdicating them. I tend to lack initiative.

For the most part, I am content with my life. I don't ask much from life and just try to go along and get along. I end up losing myself in relationship and don't stand up for what I want. Because of this tendency, I enact very strong boundaries and can be quite immovable when people ask me to change in any way or try to get me to do something.

TYPE 9- THE PEACEMAKER
My motto: *Can't we all just get along?*

Instead of being *for* something, I act *against*. It's my way holding on to my connection to myself and whatever sense of self I have. Making a commitment to a long-term relationship is challenging for me because I am so afraid that I will disappear even more. I can be pretty darned stubborn and won't be pressured to change.

▸ COMPULSIONS AND FIXATIONS: PONDERING AND DAYDREAMING / SLOTH AND LAZINESS

The way my compulsions play out is that I can neglect to take care of things I need to do—particularly when it comes to paying attention to my own growth and development. This is how my laziness and sloth show up. I become complacent and indifferent about my own life and can be that way toward others—particularly when I feel pressure. All this leads to my own stagnation.

Instead, I seek out peace and comfort through habits and routines, indifference and daydreaming. I disengage from the world, my body, and reality. I can live in my imaginary world and tend to idealize people and my family history. As a child, I tried to tune out what was happening in an effort to stay peaceful, so I escaped into my own little world.

▸ ROLE IDENTITY

I see my role as the Peacemaker—the person who helps keep things calm, keeps conflicts to a minimum, and sees others' viewpoints. I do my best to suppress whatever strong emotions arise both in others and in me. One of the ways in which I manage to stay peaceful is to idealize my past, other people, and situations.

I daydream and ponder life as a way of disconnecting. This keeps me feeling comfortable and peaceful. Other people see me as calm and easygoing. I don't think I am anyone special or important; and I am resigned to believing that the world is indifferent to me, so I will be indifferent to the world. In other words, *what's the difference?* I focus on ways in which I don't make a difference rather than see the impact that I *do* have. This keeps my role identity in place.

What if I offered opinions, said what I wanted, and stopped focusing on other people's agendas? What if I engaged in conflict or let conflict ensue, rather than trying to dampen it? I can't imagine what that would be like. If I took a stand, expressed strong emotions, and were less predictable, would I still be lovable? Would people leave me, fire me, not like me? What would happen? What am I passionate about? What do I want for my life? If I weren't the person who blends in—who is peaceful, comfortable, easygoing, kind, routine—who would I be?

▸ THE PARADOX

By continually trying to avoid conflict, I create it—when I clam up and withdraw, people are right there trying to find out what is going on with me and pry me open. Conflict ensues. I run away and people chase. The more I try to keep the peace, the more I upset others, because I don't let things unfold naturally and am constantly trying to make things OK and smooth them over.

The more I try to accommodate others and make sure that everything is copacetic, the more I forget myself. I don't share my desires, needs, or opinions, and this confirms others' perceptions that I am rather bland and don't need anything. It also keeps me from being disappointed or hurt.

People tend to overlook me because I don't share what I want, think, or feel. I'm not a passionate person. I blend into the woodwork and make myself invisible. This confirms my belief that I don't make a difference and don't matter and that the world is indifferent to me. If you don't ask anything from life, you won't get it.

▸ TEMPTATIONS ON THE JOURNEY

Act stubborn and resistant. Go along with others and their agendas. Appear to go along by giving tacit agreement, and then do what you want to do. Avoid conflict. Act self-effacing. Don't share needs, desires, or opinions. Withdraw into your imagination. Keep things harmonious and pleasant. Act indifferent. Act oblivious to what needs attention. Keep busy. Avoid prioritizing. Don't express difficult feelings or strong opinions. Leave your own needs out of the picture. Leave things open-ended. Be resistant to change.

▸ DETOUR SIGNS

Avoid discomfort. Remember, you're nobody special. Fade into the background. Be apathetic. Act indifferent. Withdraw. Stubbornness and clamming up is your source of power. Stagnation. Indecision. Rumination. Stick with the comfort of your habits and routines. Squash your anger. Throw water on your passion. Don't offer an opinion. Stay neutral. Check out.

▸ COURSE CORRECTION

Focus inside, and question your beliefs about yourself. Take initiative—be a self-starter. You will be well served to stop distracting yourself from yourself. Notice and listen to your emotions and your instincts. Connect with your desires and longing. Take action—take your first fierce step. Acknowledge your aggressive feelings; you don't have to act them out. Become comfortable being uncomfortable. Become curious about others, yourself, and the world around you. Contact your anger and use its energy to take purposeful action for your life.

▸ INTO THE SHADOW

My Wings carry my shadow, as do my Connecting Points: lands of 8, 1, 6, 3. While the healthy expressions of these four Types are companions on my journey, when I turn around to look at the shadow they cast, I see parts of me that I don't want to acknowledge. Sometimes it takes entering the shadow to uncover the gifts that are waiting there.

Type 8s carry the part of my shadow that takes a *don't mess with me* stance and uses this stance as a way to keep reality at bay. Being willful and resistant and protecting myself from the outer world is also part of my shadow. When my anger finally does come out, it erupts much like Type 8's and is directed toward other people. Being the recipient of my anger can be pretty nasty when it comes from my shadow. Not wanting to be controlled, be told what to do, or allow anyone to have power over me feels familiar.

Type 1s carry the part of my shadow that defends against criticism and is critical and judgmental of others. It is also the part of me that has unexpressed anger about not having my needs met and may let 'er rip from time to time. Perhaps I share some of the rigidity of Type 1 as well? The busyness? Focusing on the details and missing the big picture?

Part of my life journey is to make contact with the parts of me that are germane to Types 2, 4, 5, and 7. These may be qualities that I judge in others as being somehow bad or wrong or just don't relate to at all. At some point, it will be important to visit these other lands and see what they have to teach me—what treasures can be found there.

▸ HELPING ALLIES

On my right is Type 8. Although I express some of the less healthy aspects of Type 8s, I can also express some of their healthier qualities. When I feel self-confident and self-assured, Type 8 is there at my side. Type 8s have self-confidence in spades. They also have no problem holding court and commanding attention, and I admire that. Rather than fading into the background, I can access the part of me that can hold my ground and step out front and center. When I call on Type 8s, they will be there to support me.

When I am stuck in *apathy and indifference,* my hallmarks, my helping ally Type 8s can support me to break free. Type 8s are in close contact with their instincts and their anger. They use the energy of their anger and rage to take purposeful action in the world. The energy moves through them and propels them out into the world. Type 8s have the gift of being the master of their destiny, and I can do this, too—I feel it within me as a source of my own power to take charge of my life. Type 8s are the perfect companions for my journey.

On my left is Type 1, ready to help me with discipline, to take practical and sustained action, to take initiative. Both of my helping allies are gifted at taking initiative, and Type 1s are adept at creating structure and being disciplined. Type 1s are the *perfect* guides for this, and I too have these qualities within me. They help me to connect with my integrity—meaning wholeness. While I have the gift of seeing situations holistically, seeing many points of view, Type 1 has integrity within.

Self-acceptance, seeing the absolute perfection of self and the world, and serenity are the most precious gifts that Type 1s can offer me. Serenity, the ultimate gift of Type 1, is the elusive *peacefulness* I seek.

Both of my companions are known for their ability to take a stand in the world and make their point of view known. There is nothing wishy-washy about either of them. I can feel their power in me as I link my arms with theirs.

Because of indifference, one dies before one actually dies.
—Elie Wiesel

▸ **BURIED TREASURE:** TYPE 9 *ALCHEMY*

Rumination, apathy, indifference, resignation, and sloth are transformed into peace of mind, wholeness, connection, self-possession, dignity, and *authentic* harmony.

I have found the courage to face my past hurts and pains. I have taken off my rose-colored glasses and see my life and others clearly—not who I want to see but who and what is really there. My focus of attention is now my heart's desire—I have reclaimed it and use the force of my long-suppressed anger to create a life filled with purpose and passion! My gift of seeing multiple points of view is no longer in service of stifling conflict, but rather in service of building bridges and helping people to feel accepted, seen, and understood. My relationships are more vital, and I feel passionate about my life. I am in contact with my vitality and no longer feel the need to shrink or hide. I am visible, stand my ground, and offer my opinions. I am letting my star shine, and it feels great!

Conflict is the beginning of consciousness.

—M. Esther Harding, *The Way of All Women*[27]

TYPE 9

POSITIVE CONTRIBUTION	REACTIONS / STRESS
Good implementers / Followers	Don't take initiative
	Don't like to be pushed / Clam
Harmonizers / Kind / Understanding / Tolerant	Conflict avoidant
	Comfort seeking
Stabilizers	Dislike change
	Slow to act / Routine / Habit
	Risk averse
	Indecisive
	Avoid commitment
Agreeable / Accommodating / See multiple points of view	Others don't know where they stand
	Don't share opinions
	Passive-aggressive
	Withdraw
Even-tempered	Unaware of own strong feelings
	Explosive
	Anxiety / Worry / Fear / Doubt
Imaginative	Daydreamers / Lost in fantasy / Idealize

TYPE 9 JOURNAL

STOP AND REFLECT

Look at the Type 9 compulsions: Sloth, laziness, anger, and withdrawal. As you begin to explore this for yourself, you will start to see your compulsive patterns and their impact on your life.

 Recall a time when you felt the need to seek peace and comfort rather than address an unpleasant situation. Write about your mem-

ory of this. What caused you to seek comfort rather than try to resolve a situation you didn't like? What were your feelings, thoughts, reactions, and body sensations when this happened? Tell the story.

✍ Think of a time in the recent past when you *checked out*. What precipitated this? What was going on in your internal state when you did this? What were your inner dialog, feelings, and thoughts? Tell the story. How does this behavior serve you? How does it hinder you?

✍ How does this pattern play out in your life?

✍ See if you can begin to notice your compulsion to disappear into your inner world before you do it. What are the telltale signs that precede your disappearance (inner sensations, feelings, thoughts, perceptions, something that someone says or does)?

✍ How has this worked for you / benefited you?

Unraveling Your Role Identity (Review the *Role Identity* for Type 9, the Peacemaker)

✍ What has been the cost to you?

✍ List your *core fears* (for example, powerlessness, no support, loneliness, rejection, harm, deprivation, shame, exposure, feeling overwhelmed, humiliation, abandonment, pain, inability to fulfill dreams).

List your *core hurts* (for example, feeling unsupported, accused, unseen, flawed, worthless, unimportant, guilty, devalued, rejected, powerless, inadequate, unlovable).

If you no longer reacted to these fears, how would that affect the role you play?

How do your core fears and core hurts relate to each other and reinforce each other?

If you weren't playing your roles of the Peacemaker and "I'm nobody special," who would you be? What feelings come up for you when you imagine dropping these roles?

What do your core fears and hurts have to do with your role identity?

Describe and list some of the qualities your would like to have. List some descriptive words (warm, playful, powerful ...).

How did you come to believe that these fears and hurts were true and real? What is your evidence that this is true? How do you know?

What are the first steps you can take toward embodying these qualities?

What do you believe would happen if you stopped looking for this evidence and chose to look for evidence that negated these fears?

▸ TYPE 9 WORDS

Comfort, anger, appease, peace, easygoing, passion, change, fantasy, idealize, control, kindness, reality, stubbornness, commitment, power, acceptance, discipline, self-promote, pressure, anxiety.

Your Enneagram Type has a unique association with certain words related to your compulsions and patterns.

Understanding the significance of these words and how they have played out in your life will be telling for you. Being more conscious of your feelings and attitudes toward these words will help you to transform how they live within you and help you to create your life story moving forward.

Take your time with this, and find a quiet place where you can reflect. I suggest just writing about one word at a time and letting it stew inside of you while you activate your inner observer (the nonjudging observer) and peel back its meaning. You will want to come back to this word again and again.

I suggest picking the first word that calls to you in your list. Each word has both positive connotations and unhealthy expressions. Write about both. Keep digging deeper. Begin to notice as you go through your day how these words play out in your life.

For instance, *comfort*: What is your association with comfort? What does it feel like when you are *in the grip* of needing to be comfortable? What are the circumstances that evoke your need for comfort? How does it serve you? How does it create challenges and problems for you? Tell stories of times you have needed to feel comfortable at the expense of facing conflict, difficult conversations, taking care of yourself, or your own growth.

These are just some of the questions you might consider when you begin to explore how each word has shown up on your life journey. Consider how you want to bring these behaviors and qualities forward in a more conscious and intentional way.

✦ Go to the sections for your Connecting Points (Types 6 and 3) and your Wings (Types 8 and 1). Get to know these parts of yourself. Take time to explore the words for these four Types. It will be quite instructive.

▸ WHAT'S IN MY BIG BLACK BAG?
PEERING INTO MY SHADOW

✏ Take a look at your Wings and your two Connecting Points (Types 8, 1, 3, 6). What aspects of these Types do you recognize in yourself? What don't you relate to? Write about this. Start to self-observe and notice whether your self-observations are accurate. Inquire within. Ask others for their perceptions.

▸ THINGS YOU CAN DO TO MAKE A SHIFT

OFFER YOUR POINT OF VIEW

Type 9s can seem insubstantial to others because it can be difficult to feel their presence. Where do Type 9s stand, and what do they stand for? Type 9s can make themselves almost invisible. They do this by drawing in their energy and disappearing into their inner world. Practice offering your point of view and your recommendations. Realize that not everyone is going to agree with you or like what you have to say, and that's OK. It doesn't mean they won't like you. Do this in low-risk situations and see how it feels, and notice any shifts in your connections with others. Over time, increase the risk—share yourself. You may find that your relationships deepen rather than do what you fear—disconnect.

When you notice that you are accommodating other people to avoid conflict, see if you can catch yourself before doing this. Express your own needs and wants. People really do want to know what you would like and would prefer not to have to guess.

GROUNDING

When you notice yourself disappearing into your inner world, see if you can pause and focus your attention on your belly. Take a deep breath into your belly. Tune in to your body and ground yourself. Pull energy up from the center of the earth through your feet and up your spine. Continually bring your attention back to your body. Reground to help you feel more solid and confident.

VITALITY

When you notice strong feelings, such as anger or passion, starting to move through your body, allow them. Express your feelings. They may not initially come out as you would like, but with a little practice, you will be able to express your anger, disappointment, and passion! Don't worry—you won't annihilate anyone. Use the force of your feelings to help you take focused, grounded, and purposeful action.

Turn to "InsideOut—Leaders' Tool Kit." The following sections will be useful for your growth: "The Power of Presence," "Reclaim Your Passion," "Curiosity Is Your Guide," and "Centering Basic Practice."

 ## AN INSIDEOUT LEADER'S STORY: **CONTINUED CHALLENGES AT NHH**

The larger culture at NHH is not moving in the same direction as Caitlin—a direction she was hired to take. Both Lars and Caitlin experience the same entrenched culture, and Caitlin makes little progress catalyzing a shift. Caitlin and Lars are expected to be on the vanguard and were hired to help NHH reposition itself in the market. However, they aren't getting positive reinforcement from the larger culture. Where is the sponsorship?

In order for this change to happen, they need a high level of competence, commitment, and will, but unfortunately there is negative to variable commitment and will from needed sponsors (senior leaders) and the larger organization.

Lars's team members talk among themselves and express, "Why should we try to do this? We don't see many others doing this or others succeeding at it. Lars is the flavor of the month; we can outlast him until someone else replaces him."

They tentatively admit that there are aspects of the change that are exciting, but not enough to mobilize them to step into the unknown. Lars feels their continued resistance. Something has to shift. What can Lars do to catalyze a shift in the face of the organization's resistance, the lack of senior sponsorship, and his team's resistance? Lars is working on his own issues, but NHH's culture and the lack of sponsorship are out of his control. He realizes that he has to improve his ability to influence up, across, and down—this is in his locus of control.

Has Lars effectively communicated the value proposition to his team? Do they see themselves in the vision? Unless they can pull together as a team, their competitive advantage in the global market will continue to slip. Lars hears the clock ticking …

→ Lars's story continues on p. 216

PART 3:

DISCOVER YOUR ENNEAGRAM TYPE

Now that the foundation has been laid and you've become familiar with the nine Enneagram Types, it's time to discover your Type or help someone else find theirs. First, there are some important things to know before we get you sorted out!

ENNEAGRAM TEMPTATIONS:
THE ETHICS OF USING THE ENNEAGRAM

TEMPTATION #1: Use the Enneagram to *fix* other people—our partners, spouses, kids, coworkers, friends. The Enneagram is a tool for your own transformation, not to fix other people.

TEMPTATION #2: Tell people what you think their Type is, particularly if you are an Enneagram teacher or coach. Other people should have the opportunity to find their own Type, no matter how tempted you are to tell them your conclusion. You rob people of their own personal experience with the Enneagram and the self-discoveries they would make along the way to finding their Type. Unless you are living inside someone else's skin, you have no *real* way of knowing what is going on in that person's interior world. Early on, I was mistyped by so-called experts three different times (with three different Types), despite my having self-typed. These uninvited perceptions were quite unhelpful and presumptuous.

TEMPTATION #3: Don't test for readiness before using the Enneagram or working with someone's defense structures in a coaching or counseling context. Readiness means that someone has enough ego strength to face the mirror squarely and see the good, true, and beautiful along with the warts. Readiness also means that someone is motivated to make needed change. The motivation can be intrinsic or extrinsic. If you are a manager or work in human resources, or you serve as a coach, consultant, or counselor, it is up to you and the client to explore readiness to take the next step. Some people need longer than others to digest a new awareness or insight, and some will be more willing. You can help create the conditions for the client's readiness to move forward.

TEMPTATION #4: Use the Enneagram as a weapon. What if you say, "You're paranoid, just like a Type 6"? Or, "Typical Type 9, always burying your head in the sand." Or, "You can't be an effective leader. You focus too much on relationships and pleasing others because you're a Type 2." When we know someone else's Type, or we think we do, and use that information to do a gotcha, it can have a harmful effect. The Enneagram is not a weapon to use against others. Using it that way removes safety from a team environment and in a direct-report relationship.

TEMPTATION #5: Attend a workshop or two, read a book about the Enneagram, and go straight out to teach it. It takes a long time to be able to make use of the Enneagram's wisdom. You will be a far more effective teacher of the Enneagram or coach if you have a lived experience of what you are teaching. Many people understand the Enneagram cognitively, but they don't understand it experientially; they haven't applied it to their own lives. Teaching from knowledge without experience can do harm when students experience the dissonance between what you say and how you act.

TEMPTATION #6: Use the Enneagram for hiring decisions. Someone's Enneagram Type should not be a primary factor in a hiring decision. People's success resides in character, skills, background, flexibility, motivation, and the like. That said, Enneagram Type may be a factor to consider when evaluating the match between a person and his or her position, or between a person and a manager, or when team composition is involved. For instance, I know that working with someone who is task oriented, focuses on structure, and is highly dependable and responsible complements my predispositions. Certain Enneagram Types fit this description better than others. That said, my first consideration as a hiring manager is always the big picture.

KEY THINGS TO KNOW

▶ It is common to find aspects of yourself in all nine Types because there are all nine Types in each of us. However, if you are honest with yourself, you can identify one Type that's a *best fit* for you.

▶ People do not change from one Enneagram Type to another. That said, each Type is like a facet of a diamond, a part of the whole. On the journey we're about to take, we'll learn how to integrate all nine Types within us.

▶ Type is not gender specific or culture specific.

▶ Distinctions within each Type influence how that Type is expressed in different people. Not everything in the description of your Enneagram Type will apply to you all the time.

▶ The Types are value-neutral, meaning that no one Type is better than another. Numbers identify Types, and different Enneagram teachers give the Types different names.

✦ See the sections "Arrows," "Wings," and "The Vertical Dimension: Levels of Development" in Chapter 3, and "Instincts: The 27 Facets of the Enneagram," in Chapter 6.

▶ If there is a Type you don't like, pay attention. It might be your true Type. You may have something important to learn from the Type you dislike most.

CHAPTER 6
THE SORTING PROCESS

TIME TO DISCOVER WHICH ARCHETYPE IS YOURS.

HOW TO PREPARE

Make sure you have your Enneagram Typing Cards next to you, something to write with, and a notebook. Now, imagine yourself during your 20s when you go through this process. Why? Because during those years we are generally less self-aware than we are in midlife. By midlife, most of us have had enough bumps and bruises that we realize we need to pay closer attention to our inner life and the cause of our pain. We've already started making adjustments to our style and approach to people and life.

Each Enneagram Type reacts differently and has its own patterned response to adversity, challenges, and expectations. As we get older, life starts giving us feedback, and those of us who take it seriously and incorporate the feedback become less rigid and more flexible and agile. We take off our masks and begin the return journey back to our true selves. It is easier to discover your Type when you imagine your more habitual, reactive responses that were probably more prominent in your younger life.

📎 CRITICAL INFORMATION

As we go through the different Type descriptions, for the most part I will be focusing on how each Type behaves when they are in the grip of their Ennea-gram Type—In other words, when they are *doing their Type*.

This is critical to know because the descriptions won't be the most positive and desirable aspects of each Type. We can recognize ourselves more easily, as can others, when we are acting in our patterned and habitual ways.

After each step, go to the worksheet at the end of this chapter and fill in your responses.

STEP 1

Lay out the Enneagram Typing Cards in front of you, pictures facing up. Without giving it much thought, choose three to five cards you relate to most. Put them in front of you and move the others to the side.

Why do these five cards speak to you? How do they relate to the way you see yourself?

1.

2.

3.

4.

5.

STEP 2

Look at the card you believe is most likely your Type. Read the back of the card. Does this seem like you? Is one of the other cards you chose your Stress Point? This could be a clue, because chances are, the Stress Point will feel familiar. For instance, if you selected Type 4, is Type 2 also one of your selections? In the Enneagram symbol, you'll see a line with an arrow pointing from Type 4 to Type 2, which is the

Stress Point for Type 4. Read the back of the Stress Point card and see whether it describes your behavior in a stressful situation.

STEP 3

Did you choose a card that is the Integration Point for the Type you think is yours? Look for an arrow pointing *toward* the Type you chose. In our Type 4 example, the Integration Point would be Type 1.

What about the Wings (the numbers on either side of the Type you are most drawn to)? Is either of the Wings among your choices? Often, at least one of the Wings will feel familiar.

STEP 4

Take a look at the Enneagram symbol on the front of each of the cards you chose. The Type numbers are color-coded orange, blue, and green. What are the colors on your cards? List the Type numbers and colors below.

1.

2.

3.

4.

5.

STEP 5

Pick up the card that says, "Centers of Intelligence: Head, Heart, Gut," and read descriptions of the centers that match the cards you chose. Which ones describe you best? Jot down some notes.

Head (Types 5, 6, 7):

Heart (Types 2, 3, 4):

Instinctual (Types 8, 9, 1):

Which of the Types from your original selection are in the Center of Intelligence you think is yours? Jot them down below. Remember, everyone uses all three centers. When we experience the world through our feeling (Heart) center, we also think and act.

✷ For more information on the Centers of Intelligence, skip to Chapter 7, "More about the Types—the Triads."

STEP 6

Think of yourself in a social context with one other person or many. What is your strategy to deal with discomfort?

Check the description that sounds most like you, and underline the phrases that are most significant.

My strategy to deal with social discomfort is …

☐ **1. Reach out and connect with other people.**

    a. Do I ask for what I want so that others don't need to guess?

    b. Do I assume that if I don't ask, I won't get?

    c. Do I tend to go after what I want?

    d. Am I fast paced and action oriented?

    e. Do I often find myself at the center of a conversation?

    f. Do others sometimes see me as aggressive, assertive, or pushy?

☐ **2. Have a certain standard of behavior, even though I feel rebellious at times.**

    a. Do I believe you have to earn

        i. love,

        ii. autonomy, or

        iii. security?

b. Do I believe that when I do what is expected of me, I will get the love, autonomy, or security I want?

c. Do others see me as the responsible Type?

☐ **3. Focus attention on my inner world—ideas, fantasies, somewhere else I'd rather be.**

a. Do I withdraw from people?

b. Can I disappear?

c. Can I make myself small in a crowd?

d. Am I comfortable being alone?

e. Do I feel pushed by other people and then withdraw? Is my pace slower than others'?

f. Do I have a hard time taking sustained action toward a goal?

g. Do others see me as hard to get to know?

✦ To read more about the Social Styles and how they relate to each Type, skip to Chapter 7.

IF YOU CHECKED #1, these are the *Assertive* Types. Take a look at Type 3, the Achiever; Type 7, the Enthusiast; and Type 8, the Boss. Read the back of the cards and see if one of them is a *best fit*. Were any of these cards in your original selection? Which one(s)?

IF YOU CHECKED #2, these are the *Dutiful and Responsible* Types. Take a look at Type 1, the Perfectionist; Type 2, the People Pleaser; and Type 6, the Loyal Skeptic. Read the back of the cards and see if one of them is a *best fit*. Were any of these cards in your original selection? Which one(s)?

IF YOU CHECKED #3, these are the *Withdrawn* Types. Take a look at Type 4, the Individualist; Type 5, the Detached Observer; and Type 9, the Peacemaker. Read the back of the cards and see if one of them is a *best fit*. Were any of these cards in your original selection? Which one(s)?

STEP 7

There are several *look-alike* Types. They fall into three groups referred to by Riso and Hudson as the *Harmonic groups*. Each group has a coping strategy to deal with problems, conflict, and unmet needs. Each group also has its own strategy to defend against loss and disappointment. Which of the following three groups best describes how you deal with difficult situations, conflict, and problems?

GROUP 1
- Do people describe you as intense?
- Do others say you overreact?
- Do you have strong reactions to adversity, to problems, or when in conflict?
- Do you need to express your emotions in order to deal with them?
- Do you look for a response from others when you react?
- Are trust and betrayal core issues for you?

GROUP 2
- Do you avoid difficult discussions rather than risk triggering conflict?
- Do you avoid or minimize problems?
- Are you known for your positive reframe?
- Do you avoid dealing with the dark and difficult side of life and of yourself?
- Do you avoid people and situations you see as "downers," try to help or fix them, or attempt to accommodate them?
- When people approach you with their problems, is your style encouraging and optimistic?

GROUP 3

▸ Are you known to be a practical problem solver?

▸ Do people see you as an impersonal problem solver?

▸ Are you dispassionate when it comes to conflict?

▸ Do you set aside personal feelings in order to be objective, sensible?

▸ Do you avoid conflict with people whom you see as overly emotional?

▸ Is it important for you to control your emotions when dealing with conflict?

✸ If you see more than one possibility, jump to "Conflict Styles and Approach to Problems" in Chapter 7 to read about the *Harmonic groups*. You'll learn how each Harmonic group includes both similar and different behaviors.

If Group 1 best describes you, these are the *Reactive* Types, 4, 6, and 8, and one of them may be your best-fit Type. If Group 2 best describes you, these are the *Positive Outlook* Types, 2, 7, and 9, and one of them may be your best-fit Type. If Group 3 best describes you, these are the *Competency* Types, 1, 3, and 5, and one of them may be your best-fit Type.

THE BOTTOM LINE

On the surface, behaviors may appear similar, but remember the discussion of navigational systems at the beginning of this book? We talked about sonar capability to detect hidden objects. Under the surface of a visible behavior are the motivational forces that drive it. The so-called core drivers of behavior are the bottom line for distinguishing one Type from another. What need are you trying to meet? What are you trying to avoid, and how can you get your needs met? Make sure to read the Enneagram Typing Card titled "Motivational Aims." There is more information on motivations at the end of Chapter 5, "Journey of the Nine Types," in the section "Deeply Held Beliefs of the Nine Types."

Fill out the chart below to track your process, according to the following instructions.

1. List all of the Types you chose from Step 1.

2. Circle your best-fit Type based on your reading of the Type description on the cards.

3. Put a checkmark in front of the Types that are the Connecting Points for your best-fit Type if they are in your selection (Stress and Integration).

4. Put an X in front of the Wings of your best-fit Type if they are in your selection.

5. List the color code for each of those Types in the second column.

6. Circle your most dominant Center of Intelligence in the third column.

7. Put an X in the box(es) that match your dominant Center of intelligence in the third column (from your original selection).

8. Circle your dominant Social Style.

9. Put an X in the box(es) that match your dominant Social Style in the fourth column (from your original selection).

10. Circle your dominant Harmonic Style.

11. Put an X in the box(es) that match your dominant Harmonic Style in the fifth column (from your original selection).

12. Do you see a best-fit Type based on your sorting process?

If you have read about the Centers of Intelligence, Social Styles, and Harmonics, and are still unclear about your Type, take a look at Chapter 8, "Dynamics and Distinctions."

WORKSHEET FOR TYPE-DISCOVERY PROCES

ORIGINAL SELECTION LIST TYPES	**COLORS** Green Orange Teal	**CENTERS OF INTELLIGENCE** Head, Heart, Instinctual	**SOCIAL STYLES** Assertive Dutiful Withdrawn	**HARMONICS** Reactive Positive Outlook Competency

✦ When you have found your Type, you can turn to the discussions of the Centers of Intelligence, the Hornevians, and the Harmonics in Chapter 7. This section includes a wealth of information not covered in Chapter 5 on individual Types.

📎 NOTE

Not everyone finds his or her Type right away. Sometimes it takes a period of self-observation. You watch your reactions, tune in to your inner dialog, and notice what underlies your choices. This is important whether or not you have located your Type, so that you can start to get closer to yourself. *Observe*, and do not judge. Be curious and have humor. We are all doing our best, and the games we play to try to fool ourselves can be pretty funny.

INSTINCTS: THE 27 FACETS OF THE ENNEAGRAM

What are the Instincts? Earlier we looked at the three Centers of Intelligence: Head, Heart, and Instinctual (gut). Gut is where the Instincts reside. There are three fundamental Instincts: self-preservation, one-to-one, and social. In every individual, one will be dominant and one secondary, and the order will have an effect on Type behavior.

Why 27 facets? Think of the Enneagram Types as distinct yet connected facets of a diamond. Together these facets create a brilliant whole. Although there are nine fundamental Enneagram Types, there are three variations of each of the nine Types, and hence 27 facets.

Why are the Instincts important? Because they are largely unconscious drivers of behavior that explain where we put our attention, time, and energy. Instincts are very revealing when you attempt to understand relationship dynamics. If one person's dominant instinct is one-to-one and the other person's is social, they prioritize their time and attention differently. This can be a source of conflict, *or* it can be a way to help each other develop balance. You choose!

Instincts also help account for why all Type descriptors don't fit every person of that Type.

BRIEF DESCRIPTIONS OF THE THREE INSTINCTS

Number the Instincts as you see yourself. Which one gets your attention most often, what's in the middle, and what gets little or no attention?

☐ SELF-PRESERVATION INSTINCT

If your dominant Instinct is self-preservation, you will tend to focus on health, mortality, finances, home, exercise, and all kinds of self-improvement. You are likely to be practical and disciplined, self-sufficient and inwardly focused. Over-focus in these areas can lead to worry, fear, and obsessive concern about self-care.

If self-preservation is your *least* developed Instinct, you may not be in tune with your health, finances, food, and the like, and you may even be neglecting them.

☐ SOCIAL INSTINCT

If the social Instinct is dominant, you believe that there is safety in the group, and social bonding is a form of survival. You have a need to belong and a sense of social responsibility. You realize the benefits of connecting to something larger than yourself. You focus on the group and your place in the hierarchy.

If this is your dominant Instinct, you will put time and energy into groups, causes, and community. In order to be accepted in the group, you may find yourself conforming to values, beliefs, or ideals that are not your own. You may lose yourself in the larger group identity.

If the social Instinct is the *least* developed of the three, you may be unlikely to join a group, participate in your community, or be actively involved in causes. You may lack social networks. The benefits of belonging to a group are low on your hierarchy of needs.

☐ ONE-TO-ONE INSTINCT

If the one-to-one Instinct is dominant, you will need to build ties with specific other individuals for survival. You'll long for the ideal romantic partner and focus on attracting the ideal mate. You will feel incomplete without a love interest. You bring intensity, passion, and excitement to your relationships (spouse, friends, colleagues), and on the other hand, you may become needy and dependent.

Just as a social Type can merge with the group and lose identity, the one-to-one Type can experience a loss of self in a relationship with a partner.

If the one-to-one bonding Instinct is the *least* developed of the three, your relationships may take a backseat to social and self-preservation needs. Your responsibility to the group may be a higher priority than a new or existing relationship. An intimate connection could be challenging for you.

STOP AND REFLECT

Take a moment and reflect. How has your dominant Instinct played out in your life? Where do you tend focus your time, attention, and energy? Is there a pattern?

How might you bring your Instincts into greater balance?

Are you aware that your dominant Instinct is a survival strategy? Write about it.

AN INSIDEOUT LEADER'S STORY: **WHAT FINALLY BREAKS THE TRUST LOGJAM?**

In their next LT meeting, Victoria, one of the team members, volunteers, "Just tell us what you want, Lars. We don't understand what you're asking of us." This honest request helps Lars to realize that resistance may not have been the only obstacle in his way—his will against theirs. Perhaps they just don't understand.

With that, Chris suggests that Lars and his team go through a process to define a workgroup versus a team, the main difference being mutual versus vertical accountability. Once he lays this out structurally and logically, they get it—at least in concept.

Sean offers, "Sounds really different from anything we've seen at our company. The message is a good one." They no longer feel that Lars is speaking in code. Lars no longer feels unappreciated for all he is trying to do, nor invisible, as if he's talking into a void.

Previously, Lars would say, "We need to radically change the way we do business." They would say, "Hey, we're really good and we are doing really well. We are the best scientists in the world." They talked past one another, and it was polarizing. Both sides felt unseen, unheard, and positional.

How does Lars follow up on this breakthrough?

→ Lars's story continues on p. 218

CHAPTER 7

MORE ABOUT THE TYPES—THE TRIADS

This chapter is a rich resource for Type information *not* included in the individual Type descriptions. You'll find in-depth explanation of the Triads: the Centers of Intelligence, the Hornevians, the Harmonics. These are three different ways that the nine Enneagram Types can be sorted in groups of three.

The Triads will help shed light on why you may be torn between two or three different Types and what delineates one from another. These distinctions should help you nail down your best-fit Enneagram Type, if you haven't already.

You'll learn about the how the different Types lose their balance and how they can regain it (Centers of Intelligence), and the social styles and conflict styles of the nine Types.

AN INSIDEOUT LEADER'S STORY: **INVOLVEMENT**

With Chris's coaching, Lars involves the group. They begin to have quarterly off-site meetings that are part leadership development and part operational. The question is raised at their next meeting, "What are the things we need to do differently, given the results we need to accomplish?" The answer comes swiftly: "We need to move from acting like a workgroup to functioning like a team." They realize that they need to make decisions together, resolve and solve together, and maintain open lines of communication both inside and outside of their meetings.

They also identify circumstances when it's appropriate to function as a workgroup and they don't need to act as a team—instances when it will slow down what they are endeavoring to accomplish and won't add value.

While Lars is pleased with the progress, he also realizes that the LT has not yet laid a foundation of trust, and without it, the structure will inevitably crumble. They now have a conceptual understanding of how they will work together moving forward, but putting it into practice requires trust. How will Lars create an environment of trust for his team, especially when they are in fear of losing their jobs?

➜ Lars's story continues on p. 227

CENTERS OF INTELLIGENCE:
GROUPINGS OF TYPE BY PATTERNS OF THINKING, FEELING, AND ACTING

Robert Cooper, of Stanford Business School, points out that we have three brains—one in our head, one in the gut, and one in the heart—all with massive numbers of neurons. He claims that when all three brains work together, they produce the highest level of reasoning.[28] This is not a new idea. The three Centers of Intelligence have been taught since Plato's ti

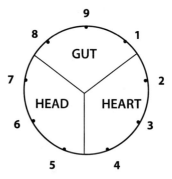

Every person habitually uses one Center of Intelligence to interpret life. The other two blindly follow its lead. The three Centers interact in a patterned way to reinforce habitual impulses that relate to the Enneagram Type.

Each Type trusts and tends to overuse one center. A second Center generally is ignored, is not trusted, and often does the bidding of the most trusted Center.

PERSONALITY:
DISTORTION OF THE CENTERS

When we filter our experience through one of the three Centers, we are in a sense running from reality. We don't trust the other Centers of Intelligence to give us guidance. We don't want to see ourselves as we are and the world as it is. A key to self-transformation, then, is to bring our Centers into balance. More on this when you learn about the Hornevian Types.

✱ Jump to "InsideOut—Leaders' ToolKit," where intuition is described and explored. You will find practices to help you take action on your intuition.

WHAT IS THE HEALTHY EXPRESSION OF EACH CENTER OF INTELLIGENCE?

When we are balanced, in the center of ourselves, not operating from personality, we make contact with our intuition. Intuition is the inner voice that is sometimes barely audible and sometimes loud and demanding. When we are integrated, we act on the voice of intuition that emerges.

The charts on the following pages summarize the ways in which each Type distorts the use of an *over-relied-upon* center.

I use the following words interchangeably for the three Centers of Intelligence because they all apply:

Action/Body/Instinctual/Gut Center

Feeling/Heart Center

Thinking/Head Center

UNDERLYING FEELINGS AND FOCUS OF THE CENTERS[29]

INSTINCTUAL CENTER

‣ Underlying feelings are anger and rage.

‣ Focus on resistance and control of themselves and the environment.

HEART CENTER

‣ Underlying feeling is shame. Envy is another emotion taught as the principal feeling for this Center.

‣ Focus on image and identity.

HEAD CENTER

‣ Underlying feelings are fear and anxiety.

‣ Focus on safety and security.

In describing the Centers of Intelligence, we start with the Instinctual Center and go clockwise. Type 8 is the first of the three Enneagram Types in the Instinctual Center.

ACTION/BODY/INSTINCTUAL CENTER

ACTION/BODY/INSTINCTUAL/GUT CENTER
ANGER / RAGE TRIAD

8 ▸ **Ruled by gut instincts**. Prone to take immediate action without pausing to think about long-term consequences or how it will affect the needs and feelings of others. Use the Action Center to be self-sufficient, letting no one have power or control over them. Act out anger and rage.

9 ▸ **Instincts are suppressed** in order to stay peaceful and comfortable and to avoid conflict. Type 9s deaden their energy and go numb to their instincts in favor of comfortable habits and routines. Suppress anger.

1 ▸ **Control or repress their impulses** and use the force of their instincts to improve themselves and the world. Become fixated on organizing the environment, correcting and perfecting everything, and criticizing what does not conform to their ideal. Control anger.

Our body is the container for our vitality and life force. When we take impulsive action, it usually comes from a sensation in our gut, often referred to as a *gut instinct*. The Instinctual Center is where we feel our impulses, be they fear, sex, anger, rage, or the need to take action.

Types 8, 9, and 1 make up the Anger/Rage Triad, and they have the closest relationship of the nine Types to their instinctual Center of Intelligence. It is the Center through which they interpret and experience reality. They use their instinctual energy to create boundaries and maintain autonomy. Types 8, 9, and 1 want to control their world without being controlled by it. All three Types have a *don't mess with me* attitude.

The most decisive actions of our life... are most often unconsidered actions.

—André Gide, *The Counterfeiters*, 1926

Type 8s trust their instincts. Using their power and energy to take action, make bold decisions, and pursue challenges almost feels like a drug fix to them. These are people of action. They express anger, act it out, let it out, and damn the torpedoes—full speed ahead! They may express anger in words, use force, speak loudly, or swear, and in all cases they unleash *big energy*. Others may feel dominated, steamrolled, terrified, or traumatized around them. Type 8s use instinctual energy to maintain control, similarly to Types 9 and 1. However, Type 8s use their energy to protect themselves from feeling vulnerable.

Type 9s access instincts and readily use the power of the Instinctual Center to protect themselves from being intruded upon by people and reality. However, they don't necessarily relate to being in contact with their instincts or vitality. While Type 8s act on and express their instinctual energy, Type 9s use it to create boundaries so that others won't intrude on their reality. With only a look, they can communicate *don't mess with me* and then snap their clamshell shut. They are known to be one of the most stubborn of the Enneagram Types.

Type 9s don't see themselves as people who get angry. Often unconsciously, they suppress their anger and can feel completely disconnected from this life force that Type 8s find so intoxicating. The suppression and denial of their anger is what creates the appearance of emotional flatness. Type 9s often report feeling frozen or numb in their body. They are scared of their own anger and are worried that it would annihilate others. In an effort to avoid losing connection with people or to preserve their false sense of emotional equilibrium, they tamp down strong feelings, thus suppressing their instincts. Type 9s resist reality in favor of idealizing people and situations. This creates the *dreamy* impression that people often have of Type 9. If Type 9s use most of their vitality to maintain these boundaries, it is unavailable to them for living and engaging more fully in the world.

Type 1s want to control all instinctual impulses, and may believe that these impulses are somehow wrong, bad, or dirty. Type 1s keep their instinctual energy and anger under tight control, repressing it and then directing its focus to perfect and organize their outer world. They know exactly where, what, and whom to perfect, because their inner critic directs the action.

Often you'll notice that Type 1s hold tension in their body and jaw, and they may appear physically stiff as they try to contain anger, rage, and impulses. Type 1s want to control their anger and both their inner and outer worlds. They use instinctual energy and drive to maintain this control. However, when they do *lose it*, their anger can be shrill or come in outbursts. While Type 9s can give you that *don't mess with me* look, Type 1s have another look—the scathing look of the authority figure to indicate that you have done something wrong.

HEART / FEELING CENTER

HEART / FEELING CENTER
SHAME / IMAGE TRIAD

2
▶ **Don't value their own feelings.** Use empathic gifts to anticipate others' needs, flatter and heap attention, and seduce in order to become indispensable. May not be in touch with their own needs and feelings because their focus is on the *other* in search of appreciation, validation, and love. Shame about not feeling lovable. Seek appreciation.

3
▶ **Repress feelings** to avoid feeling worthless or a failure. Instead, focus energy on adapting their image to appear successful, be the best, secure accomplishments and achievements—all to win approval and be admired. Self-value lies in their achievements and performance. They deceive their own heart. Shame about not feeling worthwhile. Seek admiration.

4
▶ **Amplify feelings.** Put their energy into intense feelings of sadness and longing about what they believe they are missing in life. Turn to feelings to tell them who they are. Find meaning through self-expression, creative expression and deep connection. Sensitivity. Shame about not living up to their true abilities. Seek to be seen as unique and special.

Types 2, 3, and 4 occupy the Feeling Center and are known as the Shame Triad. They have the closest relationship of the nine Types to the Feeling Center of Intelligence. Whereas Types 8, 9, and 1 filter life and experience the world through their instincts, Types 2, 3, and 4 filter and experience reality through their feelings. These Types have issues with shameful feelings. They focus attention on self-image and how others perceive them. These Types are more likely to take things personally and read into the emotions of others.

The distortion of the Feeling Center is, at core, about issues of self-worth and image (how I see myself and how I want to be seen by others). Through this distorted lens, authentic feelings are hijacked by emotional reactions when they are not appreciated, admired, or given attention. These Types believe they need approbation in order to feel loved, lovable, valuable, worthwhile, and special. They create false identities to stave off feelings of shame. They identify with the image they have created while looking to others to affirm this self-image.

The heart has reasons that reason does not know.
—Pascal

Type 2s don't feel lovable at core—the source of their feelings of shame. They attempt to manage their shame by focusing on positive feelings toward others and by being *good*. They want to be seen as a *good person* and try to get people to like them and see them as a loving individual.

Type 2s self-image is tied their roles as the people pleaser and the helper. They are in search of appreciation and hold a belief that if they help others, they will be both lovable and loved. For them, garnering appreciation is akin to getting their fix. They attempt to make themselves indispensable to a select few and assume the role of the *power behind the throne* to people in positions of power and authority. Their belief is that this will secure the approval, acceptance, and appreciation they seek.

In the absence of appreciation, shameful feelings arise about not being lovable, and this triggers their emotional reactions. Type 2s' positive feelings toward others are replaced by feelings of anger. When they don't feel appreciated (enough), they can become demanding and manipulative, and might create a situation in which others are coerced into rescuing them.

Type 3s relationship to their Heart or Feeling Center is to suppress it, just as Type 9s suppress their instincts/anger/impulses. Type 3s either are unaware of their feelings or block them. Instead, they focus on goals and achievements in order to be admired. Admiration gives Type 3s a false sense of feeling valuable and worthwhile. This is their attempt to stave off or deny their feelings of shame and inadequacy. Their feeling/emotional energy is channeled into a bias for action. These people are human *doings*; they focus on goals and take immediate action toward those goals, even at the expense of relationships.

Type 3s learn to craft an image of success, however they choose to define success, that allows them to cope with shame about not feeling valuable. They become driven to perform, achieve, and be perceived as outstanding. Their focus is on the external world and symbols of success. They will do whatever it takes to avoid failure, including deceiving others and even their own heart—all in the relentless pursuit of being affirmed as a valuable and worthwhile person.

Type 4s chosen strategy is to avoid their feelings of shame for not living up to their ideal self-image. They attempt to have others perceive them as unique and special. Type 4s do this by drawing attention to their individuality and originality. They avoid what they believe to be the ordinary and mundane, and feel the need to have a unique form of self-expression.

Type 4s craft an image of being deep, sensitive, vulnerable, authentic, loving, and compassionate. They filter reality through their feelings. If they *feel* something about themselves, someone else, or a situation, it must be true. Their self-identity can shift in sync with their mood states, without their realizing that they see and experience life through this distorted lens. Any attempt to poke holes in their idealized self-image can elicit dramatic outbursts. All of this is their attempt to avoid feelings of inadequacy and shame for not living up to their potential or their idealized self-image.

HEAD / THINKING CENTER

HEAD / THINKING CENTER
FEAR / ANXIETY TRIAD

5

▸ **Don't Focus on ideas, problem solving, conceptualizing, abstraction, observation, developing expertise** in an effort to avoid having direct contact with the messiness of life. Withdraw into their head to problem-solve and innovate. Living in the world of ideas can become a substitute for lived experience. Fear of there not being support for them and of their inability to cope with the demands of others.

6

▸ **Focus on preparing, analyzing, looking for hidden agendas/meanings** in order to survive and to feel safe and secure. The rug could get pulled out at any time. Everyone is out for themselves. The world is not a safe place. Clear thinking is blocked by the voices of "should," fear, worry, and doubt.

7

▸ **Focus on planning, synthesizing, visualizing, possibilities, and ideas** in an effort to take themselves out of the present, in order to avoid experiencing difficult feelings that might overwhelm them. Thinking can look scattered and unfocused. Fear of being deprived, of shutting down options, and of being trapped in pain and boredom.

Types 5, 6, and 7 are known as the Fear Triad, and each has its own kind of fear and unique reaction to fear, anxiety, and insecurity. It is important for the Fear Triad to quiet the mind in order to connect with their intuition and instincts. This will give rise to their confidence and ability to take focused and meaningful action in the world. These Types resist reality by filtering life through their Thinking Center. All three have issues with trust and anxiety. Type 6 is the most obviously anxious and lacking in confidence, whereas it is masked in Types 5 and 7. Type 7 can appear quite confident and Type 5 can even appear arrogant—both as a reaction to feelings of fear, insecurity, and anxiety.

Type 5s fear that they don't have what it takes to deal with the demands of the outside world. They also believe that there is no support for them. Their reaction to these fears and anxieties is to retreat into their inner world—*cave*—and to minimize their needs so that they don't have to depend on anyone. Type 5s have ambivalence about relationships, both wanting to open their heart to another and simultaneously not wanting others to depend on or need them. They generally do not trust others and let only a chosen few into their inner sanctum.

He who thinks he knows,
doesn't know.
He who knows that he
doesn't know, knows.
For in the context, to know
is not to know.
And not to know is to know.
—Tao te Ching

To suppress their feelings of anxiety and insecurity, Type 5s take life firmly into their own hands and develop their expertise in at least one area. They trust their mind and their ability to figure things out. Knowledge becomes their source of power and security. This is not the wisdom of lived experience, but comes from books, lectures, and other external sources. Type 5s become a repository for their acquired knowledge and information.

Type 5s use their mind to understand the nature of the world and therefore what they deem to be reality. Their knowledge offers Type 5 a false sense of safety and security that they need to leave their cave and participate in the world. Talk to Type 5s, and they love to tell you about what they know. The trouble is that they never feel like they know quite enough to give them the confidence they need to fully engage in the world. They can become increasingly entangled with ever more complex ideas and thoughts, confusing this with true *inner knowing and guidance.*

Type 6s strategy for dealing with feelings of fear and anxiety is to vacillate between putting their energy and attention on the external world—gathering ever more input and information—and focusing inward to analyze the situation. Too much time analyzing, and the anxiety becomes overwhelming, so they refocus and solicit input from others or external sources. They tend to be great researchers. Type 6s don't trust their own internal decision maker and second-guess themselves. They solicit the opinions of others. Yet Type 6s are skeptical of people's motivations and continually scan for hidden agendas. Ultimately, they make their own decisions regardless of vast amounts of input. Sometimes Type 6s make a decision just to quell their anxiety.

Like Type 5s, Type 6s fear the demands of others, yet are driven by an obligation to be responsible. At times, they can feel overwhelmed by this obligation and experience it as pressure. Their response to this feeling of pressure is to withdraw, which might be preceded by an emotional reaction, leaving behind what might appear to others as scorched earth. After a time of withdrawal, Type 6s can't take the anxiety; they get scared again and resurface. Thus continues this inner and outer reactive cycle.

Underneath it all, Type 6s never feel as though they are standing on solid ground and believe the rug could be pulled out from under them at any time. The voice of "what if" can paralyze them with fear. The paradox is that in a real crisis, Type 6s are usually the ones whom people follow. The immediate demands of the moment allow for no second-guessing or listening to the *should* voice. They act on their instincts and intuition, which are often right on target. All of that time planning and preparing shows its value in the exigencies of a crisis.

Type 7s, to the outside world, seem unstoppable, resilient, and courageous, and appear to take on life with full abandon. What others don't know (and what is often hidden to Type 7s) is that their bias for action is a way to escape from their inner world. The endless ideas, projects, and activity, and their constant movement, are all ways of running away from their fear and anxiety—fear of being trapped in emotional pain and fear of being deprived.

Type 7s believe that they can't count on other people, so they have to be self-reliant and go after what they want. If they don't take action, Type 7s fear that they will be trapped and deprived. This can feel like death to them. To cope with these feelings, Type 7s create distractions by keeping their mind stimulated and fully occupied with exciting possibilities and options. Not only that, but they end up taking action on many of these ideas and staying on the go. They appear to be running from one thing to another in the attempt to keep lots of balls in the air. This creates the impression that they are scattered and unfocused.

 AN INSIDEOUT LEADER'S STORY: **TRUST BUILDING**

Faced with conflict avoidance, an overly polite group glued together by a fear of job loss, skills gaps in interpersonal feedback and challenging one another's thinking, Lars knows that this will be tricky and he'll have to change his style and learn new skills right along with his LT.

Chris and Lars discuss the merits of using part of their next few off-sites for some fun team-development activities. Both of them have experience with how effective they are for building bonds among team members. Through these team-building activities, they'll also practice new skills—collaboration, giving and receiving feedback, conflict resolution, and so on.

Together, Lars and Chris develop a general plan and choose to involve the team, on a rotating basis, to manage the agenda for their off-site meetings. Lars and Chris hope this will encourage

the LT members to take more ownership for the quality and success of the meetings and for their own participation.

Lars introduces the idea of having a team session on the Enneagram at one of their upcoming off-site meetings. With some consideration, the LT agrees that it could be useful to better understand what makes each other tick and their own predispositions (motivations, reactive patterns, and strengths).

This team needs to quickly learn how to learn together—to recognize their complementary strengths, to demonstrate respect for what each brings to the team, and to leverage their strengths. Lars and Chris believe the Enneagram will be an ideal tool to support the team in these efforts.

→ Lars's story continues on p. 240

SOCIAL STYLES AND INTERPERSONAL COPING STRATEGIES

Everyone experiences discomfort or anxiety from time to time when faced with attending social or professional functions, meetings, or family gatherings, or in any kind of personal interaction. Karen Horney, a German psychoanalyst and psychiatrist, described three clusters of coping strategies that individuals use to deal with these inner stresses and to get their needs met. These strategies are so germane to our way of being that they are often used habitually and without conscious awareness.

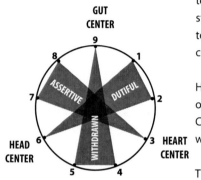

Horney describes three different ways in which people have a "sense of self" within a social context. Don Riso and Russ Hudson built on Claudio Naranjo's work and identified how the Enneagram Types fit with Horney's styles, naming them the Hornevian Types.

These three styles are as follows:

▸ **Moving Against People (Assertive)**
   Types: 3, Achiever; 7, Enthusiast; 8, Boss

▸ **Moving Toward People (Dutiful)**
   Types: 1, Perfectionist; 2, People Pleaser; 6, Loyal Skeptic

▸ **Moving Away from People (Withdrawn)**
   Types: 4, Individualist; 5, Detached Observer; 9, Peacemaker

Each of the Enneagram Types fits into one of these three coping strategies, as shown above. Let's explore each of the Enneagram Types' relationships to the Hornevian Types.

ASSERTIVE TYPES:
3, ACHIEVER; 7, ENTHUSIAST; AND 8, BOSS

The strategy that the Assertive Types use to get their needs met is to *ask or demand*. They take bold action, puff themselves up, promote themselves, and take risks. This gives them the appearance of being courageous, confident, and sometimes overconfident. People may experience them as very assertive, personable but not personal, and pushy.

WHY DO THEY COME ACROSS LIKE THIS?

All three try to keep others at an emotional distance and to distance themselves from their own heart. In fact, these Types tend to be out of contact with their own feelings and generally do not show their vulnerability.

The Assertive Types often give up on love and instead derive their satisfaction from taking on challenges, projects, and goals, and seek the admiration of others. Types 3, 7, and 8 may (unconsciously) expect to be at the center of attention and often find themselves there.

Assertive Types are action oriented, future oriented, goal oriented, and often task oriented. They are upbeat, *can do* people who see around obstacles and tend to avoid people they perceive as negative or pessimistic. You will find these Types to be naturally expressive, but that does not mean expressive of feelings. They are confident and can instill confidence in others.

 STOP AND REFLECT

How will you recognize if you are one of the Assertive Types—3, 7, or 8? If several of the statements in the following checklist apply to you (most of the time), one of these Types *may* be yours.

❑ You go after what you want and need.

❑ You may not be aware of your feelings.

❑ You are action oriented and future oriented.

❑ You may confuse being emotive, passionate, and expressive with actually experiencing your feelings.

❑ Rather than connect with your feelings, you use the fuel of your feelings to passionately take on   projects, tasks, goals, challenges, and causes.

❑ You may not be aware of the consequences of your behavior on others.

❑ People may feel steamrolled by you or tell you they think you are pushy.

❑ You may choose partners for practical reasons, rather than choosing partners with whom you have a romantic and intimate connection.

❑ Intimacy and vulnerability do not come naturally to you.

❑ Generally, you do not hold on to grudges.

❑ You don't easily take personal offense.

❑ You are a fast mover and can easily get impatient.

❑ You often feel constrained by the demands and expectations placed on you by others.

How do the Assertive Hornevian Types sync with the three Centers of Intelligence?

They are out of contact with their feelings and use the Action/Body/Instinctual Center in conjunction with the Thinking Center.

Type 3s think and act, while *repressing their feelings*. Their eye is on the goal and on success, and they attempt to ward off their feelings of shame. Their action is focused, and they have an uncanny ability to see an opportunity and jump on it. Type 3 is a focused doer; a master of efficiency; a take-action, *just do it* type of person. Relationships take a backseat to their focus on success. They think and act, think and act, think and act—and feelings are negated.

Type 7s are busy *running away from their feelings* and anxiety. They fear being trapped in painful feelings. Their thinking takes the form of dreams, visions, ideas, and possibilities, and they are great synthesizers. Unlike Type 3s, who take focused action, Type 7s attempt to take action on as many of their ideas as possible. They are experience seekers. The Action/Body/Instinctual Center becomes a slave to their generative mind. Meanwhile, they avoid their feelings for fear of being consumed by them with no way out.

Type 8s have strong gut instincts, and they use their Thinking Center to rationalize taking action on these instincts. They like to feel their power, and they intensify their sensations. Self-reliance is key to their makeup. They seek out challenges and causes to take on. Meanwhile, they harden their feelings in order to survive. They avoid showing any vulnerability, and demonstrate strength and power, so that no one can control them in any way. They trust their gut instincts about people and situations. If you pass the *gut* test, you're in, as long as you are completely loyal. Over time, by consistent demonstration of loyalty, you can earn their trust. It takes a lot of trust for Type 8s to allow others to know they care, and to express compassion and empathy. They see this as a sign of weakness. If they were to show this part of themselves, their belief is that it would be used against them.

THE KEY TO THE KINGDOM

For Types 3, 7, and 8 to become high-functioning leaders and to lead from their *best self,* the developmental opportunity is to work with the Heart Center. The first step is to slow down and notice the world around you. Rather than pushing into the world, allow the world to enter; take in impressions, notice, let your heart to be touched. Commit to people who are important to you. Be a friend—offer help. Take time for family and friends. Take the risk of sharing your feelings with those you trust, and allow yourself to show some vulnerability—for instance, "I don't know the answer," "I need some help," "I think I made a mistake," "I'm sorry." When you are willing to show vulnerability, people will be drawn to you and inspired by your courage.

Even though you slow down, you will still be productive and active, but more available to yourself and others in the present moment. You'll make better decisions, have easier relationships, and have fewer do-overs.

When you slow down and allow yourself to be touched by life, people, and the miracle of every moment, you will find the health and happiness you seek.

✹ See "Centering Basic Practice" and "The Power of Presence" in "InsideOut— Leaders' Tool Kit." You will also find exercises designed uniquely for Types 3, 7, and 8 in their respective sections.

DUTIFUL TYPES:
1, PERFECTIONIST; 2, PEOPLE PLEASER; 6, LOYAL SKEPTIC

The Dutiful Types are those people you can count on to take responsibility and help out. They tend to be loyal and committed friends, workers, and family members. They often secretly feel they are better than others—they can see how things and people could be improved, the right way to be, and how best to think about things. The strategy they use to get what they want is to *earn it*—by doing what they think is expected of them. *Should* is a word they know well, along with *duty*, *responsibility*, *commitment*, and *obligation*.

WHY DO THEY COME ACROSS LIKE THIS?

Because they believe they have to earn what they seek. Type 1s believe that if they act ethically and morally, and follow the rules, they will *earn* autonomy. Type 2s believe that if they selflessly do for others and are a *good* person, they will *earn* attention and love. Type 6s believe that if they act responsibly, they will *earn* security.

These Types are dutiful or compliant with their inner critic, who tells them what they *should* do. Their inner critic is the voice of authority, the rules, the standards, the beliefs they hold, and so on. Each of these Enneagram Types has certain standards of behavior that they believe they must uphold and are expected of them.

 STOP AND REFLECT

How will you recognize if you are one of the Dutiful Types—1, Perfectionist; 2, People Pleaser; 6, Loyal Skeptic? If several of the statements in the following checklist apply to you (most of the time), one of these Types *may* be yours.

- ☐ You are seen as dedicated, loyal, and sociable, and you volunteer your time and energy.

- ☐ You take a responsive approach to people and situations.

☐ You are seen as someone whom people can count on.

☐ You are responsible and follow through, but may ultimately resent people for asking too much.

☐ You think your dedication and responsible actions will earn you what you seek: love, safety, security.

☐ You like to be prepared.

☐ You have difficulty saying no and setting boundaries.

☐ You often think in circles, connecting every issue with every other issue and overanalyzing.

☐ You defer to other people, rules, belief systems, morals, and standards to make your decisions and set your agendas, and to know what is the "right" thing to do, say, believe, think.

☐ You find it hard to be objective about yourself and others.

☐ Your standards are very high and exacting.

☐ You learned to mistrust your own inner compass as a child, in favor of doing what you thought you should do to earn the love, acceptance, appreciation, and security you desired.

How do the Dutiful/Compliant Hornevian Types sync with the three Centers of Intelligence?

The Body/Action/Instinctual and Heart centers obscure the Thinking Center of all three Types. In an effort to uphold standards and meet expectations, each of these Types has lost contact with and/or shut down the voice of their intuition in favor of their inner critic. This is their voice of authority—*should, I need to be good, I need to be responsible*—and the voice of *the right thing to do*. Even if the Dutiful/Compliant Types can hear their intuition, they don't trust it or won't listen to it. They fear that by ignoring their inner critic, the love, appreciation, security, and autonomy they seek will be taken away.

Type 1s: Ready, set, *action*. Type 1s are in motion and do all of the things they are supposed to do. The list is made, and they take great care to do everything well—in fact, perfectly. Type 1s use their Action Center to go out and improve themselves, others, systems, processes and the world around them. Their Heart Center gets hijacked by the Action Center's agenda. Anger and resentment are repressed by their Action Center.

Type 1s feel anger toward themselves for not being perfect and toward others for not toeing the line. Resentment is anger they hold on to toward others who don't live up to their standards. They use the fuel from their anger and resentment to take action and make things right. They misuse their Action Center to control their feelings and their environment. Meanwhile, the voice of objectivity is absent. What is good enough?

Type 2s: Feelings, nothing more than feelings … Type 2s are relational. They seek connection, are empathic, and want to care for others. The Action Center supports the Feeling Center—Type 2s act on their feelings. They want to be seen as the *good one* by doing for others in order to *earn* the love and appreciation they desire. Type 2s tend to be upbeat and busy, while letting their feelings guide the way. "Am I a good enough person?" is a question that Type 2s ask.

What they need to be asking themselves is, "How good is good enough?" The Thinking Center gets hijacked by the agenda of the heart. It functions as the busy and strategic mind trying to figure out whom to do things for or what to do for others. Type 2s use manipulation and seduction to get what they want. Activating the objective mind is what Type 2s most need to do. The objective mind will enable Type 2s to see that *people pleasing* is wearing them out and often pushes people away, rather than building relationships. It is not getting them the love and appreciation they most desire.

Type 6s: Analysis paralysis—"What should I do? Should I have done that? What do you think?" asks Type 6. This is their Thinking Center at work. They don't listen to or trust their intuition in deference to their internal committee, which has hijacked their Thinking Center. Everyone on the committee has a voice and is busy viewing situations from all sides in an effort to optimize every decision. This throws Type 6s into a state of indecision, self-doubt, and paralysis.

Meanwhile, their Heart and Action centers are on the loose, trying this and that, researching on the Internet, talking with this person and that person, yet suspicious of the advice they are getting from others and wondering about their hidden agendas.

In the vast chorus of voices, the voice of responsibility is the loudest. Yet the pressure to be responsible sends Type 6s into a counter-re-action against being responsible and can result in angry outbursts. The once-responsible Type 6s can look quite self-centered. Mean-while, everyone is wondering what happened. Often, Type 6s can hear their intuition. However, it takes courage to act on it and ignore the inner committee or the wiring that tells Type 6s that they must act responsibly.

THE KEY TO THE KINGDOM

Cultivating a clear, quiet mind will allow the Dutiful Types to distin-guish their intuition from their inner critic. When the Dutiful Types begin to take action on their intuition, they become more focused, creative, and trusting of their impressions and insights, and begin to feel more secure. They no longer feel the need to rely on their inner critic, external belief systems, or authorities to tell them what to do, how to feel, and what to think and believe. Confidence in their in-ternal compass arises, and they begin to do for others from an inner desire to serve, not because they *should*.

See "Centering Basic Practice" and "Mindful-ness Meditation" in "Inside-Out—Leaders' Tool Kit." They contain exercises designed uniquely for Types 1, 2, and 6 in their respective sections.

WITHDRAWN/MOVING AWAY FROM PEOPLE
TYPES: 4, INDIVIDUALIST; 5, DETACHED
OBSERVER; 9, PEACEMAKER

Their strategy under social stress is to withdraw into their inner world of ideas, imagination, and fantasies, or to withdraw emotionally. Ba-sically, they disengage from the world and enter their interior. They are often challenged to stay grounded in their body and take action rather than escape into their inner sanctum.

WHY DO THEY DO THIS?

All three Types tend to idealize people and situations for different reasons and in different ways, and to use this strategy to keep reality at bay. The *real world* never quite lives up to their idealized version of it. Often it is more satisfying to maintain their fantasies rather than allow reality to show itself through direct experience. They can often feel closer to people from an emotional and physical distance.

Their point of view is the most important for them, and they believe they are the final authority. They tend to be the most stubborn of the nine Types.

Of the three Centers of Intelligence, the one that is least trusted and therefore least developed for Types 4, 5, and 9 is the Gut/Body/Action/Instinctual Center. They have difficulty keeping their attention in their body long enough to leave their inner world and get into sustained and practical action.

This does not mean they don't take action. What it does mean is that they tend to do only what they *like to do* or *feel like doing*, but not what practically needs to be done. If the Withdrawn Types do take action on the practical, you may see them taking shortcuts or making snap decisions just to tick an item off the list. All three feel that they have to summon up energy to face the world and deal with the demands of life. They often dream about what life should be like or how things could be, but have a hard time converting that into committed and sustained action. They can rationalize themselves out of doing anything they really don't want to do.

The paradox for Types 4, 5, and 9 is that while they often consider themselves the final authority, and rely on their own perceptions and analysis for decision making, they also have issues with self-esteem, though they may not appear that way at first. They may also believe, "I don't fit in" or "I'm different," and that people don't fully see or understand them.

Type 4s don't believe they will ever find themselves or be able to fully express their uniqueness. This belief undergirds their drive to attract attention and to stand out in a crowd.

Type 5s don't believe they have what it takes to deal with all of life's demands or the energy to deal with other people's needs. They can appear very insecure socially and even awkward. Type 5s may try to counteract their insecurity by acting arrogant and dismissive or by offering a treatise on their latest topic of interest.

Type 9s believe that they don't matter, that they are nobody special and can therefore blend into the woodwork in social settings. They are the *nice guys* or *nice gals* who go along and prefer to feel comfortable rather than use their energy to go after what they want.

 STOP AND REFLECT

How will you recognize if you are one of the Withdrawn Types—4, 5, or 9? If several of the statements in the following checklist apply to you (most of the time), one of these Types *may* be yours.

- ☐ You have different ways of "checking out/going numb."

- ☐ You have several ways of withdrawing and "proving" that you are different.

- ☐ May act mysterious.

- ☐ May be an observer rather than an engaged participant.

- ☐ May disengage even though you appear engaged and involved.

- ☐ May open a book at a dinner party or retreat to another room.

- ☐ You do what you feel like doing, not necessarily what needs to be done.

- ☐ You set yourself apart through your originality and commitment to your own ideas.

- ☐ You think through issues deeply.

- ☐ You are not confident that you can deal with people and their demands.

- ☐ You retreat to your inner world of thoughts and feelings.

☐ Your pace tends to be slower and more leisurely than most people's.

☐ You can feel trapped and/or the victim of other people's plans and ideas.

☐ You may feel a sense of hopelessness about your ability to have an impact on the world around you.

How do the Withdrawn Hornevian Types sync with the three Centers of Intelligence?

Kathy Hurley and Theodorre Donson are known for this particular understanding of the Triads—bringing the Hornevians and the Centers of Intelligence together in a very useful way—and give some valuable insights into the inner workings of each Type.[30]

Type 4s can withdraw and become resigned about relationships. They come to believe they will never have the love they want, nor feel fully seen and understood. They filter the world through their feelings (Heart Center), and their Thinking Center is at the mercy of, and in support of, their Heart Center. The Heart Center runs the show, and the Thinking Center is the best supporting actor.

Type 4s use their Thinking Center for fantasy and imagination, to envision their ideal *self* and their ideal life. Their need to be unique and special can cloud their self-perception. Their Body/Gut/Instinctual Center is often left out of the conversation—meaning that it is blocked. This keeps them stuck. Rather than taking action, they long for and idealize what they don't have. Alternatively, they are known to try on lots of different identities in search of self. They may have multiple careers or move to different areas, all in search of their unique identity.

Ironically, when Type 4s take purposeful action, they start to feel good about themselves. The way out of this self-reinforcing loop is through the Body/Gut/Instinctual Center; take practical action and act on instincts.

Type 5s withdraw into their Thinking Center. They detach, disengage, and become an observer. They escape into their imagination and fantasy life. They may retreat to problem-solve in order to come up with innovative ideas and solutions. They are most in tune with this internal world.

Their Heart Center is the best supporting actor to their Thinking Center. They think about their feelings, and think about their life, people, and situations perhaps without feeling their feelings. Type 5s can confuse this connection between their Thinking Center and Heart Center as actually feeling, and their heart is left out of the real conversation. Feelings are a bit messy, and Type 5s believe that feeling their feelings will rob them of the ability to be objective. That would leave them vulnerable and unsafe.

Type 5s can forget that they have a body and fail to pay attention to their physical world. Yet getting grounded in the physical (the Gut/Action/Body/Instinctual Center) is just what is needed. Type 5s are often known as the absent-minded professor; so completely lost in their world of thoughts and ideas, they forget to take care of themselves and the practical.

Type 9s can appear to be very busy, while their focus of attention is on their imagination and fantasies about people and life. Their Feeling Center is in support of their inner world by having feelings about what they are imagining.

Simultaneously, the energy of their Gut/Body/Action/Instinctual Center is used to keep reality at bay. The idealized world is so much more pleasant! Type 9s are reticent to take action on their own personal growth and development. When they finally do, it is often a result of their willingness to take off their rose-colored glasses and allow reality to intrude upon them.

THE KEY TO THE KINGDOM

To become a high-functioning leader and to lead from their *best self*, Types 4, 5, and 9 find their developmental opportunity in working with the Gut/Body/Action/Instinctual Center. When this Center is unlocked and available to take its rightful place in the chorus of inner

For specific suggestions, see "Centering Basic Practice" in "InsideOut—Leaders' Tool Kit." You will also find exercises designed specifically for Types 4, 5, and 9 in their respective sections.

voices, Types 4, 5, and 9 will discover both the personal benefits and joys of intentional and sustained action, of being fully engaged in the world around them, and of participating in a *real* relationship— not just their idealized version of the person who lives in their imagination. They will also realize that they have the fortitude to deal with the demands of others and life, and to make their mark on the world.

AN INSIDEOUT LEADER'S STORY: **IN THE BACKGROUND**

Chris continues to coach Lars. Lars is able to surface some of the unconscious patterns that hinder his success, both in life and at work. He sees how these patterns play out through his life. It is hard to face some of this stuff, but he knows that the time has come and he'll be a much more effective leader having taken this inner journey.

Chris helps Lars to see his strengths and how they contribute to his success. They talk about how Lars can use some of his strengths more effectively.

Lars becomes highly engaged with the Enneagram because it so accurately depicts his inner landscape and identifies things he hasn't previously been able to see about himself—his blind spots. He is very curious about his team and how they will take to the Enneagram.

He hopes it will give him more insight about how to best support them as leaders. In two weeks' time, they will be meeting off-site for two days. Meeting away from the office creates a more relaxed and comfortable environment with few distractions. Lars is glad to be able to provide the opportunity for the members of the LT to get to know each other in a different way. He is both a little anxious and curious to see what will unfold.

Once he knows their Types, Lars will have a better idea about how to work with them more effectively, by understanding what drives their behaviors, some of their likely triggers, and their strengths.

➜ Lars's story continues on p. 249

CONFLICT STYLES AND APPROACH TO PROBLEMS

One of the triadic groups identified by Riso and Hudson, called the *Harmonics*, describes how each Type is likely to respond when faced with conflict, or when confronted with a problem, adversity, and situations where their needs are not being met.[31] The reactions described below are more typical of someone under in the grip of his or her Type.

On a deeper level, this coping strategy is a defense against loss and disappointment. Although we have all three styles available to us, each Type has a predisposition for one in particular. Because the three Types making up each Harmonic Triad share a similar approach to problems or dealing with unmet needs, they can mistype as one of the other two Types in their Harmonic Triad. For instance, I have seen many Type 6s initially mistype as Type 4, Type 7s as Type 2 or 9, and so on.

REACTIVE TYPES:
4, INDIVIDUALIST; 6, LOYAL SKEPTIC; 8, BOSS

All three are provoked by issues of trust and betrayal and are described as intense.

If you need to *point out a problem* to one of these Types, don't be surprised if you get an emotional reaction. They are likely to have strong emotional reactions to adversity and conflict. Some might see them as intense, but for Types 4, 6, and 8, it helps to express their emotions in order to deal with the issue. What they are looking for from others is a *response*.

When people reciprocate emotionally—what the Reactive Types may consider feedback—they feel met. These Types have a hard time trusting people, so knowing where they stand with you helps build their trust. The Reactive Types desire trust. However, they find it difficult to let go of control because they fear betrayal.

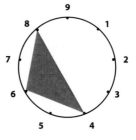

The Reactive Types

A TYPE 4 CLIENT NOTED:

Being authentic is required to have a meaningful relationship. Therefore, if I feel somebody is trying to cheat me or is phony, I consider this relationship senseless. I end up feeling intense pain and sadness.

When I explode after someone has broken their word or I have been betrayed, I usually do something provocative to draw attention to the problem. Personally I feel emotionally and physically exhausted. I also feel like I am from another planet.

What I want from others is to talk it out, I don't want to be given advice or solutions or be told that there is no problem.

Type 4, the Individualist—*"I'm upset, and I need to feel free to express myself."*

How do Type 4s trigger conflict? They can be temperamental, moody, and self-absorbed. They can react strongly to problems or perceived problems. Type 4s identify strongly with their emotional reactions and believe that what they feel about situations and people is *the truth*. They have a hard time being objective.

As was described earlier, Type 4s are one of the Withdrawn Types. Their pattern is to react and withdraw. They may not just physically withdraw; they may also withdraw into their inner world, where these problems and issues can become larger than life. This can lead to Type 4s' becoming despairing and hopeless. What they most desire is someone to *rescue* them. In this case, "rescue" means that someone makes efforts to understand them and make them feel *seen*.

Type 6, the Loyal Skeptic—*"I'm feeling pressured!"*

Type 6s are watchful, sure that people will take advantage of them. They tend to be suspicious of others' motives. When 6s let their guard down, the fear of betrayal is always lurking around the corner. Conflict can get ignited in a problem-solving situation because Type 6s tend to focus on what could go wrong. They expose and amplify every idea's potential downside. To others, they can appear pessimistic and argumentative.

When Type 6s are involved in a conflict or feel threatened in some way, their underlying anxiety and sense of inferiority can trigger defensive behavior and what others perceive as intense overreactions. Type 6s can attribute all manner of imagined motives (negative) onto others.

They get themselves into a pickle as they swing from one extreme to the other. Type 6s want to be able to trust and rely on others, but they simultaneously feel the need to be the one that others rely on. The real trouble starts when they feel pressured by people who rely on them. This tends to catalyze their reactivity and defensiveness.

As one of the Dutiful Types, their coping strategy is to act responsibly in order to earn the security they desire. Trouble can ensue when they begin feeling the pressure of others' expectations to take responsibility and when they believe others are taking advantage of their good nature.

Type 8, the Boss—"I'm angry, and you need to hear about it."

Type 8s can be impulsive, defy authority, and act confrontational and bossy—telling rather than asking. These are their reactions to problems that surface or to people whom they see as obstacles. They are not known for censoring their emotional reactions, and these sometimes larger-than-life explosions give Type 8s a feeling of vitality and power. These behaviors serve to keep others at bay and to mask their feelings of vulnerability. Type 8s believe they can power through problems and people if they need to.

They are known for their confrontational style and ability to challenge others. Like Types 4 and 6, Type 8s don't trust others easily. If they believe they have been betrayed or publicly criticized (they feel they have been rendered vulnerable in some way), Type 8s can explode, cut you out of their life, or fire you.

Their fear of being controlled or of someone having power over them also triggers Type 8s' reactivity and their desire for self-reliance.

POSITIVE OUTLOOK TYPES:
2, PEOPLE PLEASER; 7, ENTHUSIAST; 9, PEACEMAKER

If you want help seeing the silver lining on your storm cloud, talk to one of the Positive Outlook Types. These are the spin-doctors who can help you to see your problem in a positive light and make you feel good. Don't come to them if all you want is to wallow in self-pity and find a shoulder to cry on. What these three Types share is their positive or optimistic outlook and general avoidance of what they perceive to be negative people, thoughts, and situations.

The Positive Outlook Types want to feel good themselves and would like others around them to be upbeat. When problems arise, they try to put a positive spin on the situation, each Type in its own particular way.

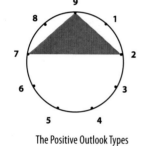

The Positive Outlook Types

When problems or potential conflict arises, the Positive Outlook Types attempt to avoid, distract from, or minimize the problem. Looking at the dark side of life or the dark side of themselves is something each of these Types would rather avoid. When they avoid dealing with problems, it creates difficulties for them and for others. *What you resist, persists.*

Type 2, the People Pleaser—*"You have a problem? I'm here to help you."*

As one of the Dutiful Types, Type 2s move toward others. They identify as a people pleaser or helper, the one who is *giving*. They want to make people feel good. This reinforces their role as a person who helps through their *good intentions*. Type 2s see themselves through the eyes of others. When they get approval and appreciation, it feeds their self-importance and positive self-image: "I am a good, caring, and loving person."

By focusing on these positive qualities and the needs of others, Type 2s avoid looking at their own neediness, hurts, and upsets. Type 2s are known to anticipate others' needs. Moving toward others in order to *help* can precipitate conflicts for Type 2s—especially when the help is uninvited.

Others may be annoyed by their tendency toward self-importance: "What would you do without me?" People may experience Type 2s as clingy or invasive. When people don't welcome the help that Type 2s offer and try to set limits for contact with them, Type 2s can become demanding, manipulative, and/or seductive.

A TYPE 2 CLIENT NOTED:

I'm the neighborhood problem solver. I sure do avoid conflict if possible. When conflict does come up and I can't avoid it, then I want to talk about it, hear what the other person has to say, and get it resolved. My urge to find a way to fix what's wrong for that person, and to make them feel better, is almost overwhelming. There is this monologue inside my head, 'You need to fix this. Find a way to make this person feel better.' I have such a strong inclination to say, 'Let's dig in and find a solution to this,' as long as I'm not part of the problem. If I deviate from this role, I'm afraid I won't be loved.

Type 7, the Enthusiast—*"Well, the good news is …"*

Type 7s' approach to problems or adversity is to put a positive spin on it; to make lemonade out of lemons; to find the good in a bad situation. While this can be quite helpful, the driving reason for their approach is escapism. Finding the good in what went wrong is a coping strategy to quell their own anxiety and to run away from their feelings of hurt, pain, and underlying fear of deprivation. Instead, they distract through constant activity and turn toward anticipating something positive in the future, seeing possibilities and options, and trying to find ways to seek satisfaction in their lives.

This can create conflicts with others who want Type 7s to sit still and *face reality*; to deal with the situation and work it through. Type 7s tend to get impatient with others and avoid people whom they perceive as needy and depressive. They have a hard time being compassionate or making a soft place for people to land. Instead, they focus on their own needs and avoid being dragged into situations that they would see as downers.

This behavior is an effort to avoid being trapped in their inner world of anxiety, unprocessed grief, sorrow, disappointments, loss, and emptiness. To Type 7s, being with people they perceive as needy or depressive for any length of time, or feeling stuck in conversations that dredge up the past, evokes their fear of being trapped. They believe others are throwing a bucket of cold water on their passion, plans for the future, and joy.

Type 9, the Peacemaker—*"I can't see the problem with my rose-colored glasses on."*

Type 9s would prefer to live in their idealized version of the world and stuff unpleasant feelings. As one of the Withdrawn Types, they happily escape into fantasy and imagination rather than face what is right in front of them. Others may perceive Type 9s as sticking their heads in the sand.

They focus on their positive feelings toward others and the world around them in order to sustain their sense of inner peace, harmony, and comfort. Type 9s' approach to problems and conflict is avoidant, and they attempt to keep the peace by being kind and accommodating. They try to take care of others' needs in order to take care of their own needs.

Type 9s can create conflict, paradoxically, by trying to avoid it. Their strategy is to be complacent, avoiding problems or denying their existence. *Things will just take care of themselves.* From Type 9s' perspective, they want stability in their lives and believe they'll attain this by maintaining the status quo. To face problems head-on would be inviting trouble. This would open the door to potential change, conflict, and loss of connection with others—what they fear most. To others, Type 9s appear stubborn, difficult, and in denial. People often tire in the attempt to engage and involve them in facing reality.

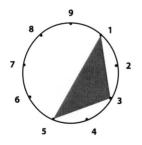

The Competency Types

COMPETENCY TYPES:
1, PERFECTIONIST; 3, ACHIEVER; 5, DETACHED OBSERVER

If you want to find an objective voice for problem solving, seek out a Type 1, 3, or 5. While they can appear dispassionate about your difficulty, they are quite helpful when you need to separate out your emotional issues from the practical and get an objective foothold on the situation. Don't approach one of these three if all you are looking for is a shoulder to cry on, a soft place to land, and an empathetic ear. The Competency Types strive to set aside their personal feelings in order to be objective, logical, sensible, and effective.

Type 1, the Perfectionist—*"I am sure we can find a reasonable solution if we can all just be sensible here."*

Finds a sensible solution: Type 1s' problem-solving approach can be very effective, and it can also create conflicts with others. They are one of the Dutiful Types who tune in to the voice of their inner critic/ internalized voice of authority to know what to do. When Type 1s decide that the way to go is to adhere to the rules, without regard to context, people experience them as rigid and uncompromising, and perhaps cold and unfeeling. Type 1s' approach sets them up as the authority—triggering all sorts of reactions in others.

From the perspective of Type 1s, they are being sensible. By following the rules, adhering to their morals or principles, they are being fair and just. They believe that they demonstrate integrity by putting aside their own needs and feelings, and working within the structure of the system. They can feel frustrated by, and be disdainful of, people who don't follow the rules.

A TYPE 1 CLIENT NOTED:

I am very practical when it comes to problems. People often come to me when they have an issue. My PA is always depressed. I try to find a practical approach to her problems and help her think differently. I find that I am good in a conflict—I can calmly find an objective voice and say something sensible to get things back on track.

This can also work against me because I want to impose my way of thinking on others. I have a hard time understanding people who have different ways of doing things, because I think my way is the right way.

I stay in control of my emotions to provide the perfect image of being strong. I will rarely let go of my emotions. I need to be able handle whatever happens. I take things in hand, organize, and make sure that everything is perfect. I have a need to be in control of whatever situation arises. I am emotional when I am on my own. I don't really hide my anger. People will know that I am angry. I am always the one to take care of all the difficult matters and be the responsible one. It can be very tiring. Sometimes I just want to let go and have some rest.

Type 3, the Achiever—*"OK, let's keep our eye on the goal and find an efficient way to resolve this."*

Finds an efficient solution: Type 3s are among the Assertive Types, who appear confident, and easily and quickly take efficient action toward goals. They can cut out what they see as *the fat* to focus on the finish line and stay on task. They happily work inside or outside the existing structure or system, and take shortcuts if necessary—whatever path will achieve results.

Their problem-solving style tends to be impersonal. Type 3s set aside their feelings to stay focused on the goal. They see others as extensions of themselves, as resources to reach the target. This type of approach can create conflict. People can see them as too competitive, uncaring, and unfeeling, and too concerned with their own success and image. Type 3s will avoid conflict with people whom they see as emotional. If you can have a pragmatic conversation with Type 3s and avoid discussions about feelings, they will engage. Type 3s can be curt, short, and deceptive, and elicit conflict just by virtue of their style.

Type 5, the Detached Observer—*"Let me think about this ..."*

Fixes problems rationally: Type 5s are among the Withdrawn Types and can detach emotionally from the situation to objectively assess it. They prefer to work outside the system and structure and make up their own rules. They withdraw into their world of ideas and may need to take time away to solve things. Type 5s prefer to figure out problems by themselves without soliciting input. They believe they have the expertise and intelligence to deal with problems. "I'll figure it out" is something Type 5s are known to say. They enjoy problem solving as an intellectual exercise. However, they are not likely to be empathic. They want to "fix it" and make it go away.

If Type 5 is in a leadership position, this may be a source of conflict. They are likely to *decide and announce* rather than engage and involve. Type 5s can create conflict by being remote, distant, emotionally detached, and isolated. People don't know how to reach them or connect with them. An attempt to draw them out can be perceived as intrusive by Type 5s, pushing them further away. They can provoke others by acting dispassionate and indifferent, as if they don't care and aren't affected. Type 5s can talk about their feelings as if they were happening to someone else.

The conflict style of Type 5s tends to take the form of intellectual arrogance, detaching emotionally, and trying to control any demonstration of emotions. When their detachment doesn't work, Type 5s can wall themselves off. They don't trust easily, don't like to lose control, and don't like to let others know that they have allowed themselves to be affected by them. Remember, Type 5s want to minimize their need for, and reliance on, others.

 AN INSIDEOUT LEADER'S STORY: **LARS PREPARES FOR THE LT OFF-SITE**

Lars and Chris schedule a couple of coaching sessions in preparation for the off-site. At this point, Lars is quite curious and wants more information about his Type and the related Types. He already sees some benefit from his work with Chris, and that gives him the motivation and confidence to continue exploring. In fact, Lars purchases a journal to capture insights he has in his sessions with Chris and throughout his day.

When the stress gets too high, Lars finds that he can slip into the denial and procrastination of the lower side of Type 9. He now has the ability to see this happening, as if he is an observer of himself. When he notices his desire to bury his head in the sand, he makes a different choice.

He also catches himself, on several occasions, ready to defend and throw out a barb to keep others away. Lars knows he needs to get to the bottom of this pattern. He is gratified that some of this stuff is coming to the surface so that he can work with it. These reactions have tripped him up on several occasions.

Lars commits to himself and Chris that he will work with both of these reactions and see if he can manage them at the off-site: burying his head in the sand and sending out the drones. Can he do it?

➜ Lars's story continues on p. 251

TRIADS AT A GLANCE ENNEACHART

Types at a Glance *Similarities and Distinctions Among the Nine Enneagram Types*

ENNEAGRAM TYPE	CENTER of INTELLIGENCE (Overrelied-upon center)	FEELING TRIAD (Underlying feelings that drive behavior)	HORNEVIANS (Getting needs met in a social context)	MOTIVATIONS and ASSOCIATED STRATEGIES	HARMONICS/HARMONIZING INTERNALLY (How each Type deals with difficulty/disappointment/not getting what they want/conflict)
8 Boss	Instinctive	Rage/Anger	Asserts	Demands autonomy	Reactive (Emotionally) React strongly and need response
9 Peacemaker	Instinctive	Rage/Anger	Withdraws	Withdraws to get autonomy	Positive Reframe Deny they have problems
1 Perfectionist	Instinctive	Rage/Anger	Complies	Earns autonomy	Competency/Efficiency Objective and logical problem solving
2 People Pleaser	Heart	Shame	Complies	Earns love	Positive Reframe Deny they have problems
3 Achiever	Heart	Shame	Asserts	Demands attention	Competency/Efficiency Objective and logical problem solving
4 Individualist	Heart	Shame	Withdraws	Withdraws to get attention	Reactive (Emotionally) React strongly and need response
5 Detached Observer	Thinking	Fear	Withdraws	Withdraws to get security	Competency/Efficiency Objective and logical problem solving
6 Loyal Skeptic	Thinking	Fear	Complies	Earns security	Reactive (Emotionally) React strongly and need response
7 Enthusiast	Thinking	Fear	Asserts	Demands security	Positive Reframe Deny they have problems

AN INSIDEOUT LEADER'S STORY: **THE LT MEETS THE ENNEAGRAM**

The day arrives and everyone is curious. None of them have heard of the Enneagram. They find themselves in an unusual setting—no tables, just chairs, sitting in a circle with banners on the wall and something taped to the floor.

Chris set this up to move them into unfamiliar territory. None of the usual props. Mobiles off. Computers off. The meeting will be heavy on activities and interaction and light on lecture. Chris wants them to have an experience of themselves, each other, and the team. After initial trepidation, they start warming to the interactive exercises.

The kinds of conversations they have with one another are ones they would probably never have outside of this context. They get to know each other from different angles and start building some bonds based on shared perspectives and different commonalities of the various Types.

The LT is largely an analytical group of scientists, so there are lots of questions and some skepticism at the outset. Chris encourages everyone to suspend judgment and to go along with the experience.

The energy is high, and most of the team members are able to identify their Enneagram Type.

Throughout the two days, they come to know one another better and talk about how to work with their differences and the benefits of having such a diverse team.

Many of them have some personal insights as well as a better sense of their team members. There is quite a bit of laughter and some groans. Lars offers coaching support to those team members who want to continue exploring. He also commits to continued teamwork using the Enneagram to help the team with their interpersonal interactions. Lars believes that this will help improve their skills at challenging one another and engaging in healthy conflict. He wants to take their work with the Enneagram to the next level so that they can see how their Type influences their styles of decision-making, conflict, and leadership.

All agreed that the meeting was valuable and rate it as a success. Now they need to put some of this into practice. The next few team meetings will reveal the value of investing the time and money in the team. Lars hopes some of them will accept his offer of coaching. He knows that without support, change won't come easily. Let's see what happens.

→ Lars's story continues on p. 253

PART 4

TYPE AND TEAM INTERACTIONS

When we work with others, the possibility to build on each other's strengths and to have conflict is ripe. This chapter examines predictable points of tension, reactive patterns, and synergies between all of the possible Enneagram Type pairs. It is not meant to be read in one sitting, but rather to be used as a resource to help you do the following:

▸ Harness the strengths of your Type and the Types of those you work with

▸ Be aware of some of the traps you may fall into when working with another Type or someone of your same Type

▸ Better understand how Types differ

▸ Discover your Type, if you are still unsure

AN INSIDEOUT LEADER'S STORY: **PROGRESS**

Lars and Chris confer, and they agree the team has started to jell. Several team members mention that their colleagues in other parts of the organization are envious of all the leadership development they are getting. Few of the team members have ever been exposed to the kinds of thinking and skill building now afforded them. They seem grateful.

During the meetings, participation increases and politeness decreases. The team starts to challenge Lars as well. He is thrown a bit off-guard; "What are you implying?" he hears himself say. His immediate reaction is that his authority is being challenged. He got what he asked for, and now he has to handle it. At least he caught himself and quickly recovered.

A few of them opt for coaching. Meanwhile, Chris is off to do an assessment of several departments that need to coordinate their work with the LT. He is looking to uncover how Lars's team is perceived—their strengths, what they do that should continue, and areas for improvement. Chris will have quite a bit of data to review at their next team off-site.

Lars and Chris anticipate that the team will soon be ready to begin developing a strategic plan. It will take a lot of innovation—outside-the-box thinking—and team trust to develop a great plan.

Caitlin continues to be a supporter and sponsor of the work that Lars is doing, and to pave the way for better sponsorship in the organization. She is still concerned about Lars's executive presence in the board meetings and asks him to work with Chris on it. If he is unable to have influence in those meetings, Lars will have an even more difficult time gaining sponsorship for his vision and strategy.

Lars has some ideas about the innovative strategy he would like to implement, but without support, he will never get approval or funding. He will also need stakeholder engagement, and this is going to be tricky. Chris's assessment will be a valuable resource when it is time to develop their stakeholder engagement plan. Meanwhile, time to up-level his game.

➔ Lars's story continues on p. 257

CHAPTER 8

DYNAMICS AND DISTINCTIONS

This chapter highlights distinguishing characteristics of the Type pairs to help you clearly see how each Type is distinct from the other. If you are trying to guess someone's Type, this section will be a valuable resource. If you are still unsure of your Type, look at the Type pair(s) you are considering to identify how they are distinct and the common behaviors they share.

The "Areas for Interpersonal Conflict" sections focus on some of our predictable behaviors when we are *doing our Type*. In team situations or in any kind of relationship, it is easy for us to trigger each other's reactive patterns, particularly in stressful situations or when the stakes are high.

Most of us are caught in a paradox. In the attempt to have our needs met, we use our tried and true coping strategies and end up creating the exact opposite of what we really want. Coping strategies work in some but not all situations. When we respond out of habit, regardless of the circumstances, we paint a canvas in one color instead of using the many colors available to us.

The "Synergistic Potential" sections illustrate productive Type interactions. When we become self-aware, we have the potential to harness differences and combine strengths of the different Type pairs. This requires us to leave our comfort zone and respond to the other person in a language he or she understands and in a way that is appropriate to the situation.

THE DIFFERENT-TYPE PAIRS

The following sections examine all possible combinations of Types except same-Type pairs. That section follows this one. It is separated out because it is treated in a slightly different way.

TYPE 8, THE BOSS, AND TYPE 9, THE PEACEMAKER

At first they seem like an unlikely pair, but I have run into many 9/8 personal and professional pairs. Each has something the other wants and needs. Types 8 and 9 are each other's Wings; therefore, they understand some of the interiority of the other. Outwardly, their behavior and body language appear substantially different.

AREAS FOR INTERPERSONAL CONFLICT

Type 9s do not like to be controlled or told what to do. When they feel pushed, Type 9s will shut down and clam up. This creates anger on the part of Type 8s, who want to pry their clamshell open. Type 8s will lose trust and question the loyalty of Type 9s when they withhold their opinion or point of view.

Type 8s are always trying to find out where Type 9s stand and what they stand for, and Type 9s are reluctant to make their opinions known for fear of creating conflict. The seeming lack of opinion and self-effacing aspect of Type 9s cause Type 8s to lose respect for them. Type 8 is full of self-confidence and opinions, and wishy-washiness can be seen as a sign of weakness to the decisive Type 8.

What gets Type 9 in trouble with Type 8 is not being forthright and straightforward. When Type 9 feels pushed by Type 8, Type 9 is likely to agree with Type 8 publicly and then do what he or she wants, which angers Type 8. Type 9s often show their anger through this passive-aggressive behavior.

Type 8s' pace is often much faster than Type 9s', and Type 9s can feel, pushed, bullied, and steamrolled by Type 8s. Type 9s will still be reluctant to stand up to Type 8s and instead will dig in their heels. These two can get into a test of wills. Type 8 uses force, and Type 9 uses sheer stubbornness and will shut them out.

SYNERGISTIC POTENTIAL

Type 9 likes the strength, power, confidence, and conviction of Type 8. Type 9 admires Type 8's ability to take on big challenges and confront others. This is someone Type 9 can follow. Type 8s can give direction to Type 9s, and they are willing to take it and implement Type 8s' plans—to a point.

Type 9 is great at seeing all viewpoints and is often humble. Type 8 admires this quality and tends to trust a Type 9. Type 9s often provide the loyalty and followership that Type 8s demand of people in their circle. Generally Type 9 is like the good soldier, willing to implement the plans of Type 8.

They share a Wing and therefore have a sense of the interiority of the other. They are also both instinctual Types, but they use their instincts in very different ways. Type 8 could take a few lessons from the kindnesses that Type 9 often bestows on others. They tend to think of others first before themselves. Additionally, Type 9s see others' points of view, whereas Type 8s are more attuned to their own point of view. Type 8s could also learn to contain some of their anger and expressiveness like Type 9, and to move more methodically and slowly, like Type 9.

Type 9 could learn from Type 8s' vitality—their willingness to experience and use the force of their anger to take action in the world. Type 8 is willing to confront others, and Type 9 needs to learn to do this as well and to realize that the relationship will survive the confrontation and will likely be strengthened by it. Rather than withdrawing, Type 9 needs to stay in the game. Type 8s are expressive of their viewpoints and opinions, and Type 9s could learn to access and share their own point of view, as well as to connect with their own desires and act on them, not just accommodate others.

TYPE DISTINCTIONS

TYPE 8 | TYPE 9

TYPE 8	TYPE 9
LEADS	FOLLOWS
DIRECT	INDIRECT
CONFRONTS	AVOIDS
PUSHES	WITHDRAWS
OVERCONFIDENT	UNDERESTIMATES SELF
RISK TAKER	RISK AVOIDANT
SHAKES IT UP	STABILIZES
LIKES CHANGE	LIKES PREDICTABILITY
IS FRONT AND CENTER	IS BACKSTAGE (secretly wants to be the star)
ACTS OUT ANGER	SUPPRESSES ANGER
ACTS ON INSTINCTS	REPRESSES INSTINCTS
IS FAST AND IMPATIENT	IS SLOW AND STUBBORN
IS WILLFUL	IS WILLFUL

 AN INSIDEOUT LEADER'S STORY: **A DIFFICULT TEAM MEMBER—TONY**

As you might imagine, not everyone on the team buys into the new world. There are a few skeptics and naysayers who show their stripes either through resistance during the meetings or in side conversations outside the meetings. The face of their resistance looks like arms crossed, lack of engagement, arriving late, or showing up unprepared. At times, their resistance is more overt and takes the form of criticism without offering solutions.

Everyone wants to be on a winning team, but those who are fearful of losing their job when layoffs come hedge their bets and keep their feet in both worlds.

Tony is one who is overtly critical of Lars. Tony resents Lars because he wanted his job and instead Lars was brought in. It was a real blow for Tony. Instead of looking to understand why he wasn't promoted and how he can improve his leadership skills, he is angry and blames others. Tony has worked hard for many years and thinks he deserves a promotion. He sees this as a fairness issue.

Tony self-identifies as a Type 1, the Perfectionist, on the Enneagram and is easy to spot when he is doing his Type. His stance, "I'm always right" and "I know what's best," leaves little room for team members to challenge his ideas.

Lars has asked the LT to show some vulnerability and step outside their comfort zone, but Tony will not open up or admit to anything. When he receives feedback, it backfires. It just makes him more wary and withholding. He continues to resist. He holds on to his anger, which comes out as sharp-edged criticism.

Lars and Chris wonder if, in addition to his disappointment over not being promoted, Tony is fearful of being laid off when the next round of layoffs is announced. He must suspect that he is at risk. The feedback he received when he was turned down for the job, through performance appraisals as well as informally, was that his work is not up to par. His team is not producing. They are demoralized because nothing they do is good enough.

Tony has been given concrete steps he can take to right the ship if he chooses to do so. But he has a very difficult time hearing critical feedback. Rather than taking it in and making some changes, he becomes angry, defensive, and resentful. He blames others for his own failings and believes that he is being unfairly singled out.

Lars remains committed to Tony's success but finds no openness or willingness to look inside and make a shift. Tony refuses the offer for coaching support. If Tony is unwilling, Lars thinks there is little he can do. It is unclear how much more time Lars will give Tony to make a turn around. His patience is wearing thin.

Tony's direct reports have lodged complaints about him. He has been described as impatient, a micromanager, authoritarian, and someone for whom nothing that people do is good enough—he reworks their work. At this point, he is better suited to being an individual contributor than a team leader. He is so terrified of making mistakes that his team is paralyzed.

Many of his troubles stem from some of the less healthy Type 1 behaviors described above. It seems the stress of the job, all of the change, and the impending layoffs have brought out his worst. Lars attempts to reach him through one-to-one conversations. Tony is forthright and says, "Look, I disagree with the direction you are taking our organization. I don't think it's the right way to go. You shouldn't ... "

Lars feels admonished. Tony avoids responding to the claims made by his team and the concerns Lars expressed. He seems intractable. This brings up Lars's insecurities and issues around loyalty. Tony holds his ground, and Lars believes that Tony is trying to sabotage and outlast him. Unfortunately, Lars hasn't developed trust with Tony and is unable to reach him.

Lars has a history of putting too much focus and energy into a couple of problem people. He second-guesses himself, waffles, and wonders about the impact on the team if he fires Tony and whether it will have a detrimental effect on the progress they have made. He feels a sense of responsibility for Tony, too. Lars is frozen with indecision (Type 6).

➜ Lars's story continues on p. 354

TYPE 8, THE BOSS, AND TYPE 1, THE PERFECTIONIST

Types 8 and 1 can initially mistype as each other and be mistaken by other people. Yet they are quite different, and upon closer examination, they are very different. They have distinct reasons for why their attitudes and behaviors may appear similar to each other's.

They both express anger, but differently. Type 8's anger feels more like a blunt instrument, and Type 1's anger comes in outbursts or can be more sharp, condemning, and shrill. Type 8 seeks justice and wants to right the wrongs, whereas Type 1 sees things more as right or wrong and wants to *teach* people what is the right thing to do and the right way to think and be, and to act with integrity.

AREAS FOR INTERPERSONAL CONFLICT

Type 1 is more inclined to be socially proper, and Type 8 is more inclined to be socially robust, to be visible, and to use language that some consider vulgar; this can irk Type 1.

Type 1s are likely to be methodical and make sure that their work is of the highest quality. This can take more time than Type 8 is comfortable with, because Type 8 would prefer to just get the job done.

Type 1s can be prone to anxiety and worry and wanting to look good. They want to be seen as good and right. They can have sleepless nights worrying about Type 8s' (or anyone's) reaction or lack of response. Type 8s can seem to let arrows and swords bounce off of them; yet secretly they do care what people think and have a teddy bear inside of the ferocious grizzly bear—they want reassurance that they are OK.

When Type 8 takes big risks (and it goes wrong!), Type 1 can become blaming and critical or take the righteous, moral high road. Type 8 is liable to take many large and calculated risks, and some will work and others will fail. Type 8s believe in themselves and want people in their circle to believe in them, too. These types of risks, especially if they offend the integrity and principles of Type 1, can be a source of conflict.

If Type 1 is the boss, Type 8 can feel very constrained and microman-aged. Type 8s are rule benders, and Type 1s are rule followers, and that entrepreneurial spirit of Type 8 will be dampened quickly. If Type 8 is the boss, Type 1 is free to innovate and take risks, something that Type 1 may not be as comfortable doing; Type 1s like to have direction and parameters, and they *do not* like to deliver a mediocre or less-than-perfect work product.

They are both anger Types, and the blustery and angry outbursts of Type 8 can be extremely offensive to a Type 1. Type 1 can have a sharper, more condemning and authoritarian type of anger that can both enrage a Type 8 and make him or her feel like a child being scolded. They both have a great need for control, and it can become of war of wills.

SYNERGISTIC POTENTIAL

Types 8 and 1 can make a very productive pairing when they use their differences as strengths. Type 1 is very responsible and follows through, handles the details, likes and imposes structure, and takes care of business. This can be reassuring for Type 8, who likes to be out there on the forefront, battling the world and dealing with the big hairy audacious challenges! Type 8s know they can relax because Type 1 is taking care of business on the home front. Type 1s appreciate the *make it happen / take charge* abilities of Type 8. It gives them a sense of security.

Where the two of them can really join forces for a common goal is that they both want to make the world a better place—Type 8s through seeking justice, righting wrongs, and using their force of will to take on the world, and Type 1s through their high ideals, their morals, and their desire to make reform through pet projects, politics, policy change, and structural change. If Type 1 is aligned with the vision and values of Type 8, he or she will be a great implementer of the vision, putting order and structure to the plan.

Type 8s can learn to honor and respect boundaries from Type 1. They can learn about being responsible and dutiful to others, not just to expect it from others. They can learn to be better planners, to be methodical, and to have respect for structure, quality output, and details. Type 1 also offers a perspective on risk (compliance, implications, and so on) to the often-risky ventures of Type 8. It would be wise to listen to the counsel of Type 1.

Conversely, Type 1 could learn to move a bit faster, be less risk adverse, and strive for excellence and not perfection. Type 1 could also learn to operate with a bit less planning and structure like Type 8, and to see things as more colorful and let go of living in a black-and-white world. Truth can be, and often is, contextual, as Type 8 teaches.

TYPE DISTINCTIONS

TYPE 8 | TYPE 1

TYPE 8	TYPE 1
BENDS THE RULES	FOLLOWS THE RULES
WANTS JUSTICE	WANTS TO BETTER THE WORLD
ACTS OUT ANGER	CONTROLS ANGER
IS LUSTY	IS MORALISTIC AND RIGHTEOUS
IS STRATEGIC AND VISIONARY	IS FOCUSED ON STRUCTURE AND TACTICS
TAKES ACTION AND DEALS WITH THE CONSEQUENCES	SEEKS PERFECTION—SLOWER TO ACT
ASKS FOR FORGIVENESS	ASKS FOR PERMISSION
WANTS TO GET THE JOB DONE	WANTS TO GET IT DONE RIGHT
CAN DEAL WITH ROUGH EDGES	WANTS QUALITY
SAYS TAKE ME AS I AM	THINKS I'M NOT GOOD ENOUGH
VULGAR LANGUAGE	PROPER LANGUAGE
BLACK AND WHITE (you are in or out)	BLACK OR WHITE (it is right or wrong)
CRITICAL AND JUDGMENTAL (*you idiot!*)	CRITICAL AND JUDGMENTAL (morally superior / the authority figure)

TYPE 8, THE BOSS, AND TYPE 2, THE PEOPLE PLEASER

Surprisingly, Type 8 and Type 2 can be mistyped—sometimes others do it, and sometimes they (especially women) mistype themselves as each other. There are many women who don't want to be seen as a Type 8 because Type 8 embodies the masculine archetype (strong, powerful, dominant, challenges others, assertive, pushy, robust, protector, lusty, rageful), just as Type 2 embodies the feminine archetype (empathic, people pleasing, concerned about their feelings as well as those of others, nurturing, manipulative).

Because a line on the Enneagram symbol connects Types 8 and 2, they share some common behaviors. Particularly under stress, Type 2 becomes quite demanding and pushy. On the other hand, Type 8 can have strong emotional reactions that appear very 2-like.

AREAS FOR INTERPERSONAL CONFLICT

In a work environment, Type 8 wants Type 2 to be more focused on business results and not on people's needs and feelings. Type 2 doesn't like the *crass* nature of Type 8s and their blatant disregard of the impact of their behavior and decisions on others.

Type 8 can appear very insensitive to the empathic Type 2. Type 2 can be put off by the direct, blunt, and sometimes offensive nature of Type 8, which can bring out the manipulative martyr in Type 2. Type 2s are also great at using their powers of seduction on the susceptible Type 8. This is where these two types can bring out the worst in each other.

Type 2s' need for affirmation and appreciation and their proclivity to take things personally is annoying, at best, to a Type 8. Type 8s' insensitivity to how they come across and lack of awareness or interest in the consequences of their behavior can be very upsetting to Type 2.

SYNERGISTIC POTENTIAL

Types 8 and 2 can make a good team and are often drawn to each other. While Type 8 tends to seek power, Type 2 is selectively drawn to be the power behind the power. Type 2 is happy letting Type 8 be front and center while controlling things from behind the curtain. Type 2 provides the loyalty and responsiveness that Type 8 demands.

Type 8 feels cared about and taken care of by Type 2 and admires Type 2's ability to be empathic and warm-hearted. When Type 8 comes home from battling evil in the world, Type 2 is there to provide the caring, hot meal, and tenderness that Type 8 so desires.

Type 8, as we have learned, demands loyalty from within the family, from friends, and in a work environment. Type 2 will provide that loyalty well past the expiration date. In exchange for running things behind the scenes and cleaning up some of the messes left by Type 8, Type 2s earn what they perceive to be the love and appreciation they desire. They also feel a sense of their own power by being a part of what Type 8 is creating. It feeds their image needs as well—being part of something important. Type 2s may put up with a lot of abuse, because they fear the consequences and the retribution that may result from severing the relationship, as well as the loss of that sense of power, protection, and appreciation they receive.

Both Types like to be positive, and this is a good place for them to find common ground. They are both dynamic and like to make things happen, and Type 2 can *draft* on the action and power of Type 8. Type 2 will be there to clean up the messes and suture the wounds.

Type 8s' Integration Point is Type 2. This translates to learning about connecting with their heart and their feelings; to demonstrating that they care and understand; to respecting people's feelings and acknowledging them. Type 2s are aware of how they come across to others and care about the impact of their behavior—an important area of development for Type 8. Type 2s know how to take care of others and pay attention to others' needs in a warm-hearted way. Type 8s can learn about compassion and empathy for themselves and for others.

Type 8 is a great teacher for many of the things Type 2s need to learn: directness, asking for what they want and not trying to seduce or manipulate to get their needs met; not taking things so personally; paying attention to the business issues, not just the people issues; and learning to take charge of their own life. Type 8s are great at receiving, and Type 2 has a lot to learn from them in this regard as well.

TYPE DISTINCTIONS

TYPE 8 : TYPE 2

TYPE 8	TYPE 2
TAKES POWER	IS THE POWER BEHIND THE THRONE
DISRESPECTS OTHERS' BOUNDARIES	INVADES OTHERS' BOUNDARIES
DEMANDS LOYALTY	DEMANDS APPRECIATION
TAKES CARE OF BUSINESS	IS A CARETAKER
STRONG-ARMS PEOPLE	MANIPULATES AND SEDUCES PEOPLE
IS DIRECT	SUGAR-COATS
IS INSENSITIVE	TAKES THINGS PERSONALLY
STEAMROLLS	ENGAGES, INVOLVES, INVITES
IS TACTLESS	IS TACTFUL
IS A VICTIMIZER	IS A VICTIM
IS BUSINESSLIKE	THINKS, IT'S THE PEOPLE!
IS LACKING IN EMPATHY	ANTICIPATES OTHERS' NEEDS
IS DEMANDING	IS DEMANDING
IS A PROTECTOR	IS A HELPER

TYPE 8, THE BOSS, AND TYPE 3, THE ACHIEVER

Types 8 and 3 can appear similar at first. Often, they seek leadership positions; are highly active, engaged, and busy; and make things happen. However, taking a closer look, one can better distinguish between the two and see how they can be a good pairing or spin off the flywheel.

AREAS FOR INTERPERSONAL CONFLICT

When Types 3 and 8 both want to be in charge and run the show, their competitive nature can be their undoing. Type 3s want to be the star of the show, be the best, and win at all costs. Type 8s want to move mountains and take on big challenges, have power and control, and make sure that no one controls them; of course, they like to win, too.

If Type 8 is the boss, Type 3s may secretly believe that they are better suited for the job and try to undermine the authority of Type 8 in order to unseat him or her. Type 8s demand loyalty, and when they uncover someone's disloyalty, that person is unceremoniously dumped. There is a *no-tolerance* policy for disloyalty, and when Type 8 forms an opinion about someone, it is unlikely that he or she will change it.

If Type 3 is the boss, he or she will enjoy the productivity and make-it-happen behavior of Type 8. However, in the case that somehow Type 8 reflects at all poorly on Type 3 in the eyes of Type 3, the micromanaging and making life miserable for Type 8 will commence, and Type 8 will not tolerate this for long. As long as Type 8s are free to run with the ball, bend the rules, and control their destiny, they will get along great. If Type 8s think they are being deceived, duped, or made to look bad in front of others by Type 3 in any way, it's *game over*. However, Type 8s may go through a lot of personal anguish first, as it will deeply undermine their self-confidence and sense of power and control.

SYNERGISTIC POTENTIAL

Types 8 and 3 can work together well, in that Type 3s will excel at promoting, marketing, and creating the right image for their family or business, while Type 8 will be the one to create the opportunities to take on big challenges and be the engine in the machine. Both are active doers—Type 3 being highly focused on the goal and efficient in getting there. Type 8 may be the one with the clearer vision of the goal and will be focused on removing the obstacles. Type 3 will have more tact and possibly suitable behavior to fit some of the social and business situations, and is best taking the lead in cases where image and tact are required. Type 3s are skilled at morphing their image to suit changing circumstances.

Type 8 is more inclined to brute force and can learn finesse from Type 3, as well as some of the more subtle and diplomatic ways to move through life and make things happen. Type 8s can also learn to keep their eye on the goal like Type 3, rather than being derailed by yet another challenge or the need for revenge when they believe they have been wronged.

Type 3 can learn more transparency and straightforwardness from Type 8. There is something refreshing about Type 8's direct, no-nonsense approach, from which Type 3 can benefit. Type 3 could also learn more about loyalty—both offering it and respecting it when it is given. Type 3s are prone to be solo performers, and while both Types know to surround themselves with people who complement their skills, Type 3s could learn from Type 8 to appreciate and take care of those in their circle.

TYPE DISTINCTIONS

TYPE 8 | TYPE 3

TYPE 8	TYPE 3
IS ASSERTIVE	IS IS ASSERTIVE
IS CONFIDENT	IS CONFIDENT
IS FOCUSED	IS FOCUSED
COMPETES TO WIN	COMPETES TO BE THE BEST
IS IMPATIENT	IS IMPATIENT
IS A DOER	IS A DOER
IS A BIG RISK TAKER	TAKES CALCULATED RISKS
BUILDS EMPIRES	BUILDS EFFICIENT STRUCTURES
WANTS JUSTICE, POWER, AND CHALLENGES	WANTS SUCCESS AND ADMIRATION
IS A PROTECTOR AND PATRIARCH/MATRIARCH	BELIEVES PEOPLE SERVE AS A MEANS TO THEIR ENDS
LEADS	LEADS
IS A VISIONARY	HAS THEIR EYE ON RESULTS
DOESN'T SHOW VULNERABILITY	DOESN'T SHOW VULNERABILITY
IS WARM AND GREGARIOUS	IS COOL AND CIRCUMSPECT
SAYS, *take me as I am*	IS A CHAMELEON
IS EFFECTIVE	IS EFFICIENT
IS DIRECT	TELLS YOU WHAT YOU WANT TO HEAR
IS ROUGH	IS POLISHED
SEEKS VENGEANCE	IS RUTHLESS
PROTECTS VULNERABILITY	IS GUARDED
THINKS, *I am who I am*	THINKS, *I don't know who I really am*

TYPE 8, THE BOSS, AND TYPE 4, THE INDIVIDUALIST

Types 8 and 4 couldn't be more different, in what motivates them and in how they act. However, they can both be emotionally explosive, which is why some people mistype as one or the other. Their differences, though, quickly come to light. Type 8 tends to lack the sensitivity that Type 4 has in spades, and this is where the differences become most stark.

They both have something the other needs, and when they see each other as their teacher or can play to each other's strengths, these two can be a powerful pairing.

AREAS FOR INTERPERSONAL CONFLICT

Both Types can be intense, like a good fight, and be emotionally explosive. Type 8 can fight with a club and brute force; and Type 4 can fight with sharp-edged objects, move into martyr and victim mode, and then retreat—which will anger Type 8. Type 4 will see Type 8 as insensitive, lacking in empathy, clueless, and uncaring, while Type 4 desperately wants to be understood and seen, cared about, and soothed. Type 4s will hang on to their hurt for a long time, while Type 8s can get their feelings out, think the storm has passed over, and move on. Until they realize that it hasn't …

Type 8s abhor weakness in themselves; thus, when they see others as weak, they react. Because Type 4 is sensitive, temperamental, needing to being seen—and basically a *feeling*-type person—Type 8 will see all of that as weak and will be dismissive and condemning of Type 4.

Type 4s are more self-referenced and have their own way of doing things and own idea about how things should be done. If Type 8s are feeling out of control, they will start clamping down on Type 4s in an effort to regain control. Type 4s can react by withdrawing, which will anger Type 8s, causing them to feel even more out of control and begin questioning the loyalty of Type 4. Type 8 may start to intimidate and place strong demands on Type 4.

SYNERGISTIC POTENTIAL

Type 4 has a sensitivity to people and situations that is often a blind spot for Type 8. The two together can be a powerful combination in this regard, similar to the Types 8 and 2 pairing. Type 4s give tacit permission for Type 8s to express their creative side, which is something they may keep hidden for fear that it makes them appear too *soft* or vulnerable.

Type 4s can offer innovative, creative, and elegant solutions to challenges that complement Type 8s' proclivity for acting impulsively and pushing through decisions through force of will. Type 4s will be more effective at client relations, because they bring sensitivity to client needs, and deeply think through client issues and challenges to come up with creative solutions.

Type 8s will be the ones to take the lead, making things happen and opening doors for Type 4s to step through. They can take a protective, almost parental and tender stance with Type 4s, whom they see as more vulnerable and sensitive to the world.

Type 8s are people of action, and this is often challenging for Type 4s—to take practical and purposeful action in the world, to go after what they want, to be objective about their gifts and talents, and not to take things so personally. Type 8s are gifted and manifesting, and Type 4s are likely to be more comfortable longing for what they don't have rather than going after it. Type 4s are in constant search of their unique identity, a way to uniquely express themselves.

Type 8s are deeply connected to their instincts and are willing to take action on them. They tend to look forward in life, and Type 4s can learn from this, as they often live life looking in the rearview mirror and inside themselves.

TYPE DISTINCTIONS

TYPE 8 | TYPE 4

TYPE 8	TYPE 4
COMMANDS ATTENTION	CREATES DRAMA TO GET ATTENTION
LIKES TO BE RECOGNIZED	LIKES TO BE SPECIAL AND DIFFERENT
IS INSENSITIVE	IS OVERLY SENSITIVE
IS INTENSE	IS INTENSE
ACTS	FEELS
USES SIMPLE LANGUAGE OF ACTION	USES FEELING LANGUAGE
SAYS, *Just do it!*	DOES WHAT THEY FEEL LIKE DOING
EXPRESSES THEMSELVES THROUGH PHYSICAL ACTS	EXPRESSES THEMSELVES THROUGH CREATIVITY AND SENSITIVITY
FOCUSES ON THE FUTURE	FOCUSES ON THE PAST
IS IMPERSONAL	TAKES THINGS PERSONALLY
ACTS OUT ANGER AND RAGE	IS TEMPERAMENTAL AND MOODY
IS ROUGH EDGED	IS SHARP EDGED
QUICKLY MOVES ON AFTER CONFLICT	HANGS ON TO CONFLICT AND HURT FEELINGS
GOES OUT AND GETS IT	LONGS FOR IT
DEMANDS AND PUSHES	WITHDRAWS AND REJECTS

TYPE 8, THE BOSS, AND TYPE 5, THE DETACHED OBSERVER

Types 8 and 5 are a very common pairing, both in business and relationship contexts. They have something the other needs. They sometimes mistype as the other, largely because they recognize themselves in both. Type 5 is the Stress Point of Type 8, and Type 8 is the Integration Point of Type 5. You can find either Type leading organizations, and both can be ambitious and visionary. However, their motivations, styles, and approaches are quite distinct.

SOURCES OF INTERPERSONAL CONFLICT

Neither Type 8s nor Type 5s are necessarily adept in social settings. Type 8s tend to be unaware or uncaring of how they come across and can easily dominate a conversation. Type 5s can appear uncomfortable socially, withdrawing into themselves or the study. Often, when they do engage in conversation, they are likely to draw attention to themselves by telling you about what they know, their area of expertise.

Type 8s tend to speak off the cuff, and to be seen as too direct, insensitive, arrogant, and sometimes rude and crass. They tend to hold court and be the focal point in the room. Yet Type 8s can also be seen as gregarious and lively once they get going. Type 5s will often back off and withdraw in reaction. Type 5s can be seen as socially maladroit; and at times they will walk away from conversations in the middle of them, make abrupt and arrogant comments, or talk at people about their areas of interest with little regard for their audience. Type 8s can become extremely annoyed at Type 5s' lack of social graces and think of them as nerdy and socially unsophisticated.

They can both come across as arrogant and intimidating. Type 8s have the *I know what's best* and *We are going to do it my way* arrogance, and Type 5s have intellectual arrogance. Type 8s can be physically intimidating by using their body, their anger, their force of personality, and their accusations and condemnation. This gives them a feeling of control and keeps people at a safe distance from their heart or other vulnerable areas.

Similarly, Type 5s can be intimidating, because they often look at you without saying a word; and the silence, along with the poker face, feels distant and unapproachable, which is one of the ways they maintain control and keep people at a distance. When that doesn't work, a cutting or cruel remark usually does the trick.

When these two personas meet, there is little trust, which is a significant issue for them both. They can fight, and fight dirty, but Type 5s will usually win the battle (in the short term) because they act indifferent, as if arrows just bounce off of them. Type 5s retreat. They have minimized their needs, allowing them to walk away from a situation and still be intact. This can enrage Type 8s, who feel a complete loss of control.

The biggest source of their conflict is when Type 5s feel pushed, challenged, and invaded by Type 8s, which is often the case. When this happens, Type 5s retreat, and this evokes anger and rage from Type 8s. When Type 8s push more, Type 5s retreat more deeply and take longer to resurface.

SYNERGISTIC POTENTIAL

Type 5s are innovators, and Type 8s are great at bringing innovation into the world. Their energies complement each other. Type 8s are expansive, generally outspoken, gregarious and lively, and quick to act; they follow their instincts and exude power and confidence. Type 5s are more deliberate in their pace and timing, are more contained and poker faced, hold their cards closer to their chest, are focused on developing and sharing their expertise, and can bring needed rigor and depth to the impulsive Type 8s. Type 5s often work behind the scenes and don't focus on drawing attention to themselves. This is good for Type 8s, who command attention and are more than comfortable in that milieu. Can you imagine a Type 8 venture capitalist with a Type 5 inventor? This illustrates their synergy.

Type 8s can learn to deepen their knowledge and expertise—or at least slow down for others to develop it before leaping ahead. They can learn patience. They can also learn to add analytical rigor to their decision making, something Type 5s do naturally. Type 8s can learn to control, contain, and focus their energy, and to be less aggressive and impulsive. Type 8s would benefit from more observation and more curiosity, which are highly developed in Type 5s. Type 8s can also benefit by creating more of a *pull* rather than a *push*.

Type 5s have much to learn from Type 8s about personal power, taking charge, making things happen, and standing up for themselves. Type 5s, like Type 1s, want to control their anger. Type 5s do not like to show vulnerability, like Type 8s. However, Type 5s experience a feeling of loss of control when they show their emotions—when they believe they let someone see that they "got to them." Type 5s can learn to express their emotions and let go of trying to control them—to stay on the playing field rather than detach and retreat.

Type 5s don't often feel like they can handle life's demands, and Type 8s want to take on the world. Type 5s can learn to set boundaries by becoming more grounded in their bodies, much like Type 8s. This would give them the power to stand their ground and take care of themselves without the need to withdraw into their head or withdraw physically to protect themselves. Through the body and the heart, they become more engaged in life. Type 8s are great teachers for this type of full-body engagement with the world.

TYPE DISTINCTIONS

TYPE 8	TYPE 5
ENGAGES	OBSERVES
RELIES ON GUT INSTINCTS	ANALYZES
IS FOCUSED ON THE CHALLENGE	IS FOCUSED ON KNOWLEDGE ACQUISITION AND EXPERTISE
OVERCOMES CHALLENGES	FIXES PROBLEMS AND INNOVATES
IS LOUD	IS CUTTING AND SARCASTIC
IS AT THE CENTER	IS IN THE BACKGROUND
TRUSTS INSTINCTS	TRUSTS MIND
HAS BROAD NETWORK AND FEW TRUSTED FRIENDS	HAS FEW TRUSTED FRIENDS
IS A RISK TAKER	IS A RISK TAKER
IS BOLD	IS SUBDUED
IS PHYSICALLY COMMANDING	IS INTELLECTUALLY COMMANDING
IS ENTERTAINING	IS NERDY
IS A NATURAL PEOPLE LEADER	LEADS WITH EXPERTISE
LEADS BY WALKING AROUND	LEADS BY REMOTE CONTROL
IS FAST PACED	IS SLOWER PACED
LEARNS BY EXPERIENCE	LEARNS THROUGH BOOKS (intellectual pursuits)

TYPE 8, THE BOSS, AND TYPE 6, THE LOYAL SKEPTIC

Types 8 and 6 often mistype and are mistyped. When Type 6s become *counterphobic* (acting against their fears rather than being paralyzed by them), they can appear very 8ish. They can both be emotionally explosive and assertive. At closer look, though, they are very different. The self-confidence and decisiveness of Type 8 are quite different from the insecurity and indecisiveness of Type 6.

If it is a male/female pairing, I refer to them as *Hera and Zeus*, especially if both have more highly developed social instincts. These two can be the consummate power *partners*.

SOURCES OF INTERPERSONAL CONFLICT

Type 8s have grand ideas, think big, and are comfortable taking risks. Type 6s focus on worst-case scenarios and what-ifs. Type 8s perceive this as insecure and cowardly behavior, and feel as if Type 6 threw a bucket of cold water on their ideas and plans. This can lead to belligerent acts by Type 8 and leave Type 6 feeling disregarded or dismissed.

Type 6s can often feel bullied by Type 8s and become tired of playing second fiddle to them, their grand plans, and their need to be on center stage. Type 8 can tire of Type 6s' need for security, lack of self-confidence, need for reassurance, indecisiveness, and doubting nature.

Type 6 tends to be conflict avoidant, and Type 8 tends to be confrontational. This can create issues for the two of them, because Type 6s will deny that they are angry or that something is bothering them; yet they will act out their anger. It is tough for Type 6s to confront other people directly without attacking and blaming. This can erode trust between Type 8s and Type 6s. Type 8s can exact a pound of flesh with their own rage and have a hard time controlling it, once they get going.

When Type 6s get pushy, they can resemble Type 8s. While they both push, neither likes to be pushed. Type 6s have a cutting, sarcastic anger, whereas Type 8s hit you over the head with a blunt instrument. Type 6s don't trust that people are honest about their true agenda and wonder, "What do they really want?" whereas Type

8s have a hard time trusting that people are being straightforward with them about what they think, where they stand, and where their loyalties lay.

SYNERGISTIC POTENTIAL

Type 6s like to be protected and feel safe, and Type 8s like to protect. Type 6 can be very loyal, and Type 8 demands loyalty. Both Types are very active and busy. Type 8s have a more focused and intentional way of being active, while Type 6s keep busy trying to allay their own anxiety. Both can accomplish a great deal when they work in tandem.

As long as Type 6s are willing to follow Type 8s' lead, the two can make a great team. Type 8s are big risk takers, and Type 6s will do what it takes to help Type 8s in their endeavors, all the while warning about what could go wrong. Type 6s have ideas but fear taking the necessary risks to make them a reality. When Type 6s know that Type 8s are standing there, ready to catch them if they fall, Type 6s feel safe taking risks.

Type 8s are impulsive and act before fully thinking things through and weighing the potential consequences. Type 6s can be very helpful to Type 8s by looking at worst-case scenarios and potential pitfalls, as well as creating back-up plans. Type 8s are full steam ahead, and Type 6s pay attention to the dangerous creatures lurking below that can trip up the best-laid plans of Type 8s. Type 6s are skilled at preparing for eventualities that may come. Because Type 8s are very direct and clear about who they are, where they stand, and what they want, they tend to build trust with Type 6s quickly.

Type 8s can learn to pay more attention to the potential downsides of their actions and plans, and to manage to them. Type 6s are gifted at making plans, preparation, and research, and bring intellectual rigor. If Type 8s don't choose to develop those abilities, they will value Type 6s' contribution to their endeavors.

Type 6s' areas for growth include self-confidence, the courage to take action on their ideas, and being less risk adverse—all qualities that Type 8s have in spades. Type 8s trust their gut instincts, and while Type 6s may be aware of their instincts, the voices of self-doubt and *should* usually win. Type 8s have something to teach Type 6s about listening to, trusting, and acting on their instincts. Type 6s can teach

Type 8s about humility, and to slow down and look at the potential consequences of their actions.

TYPE DISTINCTIONS
TYPE 8 | TYPE 6

TYPE 8	TYPE 6
PROTECTS	LIKES TO FEEL SAFE AND PROTECTED
OPPOSES AUTHORITY	PLAYS DEVIL'S ADVOCATE
DEMANDS LOYALTY	IS LOYAL AND RESPONSIVE
GIVES ORDERS	IS RESPONSIVE TO ORDERS
IS A RISK TAKER	IS RISK AVOIDANT
HAS A POSITIVE OUTLOOK	SEES PROBLEMS
IS UNPREDICTABLE	LIKES PREDICTABILITY
IS SOMEWHAT PREPARED	IS OVERPREPARED
IS GOOD IN CRISIS	IS GOOD IN CRISIS
IS BUSY AND PREOCCUPIED	IS BUSY AND PREOCCUPIED
THINKS, *Just do it!*	IS PARALYZED BY FEAR AND ANXIETY
IS QUICK TO ACT	OVERTHINKS
IS OVERCONFIDENT	HAS SELF-DOUBT AND INSECURITY
TRUSTS THEIR INSTINCTS ABOUT PEOPLE	NEEDS PEOPLE TO EARN THEIR TRUST (over and over)
PUSHES	ENCOURAGES
IS JUDGMENTAL	IS JUDGMENTAL

TYPE 8, THE BOSS, AND TYPE 7, THE ENTHUSIAST

Types 7 and 8 can be look-alike types and share some of the same behaviors. They both are assertive, appear confident, ask for what they want, make things happen, can be the center of attention, and naturally lead. Yet, a closer look shows that they are also very different, and the motivations for how they act are different. Because each is one of the other's Wings, they understand the interiority of the other.

They both have one of the same blind spots—their heart. Patience, slowing down, and developing compassion and empathy are things that both need to integrate in their lives. However, at closer look, their differences are revealed. Types 7 and 8 can make a great team when they play to the strengths of both of them and are aware of their points of tension.

SOURCES OF INTERPERSONAL CONFLICT

Neither Type 7 nor Type 8 likes to be told what to do. Type 8s will defy authority and ask for forgiveness (or not) later, and ultimately believe they can do a better job than their superiors. Type 8s want to run the show and have others follow them. Type 7s' approach is to equalize authority—to speak to authority as their equal. If Type 8s try to rein in Type 7s, cut them off at the knees, or take a *power over* and authoritarian approach to Type 7s, this will be a source of conflict for the two.

Type 7s' leadership style is very hands off—"Come to me with questions if you have them; otherwise, I trust you to do your job." What can be a source of frustration for Type 8s is that Type 7 leaders tend to err on the side of trying to implement too many ideas at once and have a hard time closing down options. This type of leadership style will disrupt Type 8s' ability to see a challenge, focus on it, move through or around it, and conquer it. They won't be able to focus and consolidate their energies, and ultimately they won't feel effective or successful. If Type 7 is the boss, Type 8 will be frustrated at the lack of focus and the loose way that things are run.

It would be easy for Types 7 and 8 to get into power struggles, both using their force of will. Because they are each other's Wing, there is a way in which they understand the interior world of the other and have a common need for self-determination. Type 8s can become bored with and uninterested in Type 7s' fascination with theories, models, possibilities, and ideas. Type 8 wants Type 7 to get to the bottom line. "Give me the headlines," "Make a recommendation," "Give me your opinion and back it up," "Make sure you have all your ducks in a row." Type 8 will test you.

SYNERGISTIC POTENTIAL

Type 8s bring solidity and an ability and willingness to push through challenges; and they are more willing to take big risks and go on gut instinct. Type 7 is generally not interested in the responsibility of running an organization, whereas Type 8 has no issue with taking on the responsibility and looks for it. Type 7s value their own freedom too much to take on larger responsibilities for long.

If Type 7s are the boss, they may easily turn over the running of their organization to Type 8s; in fact, Type 7 might look for Type 8 to take charge and run with the ball. If Type 8s are the boss, as long as they give Type 7s plenty of freedom to do their work, be creative, and be autonomous, and Type 7s keep Type 8s informed, do their job well, and are loyal, they will get along well together.

When Type 7s can rely on Type 8s to bring focus and decisiveness, and Type 8s give Type 7s new challenges to spearhead, this can work. Type 7s are not known to micromanage and are happy to be the inspirational and visionary leader. Type 7s bring a more playful and fun spirit into the dynamic, as well as intellectual and analytical rigor. They are well informed and tuned in to the cutting edge. They are also idealistic and want to make a difference in the world.

Type 7s fly off in multiple directions, and Type 8s bring the solidity and forward momentum that Type 7s need. Additionally, Type 8 embodies the *adult archetype*, whereas Type 7 embodies the *Peter Pan archetype* that doesn't want to fully take on adult responsibilities and commit to a person or direction. Type 8 is the perfect teacher for what Type 7 needs.

Type 8s can learn to be more spontaneous, playful, and light, like Type 7s; to appreciate their intellect as much as their gut instincts; and to be patient and respectful of their intellect. Type 7 brings forth an amazing curiosity and sense of wonder about the world and the people in it. Type 8s would do well to develop and value this in themselves.

Type 7s and Type 8s can make a powerful hand-in-glove pair when they see the strengths in each other and harness them.

TYPE DISTINCTIONS

TYPE 8 | TYPE 7

TYPE 8	TYPE 7
IS CONFIDENT	IS CONFIDENT
PUSHES	PUSHES
LEADS	LEADS
BUILDS EMPIRES	BUILDS NETWORKS
IS INTENSE	IS PLAYFUL
IS A PROTECTOR	IS INDEPENDENT
BENDS THE RULES	COMPLAINS ABOUT THE RULES
IS FOCUSED	IS SCATTERED
ACTS FIRST	THINKS AND ANALYZES FIRST
IS QUICK TO DECIDE	IS SLOWER TO DECIDE (WEIGHING OPTIONS)
COMMITS	KEEPS OPTIONS OPEN
IS UNPREDICTABLE	IS SPONTANEOUS
IS IMPATIENT	IS IMPATIENT
IS BLUNT	IS SHARP EDGED
IS A MANIFESTER	IS A VISIONARY
LIKES CHALLENGES	LIKES CHALLENGES
SUBORDINATES AUTHORITY	EQUALIZES AUTHORITY

TYPE 9, THE PEACEMAKER, AND TYPE 1, THE PERFECTIONIST

Types 9 and 1 can seem very similar on the surface, and sometimes they mistype as each other. They both can be very busy doers and have issues with the expression of anger. Type 9s tend to be out of contact with and suppress their anger, whereas Type 1s try to control it. Neither is fond of change when it is imposed, and they both lean toward stability.

SOURCES OF INTERPERSONAL CONFLICT

Type 1 and Type 9 are each other's Wing and therefore have an experience of the other's interiority. Both Types share a propensity to be critical and judgmental. However, you will not often see Type 9s express their criticisms and judgments publicly.

Because Type 1s are practical, task-oriented list makers, and providers of structure, they like to have order around them. Type 9s can evoke their criticism because Type 9s may not attend to the practical, but rather what they feel like doing. Type 1s are ready to take on that to-do list, up and out of bed, ready to go. Type 9s' pace is slower and more leisurely.

Type 1s can be quick to express their irritation and anger, while Type 9s suppress it for fear of creating conflict. Type 9s will use a more passive-aggressive method to demonstrate their displeasure. Their anger can show up as acting noncommittal, clamming up, stubbornness, slowing their pace, and making sharp comments that can appear to come of the blue.

If Type 9s believe that someone important to them is being criticized in some way, they will assert themselves to stand up for that person. This is an effort to protect someone as well as to keep the peace. Type 9s have an uncanny ability to see many viewpoints, whereas Type 1s align their words and actions with their inner voice of authority and critic. They often believe they know The Truth, and they are right! This is almost in direct opposition to the way Type 9s operate.

Type 9s will have difficulty working for Type 1s if they are the target of Type 1's critical voice. Type 9 will also have difficulty with the order-imposing, micromanaging style of Type 1. Type 9 likes to be forever young, and Type 1 acts as the responsible adult, so authority issues may surface for Type 9, who can bring out the parental authority style of Type 1.

SYNERGISTIC POTENTIAL

When Type 1s pair up with Type 9s, they will bring structure and order to Type 9s' more creative approach to work. Type 1s will draw attention to quality of process and output, and will ensure that things conform to rules, standards, and regulations. When Type 1s take responsibility, you can count on them to deliver and follow through. Type 9s bring a positive outlook and a steady, calm approach to whatever they do. They are often kind, gentle, warm, and caring, taking a bit of the edge off of the more rigid Type 1s.

Both are action oriented and together can accomplish a lot. Both also tend to have high ideals and may share common values that propel them toward common goals. They both like a certain amount of predictability and tradition. Type 1 can be a grounding, practical counterweight to the sometimes-ethereal Type 9. Type 9 may bring a good-enough attitude to the unreachably high standards of Type 1.

Type 1s can teach Type 9s about connecting more with their anger; taking practical action; being more grounded in the here and now; forming and expressing opinions, wants, and needs; and taking responsibility for, and being an authority in, their own lives.

Type 9s can teach Type 1s relaxation; to slow down; to be more spontaneous and childlike; to tap into their own imagination; to be open to other ways of thinking, other beliefs, and other ways of doing things; and to see more shades of color in the world.

TYPE DISTINCTIONS

TYPE 9 | TYPE 1

TYPE 9	TYPE 1
IS ACCEPTING	STRIVES TO IMPROVE
REPRESSES ANGER	CONTROLS THEIR ANGER
DOESN'T SHARE OPINIONS	EXPRESSES STRONG OPINIONS
SEES ALL POINTS OF VIEW	HAS A CLEAR SENSE OF RIGHT AND WRONG
IS PASSIVE-AGGRESSIVE	HAS SHARP-EDGED CRITICISM AND IMPATIENCE
IS A STABILIZER AND CHANGE AVOIDANT	IS SLOW TO CHANGE
IS INDECISIVE	IS DECISIVE
IDEALIZES THE PAST	IS IDEALISTIC ABOUT THE FUTURE
IS NONCOMMITTAL	COMMITS
HAS ANXIETY AND WORRY	HAS ANXIETY AND WORRY
HAS A CREATIVE APPROACH	HAS A STRUCTURED AND ORGANIZED APPROACH
IS EVEN-TEMPERED	EXPRESSES ANGER AND RESENTMENT
IS EASYGOING	FOLLOWS THE RULES
IS IDEALISTIC	IS IDEALISTIC
IS KIND AND SOOTHING	IS RESPONSIBLE AND GIVES DIRECTION

TYPE 9, THE PEACEMAKER, AND TYPE 2, THE PEOPLE PLEASER

Types 9 and 2 are often mistaken for each other. Both express kindness and can be warm. Both are positive-outlook Types, and both are people pleasers but for very different reasons. Type 9s wish to keep the peace (inside themselves and therefore around them); Type 2s want to feel lovable, and the way they do that is to focus on taking care of others' needs, hoping for appreciation.

Type 9s are self-referenced, meaning that they look to themselves for making decisions, for sense of style, for making change in their life, and for whether or not they will do something, rather than soliciting or inviting input. Type 2s are other-referenced, meaning that they seek approval from others to know that they are OK, look good, are wearing the right clothes, are making good decisions, are decorating in a style that is appealing, and so on.

SOURCES FOR INTERPERSONAL CONFLICT

Type 9s are more contained and withdraw into themselves and away from people when they feel pressured or pushed in some way, or to avoid conflict. Type 2s move toward people when they are scared or upset and need connection. This can create a push-pull between the two.

Type 9s use their energy to maintain their boundaries, so they are not affected by the world around them. This is in response to their propensity to merge with others. It is an either/or for them. Type 9 may feel a bit overwhelmed, smothered, or pushed by the sometimes-demanding nature of Type 2.

Type 9 is well boundaried, and Type 2 has much softer boundaries. Type 2 can feel a deep sense of loss of connection when Type 9 withdraws, can take it very personally, and can feel hurt by Type 9's need to have time away and alone. Type 9s can feel invaded by Type 2s, who may ignore others' emotional and physical boundaries in their need to maintain a relationship connection in order to feel valued and lovable.

Type 2s can be emotionally explosive and demanding, sending Type 9s right into their shell. Type 9s' disappearance, both energetic and physical, can create a lot of emotional angst for Type 2s and often precipitates the conflict that Type 9s try to avoid. Type 2s can feel shut out and a loss of connection. It is easy to see this push-pull dynamic.

SYNERGISTIC POTENTIAL

Both will be kind and caring of each other, tend to avoid conflict, and are active. Type 2 is generally seen as a "people person" and is likely to be the social one in a work or love partnership. Neither Type is necessarily goal oriented, and both can be good team players. Type 2 is, more often than not, focused on people and relationships. Type 9 is attuned to others' points of view and is accepting of differences. Type 2 is tuned in to helping others and anticipating their needs, and Type 9 focuses on accommodating others' needs. They are both drawn to work as facilitators in many fields, such as education and business.

Type 2s have the *come on, let's go* energy that can pull Type 9s out of their complacency. Type 2 can have a hedonistic, fun sensibility and energy that can enliven Type 9. Type 9s will appreciate Type 2's sensitivity to their feelings and their empathy.

Type 9 is more contained and boundaried, and can be a good role model of this for Type 2. Type 9 tends to be more objective, whereas Type 2 takes things personally. Learning to be more objective will serve Type 2 quite well. Type 2s can teach Type 9s about contacting their feelings and vitality, about expressing love and affection, and about partnership.

TYPE DISTINCTIONS

TYPE 9 | TYPE 2

TYPE 9	TYPE 2
ACCOMMODATES	HELPS
FIXES THINGS	FIXES PEOPLE
SEES ALL POINTS OF VIEW	SEES WHAT OTHERS NEED
IS SELF-REFERENCED	IS OTHER-REFERENCED
IS CALM	IS EMOTIVE
WITHDRAWS WHEN PUSHED OR IN FEAR	MOVES TOWARD PEOPLE WHEN FEARFUL
IS AFRAID TO LOSE CONNECTION	IS AFRAID OF NOT BEING VALUED
THINKS, *I am nobody special*	THINKS, *I am not lovable*
IS HIGHLY BOUNDARIED	CROSSES OTHERS' BOUNDARIES
IS THOUGHTFUL	IS THOUGHTFUL
SEEKS HARMONY	IS PEOPLE PLEASING
IS INCLUSIVE	IS INCLUSIVE
IS IMPERSONAL	IS PERSONABLE
IS OBJECTIVE	TAKES THINGS PERSONALLY
IS CONSIDERATE AND KIND	IS CONSIDERATE AND KIND
IS PASSIVE AND RECEPTIVE	REACHES OUT AND MOVES TOWARD
HAS A POSITIVE OUTLOOK	MAKES A POSITIVE REFRAME

TYPE 9, THE PEACEMAKER, AND TYPE 3, THE ACHIEVER

Types 9 and 3 make an interesting pair. When Type 9s are emotionally healthy, they automatically begin to adopt some healthy Type 3 behaviors, such as focused action toward their goals and dreams, and letting their star shine. They wake up from a dreamlike state. On the other hand, when stressed, when there is conflict, or when the stakes are high, Type 3s will check out like average and unhealthy Type 9s. They become stubborn, withdraw, and lose contact with their vitality.

SOURCES OF CONFLICT

If Type 9s start becoming complacent—if they don't take on the tough conversations with their colleagues, boss, or direct reports—Type 3s will quickly pounce on them. Conversely, Type 9s may tire of Type 3s' need to be the star. This is secretly what Type 9s desire for themselves. They may resent Type 3's need to be center stage and have general disdain (though they may not show it) for people who want to stand out.

Type 3s are one of the Assertive Types, and Type 9s can feel pushed, challenged, and manipulated by them. Type 3s are masters of a *just do it*, take-action, goal orientation, and of efficiency. Type 9s' more complacent style—*don't stir the pot*, take things slowly—plus their desire to hear all points of view and their focus on stability can create a polarizing effect.

Relationships take a backseat to the goals for Type 3s, who appear shiny and polished. The more self-effacing, bland, easygoing, and stubborn Type 9s, who don't like to be pressured, could aggravate Type 3s. Type 3s may see Type 9s as obstacles on their path to the goal, and may decide to move Type 9s out of the way.

SYNERGISTIC POTENTIAL

Under normal circumstances, Type 9s will quietly go about their work and will take a backseat to Type 3, and happily do so as long as they are left alone. Type 3s will see Type 9s as a natural extension of themselves and expect that they will do what it takes and make Type 3 look good. As long as Type 9 is given lots of autonomy, this can work.

Type 9s appreciate and admire Type 3s' ability to make things happen, ability to win people over, and vitality. Type 3s can be truly heroic in their quest for success. Type 9s will value the autonomy that Type 3s give them to do their work. Type 9s may also enjoy the competitive nature of Type 3s, even though it goes against their egalitarian outlook.

Type 3s value the stabilizing effect of Type 9s, especially when coming out of a time of change. Additionally, they can see value in Type 9s' kind, easygoing way with people, and their ability to smooth things over, especially after Type 3s have created lots of turbulence. They appreciate the calm steadiness of Type 9s and their ability to function autonomously.

Type 9s can learn to take focused action toward a goal; that there are times to let themselves shine and make their voice heard; that healthy competition can be a positive force; and to take risks and shake things up from time to time.

Type 3s can learn to relax and slow down, be more humble, pay attention to other viewpoints, and be kinder to others; can learn that effectiveness is as important as efficiency; and can learn that healthy competition is good, but competition at any cost, only to win, is counterproductive. This is some of what Type 9 and Type 3 can offer each other.

TYPE DISTINCTIONS

TYPE 9 | TYPE 3

TYPE 9	TYPE 3
IS BEHIND THE SCENES	IS FRONT AND CENTER
WANTS AUTONOMY	WANTS TO WIN
IS A PEOPLE PLEASER	DECLARES, PEOPLE PLEASE ME
IS TACTICAL	HAS GOALS
SEEKS PEACE AND EASE	SEEKS SUCCESS AND ADMIRATION
THINKS, *I'm nobody special*	THINKS, *I'm not worthwhile or valuable*
IS ACTIVE: DOES WHAT THEY FEEL LIKE DOING	IS ACTIVE: FOCUSED ACTION TOWARD GOALS
SEES MANY POINTS OF VIEW	SEES CONTEXT AND FITS IN
IS RELAXED	SAYS, *just do it!*
IS A STABILIZER AND COMPLACENT	IS A CHANGE MAKER
WANTS TO GET ALONG	WANTS SUCCESS
LACKS CONFIDENCE	IS OVERCONFIDENT
WANTS OTHERS TO SHINE	WANTS TO SHINE AND BE THE STAR
HAS A POSITIVE OUTLOOK	IS OPTIMISTIC
IS CONFLICT AVOIDANT	IS CONFLICT AVOIDANT
IS ACCEPTING	IS STRIVING
SEEKS COMFORT AND SECURITY	SEEKS EXCITEMENT AND AMBITION

TYPE 9, THE PEACEMAKER, AND TYPE 4, THE INDIVIDUALIST

Types 9 and 4 can be look-alike Types. Both withdraw when they are stressed or upset, but they look very different when they do. Usually there is some drama involved when Type 4s pull away, whereas Type 9s *check out* and quietly become unavailable or close up like a clamshell.

SOURCES OF CONFLICT

They can mutually reinforce each other in ways that are unhelpful. Both Types have a predisposition to miss the mark and never take aim at practical action toward their goals or vision. They both like to do what they feel like doing and not necessarily what is practical or purposeful. This could be a source of conflict when they are working together or in a relationship, and each is waiting for the other to take action.

SYNERGISTIC POTENTIAL

In many ways, these two Types are quite similar, but their outward style is very different. They benefit each other when Type 4s support Type 9s to make their mark on the world and give them permission to stand out, stand up, and be counted. Type 9 can help Type 4 with the opposite—stop striving to be different and unique; there are times when blending in is a good approach.

Type 9 often feels invisible and will appreciate being *seen* by Type 4. This can build a strong bond between them. The calm, accepting nature of Type 9 will be greatly appreciated by the more tempestuous Type 4. Type 4s long to be accepted for who they are, and Type 9s are just the people to do that. Because they both withdraw in a stressful situation, they will relate to that aspect of each other.

Professionally, these two could be a very creative pair. They both feel comfortable in the imaginary realm and enjoy bringing their creative expression out into the world. Type 4s like to create beauty around them and could spice up the otherwise more simple and plain Type 9s.

The easygoing and accepting nature of Type 9 is a good counterpoint to the more temperamental and moody nature of Type 4. Type 9s are so conflict avoidant that being with Type 4s could help Type 9s become more comfortable letting out their own emotions and strong feelings. Conversely, Type 4s could learn not to be run by their own emotions.

Type 9s have a keen ability to see multiple viewpoints, and Type 4s could learn to be more objective and see that their feelings about others are not always *the truth*. Type 9s will appreciate the sensitivity of Type 4s and their willingness to go into the depths of their feelings—a place that is not necessarily comfortable for Type 9s.

Type 4s are mired in the past and what went wrong, whereas Type 9s idealize the past. Both can be teachers for each other and support each other to experience life in ways that they typically don't.

TYPE DISTINCTIONS

TYPE 9   TYPE 4

TYPE 9	TYPE 4
IS PRIVATE	IS PRIVATE
IS KIND TO OTHERS	IS SENSITIVE TO OTHERS
DOES WHAT THEY FEEL LIKE DOING	DOES WHAT THEY FEEL LIKE DOING
IS EASYGOING	IS TEMPERAMENTAL
IS IMAGINATIVE	IS CREATIVE
SEEKS CONNECTION AND AUTONOMY	SEEKS CONNECTION AND AUTONOMY
HIDES SENSITIVITY	EXPRESSES SENSITIVITY
WANTS TO BLEND IN	WANTS TO STAND OUT
IS EASYGOING	IS TEMPERAMENTAL AND MOODY
IS DREAMY	HAS DREAMS AND LONGS FOR THEM
IS ACCEPTING	FEELS LONGING
IS RESERVED	IS EXPRESSIVE

TYPE 9, THE PEACEMAKER, AND TYPE 5, THE DETACHED OBSERVER

Types 9 and 5 can be look-alike Types. They both contain or conserve their energy and vibrancy, withdraw when they are feeling stressed and pushed, can appear quite stubborn, have a slow pace, are unlikely to take initiative in relationships, and tend to lose focus on the practical in deference to what they feel like doing in the moment.

POTENTIAL SOURCES OF CONFLICT

Type 9s avoid confrontation and are not in touch with strong feelings or emotions, particularly anger. When pushed, they have been known to make withering comments that can be quite hurtful. Type 5s don't like to lose control, and instead of expressing anger directly, they will make biting, cutting, and sarcastic comments or emotionally detach. Type 5s use their strong intellect to swat at you. Between these two stubborn Types, there can be a standoff. It's a guess as to who can outlast the other.

Both Types lose contact with their vibrancy, instinctual energy, and life force, and this is their mutual blind spot. Type 9s suppress their anger and are unaware of it, whereas Type 5s try to maintain control of their anger, emotions, and expression of feelings. Type 9s suppress their vital energy and are therefore often unaware of its lack. Because of this, they can come across as both dreamy and having a flat affect. Others may perceive Type 9s as boring and without opinion or direction.

Type 5s, on the other hand, rely on their intellect. They tend to conserve their energy and focus it on their innovative, analytic, theorizing mind. They come across as rather controlled. They live in their world of ideas about life and often confuse it with actually experiencing life. This gives them the appearance of the absent-minded professor who forgets to take care of the practical matters of life and the physical world.

Together, they can both be busy. Type 9s can be quite active, whereas Type 5s can be busy reading, in front of the computer, taking courses, or acquiring information in some way. Their busyness is a way of self-forgetting; and again, this is their mutual blind spot and a potential source of frustration that they may have with each other.

There may not be much visible conflict in this relationship, because they both withdraw and avoid, and they are both self-referenced, so they may not seek the other out. This could be a very quiet relationship. Type 5 can be quite ambitious and goal oriented, and may be frustrated by the lack of ambition in Type 9.

SYNERGISTIC POTENTIAL

They are likely to get along well because they share a similar pace, don't cross each other's boundaries, understand the need for private space and time, and have a kind of *live and let live* stance on life. Type 5's need for acceptance will be met here. They will appreciate the kind, caring nature of Type 9 and be able to let down their guard a bit and relax.

Type 9's need for autonomy will also be met in this relationship. Like the Type 4–Type 9 pair, these two share a profound connection to the imaginary realm. There is a lot of creative potential they can tap into. When Type 9s are willing to let go of the belief that they are nobody special and are ready to become more visible in the world, they can share and participate in the ambitions and plans of Type 5s. When both become more grounded in their bodies, their potential for manifestation is great!

If they can honestly see themselves in the other, they may be able to have some profound insights about their own blind spots. Type 5s can learn from the kind and considerate Type 9s, who think of others and extend themselves on behalf of others. They can also learn from the humility of Type 9. Type 9s are more in touch with their childlike innocence, which Type 5s seem to have lost at an early age.

Type 9s can learn from the focused ambition of Type 5s, to be more curious about how the world works, and to deepen their understanding of life. Type 5s are deep thinkers and generate innovative ideas, which they bring into tangible form. Type 9s can learn about this from Type 5s.

TYPE DISTINCTIONS

TYPE 9 | TYPE 5

TYPE 9	TYPE 5
WITHDRAWS ENERGY AND GOES INTO CAVE	WITHDRAWS INTO WORLD OF IDEAS AND INTO CAVE
IS CREATIVE	IS INNOVATIVE
DOES WHAT THEY FEEL LIKE DOING	DOES WHAT THEY FEEL LIKE DOING
IS DISCONNECTED FROM ANGER	CONTROLS ANGER
IS WARM AND KIND	IS DISTANT AND WILL USE REASONING SKILLS TO HELP
LEADS FROM A DISTANCE	LEADS FROM IVORY TOWER
IS INDECISIVE AND A CONSENSUS BUILDER	DECIDES AND ANNOUNCES
FINDS IT HARD TO COMMIT	COMMITS AND FOCUSES
RESPECTS BOUNDARIES	RESPECTS BOUNDARIES
IS PRIVATE	IS SECRETIVE
IS HUMBLE	IS ARROGANT
WANTS AUTONOMY	WANTS AUTONOMY
NEEDS PERSONAL SPACE	NEEDS PERSONAL SPACE
IS RESERVED	IS RESERVED
IS AN IDEALIST	IS A REALIST
IS UNCOMPLICATED	IS COMPLICATED
WANTS TO MAINTAIN CONNECTION	WANTS TO BE UNDERSTOOD

TYPE 9, THE PEACEMAKER, AND TYPE 6, THE LOYAL SKEPTIC

Types 9 and 6 are another interesting pair. I have met many 9/6 couples. Because they share a line on the Enneagram symbol (Type 6 is the Stress Point for Type 9 and Type 9 is the Integration Point for Type 6), they are good mirrors for each other and share some similar patterns of behavior.

SOURCES OF CONFLICT

There is an earnestness to Type 6s, a desire to help and fix that can feel pushy and parental. Their incessant *need to know* can wear down the more patient Type 9s, who often lack an intellectual curiosity and are not prone to research like Type 6s. This need probe into things, and *to know* and understand in order to feel more secure, can feel onerous to Type 9s.

Type 9s are a positive-outlook Type and have a more *stiff upper lip* approach to life. When Type 6s start up with their fear-based *what if* and *the sky is falling* and complain about what is wrong with the world or others, this can really rub Type 9s the wrong way. Type 9s act kind initially but may end up withdrawing because they can't tolerate Type 6s' negativity. It ruins their idealized view of life and the world. They don't want to have to deal with the messiness of life. *And* Type 6 is their Stress Point, so while it is familiar territory, they don't want to be taken there as a reminder of what they can also be like, and they don't want their own fears and anxieties activated.

If Type 9s are stressed, the two become worried and anxious together, and this can be counterproductive. Type 6s can be more active and out in the world, and Type 9s may feel like they are being dragged along unwillingly. Type 6s tend to be more socially minded.

While both Types are conflict avoidant, they have different strategies. Avoidance and smoothing things over is Type 9s' strategy. They tend to avoid expressing strong opinions or raising issues with people. This makes them rather easygoing and generally likable. However, by avoiding conflict, they are actually inviting it and encouraging the prying they so dislike. Type 6s' strategy is to act out their anger by doing things they think might hurt you in some way to retaliate, making a preemptive strike, or making a cutting remark; but they are unlikely to address the issue head-on. Both Types want to avoid conflict, and their avoidance of conflict or denial of problems or issues can be a source of difficulty for them.

Type 6s' need to know can feel intrusive, and Type 9s tend to be very boundaried and private. Type 9s can feel pushed, invaded, and overwhelmed by Type 6s' anxiety. Because Type 9s are more in the moment, this planning and preparing for all contingencies by Type 6 could either be welcomed or feel constraining.

SYNERGISTIC POTENTIAL

Type 9s are easygoing, and this is not a word usually applied to Type 6s, who are often anxious, worried about what could go wrong, and mistrusting of others' motives. Type 6s will appreciate the accepting nature of Type 9s and the calm steadiness that can help them to relax and feel better about themselves. Type 9s can provide the stability and the rudder in the water that gives Type 6s more confidence that they can ride out the storm. Type 9s also instill trust in Type 6s because of their kindness, warmth, and lack of reactivity to the stormier moods of Type 6s.

Type 9s appreciate Type 6 as a fellow playmate and adventurer in life. Type 6s provide the vitality and energy to propel the two forward. Type 9s also appreciate the planning and preparedness of Type 6s, who take care of business and make sure that there are provisions for the family, the business, and so on. Type 9s know that they can count on Type 6s to be responsible for what they have agreed to do.

Type 6s are often skilled in research, marketing, and teaching, and they like to lead teams. Type 9s are good team players, and the two could work well for each other or together. Type 9s are often drawn to working with groups—facilitating, mediating, teaching. Type 6s can be found in the fields of architecture, sculpting, and other arts. I have seen Type 9s drawn to architecture as well. Their interests can be similar and complementary.

Type 9s can learn from the action-oriented Type 6s—from their willingness to research and prepare and move their life forward in a concrete way. Type 6s extend themselves and their energy more into family, community, and their organizations. Type 9s could be more expansive with their time and energy and extend themselves in these directions. Type 6s can learn to take a more leisurely pace in life like Type 9s, who manage to surf the waves of life more gracefully without getting knocked off their board or worrying that they will be knocked off. Type 6s can take cues from the calm steadiness of Type 9s.

TYPE DISTINCTIONS

TYPE 9	TYPE 6
SEEKS SECURITY	SEEKS SECURITY
SEEKS STABILITY	SEEKS PREDICTABILITY
SEEKS AUTONOMY	IS A TEAM PLAYER
IS COUNTERCULTURAL	IS REBELLIOUS
IS CONFLICT AVOIDANT	IS CONFLICT AVOIDANT
IS TRUSTING	IS DOUBTING AND SKEPTICAL
TRUSTS FIRST	SAYS, EARN MY TRUST
GOES INTO FANTASY	GOES INTO ANALYZING
IS OUTWARDLY CALM	IS ANXIOUS
IS SPONTANEOUS	IS PREPARED
IS EASYGOING	IS INTENSE
IS LIKABLE	IS ADMIRABLE

TYPE 9, THE PEACEMAKER, AND TYPE 7, THE ENTHUSIAST

Type 7s come across as confident, socially competent, quick-witted, and high energy. Initially, this can be very compelling for Type 9s, who want more of all this for themselves. Type 7s may feel as if they have found a playmate, someone to go along with their plans, and may appreciate the more contained, thoughtful nature of Type 9s.

SOURCES OF CONFLICT

Pace. Type 7 thinks fast, talks fast, moves fast, and wants to *do it all!* While Type 9s can be very active, they don't want to feel pushed by Type 7s' need for constant activity and their agenda. In fact, the more Type 7s try to pull Type 9s along, the more withdrawn, resistant, and stubborn Type 9s get.

Change. Type 9s like stability, familiarity, and habit. These are almost dirty words to Type 7s, who long for change, variety, and stimulation. Type 9s can feel like a stick in the mud to Type 7s, and Type 9s can be completely overwhelmed and pushed to the point of anxiety and complete withdrawal by Type 7s.

Passive/Assertive. Type 7s can tire of the need to be the engine of the relationship, the one to have the ideas, take action, and make their needs known. Type 9s admire this assertive, *go get 'em* quality and desire it for themselves. At the same time, they feel pushed and inadequate.

Contained/Expressive. Type 9s are more often found in the background, whereas Type 7s are usually in the center of activity or a conversation, and this can be annoying for Type 9s, who think one should play *small* while secretly wanting to be the star. When they try to change each other, this can only result in conflict and distress.

SYNERGISTIC POTENTIAL

They both see life from a positive vantage point and therefore relate to and appreciate that in each other. They can be great playmates and adventurers. Type 9s can be a nice stabilizing force in the more changeable and sometimes chaotic world of Type 7s.

Type 9s can learn from the more action-oriented, assertive, *go after what you want* Type 7s, who take action on their dreams. Type 7s are quite visionary, and Type 9s are more accepting of "what is." Somewhere in between would be beneficial for them both. Confident Type 7s can inspire the more self-effacing Type 9s.

Type 7s are drawn to Type 9s because they know they need to be more contained, introspective, and quiet, and to have more stability—just as Type 9s can learn from Type 7s' dynamism, vision, comfort with change, resilience, and willingness to be expressive of emotion. Type 7s are the yang to Type 9s' yin.

TYPE DISTINCTIONS

TYPE 9	TYPE 7
HAS A POSITIVE OUTLOOK	HAS A POSITIVE OUTLOOK
IS IDEALISTIC	IS IDEALISTIC
IS PASSIVE	IS ASSERTIVE
DOESN'T MAKE WANTS KNOWN	ASKS FOR WHAT THEY WANT
FOLLOWS	LEADS
FOLLOWS	INITIATES
IS SLOW TO CHANGE	SEEKS CHANGE
SEEKS STABILITY	SEEKS VARIETY
IS RESERVED	IS EXPRESSIVE
SEEKS STABILITY	SEEKS CHANGE
IS SLOW	IS FAST
SEEKS AUTONOMY	SEEKS FREEDOM
HAS AN IMAGINATIVE MIND	HAS A SYNTHESIZING MIND
GOES ALONG WITH	GOES OUT AND GETS IT
IS WILLFUL	IS WILLFUL
IS INDIRECT	IS DIRECT
IS CONFLICT AVOIDANT	IS CONFLICT AVOIDANT

TYPE 1, THE PERFECTIONIST, AND TYPE 2, THE PEOPLE PLEASER

Both are busy Types, responsive and responsible. These are people you can generally count on. However, the differences between the two are often quite visible. Type 1s can appear a little distant and reserved, whereas Type 2s are generally a warm embrace. Type 1s are inspiring when their work is aligned with their ideals and values, and Type 2s are likely to be warm, caring leaders who bring people together.

Type 2s don't know when to stop helping and giving, and they completely exhaust themselves in the process. Type 1s don't know when to stop improving themselves and others, because there is no such thing as the perfection that Type 1s seek. They exhaust themselves as they endeavor to improve everyone and everything.

Their shared ideals, responsible nature, and thoughtfulness are sources of connection for the two. People experience both of these Types as devoted friends, colleagues, spouses, and parents.

SOURCES OF CONFLICT

Where these two can tango has to do with what they both respect in the other and value in themselves—their idealism and sense of responsibility—but they may differ in how they demonstrate it. The dance gets awkward when Type 2 feels constrained by Type 1's right/wrong approach. Type 2s are happy to bend the rules to fit the situation, especially when it comes to helping other people. This is generally a no-go for Type 1s, who not only like to make the rules but are happy to enforce them as well.

Type 1s are focused on being *good*, and on quality, structure, and order. They have a moral compass that tells them right and wrong, and they are on a mission to improve their world and themselves. Every nit must be picked. The best analogy I can think of to depict the dynamic tension between Types 1 and 2 is the following: Type 2 is a social worker who is trying to help a family stay together, but the way the laws are written prevents it. The laws don't allow for the context to drive a decision that puts the family front and center. Type 2s are very context oriented, working with each unique situation to define a path forward, and see laws as arbitrary and constraining.

Type 1s believe it is their job to maintain standards and do what is right, which is to play by the rules. They are clear about what lines can and cannot be crossed. They want to be impersonal and objective about people and situations, to be fair. Type 2s can play favorites, which offends Type 1s' sensibilities.

Both believe they are being responsible and doing what is best, and they each have a different worldview that supports and guides their actions. Type 1s are responsible and dutiful to the inner critic, and they believe in objective and logical problem solving—which in this case is concrete and tangible. Type 2s' focus is on others and the feelings of others, and they seek appreciation and approval. Their approach is intangible and contextual.

SYNERGISTIC POTENTIAL

When Type 1 and Type 2 are focused on the same goals, they can play to each other's strengths. Type 1s are great at creating the structure and the plan, tracking progress, attending to quality, and checking for alignment with other aspects of the business. Type 1s can take the ball and run with it, especially when they know what is expected and where they are going. Type 2s will have their eye on the impacts on people, on building relationships, and on the network; and they will have their finger on the pulse of the team, the larger organization, and the clients.

If Type 1s are in charge, Type 2s can be loyal implementers behind the scenes and will clean up any people issues created by the Type 1s. On the other hand, if Type 2s are in charge, they will be out there connecting with people and engaging and involving the voices of the organization. Type 1s are great at putting structure to and organizing what comes out of the data or information gleaned by Type 2s, and they will make sure that business is being taken care of at the office.

Type 1s need a little bit of the warmth and softening of Type 2s, and Type 2s need a little less focus on people and more on structure, goals, and the business at hand. Type 1s demonstrate what Type 2s need—objective problem solving as well as taking care of themselves. Type 2s can help Type 1s to connect with their empathic nature, first and foremost toward themselves.

TYPE DISTINCTIONS

TYPE 1	TYPE 2
IS FRIENDLY	IS WARM
IS PERSONABLE	IS PERSONAL
FOCUSES ON STRUCTURE AND ORDER	FOCUSES ON PEOPLE
FOCUSES ON IMPROVING	FOCUSES ON HELPING
VALUES QUALITY	VALUES CUSTOMER RELATIONS
VALUES RULES AND LAWS	VALUES PEOPLE FIRST
FEELS IMPERFECT	FEELS UNLOVABLE
WANTS TO BE RIGHT, GOOD	WANTS APPROVAL, TO BE A GOOD PERSON
ORGANIZES THE ENVIRONMENT	ORGANIZES PEOPLE
IS RESPONSIBLE	IS RESPONSIBLE
IS RISK AVOIDANT	IS RISK AVOIDANT
OVEREXTENDS	OVEREXTENDS
IS RESERVED	IS EXPRESSIVE

TYPE 1, THE PERFECTIONIST, AND TYPE 3, THE ACHIEVER

Together, 1s and 3s can accomplish almost anything when they join forces. They both like to appear competent and tend to look put together and polished to the outside world. In fact, these two often are mistyped for the other.

SOURCES OF CONFLICT

Areas of tension will be Type 1s' need to have everything just right and follow all of the rules. They have a tendency for such high standards and *staying between the lines* that Type 3s will feel hampered. Type 3s are known for taking efficient action, making things happen quickly, and taking measured risks. They are focused on results and, if not careful, will overpromise and underdeliver. Type 1s can slow Type 3s down because of their focus on quality and perfection. There are times when Type 1s can't see the forest for the trees and lose sight of the goal. Type 3s have their eye on the customer and focus on results! Both are busy and active.

Whether these two are in a working or a romantic relationship, Type 3s will have a tendency to put work, goals, image, and success first and the relationship in the backseat. In fact, Type 1s can feel like just a cog in Type 3s' wheel. When Type 3s are not in contact with their heart's desire and are focused only on their goals, their success, and seeking admiration, this will set off the integrity alarms for Type 1s.

Should Type 3 cut corners to achieve success, Type 1 will become the disapproving authority figure and endeavor to get Type 3 back on track. If unable to do so, Type 1 will lose respect for Type 3 and see them as deceptive. Type 1s are, in fact, the conscience for Type 3s. Type 3s will see Type 1s as rigid and a barrier to success.

SYNERGISTIC POTENTIAL

They are both active and high energy and like to make things happen. Both have high standards, but the drivers for these high standards are different. Both Types can be quite idealistic, and when these high ideals are shared and they both focus their energy on making a difference, they can be quite a force.

Type 1s slow down Type 3s to make sure that quality is attended to, and Type 3s help Type 1s to take risks and let go of the need to have every detail worked through. Type 3s have a great capacity to see opportunity and success, visualize the goals, and take focused action to achieve those goals. They are confident and comfortable promoting themselves to secure success. Type 1 admires this about Type 3 and can be a responsible agent on behalf of Type 3 and their shared vision. Type 1s will be diligent and attend to the details, procedures, and actions to bring ideas into tangible form.

When Type 3s' compulsion to deceive kicks in, Type 1s are the place to look for inspiration. Healthy Type 1s model integrity, quality, thoughtfulness, planning, and high standards.

Type 1s can be inspired by the *just do it* nature of Type 3s, who go out and make things happen. Type 3s can also inspire Type 1s to have bigger goals and aspirations for themselves and to believe in themselves. They can help Type 1s loosen up a little bit, to learn *good enough.*

Type 3s can also lean on Type 1s so that they don't have to do it all alone. Type 1s will work right alongside Type 3s. Type 3s can also look to Type 1s for goals that are more in alignment with their values and less focused on maintaining or creating the right image.

TYPE DISTINCTIONS

TYPE 1 | TYPE 3

IS COMPETENT	IS COMPETENT
HAS HIGH STANDARDS	HAS HIGH STANDARDS
IS TASK FOCUSED	IS A TASKMASTER
WANTS TO BE RIGHT	WANTS TO BE ADMIRED
FOCUSES ON STRUCTURE	FOCUSES ON RESULTS—SUCCESS
FOCUSES ON TASK COMPLETION	FOCUSES ON ACHIEVING GOALS
IS A DOER	IS A DOER
HAS A FEAR OF BEING BAD	HAS A FEAR OF BEING WORTHLESS
IS RISK AVOIDANT	IS A RISK TAKER
FOCUSES ON QUALITY	FOCUSES ON EFFICIENCY
IS CONFLICT AVOIDANT	IS CONFLICT AVOIDANT
DOES IT THE RIGHT WAY	IS EXPEDIENT
IS POLISHED	IS POLISHED
FEARS MAKING MISTAKES	FEARS FAILURE

TYPE 1, THE PERFECTIONIST, AND TYPE 4, THE INDIVIDUALIST

Because a line on the Enneagram symbol connects these two Types, they can be mistyped under certain circumstances. I have seen very 1ish-looking Type 4s and very 4ish-looking Type 1s. The perfectionist can come out in both of them, and their focus is on how things aren't as they should be, but for different reasons. Type 1s look to improve *what is*, and Type 4s long for *what isn't*. They both have high standards and can be uncompromising. At close examination, they are quite different from each other, with different motivational aims, but will have a shared understanding of the other because they are directly connected.

SOURCES OF CONFLICT

Types 1 and 4 are connected by a line on the Enneagram Symbol, which means that Type 1 under stress will take on some of the less healthy behaviors of Type 4, such as being moody, needing to be seen as special, being dramatic, and going into some darker moods. When Type 4 becomes moody and melancholy, it may trigger reactions in Type 1 because this is a part of them they don't like and therefore don't want mirrored to them. Type 1's reaction could be impatience, frustration, and a critical, *pull yourself up by your bootstraps and get on with it* approach.

This may trigger an emotional reaction in Type 4s, because they may feel unseen, misunderstood, or unsupported, and it reinforces their *nobody understands me, I'm different* belief. Type 1s have to be judicious with their critical voice toward the sensitive and temperamental Type 4s. Type 1s are also very action oriented and practical. Conversely, Type 4s have a more leisurely pace and take action on what feels right in the moment.

The tension between the two will be somewhat chaotic. The *I gotta be me* nature of Type 4s means that things can change at any moment, depending on their mood. This can be unsettling for Type 1s, with their need and desire for structure, organization, planning, predictability, responsibility, and practicality. Perhaps Type 4s can loosen up Type 1s a bit, and Type 1s can rein in Type 4s a bit—however, these dynamic pulls will always be at play.

SYNERGISTIC POTENTIAL

What do Type 1s offer Type 4s? Practical, actionable goals, discipline, and structure to the more free-form Type 4s, who need freedom of self-expression. Type 4s are visionary, and Type 1s can provide the structure and practicality to bring their vision to life.

Type 1s are committed and responsive. This will help build trust with Type 4s. Type 1s offer stability to the more emotionally volatile Type 4s, who are often disappointed by others and have a belief that they will be rejected.

Type 4s bring genuineness, sensitivity, and a romantic quality to their relationships. They also bring flair and freedom of style to the more crisp and restrained style of Type 1s.

Type 4s take on the healthier qualities of Type 1s when they are relaxed and are not in the grip of their Type. This is demonstrated most clearly when Type 4s are disciplined enough to take action on their vision. Type 1s can help Type 4s to look outside themselves to get other reference points—to be more objective and less storm-tossed by their changing moods.

Type 1s can learn to take a more leisurely pace like Type 4s. Type 4s also demonstrate sensitivity to others. Because Type 1s excel at checking things off the to-do list and keeping things in perfect order, balancing this propensity with the more relaxed and introspective style of Type 4s will be beneficial. Type 1s are so tuned in to the right way to do things, it is challenging for them to express their creativity, which is also where Type 4s excel.

TYPE DISTINCTIONS

TYPE 1 | TYPE 4

TYPE 1	TYPE 4
IS DISCIPLINED	IS DISCIPLINED WHEN THEY FEEL LIKE IT
FOCUSES ON BEING RIGHT	FOCUSES ON BEING UNIQUE
IS ACTION ORIENTED	4'S MOOD DRIVES ACTION
IS PRACTICAL	IS CREATIVE
IS ACTIVE	IS PASSIVE
IS STRUCTURED	IS SPONTANEOUS
IS COOL	IS WARM
IS RESPONSIBLE TO OTHERS	IS RESPONSIBLE TO SELF
IS FORMAL AND HAS SELF-RESTRAINT	IS EMOTIONAL AND INTENSE
MOVES TOWARD	WITHDRAWS FROM

TYPE 1, THE PERFECTIONIST, AND TYPE 5, THE DETACHED OBSERVER

Types 1 and 5 are look-alike Types. They can be cool and reserved, slightly detached; they like to appear competent; and they act judgmental. Type 1s want to impose order on their outer world, and Type 5s want to impose order on their inner world. They both try to control their anger. Type 1s' anger and hurt leaks out through judgmental comments, criticism, and corrective action. Type 5s use cutting remarks and reject when they are angry enough. Type 5s are detached from their feelings and talk about their feelings rather than have them. They will act angry rather than expressing anger directly.

SOURCES OF CONFLICT

Types 1 and 5 can be triggered by each other's judgmental nature. The socially adept Type 1s have a hard time tolerating the irreverent Type 5s and their style of dress, socially inappropriate comments and behavior. Type 5s don't appreciate the need for such outer perfection and order, either in their physical environment or in their social or business environment, and don't appreciate the attempts by Type 1s to correct and perfect.

Type 1s are idealistic and like to put their energy into reforming people, systems, and themselves. They are challenged by Type 5s' apparent dispassion about righting the world's wrongs. They will perceive Type 5s as solely having intellectual curiosity about the world situation. Type 5s are often private about putting their money and energy into causes that matter to them.

SYNERGISTIC POTENTIAL

In a business context, these two can do quite well together, once they harness each other's strengths and respect their differences. Type 1s can help bring Type 5s' ideas into form, to prioritize and attend to the details.

Type 5s like to problem-solve and innovate—which could be just what Type 1s need. Type 1s respect the focus, expertise, and innovative mind of Type 5s. Type 5s enjoy the predictability, stability, and detail orientation of Type 1s, as well as their ability to implement in a practical, process-oriented, quality-driven way the raft of ideas that Type 5s wish to make tangible.

Type 5s long to be supported, to let down and express needs. Yet they have spent their lives minimizing their needs so that they don't have to rely on anyone. Type 1s can provide some of the support, commitment, and solid ground that Type 5s believe they are lacking.

Professionally, Type 5s tend to take risks, which is not something that Type 1s are prone to do. They tend to be more cautious and like to plan. Seeing how Type 5s are able to take the risk to put their ideas out in the world can be emboldening for Type 1s.

Type 1s are closely aligned with their values and live in accordance with them. This is not necessarily something that Type 5s focus on. Both can use each other as mirrors to see the harm that comes from passing judgment: Type 5s use their intellectual arrogance, and Type 1s use their moral superiority. Type 5s can learn from the social graces of Type 1s, and Type 1s can learn a little more spontaneity, slower pace, and relaxed attitude from Type 5s. Type 1s can be impatient and have a hard time sitting still.

TYPE DISTINCTIONS

TYPE 1	TYPE 5
JUDGES	JUDGES
IS RESTRAINED	IS CONTAINED
REPRESSES ANGER AND EMOTION	CONTROLS THE EXPRESSION OF ANGER AND EMOTION
MOVES TOWARD	WITHDRAWS
IS DISCIPLINED	IS FOCUSED
WANTS TO BE RIGHT	WANTS TO BE THE EXPERT
IS SOCIALLY APPROPRIATE	IS SOCIALLY AWKWARD
CARES WHAT OTHERS THINK	DOESN'T CARE WHAT OTHERS THINK
IS AN OBJECTIVE PROBLEM SOLVER	IS AN OBJECTIVE PROBLEM SOLVER
IS STRUCTURED AND ORGANIZED	MANAGES THE PILES
IS AN IDEALISTIC LEADER	IS AN EXPERT LEADER
IS WELL BOUNDARIED	IS WELL BOUNDARIED

TYPE 1, THE PERFECTIONIST, AND TYPE 6, THE LOYAL SKEPTIC

Types 6 and 1 often mistype themselves as the other. Why is this so? Both Types are busy doers and act responsibly in the world. They are intense in their communication and have strong opinions and judgments. Both have anxiety that propels them into activity. Both can delay pleasure until the hard work is done.

Type 1s want to take action because they are driven by a sense of right and wrong, an idealistic picture of how their world should be, and a duty to help improve and better it. Type 6s are driven by a need to allay their fears about the potential for bad things to happen, both to themselves and others. Type 6s believe that the rug could get pulled out from under them at any time.

SOURCES OF CONFLICT

Dynamic tension occurs when they trigger each other's predisposition for worry and anxiety and their tendency to listen to the *shoulds* rather than what they really want to do.

Type 6s' *should* voice has more to do with their belief that they are the responsible ones; they must act responsibly and do what others ask of them. Type 1s' *should* voice has to do with a need to be the good one, to be perfect, and to conform to an inner authority that has clearly defined lines drawn between right and wrong. Both grow to resent their roles.

Type 6s can feel overwhelmed by their commitments and react against them when they start feeling internal pressure to take responsibility and deliver on expectations. They become reluctant to honor requests, and their behavior can seem selfish and self-centered to others. This reaction can leave Type 1 perplexed and wondering what happened to the otherwise responsible Type 6. Type 1s can tire of taking on the role of the authority figure and trying to be perfect, striving to meet unachievable standards. This can cause them to do things that are contrary to what would be perceived as good, ethical, and moral, leaving Type 6s and others wondering what happened to the otherwise predicable Type 1.

SYNERGISTIC POTENTIAL

Together they can make a good team because both are caring team players who will do what it takes to get the job done. Types 1 and 6 are also the consummate planners. Type 1s pay more attention to outer structure, process, details, and putting order to things, whereas Type 6s focus on team roles and responsibilities, researching solutions, looking for what could go wrong, and making arrangements for those eventualities.

Type 6s are not as likely to stay between the lines as Type 1s are, due to their inherent rebellious nature. They are often a little more playful and irreverent. Type 6s can be quick-witted and are more inclined to overanalyze a situation and be stuck in self-doubt. Type 1s have a clearer decision-making style and use their moral compass—their sense of right and wrong, their ideals, and what the rules say—when making their decisions. Type 1s can help Type 6s with objective decision making. Type 6s can help Type 1s see what potential issues may arise as they implement their plans.

Type 1s play the role of the responsible authority figure, and Type 6s are more likely to play the responsible leader, employee, team player, friend, husband/wife/partner. It is easy to see how they play complementary roles in work and life.

Both Types 1 and 6 have a bias for action and activity. They are both driven by their anxiety, and Type 6s are also driven by their insecurities. Type 1s are active, generally in an disciplined, focused, and structured way. Type 6s can learn from Type 1s in this area because they act impulsively as a way to alleviate anxiety, which might include changing jobs, moving, traveling, taking workshops, continuing education, and so on. Type 6s' insecurity drives a belief that they aren't *enough* and need to know more before they can take focused action toward a concrete goal.

TYPE DISTINCTIONS

TYPE 1	TYPE 6
IS ANXIOUS	IS ANXIOUS
IS RESPONSIBLE	IS RESPONSIBLE
IS HARDWORKING	IS HARDWORKING
IS RISK AVOIDANT	IS RISK AVOIDANT
IS DECISIVE	IS INDECISIVE
IS SELF-EFFACING	IS SELF-DOUBTING
IS COOL	IS WARM
IS LOYAL	IS LOYAL
IS EMOTIONALLY RESTRAINED	HAS EMOTIONAL OUTBURSTS
GIVES SHARP-EDGED CRITICISM	IS SARCASTIC AND CUTTING
MOVES TOWARD	MOVES TOWARD AND THEN WITHDRAWS
IS DISCIPLINED	IS RELIABLE

TYPE 1, THE PERFECTIONIST, AND TYPE 7, THE ENTHUSIAST

They can be look-alike Types because they are both planners, idealists, active, and doers. A line on the Enneagram symbol connects Types 1 and 7, so it stands to reason that they would share some common traits. When Type 1s are relaxed, they can take on some of the healthier Type 7 behaviors. Under these circumstances, the otherwise more restrained and controlled Type 1s become playful and spontaneous, and soften.

Conversely, when Type 7 goes to Type 1 under stress, the playful and fun-loving Type 7 can become sharp-edged, defensive, critical, and tight. Type 7 can also become angry and critical, blaming and judging. Steer clear.

SOURCES OF CONFLICT

The dynamic tension for these Types is the pull between discipline and play, structure and emergent form, advance planning and spontaneity, and following the rules / bending the rules. As long as Type 1s don't start moralizing or criticizing or try to rein in the free-spirited Type 7s, Type 7 will enjoy and benefit from the kind and giving nature of Type 1s and be open to what they have to teach.

However, if Type 7s become too scattered, self-centered, and unreliable, Type 1s will act disapproving and disappointed. Tension between the two will ensue. The critical voice will come out, and Type 7s become frustrated and angry while feeling scolded under the disapproving glare of Type 1s. Type 1s will brand Type 7s as unreliable; and Type 7s will think that Type 1s act like a stick in the mud and are too rigid, and they will shy away from the critical Type 1s.

Type 7s are sensitive to criticism. In the face of this, Type 1s will have to be sparing with their critique and more constructive and supportive, rather than engaging in finger pointing and finger wagging. Type 7s are allergic to the word *no* and prefer to bend the rules, much like Type 8s. The follow-the-rules Type 1s and bend-the-rules Type 7s will have to find a way to *bend* toward each other.

SYNERGISTIC POTENTIAL

Types 7 and 1 can make a powerful pair. They both have high ideals, want to make the world a better place, like to plan for the future, are doers, and can greatly enjoy each other's company. Type 1s take action on their ideals and are guided by an inner compass that points directly to right and wrong, whereas Type 7s are optimistic and idealistic in a broader sense. Type 1s are more likely to take practical action on their values and to use the force of their moral convictions.

Type 1s like to plan because they enjoy structure and predictability, while Type 7s like to plan in the abstract—to envision a wonderful and idealized future where anything is possible. This will bring spontaneity and visionary thinking to the otherwise structured and disciplined Type 1s.

Type 1s can enjoy the free-spirited, joyful, playful nature of Type 7s, who give tacit permission to Type 1s to relax and let go of their role as the authority. Conversely, Type 7s benefit greatly from Type 1s' ability to provide disciplined, forward movement for their ideas and visions. Type 7s can feel a sense of relief when Type 1s come to the rescue, creating structure and a step-by-step approach to implement their ideas. They will also make sure that Type 7s adhere to whatever rules, regulations, and guidelines exist.

TYPE DISTINCTIONS

TYPE 1	TYPE 7
IS STRUCTURED	HAS MANY BALLS IN THE AIR
HAS IDEALS	IS IDEALISTIC
FOLLOWS THE RULES	BENDS THE RULES
IS SERIOUS	IS PLAYFUL
IS TASK AND GOAL FOCUSED	IS VISIONARY AND STRATEGIC
LEADS WITH AUTHORITY	IS AN INSPIRATIONAL LEADER
IS OTHER CENTERED	IS SELF-CENTERED
MOVES TOWARD	ASSERTS
TAKES RESPONSIBILITY	AVOIDS RESPONSIBILITY
IS CONTAINED	IS UNRESTRAINED
IS COOL	IS WARM
IS POLISHED	IS CASUAL
IS A RISK AVOIDER	IS A RISK TAKER
IS DETAIL ORIENTED	IS BIG-PICTURE ORIENTED
IS A PLANNER	IS A PLANNER
IS METHODICAL	THINKS THE DEVIL'S IN THE DETAILS
IS EASILY FRUSTRATED	IS EASILY FRUSTRATED
IS ON TIME	RUNS LATE OR JUST IN TIME
IS RIGID	IS FLEXIBLE

TYPE 2, THE PEOPLE PLEASER, AND TYPE 3, THE ACHIEVER

A visible difference between Types 2 and 3 lies in how they relate to people. Type 2s' primary focus is on relationships, whereas Type 3s' focus is on their own success and achievements. People are a means to their ends. Often Type 3s' relationships suffer because they are secondary to Type 3s' achieving their goals.

Type 2s' focus is to help others, make themselves indispensable, and be appreciated, all to affirm that they are lovable and needed. Type 3s put time and energy toward achievements that will bring them success and admiration to affirm that they are worthwhile and valuable.

SOURCES OF CONFLICT

Tension arises when Type 2s feel cut off from Type 3s when 3s put their career, goals, and success before attending to their relationship. This can cause hurt and pain for Type 2s. Type 3s can be cold, calculating, and hard-edged, and can lack empathy—all behaviors that are particularly tough for Type 2s. Type 3s may enjoy the warmth and caring of Type 2s. However, when Type 2s demand connection, time, and an emotional response, Type 3s can shut down. They believe there is no time for this, and it reminds them of their loss of contact with their own heart—something they would rather not see.

SYNERGISTIC POTENTIAL

Types 2 and 3 can be a powerful pair, particularly in a social context. Type 2s are warm and gracious, empathic and helpful, complemented by Type 3s, who are socially aware and adapt to suit the situation. Together the two will sparkle. Type 2s willingly help Type 3s shine both socially and professionally.

Professionally, if Type 3s are the boss, they can harness Type 2s' people skills, their ability to engage and involve others, their empathic skills to create a humane work environment, and their desire to bring meaning to the work that people do. You can find Type 2s cleaning up after Type 3s leave a trail of shattered people. If Type 2s are the boss, they can harness the ability of Type 3s to focus on the larger business issues, know how to manage up, and take action toward goals and objectives. Type 3s will focus on the business, understanding what they need to accomplish and carve out a clear and efficient path to achieve their goals. They will be great at promoting their ideas and plans. Give them autonomy, but not too much, because they probably think they can do a better job than you.

TYPE DISTINCTIONS

TYPE 2	TYPE 3
IS IMAGE FOCUSED	IS IMAGE FOCUSED
IS WARM AND EXPRESSIVE	IS COOL AND EMOTIONALLY RESTRAINED
WANTS APPRECIATION	WANTS ADMIRATION
IS PEOPLE FOCUSED	IS GOAL FOCUSED
TAKES THINGS PERSONALLY	TAKES THINGS PERSONALLY
FEARS LOSS OF CONNECTION	FEARS FAILURE
IS THE POWER BEHIND THE THRONE	SITS ON THE THRONE
IS RISK AVOIDANT	IS A RISK TAKER
SEEKS ATTENTION	SEEKS ATTENTION
IS PERSONALLY AND SOCIALLY AMBITIOUS	IS PERSONALLY AND SOCIALLY AMBITIOUS
USES CHARM	USES CHARM
IS OUTGOING	IS OUTGOING
MOVES TOWARD	IS ASSERTIVE
IS RESPONSIBLE	IS AMBITIOUS
PUTS THE SPOTLIGHT ON OTHERS	SEEKS THE SPOTLIGHT
IS ENERGETIC	IS ENERGETIC
BELIEVES THEY ARE VALUED FOR WHAT THEY DO FOR OTHERS	BELIEVES THEY ARE VALUED FOR WHAT THEY DO
FOCUSES ON RELATIONSHIPS	FOCUSES ON GOALS AND SUCCESS

TYPE 2, THE PEOPLE PLEASER, AND TYPE 4, THE INDIVIDUALIST

Types 2 and 4 both like to help other people, but for different reasons. Type 2s like to make themselves indispensable (selectively) to others, and Type 4s like to be seen as sensitive and intuitive—to be uniquely able to help.

They can mistype as each other, particularly because they are both in the Heart Center of the Enneagram and are connected by a line on the Enneagram symbol. Type 2s integrate at Type 4, where they access depth of sensitivity and can tap into their unique, creative expression. Type 4s access some of the less healthy qualities of Type 2s when stressed and the stakes are high. This can bring out Type 4s' need to help by advice giving, disrespecting others' boundaries, and playing the victim ("I've been wronged"). Type 4s are likely to create some kind of drama ("I am hurt; nobody understands me") and then withdraw from the situation, while hoping someone will rescue and soothe them.

SOURCES OF CONFLICT

Striking an emotional balance is tough for these two. They both can have emotional outbursts and compete for attention, and Type 2s may feel unappreciated by Type 4s, who can be very self-absorbed. Type 4s often feel like outsiders and can become envious of Type 2s' sparkle and ease with people.

Type 4s may feel that their emotional and physical space is being invaded. Type 2s' demanding nature and exaggerated self-importance can either push Type 4s away or cause them to lash out. Type 2s will have a hard time when Type 4s pull away and want space. They can be hurt by the temperamental nature of Type 4s.

There is an emotional push-pull between the two. Type 2s' focus is on others' emotions, and Type 4s' is on their own emotions. They will both see the other as out of balance. Yet they have the possibility of teaching one another emotional balance.

SYNERGISTIC POTENTIAL

Type 2s have a positive outlook, are sensitive to power dynamics, and are action oriented. They can pull Type 4s out of their glass-is-half-empty frame with encouragement and kindness and inspire them to action. If Type 4 is willing, Type 2 can help them to be more politically sensitive to an organization's dynamics so that they don't shoot themselves in the foot. *I gotta be me*, regardless of the circumstances, can be career limiting for Type 4s.

Given the empathic nature of Type 2s and the sensitive nature of Type 4s, these two can be a great support to one another. When Type 4s are stressed and withdraw, there is no one better suited than Type 2s to go after them and make them feel special and loved.

They will share their mutual appreciation of creative expression, and Type 2 can be Type 4's biggest fan and supporter. Type 4 feels genuine love, acceptance, and understanding from Type 2.

Type 4s are not put off by the emotionality of Type 2s, because they are similarly wired. Their emotionality, creative expression, sensitivity, mood swings, and image consciousness will feel familiar to both; they will have an innate understanding of one another.

TYPE DISTINCTIONS

TYPE 2	TYPE 4
SEEKS WARMTH AND CONNECTION	SEEKS WARMTH AND TO BE SEEN
TAKES THINGS PERSONALLY	TAKES THINGS PERSONALLY
IS AN INSIDER	IS AN OUTSIDER
IS SENSITIVE TO OTHERS	IS SENSITIVE AND SELF-REFERENCED
MOVES TOWARD	WITHDRAWS
DOES WHAT FEELS RIGHT	DOES WHAT THEY FEEL LIKE DOING
FOCUSES ON OTHERS' NEEDS	FOCUSES ON OWN NEEDS
FOCUSES ON OUTER WORLD	FOCUSES ON INNER WORLD
THINK THE GLASS IS HALF-FULL	THINK THE GLASS IS HALF-EMPTY
WANTS TO BE APPRECIATED	WANTS TO BE SEEN AS UNIQUE
IS DEMANDING AND MANIPULATIVE	IS TEMPERAMENTAL AND MOODY
PRIDE GETS IN THEIR WAY	ENVY GETS IN THEIR WAY
FOCUS ON BEING NEEDED	FOCUS ON WHAT IS MISSING IN THEIR LIFE
IS THE POWER BEHIND THE THRONE	IS A UNIQUE CONTRIBUTOR
WANTS TO BE ADMIRED	WANTS TO EXPRESS THEIR CREATIVITY

TYPE 2, THE PEOPLE PLEASER, AND TYPE 5, THE DETACHED OBSERVER

Type 5s are drawn to the world of ideas and innovation. They want to be valued as the expert in their chosen subject(s). Type 2s are drawn to the world of people and relationships and want to be needed. Type 2s don't want their neediness to show, nor do they easily accept help; and Type 5s believe they don't have needs and are perfectly self-sufficient. Will their differences keep them away from each other, or will they realize that each has what the other needs most?

SOURCES OF CONFLICT

Under typical circumstances, when Type 5 endeavors to draw a line around their space and focus on their ideas, they will feel an emotional pull from Type 2 or feel invaded by them. Type 5s see Type 2s as emotionally needy and intrusive when Type 2s try to build a bond and dependency that Type 5s try to avoid. Type 5s are extremely private, and they permit only a trusted few to get close.

Type 5s enjoy connection, but on their terms, and will feel smothered by Type 2s when they try to anticipate Type 5s' needs while Type 5s conversely attempt to minimize their own needs. Type 2s' identity is built around being the pleaser and helper, and Type 5s' identity is built around being self-sufficient. If Type 2s do something to please Type 5s, there is a good chance that they won't receive the appreciation and approval they desire.

If Type 5 is the boss, it would be easy to allow Type 2 to handle the relationship side of things because they are so skilled in this arena. This gives Type 2s a sense of power and control. If the Type 5 boss is aware of this, they'll stay more closely connected to the team despite their desire to wall off.

If Type 2 is the boss, it is advisable for them to tap into the knowledge and expertise of Type 5 but leave them to do what they do best, and don't try to force them to reveal or connect. Create opportunities for this to happen, but don't push.

SYNERGISTIC POTENTIAL

Type 5s really do want to be loved and supported but secretly believe there is no support for them. Should Type 5 allow Type 2 to be the helper? Can they graciously receive the support that Type 2 offers? If Type 2 can give without reciprocal expectation, this could work.

Type 2s can learn from the more objective Type 5s not to take things personally, and Type 5s could learn from the generosity and warmth of Type 2s. Socially, Type 2s will take the lead and can introduce Type 5s into various social worlds. Type 5s do not tend to play the role of social initiator, so they can complement one another in this way.

Professionally, Type 2s connect and network, build relationships, and tune in to the heartbeat of the company. Type 5s lead by remote control and don't make themselves particularly accessible to members of the organization. They are busy innovating and researching, looking into the future and focusing on the road ahead. In this sense, the two can capitalize on their individual strengths and bring all of them to bear on making the organization thrive.

Both meet at Type 8. Type 2s go to Type 8 when stressed, and they become demanding, pushy, possessive, and confrontational. Type 5s go to Type 8 when they are relaxed and emotionally healthy; they become more assertive and powerful as well as protective and warmhearted. When this happens, Type 2s may feel the support they truly desire.

Under normal circumstances, Type 2s expect others to magically anticipate their needs and act on them or respond in kind to their generosity. However, Type 2s go to Type 4 when relaxed and emotionally healthy. They contain their energy, look inward, and tune in to their own needs and take action on them. Type 5s appreciate that Type 2s are taking care of themselves and are more sensitive to Type 5s' needs for space and privacy.

TYPE DISTINCTIONS

TYPE 2 | TYPE 5

TYPE 2	TYPE 5
IS INTERPERSONALLY WARM	IS INTERPERSONALLY DISTANT
CONNECTS	DETACHES
WANTS TO BE NEEDED	DOESN'T WANT TO HAVE NEEDS
IS SOCIALLY ADEPT	IS SOCIALLY AWKWARD
IS GENEROUS WITH ENERGY	IS SELFISH WITH ENERGY
WANTS TO BE LIKED	WANTS TO BE THE EXPERT
IS SUBJECTIVE	IS OBJECTIVE
LEADS WITH PERSONAL WARMTH	LEADS THROUGH EXPERTISE (GURU)
FILTERS LIFE THROUGH FEELINGS	FILTERS LIFE THROUGH INTELLECT
IS A RISK AVOIDER	IS A RISK TAKER
IS A PRACTICAL HEDONIST	FORGETS TO TAKE CARE OF THE PRACTICAL
WANTS TO BE APPRECIATED	WANTS EMOTIONAL DISTANCE
IS OTHER FOCUSED	IS SELF-FOCUSED

TYPE 2, THE PEOPLE PLEASER, AND TYPE 6, THE LOYAL SKEPTIC

Types 2 and 6 are look-alike Types because they both are active, feel responsible, and often do things for other people. They are both known to complain, and they can both use flattery (although Type 2s are the masters at flattery). However, that is where many of the similarities end. Type 2s are in the business of helping others. They believe they have to *earn* love, approval, and appreciation—that if they do things for others, they will not be abandoned or rejected. Type 6s believe they have to *earn* their security by anticipating danger on the road ahead and planning for these eventualities. They have issues with self-doubt about their decisions, abilities, and so on. They are naturally skeptical of others' motives, and this could be a challenge for a Type 2.

Type 2s have a hidden agenda—to make themselves indispensable—and they will flatter and manipulate to achieve their ends. Type 6s are constantly scanning for others' hidden agendas and believe that everyone is ultimately self-serving. Can Type 6 trust Type 2? Can Type 2 get power, appreciation, and approval from Type 6?

SOURCES OF CONFLICT

Type 2s can be put off by the natural mistrust of Type 6s and their *what could go wrong* stance. By nature, Type 2s have a positive outlook and will feel the wet blanket of Type 6 as dampening their spirit. Each has a powerful inner critic that never seems to rest, and they are liable to trigger that in the other. Their inner critic is the *should* voice, and it is tough for both of them to listen to their inner guidance and instincts over the din of their inner critic.

Type 2's critical voice can be directed toward Type 6 and sound like, "You don't appreciate all I do for you. You don't make time for me. You don't tell me you love me. Why don't you call … ?" Type 6 may respond, "I feel pressure from you. I don't want to feel responsible for … I don't want to say things just because you expect it." Type 6s feel pressure when they believe they are responsible for meeting others' expectations of them.

Type 2s will be initially appreciative of and intrigued by the analytical nature of Type 6s, but when it comes to matters of the heart, they will feel hurt and disappointed. Type 2s want Type 6s to connect at the heart level, whereas Type 6s like to contribute by being the champion, responding in a crisis, problem-solving, and doing research to find out the best way to proceed.

Type 2s are prone to emotional outbursts and become demanding and possessive, especially when they feel that the connection could be severed. When their reactivity pushes the other person further away (the paradox for Type 2s), they can become manipulative and seductive, doing whatever it takes to lure Type 6 back. This will increase the feeling of mistrust in Type 6, who is always on the lookout for hidden motives; yet they also feel responsible for the upset created, and the *should* voice gets activated.

Type 6s' ability to be self-centered and selfish is seductive for Type 2s, who want to meet their needs. It is simultaneously a source of conflict because Type 2 feels that they are being held at arm's length and kept at a distance, and feel unappreciated, while Type 6 is busy taking care of their own needs. Their conflicts can have a push me–pull you nature.

SYNERGISTIC POTENTIAL

Type 2s tend to decide impulsively, and Type 6s are indecisive. If Type 6 is the boss, Type 2 should prepare to answer all questions and concerns, be armed with concrete facts and data, and not expect an immediate answer. Type 2 should not become defensive in response to the questioning Type 6. They are prepared, and they expect you to be prepared. Still, even though Type 6 has all of the information they could possibly need, they can go around in circles and weigh one thing against another without resolve.

If Type 2 is the boss, see if you can encourage Type 6 to listen to their intuition. They can be so caught up trying to optimize decisions, do the responsible thing, and prevent all possible eventualities that could derail their decision that they become paralyzed. You may have to be the ultimate arbiter and base your decision on the information gathered by Type 6. You will have more data than you can imagine and will be aware of the risks involved. This will balance your impulsive inclinations.

If Type 6s learn to trust Type 2s and they both learn to receive assistance from the other, they could make a powerful work team—they are both natural team players and will respect that in the other. Type 6s create organizational structure, while Type 2s attend to customer service, promotion, employees, HR, and OD activities.

Type 6s appreciate the warmhearted nature of Type 2s, their action orientation, and their positive outlook. Type 6s can learn from Type 2s' natural people skills, the empathic nature of Type 2s, and how they tune in to the aspirations of people on their team. Type 2s understand customer service, and Type 6s understand market research—they have an innate ability to tune in to the market as Type 2s tune in to people.

Type 6s tend to commit deeply, and this will be a source of comfort for Type 2s. Type 2s will enjoy the analytical rigor that Type 6s bring to the table—their ability to think through and plan for contingencies, taking care of the practical. With all of that, together they can really pull off some wonderful things together!

TYPE DISTINCTIONS

TYPE 2	TYPE 6
IS RESPONSIBLE	IS RESPONSIBLE
IS WARM	IS WARM
IS TRUSTING	IS SKEPTICAL
WANTS INTIMACY	WANTS SECURITY
IS TEAM ORIENTED	IS TEAM ORIENTED
IS IMPULSIVE	IS CAUTIOUS
FOCUSES ON FEELINGS	IS ANALYTICAL
IS SPONTANEOUS	BELIEVES, BE PREPARED
FOCUSES ON THE POSITIVE	FOCUSES ON WHAT COULD GO WRONG
WANTS APPRECIATION	WANTS APPRECIATION
IS SOCIALLY GRACEFUL	IS SOCIAL
BELIEVES THEY MUST EARN LOVE	BELIEVES THEY MUST EARN SECURITY
TUNES IN TO PEOPLE	TUNES IN TO THE MARKET

TYPE 2, THE PEOPLE PLEASER, AND TYPE 7, THE ENTHUSIAST

Types 2 and 7 often mistype as the other, at least initially. While Type 2s want to help (by doing things for others or lending an empathic ear), Type 7s are more helpful by *fixing*—using their intellect, analytical skills, and resources to problem-solve. They both are drawn to working with people, but Type 2s are often found in the helping professions, such as customer service, social work, HR, medicine, and psychology. The consulting, coaching, and facilitating professions are filled with Type 7s.

SOURCES OF CONFLICT

Tension ensues when Type 2s want to delve into the inner world of Type 7s, who are often running away from their past, painful feelings, and memories. If Type 7 thinks Type 2 is trying to invade their inner space, they are likely to run in the opposite direction. Type 7s are well boundaried around deeply personal matters and their feelings, and when Type 2s don't respect those boundaries, Type 7s take off. This can be painful for Type 2s, who will feel abandoned and rejected. Meanwhile, Type 7s are suspicious of the motives of Type 2s—what are they trying to find out, and what are they going to do with the information? Will it be used against me? Are they trying to endear themselves to me in some way, and why?

Normally, Type 7 is more comfortable moving toward people and has difficulty when people move toward them. "What do they want from me?" This is the inner voice of Type 7. If Type 7 feels the neediness of Type 2, they will take off. However, it is important for Type 7s to get in touch with their own neediness. Type 7s also like to spread themselves out among lots of activities, friends, interests, and so on, and if Type 2 doesn't offer Type 7 the freedom they feel they need, Type 7 will be on the run again.

Both Types are more comfortable moving toward others rather than being pursued; giving is easier than receiving. Both maintain the illusion of control this way. Type 2s can perceive Type 7s as impatient, preoccupied, selfish, and emotionally unavailable. They may be fun to talk with about plans and ideas, but Type 2s may not find Type 7s particularly emotionally satisfying, compassionate, or warmhearted. This could be a source of dissatisfaction.

SYNERGISTIC POTENTIAL

Often the two Types are drawn to each other because they both tend to be a bit gregarious and high energy. Type 2s like to join Type 7s in their adventures, and Type 7s are grateful to have a playmate to take along. Both are positive-outlook Types and can make the best of a bad situation. Type 7s are comfortable being at the center of attention, and Type 2s are OK taking a backseat, at least for a while.

Type 2s commit deeply, whether to the family, to a friendship at work, or in a relationship, and Type 7s can learn about this from them. Type 2s know how to be a compassionate presence for others, which is something Type 7s would be well served to develop. Type 2s can learn from Type 7s not to take things as personally, to be more independent and respect others' boundaries.

Both in work and in personal relationships, these two can make a great team and have a lot of fun in the process!

TYPE DISTINCTIONS

TYPE 2	TYPE 7
WANTS TO HELP	WANTS TO FIX
IS SPONTANEOUS	IS SPONTANEOUS
IS POSITIVE	IS POSITIVE
IS ENERGETIC	IS ENERGETIC
IS PLAYFUL	IS PLAYFUL
IS WARM AND PERSONAL	IS WARM AND PERSONABLE
TAKES THINGS PERSONALLY	IS LESS LIKELY TO TAKE THINGS PERSONALLY
IS OTHER CENTERED	IS SELF-CENTERED
IS EMOTIONAL	IS ANALYTICAL
IS AN ENGAGING LEADER	IS A VISIONARY AND INSPIRATIONAL LEADER
IS IDEALISTIC	IS IDEALISTIC
IS RISK ADVERSE	IS A RISK TAKER

TYPE 3, THE ACHIEVER, AND TYPE 4, THE INDIVIDUALIST

While Types 3 and 4 are neighbors on the Enneagram, and both occupy the Heart Center, they are very different Types. They may look alike in that they both want to be noticed and admired, even envied. Type 3s want to be admired for their achievements, and Type 4s want to be envied for being unique or special in some way. They both are concerned about their image, are likely to take things personally, and are familiar with feelings of shame. Type 3s have shame about not feeling valuable or worthwhile, and Type 4s have shame about not living up to their idealized self-image.

Where they differ is in their pace (fast versus *as the spirit moves*) and how their focus on image is played out. Type 3s want to fit into each unique circumstance and to craft an image of success in their milieu, while Type 4s will find a way to draw attention and stand out—the shape shifter versus the tulip in a field of hyacinths. Type 3s want to be outstanding, and Type 4s want to stand out.

SOURCES OF CONFLICT

The dynamic is push-pull with these two. Type 3s want to make their mark on the world, and Type 4s have a hard time getting going and finding their true calling. Type 3s are clear and directed—they have their goals in sight and are on their way. Type 4s see themselves as different and unique and look for creative ways to express themselves.

Type 3s want to be the star, and their star quality can evoke Type 4s' envy. The temperamental Type 4s' glass tends to be half-empty. They can appear fragile, and their energy fluctuates with their mood. Type 3s try to repress their emotions and tend to stay upbeat and focused. Type 3s see the goal and go for it; Type 4s have a dream and long for it. Type 3s are known to wear different masks to suit the situation. Type 4 is about being authentic, and they abhor people they see as phony. These two very different approaches to life can grate on each other; yet somewhere inside, they both know they can learn from each other.

SYNERGISTIC POTENTIAL

Type 3s run toward their goals and away from their shame. They have lost contact with their heart's desire while internalizing the high expectations of their parents. Type 4s try to find their heart's desire, to be their idealized self. Type 3s are outer directed and Type 4s are inner directed. These two can help each other. Type 4s can help Type 3s reconnect with their feelings and desires, and Type 3s can help Type 4s take practical action toward bringing their dream into tangible form. "Just do it!" says Type 3.

Type 3s can help Type 4s see through more objective eyes rather than being storm-tossed by their feelings and mood states. Type 4s are sensitive and empathic toward others, and Type 3s can learn from this. Professionally, they make good counterparts. Type 3s have the capacity to take the creative expression of Type 4 and market it, bring it out into the world, and sell it. Type 3s can learn to have a more leisurely pace like Type 4, connect to their authenticity, and tap into their own creative potential and deeper sensitivities—to take time to smell the flowers and appreciate the beauty around them. Type 4s can help Type 3s soften their edges, and Type 3s can help Type 4s take action and focus on goals.

TYPE DISTINCTIONS

TYPE 3 | TYPE 4

TYPE 3	TYPE 4
WANTS TO BE ADMIRED	WANTS TO BE SPECIAL AND UNIQUE
ASSERTS	WITHDRAWS
BLOCKS THEIR FEELINGS	ACTS ON THEIR FEELINGS
IS EFFICIENT	IS A DILETTANTE
WANTS TO BE THE STAR	WANTS TO STAND OUT AND BE UNIQUE
WANTS TO BE IN CHARGE	WANTS TO DO THEIR OWN THING
IS ACHIEVEMENT ORIENTED	IS ORIENTED TOWARD CREATIVE EXPRESSION
FOCUSES ON SUCCESS	FOCUSES ON WHAT'S MISSING
IS INSENSITIVE	IS SENSITIVE
IS COOL AND IMPERSONAL	IS WARM AND GUARDED
IS FAST PACED	MOVES AT THEIR OWN PACE
IS A CHAMELEON	THINKS, I GOTTA BE ME
IS CHARMING AND EMOTIONALLY REPRESSED	IS MOODY AND TEMPERAMENTAL

TYPE 3, THE ACHIEVER, AND TYPE 5, THE DETACHED OBSERVER

Types 3 and 5 can be mistyped by others and mistype themselves as the other. Outwardly they both seem a little cool, objective, and controlled. They both want to be seen as competent and can be ambitious. Both find themselves in leadership positions, appearing confident and self-promoting. However, their motivations are different.

Type 3s want to achieve success and are very image conscious. If Type 5s are image conscious, it is to craft an image as the expert or guru. Type 3s want the admiration that comes with success, whereas Type 5s desire recognition for their ideas, innovations, and expertise—to be seen and sought out as the expert.

The underlying motivation for Type 5s is to have the freedom to focus on knowledge acquisition and to innovate. Type 3s are motivated by results and winning. They surround themselves with symbols of success and want to be admired for their achievements.

SOURCES OF CONFLICT

In an effort to move things forward, Type 3 may get out ahead of Type 5. Type 5s don't like to be rushed or pushed, and this is a potential source of tension for the two. Type 5s want to communicate their complex ideas and thoughts. Their communication style may not have much affect—it can be a bit dry and intellectual. Type 3s can be slick, use marketing lingo and spin, and communicate the surface of ideas.

Type 3s tend to be socially savvy, and Type 5s are known to be socially awkward. This could be difficult in a partnership, both professionally and personally. Type 3s care about how they are perceived, and Type 5s are more iconoclastic.

Type 5s trust a very few people; and Type 3s, in their effort to get ahead and promote their latest idea, plan, or project, may misrepresent or cut corners. This would be an affront to Type 5s and their expertise.

SYNERGISTIC POTENTIAL

The two together could be a powerful team. Type 3s can pull Type 5s out of their cave and into the larger world. They would be perfect for promoting and marketing the otherwise recalcitrant Type 5 and their innovative ideas. Type 3s tend to cut corners on the way to their goals, and Type 5s can bring some intellectual rigor to Type 3s' ideas and help them to be innovative in their approach.

This pairing is more suited to a business partnership than to a personal partnership because they both tend to be cut off from their feelings. Relationships take a backseat to the achievements of Type 3s and to Type 5s' desire to focus on ideas and innovation. In the case of a romantic partnership, it will be important to make sure their focus isn't weighted too heavily toward their professions, or it will become more of a practical partnership than a romantic one.

If Type 3 is the boss, they would be well served to give Type 5 lots of space and time to innovate. Micromanaging Type 5s would not work. However, it will be important to set clear expectations with concrete deliverables, *and* to allow plenty of space for thinking and time for their *Eureka!* moments.

If Type 5 is the boss, they would be well served to let Type 3 promote and market their ideas, create space for Type 3 to shine, make sure they are given plenty of recognition, and set clear goals for their work—then let 'em go!

TYPE DISTINCTIONS

TYPE 3 | TYPE 5

TYPE 3	TYPE 5
IS COMPETENT	IS COMPETENT
WANTS TO BE SUCCESSFUL	WANTS TO BE THE EXPERT (GURU)
WANTS TO BE ADMIRED	WANTS RECOGNITION FOR THEIR EXPERTISE
WANTS TO FEEL WORTHWHILE AND VALUABLE	WANTS TO FEEL SAFE AND SUPPORTED
AVOIDS CONFLICT	AVOIDS CONFLICT
ASSERTS	WITHDRAWS
FOCUSES ON SYMBOLS OF SUCCESS	FOCUSES ON IDEAS
PACE IS FAST	PACE IS SLOW
REPRESSES THEIR FEELINGS	THINKS ABOUT THEIR FEELINGS
IS OUT IN THE WORLD AND ENGAGED	IS SAFE IN THEIR IVORY TOWER
LEADS BY MANAGING UP, MEETING GOALS, AND MAKING THINGS HAPPEN	LEADS AS THE EXPERT AND INNOVATOR
CAN BE COLD AND RUTHLESS	CAN BE CRUEL AND CUTTING
IS OBJECTIVE	IS OBJECTIVE AND DETACHED
COLLECTS AWARDS	COLLECTS KNOWLEDGE
PROTECTS THEIR HEART	PROTECTS THEIR INNER WORLD (TO INCLUDE THEIR HEART)

TYPE 3, THE ACHIEVER, AND TYPE 6, THE LOYAL SKEPTIC

Types 3 and 6 are connected by a line on the Enneagram symbol, and therefore they share some behaviors. When Type 3s are relaxed and emotionally healthy, they access some of the healthier aspects of Type 6. They become more responsive to others and don't think of other people as merely resources to achieve their own ends. They take more time to do a good and thorough job with the proper analysis behind it.

When Type 6s access the qualities of Type 3, however, it is often in times of stress, and their feelings of insecurity get triggered. They take on the less healthy aspects of Type 3 and can become showoffs, need to self-promote, become image conscious, deceive themselves and others, and be pushy and untrustworthy. When emotionally healthy, Type 6s pull on the healthiest qualities of Type 3. They believe in themselves, take action on their goals, become socially confident, and can be truly heroic.

SOURCES OF CONFLICT

A big challenge for these two is that Type 6s have issues with trust. Because Type 3s often wear a mask to match the image they want to project, Type 6s' internal alarms go off. They will look for Type 3's hidden agenda and wonder about their authenticity. If Type 3s become controlling in their singular pursuit of the goal, this may cause Type 6s to challenge their authority, act out, or maintain their distance. Type 6 is a loyal team player but wants to feel appreciated and valued and not a cog in someone's wheel.

When Type 3s accept a challenge and promise to deliver, they want to win at all costs and will take the most efficient route to cross the finish line. They will be inclined to turn a deaf ear to Type 6s, who want them to see the pitfalls in the plan and what could go wrong, and to take the time to prepare accordingly.

Type 3s are speedy and efficient and may not appreciate being slowed down by Type 6s, who want to *know* and be fully prepared. Type 3s may also experience the worry and anxiety of Type 6s, which triggers the worry and anxiety in themselves that they don't want to acknowledge. Type 3s are decisive and confident and become annoyed by the indecisive, doubting, and insecure Type 6s.

SYNERGISTIC POTENTIAL

These two can make a good team. Type 6s will responsibly follow through and take care of the research, planning, and preparing, while Type 3s are off promoting and managing up. Type 3s will take the risks that Type 6s would be unlikely to take and have the confidence to make things happen. Type 6s will hold down the fort and do the less glamorous work. Type 6s also focus on the team and the group, whereas Type 3s are focused on reaching the goal as efficiently as possible.

Both Types excel in the marketing arena. Type 3s are the true marketers, and Type 6s are great market researchers and researchers in general. Type 6s also have good marketing abilities and excel at promoting products and other people. Type 6s can be great champions of Type 3s when they have earned their trust.

TYPE DISTINCTIONS

TYPE 3 | TYPE 6

TYPE 3	TYPE 6
THINKS DIRECT REPORTS EXIST TO HELP THEM ACHIEVE THEIR GOALS	TEAM'S PURPOSE IS TO MOVE THE ORGANIZATION FORWARD
ASSERTS	MOVES TOWARD
WANTS TO BE THE STAR	WANTS TO CONTRIBUTE
FEARS BEING WORTHLESS	FEARS THE WORLD—IT IS NOT A SAFE PLACE
IS GOOD AT MANAGING UP	IS GOOD AT MANAGING
IS ACTION ORIENTED AND IMPULSIVE	IS ANALYSIS ORIENTED AND PREPARED
IS CONFLICT AVOIDANT	IS CONFLICT AVOIDANT
IS IMPERSONAL AND PRIVATE	IS DOUBTING AND SKEPTICAL
CUTS CORNERS WITH THE GOAL IN SIGHT	OVERANALYZES AND SECOND GUESSES
IS OVERCONFIDENT	LACKS CONFIDENCE
IS OVERLY OPTIMISTIC	IS OVERLY WORRIED AND ANXIOUS (WHAT COULD GO WRONG?)
TAKES CALCULATED RISKS	IS RISK ADVERSE
NEEDS TO LOOK GOOD	NEEDS TO KNOW
THINKS, *I am running so fast, I don't feel the ground*	THINKS, *there is no solid ground*
OVERPROMISES	OVERCOMMITS
HAS A FEAR OF FAILURE	HAS A FEAR OF WHAT COULD GO WRONG

TYPE 3, THE ACHIEVER, AND TYPE 7, THE ENTHUSIAST

Outwardly, these two Types look similar. Both tend to be personable but not personal, busy and productive, assertive, positive, and charming; and both tend to find themselves either leading organizations or being entrepreneurs. Where they differ: Type 7s tend to be high verbal, talk fast, take a creative approach, generate lots of ideas, and have a hard time shutting down options, and they can appear scattered in their actions and thoughts. Type 3s are noticeably more focused, contained, directed, and efficient—they don't take time for idle chitchat.

SOURCES OF CONFLICT

Type 3s are good self-promoters, and Type 7s like to promote their ideas. Type 7s are generally open, curious, and consumers of information. Type 3s are more circumspect, guarded, and focused on their achievements.

Type 3s and Type 7s can have an edge. Type 7s' edge gets sharp when they feel criticized or overwhelmed due to overcommitment, or when others they depend on can't move or think as fast as they do. They become impatient and defensive, angry, critical, and judgmental. Type 3s' edge comes out when they are focused on winning at all costs. Relationships and people's feelings are set aside as they cut through everything, working day and night to get the job done. This is when Type 3s appear somewhat cold and hard-hearted. They *do what it takes* and expect others to do the same.

Type 7s don't appreciate being told what to do, harassed, or micromanaged in any way. They may see Type 3's behavior as self-serving, and Type 7s will have trust issues with Type 3, because they can set off Type 7's anti-authority and skeptical buttons. When Type 3s lead by fear and intimidation, the once-confident Type 7s can become flooded with fear and anxiety, and their self-confidence can plummet.

Type 7s can be put off by the self-promoting, workaholic style of Type 3s. Type 3s can become annoyed by the lack of focus they see in Type 7s and may resent their ability to attract attention and be at the center.

SYNERGISTIC POTENTIAL

Types 3 and 7 can make a good team because they are action oriented and know how to make things happen. They can complement each other in many ways. Type 7s are tuned in to what is going on in the organization via their vast network. They are also tuned in to what is going on in the market for the same reason. They are consumers of vast amounts of information in multiple sectors because of their wide-ranging interests.

Type 3 can bring closure and focus to Type 7's ideas and plans, and help move their plans into action. Type 3s will help Type 7s keep the goal in front of them, *manage up* effectively, and take a streamlined approach. Type 3s and Type 7s both like to appear competent, and Type 3s will be happy to give Type 7s lots of freedom as long as Type 7 makes Type 3 look good. Type 3s appreciate and respect Type 7s' quick mind, as well as their resilience (remember, Type 3s fear failure).

In relationship, these two could have a good time together because they both like to be active and *out there.* They will enjoy interesting conversations, moving toward joint visions, and manifesting their dreams. Type 3s appreciate the fun-loving, adventurous nature of Type 7s.

They will be challenged by their shared blind spot—focusing on the *doing*, the practical, and not paying attention to their feelings and relationship. They could end up having a relationship that focuses on work if they are not careful. However, when they both come in contact with their hearts, they will be unstoppable.

TYPE DISTINCTIONS

TYPE 3 | TYPE 7

TYPE 3	TYPE 7
IS FOCUSED ON THE GOAL	IS EASILY DISTRACTED
IS EFFICIENT	MULTITASKS AND HAS MANY BALLS IN THE AIR
IS SELF-PROMOTING	PROMOTES IDEAS AND VISION
IS CHARMING AND COOL	IS CHARMING AND FUNNY
IS DECISIVE	KEEPS THEIR OPTIONS OPEN
IS IMPERSONAL	IS PERSONABLE
LEADS BY COMPETING TO BE THE BEST	LEADS BY INSPIRING AND NETWORKING
HAS A CAN-DO-IT ATTITUDE	IS OPTIMISTIC
FEELINGS ARE REPRESSED	DISTRACTS FROM FEELINGS
IS BUSY	IS BUSY
IS ASSERTIVE	IS ASSERTIVE
WANTS TO BE THE STAR	WANTS TO BE AT THE CENTER
IS GOAL FOCUSED	IS FREEDOM FOCUSED

TYPE 4, THE INDIVIDUALIST, AND TYPE 5, THE DETACHED OBSERVER

Types 4 and 5 are occasionally mistyped for each other. They are comfortable with *the dark side* of life, can submerge themselves in fantasy, reject before being rejected, feel mis-seen and misunderstood, and withdraw when they are disturbed or upset.

How to distinguish them? Type 4s wear their mood on their sleeves, and Type 5s manage to keep an unaffected exterior. Type 4s can be rather dramatic in their expression, whereas Type 5s tend to be contained and controlled. It is often hard to guess what is going on beneath the surface of Type 5s.

SOURCES OF CONFLICT

Type 5s will be put off by the emotional demands of Type 4s. Type 5s don't like intrusions. They feel drained by people who place demands on their time and energy. Type 5s may not appreciate Type 4s' need to stand out and be different. Type 4s dislike the cold rationality of Type 5s and their lack of emotionality and sensitivity. Type 4s need to feel free to fully express their feelings and emotions. If Type 5s cannot tolerate this, Type 4s won't feel met by them.

Both tend to withdraw when they feel discomfort, shame, fear, or stress. Who will reemerge first? Who will make the first move?

Together, their blind spot is attending to the practical. Each one can get lost in their inner world and forget earthly matters. Type 5s will be lost in ideas, and Type 4s will lose themselves in examining their feelings. Both would be well served to connect with their instincts, take purposeful action, and turn their attention outward.

SYNERGISTIC POTENTIAL

Type 5s have keen insights into people, and Type 4s will feel seen by them. Type 5s are unlikely to react to the emotionality of Type 4s, which could be useful for Type 4s. Because of Type 4's profound sensitivity, Type 5 may feel understood by Type 4. Both of these needs are extremely important to each Type.

Type 4 can bring the innovations of Type 5 to fruition with their unique creative expression. Type 4s are able to help Type 5s get in closer contact with their feelings, and Type 5s can help Type 4s become more objective about their life and reality. When problems or adversity arise, Type 5s offer an objective and innovative problem-solving approach, and Type 4s offer a sensitive and creative approach.

TYPE DISTINCTIONS

TYPE 4 | TYPE 5

TYPE 4	TYPE 5
WITHDRAWS	WITHDRAWS
WANTS TO BE SEEN	WANTS TO BE UNDERSTOOD
WANTS TO BE UNIQUE	WANTS TO BE THE EXPERT
FOCUSES ON WHAT IS MISSING	FOCUSES ON IDEAS AND MASTERY
CONFUSES THEIR FEELINGS WITH THEIR IDENTITY	CONFUSES THEIR IDEAS ABOUT LIFE WITH REALITY
FILTERS LIFE THROUGH THEIR FEELINGS	FILTERS LIFE THROUGH THEIR MENTAL CONSTRUCTS
IS EMOTIONALLY INTENSE	IS EMOTIONALLY CONTROLLED
TAKES A CREATIVE APPROACH	TAKES A PROBLEM-SOLVING APPROACH
CAN GET LOST IN FANTASY	CAN GET LOST IN FANTASY AND IDEAS
IS GENERALLY WARM AND SENSITIVE	CAN BE IMPERSONAL AND INSENSITIVE
DISENGAGES	DETACHES
REJECTS	REJECTS
MERGES FEELINGS, MEMORIES, AND THOUGHTS	COMPARTMENTALIZES FEELINGS, MEMORIES, AND THOUGHTS
IS EMOTIONALLY DEMANDING	IS EMOTIONALLY WITHHOLDING

TYPE 4, THE INDIVIDUALIST, AND TYPE 6, THE LOYAL SKEPTIC

Types 4 and 6 can mistype as each other—in fact, I have seen it on many occasions. Both seem to be drawn to the arts, have strong emotional reactions, and can complain about what is wrong with their life, what's missing, what's not working … However, the focus of their attention and life scripts is different.

Type 6s are more attuned to what could go wrong, are concerned with survival issues, believe the world is unsafe, and are in search of security and ways to quell their anxiety. They believe that people have ulterior motives and hidden agendas, so they become suspicious and skeptical. Type 4s are more attuned to what is missing in their life and life in general; they envy others who seem to have what they long for and wonder why others have what they don't. Type 4s have an idealized version of themselves and long for it to be real. They are more melancholic, sensitive, and inward focused.

SOURCES OF CONFLICT

Type 6s want to dutifully meet the emotional demands of Type 4s while being confused about whether they are responding because they *should* or because this is what they want to do. Type 6s get tied up in knots when they need to make a decision. There is a committee of internal voices offering a myriad of factors to be weighed for each decision. They lose contact with their instincts in favor of trying to act responsibly. Often this creates a counter-reaction in Type 6, and it leaves Type 4 in emotional distress.

They do a dance of approach and withdraw, which is unsatisfying for both. Type 6s can become annoyed when they perceive that Type 4s do things to draw attention to themselves or to make them stand out and be different. Their inaction, or trying this and that, may also be a source of annoyance for Type 6s. Type 4s dislike when Type 6s throw a wet blanket on their ideas with their fear of what could go wrong, and Type 4s want to be free to pursue their dreams, which may stir up feelings of insecurity in Type 6s, who are security seekers.

SYNERGISTIC POTENTIAL

Both Types have a bent for creative expression, and both are fairly independent. Type 4s appreciate the solidity of Type 6s and their caring warmth. Type 6s are known to be great promoters of other people, and Type 4s will enjoy the benefits of that. Type 4s are also champions of those they care about, and Type 6s appreciate their support. Type 6s bring practical and analytical rigor to their partnership, while Type 4s bring a depth of introspection and emotional sensitivity that Type 6s may lack. Type 4s are emotionally honest, and this will build trust with Type 6s.

Because Type 6s tend to be active, they invite and inspire Type 4s to shift their mood and move into action. Type 6s pay attention to the practical, and they plan and prepare, which Type 4s appreciate.

Professionally, they will enjoy each other's creativity. If Type 6 is the boss, it will be important to let Type 4s have a lot of room to do their work in their own unique way, to harness their people skills, and to appreciate who they are. If Type 4 is the boss, recognize that Type 6s will follow through, be thorough, and bring analytical rigor to their work; and make sure to acknowledge and use their ability to see pitfalls and develop contingency plans, as well as their skills as team leaders.

TYPE DISTINCTIONS

TYPE 4 | TYPE 6

TYPE 4	TYPE 6
WITHDRAWS	MOVES TOWARD AND WITHDRAWS
IDEALIZES	ANALYZES
PROJECTS THEIR FEELINGS	PROJECTS THEIR FEARS
FILTERS THROUGH THE HEART	FILTERS THROUGH THE HEAD
IS DECISIVE AND SELF-REFERENCED	IS INDECISIVE AND OTHER-REFERENCED
IS CREATIVE	IS CREATIVE
IS MELANCHOLIC	HAS WORRY AND ANXIETY
FOCUSES ON WHAT IS MISSING	FOCUSES ON WHAT COULD GO WRONG AND WHAT'S NOT WORKING
IS NOT FOCUSED ON THE PRACTICAL	PLANS, PREPARES, ORGANIZES
IS AN INDIVIDUAL CONTRIBUTOR	IS A TEAM PLAYER
DOES WHAT THEY FEEL LIKE DOING	ACTS RESPONSIBLY
IS SENSITIVE	FEELS RESPONSIBLE
MOVES AT THEIR OWN PACE	IS BUSY DOING
DWELLS ON WHAT WENT WRONG (past problems)	DWELLS ON WHAT COULD GO WRONG (future problems)
ENVIES OTHERS (they have what I don't)	DOESN'T TRUST OTHERS (they want what I have)

TYPE 4, THE INDIVIDUALIST, AND TYPE 7, THE ENTHUSIAST

Types 4 and 7 can mistype as each other. They can try on many different careers and places to live, and can explore personal growth. However, they behave this way for different reasons. Type 4s are searching for their true identity, and Type 7s are running away from their past, from emotional pain, and toward an anticipated, pleasurable future. Also, Type 7s don't want to close down options, and one way to accomplish that is to never fully commit to one direction.

However, in most ways, Types 4 and 7 are opposite sides of the same coin, looking in different directions. Type 4s get stuck in the past and what went wrong, and Type 7s are focused on the future: planning, anticipating, and visualizing possibilities. Both of these strategies keep them away from the present moment—the here and now. Type 4s hang on to strong feelings and memories from their past, and Type 7s quickly leave the past behind in favor of an anticipated, exciting future.

SOURCES OF CONFLICT

Type 4s tend to envy Type 7s' ease with people. Type 7s often are annoyed by yet admire Type 4s' softness and sensitive nature—something Type 7s would be wise to cultivate.

Types 4 and 7 can rub each other the wrong way when stressed. Type 7s will be annoyed by Type 4s' need to be special, to be seen as the "sensitive one"; by their moodiness; and by the way they draw attention to themselves. Type 7s annoy Type 4s when they are insensitive, impatient, or the center of attention, and when they are unwilling to take the time to discuss whatever upsets have occurred for Type 4s. Type 4s want to deeply process emotional affronts or hurts, and Type 7s would like to get it over with quickly and move on. They need to be careful not to judge each other for their differences or try to pull the other out of their moods. Type 7s will feel brought down out of their happy, positive frame, and Type 4s don't want to have their feelings dismissed or disregarded.

SYNERGISTIC POTENTIAL

Type 4s will be balanced by the action-oriented, practical, analytical, and positive outlook of Type 7s, and Type 7s will be balanced by Type 4s' ease in contacting their feelings, ability to grieve, sensitivity, ability to bring ideas into creative expression, and slower pace.

When Type 4s have mood swings, an approach that will serve both of them is for Type 7 to be present and soothing with Type 4—don't try to fix them, make it better, or do anything. Express empathy and listen. Soften your heart. When Type 4s can allow themselves to be inspired by Type 7s, join them in some fun and activity, or take purposeful action, this will enable Type 4s to take a joyful and positive stance, and to move toward bringing their creativity into tangible form. They can be great teachers for each other.

In a professional/work setting, neither likes to be managed closely. Type 7s appreciate a boss who is available for advice, counsel, mentoring, direction, and support, and then leaves them alone to take the ball and run with it. Type 4s like the freedom to take a creative approach to their work and need to feel seen, understood, and appreciated for their unique contribution. Type 4s can choose a variety of different careers, but the common thread is their need for approaching their work in a creative way. That could mean law, accounting, or running a boutique. They like to make an impact on the business and know that it is valued by their clients, colleagues, and superiors.

Together these two could make a powerful pair. Type 7s inspire and encourage, manage multiple projects simultaneously, synthesize, and network, and they are highly productive. Type 4s are sensitive to others, value authenticity, will employ their creativity when given something to sink their teeth into and the freedom and support to make it happen, and often create beauty around them. Together they can bring ideas and projects to fruition that are visionary and creative, and can engage and involve others to contribute their best.

TYPE DISTINCTIONS

TYPE 4 : TYPE 7

TYPE 4	TYPE 7
WITHDRAWS	ASSERTS
BELIEVES THE GLASS IS HALF-EMPTY	BELIEVES THE GLASS IS HALF-FULL
IS MELANCHOLIC AND MOODY	IS UPBEAT AND ENTHUSIASTIC, WITH A POSITIVE OUTLOOK
LIKES TO BE UNIQUE AND SPECIAL	IS COMFORTABLE BEING THE CENTER OF ATTENTION
GOES AT THEIR OWN PACE	IS FAST TALKING AND FAST PACED
IS SENSITIVE TO OTHERS	CAN BE INSENSITIVE AND IMPATIENT
WITHHOLDS	PUSHES
ENVIES OTHERS	ENCOURAGES OTHERS
LONGS FOR IT	GOES OUT AND GETS IT
HAS UNIQUE EXPRESSION	IS A SYNTHESIZER OF IDEAS
IS PRIVATE	IS PERSONABLE
IS IN SEARCH OF THEIR UNIQUE IDENTITY	LIKES VARIETY
FILTERS LIFE THROUGH FEELINGS	FILTERS LIFE THROUGH THINKING
IS DECISIVE	IS INDECISIVE
IS WARMHEARTED	FEELINGS ARE REPRESSED
FOCUSES ON THE PAST	FOCUSES ON THE FUTURE

TYPE 5, THE DETACHED OBSERVER, AND TYPE 6, THE LOYAL SKEPTIC

Types 5 and 6 are both in the Head/Thinking Center and Fear/Anxiety Triad of the Enneagram. They are analytical and fearful but manifest these traits differently. Type 5s look below them and inside themselves and see a void. They feel an inner emptiness and lack faith that there is support for them. They decide that the head is a safe place to reside and that by acquiring knowledge and developing their expertise, they will fill up their inner emptiness and create security for themselves.

Type 5s don't trust easily and have only a few chosen intimates. Type 6s look below their feet and see that they are standing on a fault line. The earth could shake at any time and bad things happen. They feel out of control and unsafe. Type 6s expend a lot of energy preparing for what could go wrong in order to feel safe and in control—this involves research, planning, creating backup plans, asking others for advice, and so on. Then again, they don't really trust other people either, because they are always suspicious of others' motives.

SOURCES OF CONFLICT

Because Type 5s are allergic to intrusions, they have a difficult time with the sometimes-intrusive Type 6s who have a *need to know*. When Type 5s detach and withdraw, it amps up the anxiety of Type 6s. They move toward Type 5 to quell their anxiety, which can precipitate Type 5's need to protect themselves even more. Type 6s can feel walled out by Type 5s and unappreciated. They may also resent being left with the responsibility to manage all of the practicalities. Type 6s can perceive Type 5s as being a little too "heady" and lacking in spontaneity, playfulness, and excitement.

On the other hand, Type 5s are unlikely to match the emotional intensity of Type 6s. When Type 5s take a nonreactive posture, use some gentle humor, and are *present* with Type 6s, it can bring them back to a calm reasonableness.

Their biggest shared blind spot is overreliance on their analytical minds. Too much analysis gets, well, too much analysis. Type 5s have ideas *about* things, and like to theorize. Type 6s can get paralyzed by analysis, concerns about future problems, and an active internal board of directors that wants to optimize decisions. Both trust their minds to the exclusion of their other intelligences.

Type 5s don't often give much direction, and Type 6s want direction and to be supported. Type 5s want Type 6s to act autonomously, and Type 6s want Type 5s to help with decision making. Type 5s get annoyed by the what-could-go-wrong focus of Type 6s when Type 5s propose ideas, while simultaneously appreciating the thinking behind Type 6s' concerns.

SYNERGISTIC POTENTIAL

Types 5 and 6 would be a highly intellectual pair. They share their love of information, ideas and analysis, being informed, reading, and continual education. Type 6s feel safe with Type 5s because they are fairly self-contained, and they problem-solve and think objectively, are contained and calm, and don't appear to want or need anything. When problems or adversity arises, cool-headed Type 5s can step back and come up with unique solutions to the problem—they love to fix problems and don't seem to get rattled by them. This will calm Type 6s' anxiety and help them feel they are standing on solid ground. Type 5s will feel supported by Type 6s' practical nature. They will appreciate being able to count on Type 6 to take responsibility and follow through.

Professionally, these two can be a powerful pair—the innovator and the market researcher. Type 5s are great at coming up with ideas, and Type 6s are great at taking responsibility for making things happen. Type 5s are less relational, and Type 6s can be more sociable and can help bring Type 5s out of their cave. Type 6s are prepared and thorough. Type 5s can see things from an objective place.

TYPE DISTINCTIONS

TYPE 5 | TYPE 6

TYPE 5	TYPE 6
WITHDRAWS	MOVES TOWARD AND WITHDRAWS
WANTS TO BE THE EXPERT	WANTS TO BE PREPARED
DETACHES AND PROTECTS INNER RESOURCES	IS SUSPICIOUS AND SKEPTICAL
FEARS THAT THERE IS NO SUPPORT FOR THEM	FEARS THAT THE WORLD IS AN UNSAFE PLACE
FILTERS LIFE THROUGH THEIR HEAD AND INTELLECT	FILTERS LIFE THROUGH DUTY AND RESPONSIBILITY
HAS A BUSY MIND	HAS A BUSY MIND
LIKES TO TELL WHAT THEY KNOW	LIKES TO SHARE INFORMATION AND RESOURCES
TRUSTS THEIR IDEAS	DOESN'T TRUST THEMSELVES OR OTHERS
HAS A HEAD FULL OF IDEAS	HAS A HEAD FULL OF DOUBTING WHAT-IF VOICES
IS IMPRACTICAL	IS PRACTICAL
IS CONFLICT AVOIDANT	IS CONFLICT AVOIDANT
FOCUSES ON MASTERY, HOW THINGS WORK	FOCUSES ON WHAT COULD GO WRONG
CAN BE SOCIALLY AWKWARD	CAN BE SOCIALLY AWKWARD BUT WARM AND ENGAGING
IS COOL AND IMPERSONAL	IS WARM AND PERSONABLE, AND SOMETIMES GREGARIOUS
IS A LEADER BY REMOTE CONTROL	IS AN INVOLVED LEADER WITH TEAM FOCUS
EXCLUDES SELF	HAS ISSUES OF INCLUSION AND EXCLUSION

TYPE 5, THE DETACHED OBSERVER, AND TYPE 7, THE ENTHUSIAST

Both Types are in the Head/Fear Center of the Enneagram and hold a belief that there is no support for them. However, both react to their fears differently. Type 5s *pull in*, and Type 7s are *on the go*.

Type 5s minimize their needs, detach emotionally, compartmentalize people and situations, and conserve and hoard their energy (and things) so that they don't need to rely on anyone. Type 7s are afraid of being deprived. *Carpe diem!* They live for today and taste everything at the buffet just in case the opportunity won't come along again. They believe that there is no one available to take care of them and they are on their own. It is up to them to make things happen.

SOURCES OF CONFLICT

Type 5s can feel pushed by Type 7s: their pace is fast, they're ready for action, and they are happy *doers*. Type 7s seek change, adventure, and excitement, and have joie de vivre! Type 5s' pace is slower, more leisurely, and they like to have time alone with their ideas, to read, explore, acquire information, and so on. Type 7's enthusiasm can feel dampened and stifled by the oft-stubborn Type 5, who wants to control their emotional expression and conserve their energy, and doesn't want to be pulled along. Type 5s feel the pull to join Type 7s in their enthusiasm for all things, and they might resist to maintain a sense of control.

Type 7 wants to be involved in decision making, and Type 5's *decide and announce* style can be seen as demeaning. It can also reinforce the *I don't wanna grow up* persona of Type 7, who can then abdicate responsibility. However, this will invariably come back and bite them. This can be a professional challenge if the two are collaborating. Type 5 can show up with a finished product (in their mind) without having solicited input from Type 7.

When stressed, Type 7s can become impatient, upset, perfectionistic, and critical. Type 5s have difficulty dealing with their big energy and anger—in fact, they won't. They'll withdraw, perhaps after uttering some cruel, cutting remark. Once Type 5s detach, they may just decide *that's it* and disengage completely. This can activate assertive

Type 7s' desire to try to regain the trust of Type 5; however, when it's over, it's over.

Because both Types are highly independent, this can work for a while in a love relationship. However, over time, both people will feel like two independent operators living under the same roof. The collaborative potential is lost, and their sense of isolation becomes amplified. Their mutual feeling of isolation and lack of a compassionate presence reinforces their underlying belief that there is no support.

They are both in a double bind. Each Type wants to connect and desires support, but at what cost? For Type 7, the fear is loss of freedom. For Type 5, the fears are of exposure, of their own neediness, and of letting go of control. Type 5 withdraws and pulls up the drawbridge. This reinforces Type 7's belief that there is no one there for them and they need to be self-reliant. They begin to envision happy options and take steps toward that vision. This evokes loneliness for them both, and Type 5's feelings of emptiness become acute. Both of them need emotional support, and neither is skilled at either giving or receiving it—despite their desire and need for it. They both run, but in different directions.

SYNERGISTIC POTENTIAL

Types 5 and 7 are often drawn to each other—both being Head Types, they love to talk about ideas, concepts, and theories with each other. A line on the Enneagram symbol connects them, and each seems to want what the other has.

Type 7 is out and about and engaged in the world, full of enthusiasm, excitement, and possibilities. They can grab Type 5 by the hand as if to say, "Come on, let's go! Let's make it happen. Let's have an adventure!" and they help pull Type 5 out of themselves to engage in the world.

Conversely, Type 5 is a grounding influence for Type 7's "keep several balls spinning in the air" energy. Type 5's energy is more contained and focused and can help Type 7 to slow down and be more introspective. Type 5s have the patience, objectivity, depth, focus, and inner guidance that Type 7s need and desire.

Under stress, Type 5s can take on some of the less healthy qualities of Type 7s and become distracted, try to implement multiple ideas at once, and not take the time they need to do their due diligence. They can also become much more fearful of there being no solid ground beneath them. When this happens, Type 7s can access their 8 Wing, becoming centered, grounded, and solid. Then they have a firm grip on the tiller and don't get pulled off course by Type 5. They bring Type 5 back to center again, and quell their anxieties and worries.

Professionally, these two can be quite a team, with their innovative, visionary, creative potential.

 ## AN INSIDEOUT LEADER'S STORY: **TEAM MEETINGS CONTINUE**

A few off-site meetings occur. The leadership development that the team members receive is appreciated, and they find it to be illuminating. Their work with the Enneagram continues and has become an integral part of their meetings as a way to leverage strengths and manage reactions.

They make great progress on their strategic plan, and some of their innovative ideas are quite counter to NHH's culture. They choose not to see this as an obstacle for the time being, but to forge ahead and develop what they believe will be a successful plan.

Their work requires crossing silos and building relationships outside the organization. They are becoming an x-team (teams that balance internal processes with an external focus) embedded in a very different culture. Lars and Chris are concerned about whether the organization's immune system will see them as an invader and spit them out. Caitlin is struggling, and they are all dealing with organizational buzz that they are renegades. Will the team stick together even if they become outliers at NHH?

Lars knows that for them to succeed, he needs a real LT, meaning a leader-full team, so he stays the course and continues with his leadership development efforts, the Enneagram being the centerpiece. He can see that some of the team members are growing and others are struggling. Can they move fast enough? Tony seems to have come around a bit, carried by the thawing of others on the LT and their genuine engagement on the team.

While Lars is pleased at the progress, he is still impatient, and the pressure is on for results.

➜ Lars's story continues on p. 374

TYPE DISTINCTIONS

TYPE 5 | TYPE 7

WITHDRAWS TO GET NEEDS MET	ASSERTS AND ASKS FOR WHAT THEY WANT
THINKS AND SPEAKS ABOUT IDEAS, CONCEPTS, THEORIES	THINKS AND DIALOGS ABOUT IDEAS, CONCEPTS, AND THEORIES
WANTS TO BE THE *expert*	WANTS TO BE COMPETENT
IS DEEP	IS BROAD
HAS UNDERLYING FEAR AND ANXIETY	HAS UNDERLYING FEAR AND ANXIETY
TRUSTS THEIR HEAD	TRUSTS THEIR HEAD
THINKS ABOUT THEIR FEELINGS	ACTS OUT AND SPEAKS ABOUT THEIR FEELINGS
OBSERVES	INTERACTS
DETACHES	CONNECTS
IS SERIOUS AND CONTAINED	IS PLAYFUL AND EXPRESSIVE
IS SOCIALLY UNCOMFORTABLE	IS SOCIALLY SKILLFUL
IS FOCUSED	IS SCATTERED
DECIDES AND ANNOUNCES	GATHERS INPUT AND DECIDES
LEADS BY EXPERTISE	LEADS BY INSPIRATION
LEADS BY REMOTE CONTROL	LEADS BY EXPECTING PEOPLE TO TAKE INITIATIVE *(let me know if you need me)*
LIKES FILM NOIR	LIKES HAPPILY EVER AFTER
HAS TRUST ISSUES	HAS TRUST ISSUES
VALUES PRIVACY AND SECRECY	IS OPEN AND PERSONABLE
WITHHOLDS INFORMATION	SHARES INFORMATION
HIDES VULNERABILITY	HIDES VULNERABILITY
IS SELF-FOCUSED AND SELF-REFERENCED	IS SELF-CENTERED

TYPE 6, THE LOYAL SKEPTIC, AND TYPE 7, THE ENTHUSIAST

Types 6 and 7 are both prone to anxiety. It isn't often apparent to others or to themselves that anxiety and fear are at play for Type 7s. Type 6s know themselves to be worriers and anxious. Type 7s are so busy running away from uncomfortable feelings that they are often unaware of their own fear and anxiety. Type 7s are worried that there isn't enough to go around and somehow they will be deprived and trapped without. They deal with their anxiety and fear by running away from it through lots of activities and plans, fast talking, looking to the future, and keeping several balls in the air. Type 6s try to calm their own fears and anxieties by planning, preparing, asking questions, and researching things thoroughly. When they *know* what to expect and they can be *prepared*, Type 6s believe they will feel secure.

SOURCES OF CONFLICT

Types 6 and 7 find themselves at odds when the responsible Type 6 runs into the freedom-seeking, noncommittal yet overcommitted, wanting-to-play Type 7. When Type 7s don't follow through, Type 6s see them as flaky and unreliable, and then dismiss them.

Type 7s become frustrated when Type 6s throw their wet blanket onto the fire of Type 7s' optimism or latest ideas. Type 6's skepticism and *what could go wrong* focus can feel suffocating to Type 7. Type 6s are known to question, drill into things, and play the devil's advocate. If Type 7s aren't aware of what Type 6s are doing—making sure that their ideas can really fly—this can send Type 7s into despair, frustration, or a defensive reaction.

Type 7s can throw out random comments or ideas that Type 6s take literally. Type 6s become mistrusting of Type 7s if they don't follow through. In the future, Type 6 may be vigilant in search of more evidence that Type 7 is not to be trusted.

SYNERGISTIC POTENTIAL

Types 6 and 7 are Head Types—meaning that this is their comfort zone. They can enjoy bantering with each other, and often Type 7s have the ability to get Type 6s to laugh at themselves. They will appreciate each other's intellect and curiosity. They'll share books, their networks, and educational resources.

Type 7 can bring levity and playfulness to the otherwise more intense and serious Type 6. Type 6s model commitment, follow-through, and thorough preparation for Type 7s.

These two make a good team because they are both active, intellectually curious, and sociable, and they like to make things happen. Type 6s help Type 7s to look before they leap, and Type 7s help Type 6s to become more trusting of themselves and their intuition, more confident, and more playful and light. An interesting distinction and opportunity for these two is that Type 7s focus on the system—interconnection and potential impacts, both upside and downside—and Type 6s focus on risks—things that could go wrong along the way, cause and effect. Type 7s' inner eye sees a mind map or pinball machine lighting up with all of the places that a decision could touch.

Type 7s are great initiators of ideas and projects, are visionary, take risks, and are strategic. Type 6s are great at making sure that all aspects of the plan or idea are thought through and are able to take the idea all the way to completion. Type 7s are instrumental in helping Type 6s to develop self-confidence. Type 7s trust people to do their job, give lots of freedom, and are encouraging. Type 6s are great supporters and are reliable. Together, they make great things happen.

TYPE DISTINCTIONS

TYPE 6	TYPE 7
FEELS THEY SHOULD BE RESPONSIBLE	DOESN'T LIKE TO ASSUME RESPONSIBILITY
DEALS WITH FEAR ABOUT WHAT COULD GO WRONG BY BEING PREPARED	DEALS WITH FEAR ABOUT WHAT COULD HAPPEN BY KEEPING OPTIONS OPEN
FOCUSES ON WHAT COULD GO WRONG	FOCUSES ON PLEASURABLE FUTURE PLANS AND POSSIBILITIES
DOESN'T TRUST THEMSELVES AND OTHERS	DOESN'T TRUST THAT THERE IS ENOUGH
TENDS TOWARD WORRY AND ANXIETY	HAS ANXIETY
IS ANALYTICAL	IS ANALYTICAL
LACKS CONFIDENCE	IS CONFIDENT
MOVES TOWARD	ASSERTS
FOCUSES ON WHAT COULD GO WRONG	HAS AN OPTIMISTIC OUTLOOK
CAN BE SOCIALLY AWKWARD	IS SOCIALLY ADEPT
IS A RESPONSIBLE LEADER	IS AN INSPIRATIONAL LEADER
IS CONFLICT AVOIDANT	IS CONFLICT AVOIDANT
IS COMMITTED	HAS A HARD TIME COMMITTING
IS SKEPTICAL OF OTHERS	TRUSTS UNTIL PROVEN OTHERWISE
RESPECTS AUTHORITY OR DEVIL'S ADVOCATE	EQUALIZES AUTHORITY

SAME-TYPE PAIRS

I have segmented out *same-Type* pairs (for example, Type 3 working with another Type 3) because I treat them differently than Type pairs that aren't the same. It stands to reason that interacting with someone of the same Type can trigger reactions simply because we look in the mirror and see things we don't like about ourselves. Additionally, when we work with someone of our Type, we may share common strengths and blind spots. For this reason, it is important to tune in to how each Type acts when they are *doing their Type* versus when they are less defended and more self-aware.

When two people of the same Type work together, it is important to look at additional factors that delineate people of the same Type. The level of emotional health and the primary *Instincts* driving behavior (one-to-one, social, self-preservation) are important determiners of how people of the same Type can show up differently. These important drivers are survival instincts, and people of the same Type can have three distinct ways of creating safety for themselves (see "Instincts: The 27 Facets of the Enneagram" in Chapter 6). Therefore, I include a very brief description of the three Instincts for each same-Type pair.

If you are two people of the same Type, see if you can identify your predominant Instinct, and then explore how you can use your differences as strengths. For example, if two Type 1s work together, and one's focus is on their self-preservation needs and the other's focus is on their social needs, their energy will be put to use in different ways, and their outward manner will appear different.

TYPE 1, THE PERFECTIONIST, AND TYPE 1, THE PERFECTIONIST

Emotional health: Average healthy Type 1s will be more rigid and rule bound, convinced of their *rightness*, and driven by a need to perfect and organize. Healthier Type 1s will be more flexible, contextual, accepting, and expressive of what bothers them.

Instincts: One-to-ones are likely to put their time and attention into perfecting and attending to their primary relationships (boss, employee, partner, children, close friends). Type 1s are connected to their ideals; however, those who are driven by the social Instinct express their ideals by getting involved in causes. Those driven by self-preservation tend to be more focused on creating order, structure, health, and home.

That said, both share a disciplined approach to work, attend to the quality of their work, are busy doers, are critical, and express their anger with an air of moral authority and superiority. Fairness and acting appropriately is important.

AREAS FOR INTERPERSONAL CONFLICT

They can have points of tension about what is *right,* good enough, and the best structure. They may each have a different design sense or way of organizing, and both believe their way is right. Type 1s have strong viewpoints and happily share them. They can feel criticized and nitpicked by the other, controlled, and micromanaged.

Type 1s want to do the best job and deliver high quality. There is constant room for improvement, and they can trigger each other's inner critic. If they are working on a project together, it can go way out of scope because of their standards for perfection. They can work themselves to exhaustion, each upping the ante.

Type 1s have high expectations for a job well done. This is what you are paid to do, so *thanks* are not necessarily forthcoming for hard work, sacrifice, and long hours.

They may trigger each other's worry and anxiety, risk aversion, and critical voice.

SYNERGISTIC POTENTIAL

Two Type 1s together produce high quality. They both take responsibility to deliver what they promise, will be a powerful pairing if they share ideals, and will deal fairly with one another. Because they defer enjoyment until the work is done, they will be on the same page and stick it out together through completion.

They will appreciate each other's methodical and orderly approach to work, thoroughness, and adherence to standards.

TYPE 2, THE PEOPLE PLEASER, AND TYPE 2, THE PEOPLE PLEASER

Emotional health: Average healthy Type 2s will focus on the needs of select others, self-image, and being appreciated. They believe that by aligning with and supporting others in positions of power, they derive their own power and value. They may be demanding, intrusive, and needy. Healthier Type 2s ask for what they want and need, are more balanced between other-focus and self-focus, readily accept support, and step into their own position of power.

Instincts: A one-to-one Type 2 is the most likely to attach to someone in a position of power in order to derive a sense of worthiness. They are also the seducers and can charm and reel you in. The one-to-one Type 2 is a great gatekeeper and at the same time can be intrusive and clingy. Self-preservation Type 2s like to give in a more material way. Along with that comes a sense of entitlement. Healthy social Type 2s will orchestrate volunteer drives, for instance. They express their *goodness* in a social context. They can also manipulate the group to maintain their social standing—perhaps playing people off one another.

AREAS FOR INTERPERSONAL CONFLICT

If both Type 2s are peers and work for the same boss, they can compete for attention and approval from the boss and the team. They are masters of manipulation and seduction and will compete on these grounds as well. As the boss, it would be wise to be aware of this propensity and not take the bait. Equally important will be to give recognition and express appreciation to both.

Type 2s are not often in tune with their own needs; rather, they tend to be aware of the needs of others. Their pride gets in the way, and they don't readily accept help, nor are they often open to constructive feedback. This can make it difficult to work together in a supportive way and to work through conflict that arises. Often it can lead to emotional outbursts when their manipulation for approval and attention isn't working.

SYNERGISTIC POTENTIAL

Type 2s are above all relational. They are usually warm, caring, and empathic. If both set aside their pride, they can make a great supportive team. A Type 2 boss will excel at expressing appreciation, and a Type 2 employee will try to make the boss look good. In a team environment, they can both look out for the emotional needs of the team members and create a nurturing, supportive environment in which to work. Type 2s tend to be upbeat, positive, and high energy, and can bring that to their working relationship as well as to the organization. They will excel at working across organization boundaries.

TYPE 3, THE ACHIEVER, AND TYPE 3, THE ACHIEVER

Emotional health: Type 3s of average health will compete to be the best at the expense of others and do what it takes to achieve success. They will cut corners and focus on the most effective way to get to the goal. They seek the validation and admiration of others for their achievements. They are chameleons who know how to fit in and play their role in order to achieve their ends.

Healthier Type 3s are interested in helping others shine, such as their boss, colleagues, and people who work for them. They often enjoy the role of mentor. They know how to make things happen and get the job done. They are generally positive in their outlook, supportive, and high energy, and the room can light up when they enter. Often these are great promoters of themselves and others, and are marketers.

Instincts: One-to-one Type 3s are the most likely to appear shiny and polished. They want to be attractive to others. Social Type 3s focus on social status. They want to know where they stand in relation to the team or organization and will compete for status. Self-preservation Type 3s' focus is on the material. They look for validation based on what they have acquired.

AREAS FOR INTERPERSONAL CONFLICT

Competition for validation, achievement, and success could be the undoing of both of them. There is enough room for only one star. Who is it going to be? Backstabbing and attempts to undermine are possible when both share a common goal and are competing to be the best. Neither is willing to be the one who *fails*. When this is a boss/employee relationship, if the boss only views the other Type 3 as a means to allow them to shine and take credit, not only will this be demoralizing for the employee Type 3, but over time their motivation and productivity will decline and they may withdraw.

Relationship often takes a back seat to their goal orientation. When they don't take time to build trust and a bond with the other, conflict and misunderstandings can result. Both are too busy *doing*. If one is the boss and the other the employee, admiration that the employee seeks may not be forthcoming. Average healthy Type 3s can be spare with praise and encouragement, and they are more likely to keep setting the bar higher. Type 3s focus on quickly and efficiently getting the job done and expect you to do the same.

Short, brusque, efficient e-mails and social interactions can be misinterpreted and evoke a Type 6 reaction—fear, looking for hidden meaning and agendas, worry and anxiety. Type 3s care more than other Types about appearance and want to avoid failure at all costs. They can hurl accusations or try to undermine the other.

SYNERGISTIC POTENTIAL

It is not unusual to see sales and marketing organizations heavily populated by Type 3s. They like to compete to win. They can egg each other on to win the annual sales junket or make the Circle of Excellence. They are most likely individual performers rather than team players.

If it is a boss/employee relationship, they will happily form an efficient, can-do, go-get-'em team. The environment in both situations is upbeat, focused, high energy, and hardworking. A Type 3 boss will recognize the need to set clear, achievable but tough goals in order to get the best out of a Type 3 employee. They will also know to provide incentives and recognition to keep Type 3s motivated. Taking another Type 3 under your wing and acting as mentor can be a great professional growth opportunity.

Time to build the relationship and for play as well as connecting on a more personal level strengthens their bond, and healthy Type 3s know to make room for this.

TYPE 4, THE INDIVIDUALIST, AND TYPE 4, THE INDIVIDUALIST

Emotional health: Type 4s of average emotional health tend to be more melancholic and self-absorbed, need to be seen as unique and special, and will use drama to get attention. They have a hard time with sustained action. Type 4s often feel that they fall short of their ideal self-image, which evokes feelings of shame. Healthier Type 4s have more clarity about their unique gifts and skills and use them. They are self-accepting, action oriented, profound in their thinking, and sensitive to the needs of others.

Instincts: One-to-one Type 4s are more focused on forming connections with others and are known to be intense. Social Type 4s are more prone to want to stand out on the team and be seen as unique and special. Self-preservation 4s will express their *uniqueness* by surrounding themselves (and/or wearing) things that have meaning.

AREAS FOR INTERPERSONAL CONFLICT

Two Type 4s working together can be quite competitive. Who is the most profound and sensitive or the most unique? They can secretly envy each other, and this will ultimately lead to conflict or at least create a difficult team environment. Each wants to authentically express who they are.

Although they share a need for a creative outlet, finding a common expression for their creativity will be a challenge. Imagine two Type 4s working together on a design for the next iPad. They both desire to do something meaningful but in their own authentic way.

Type 4s tend to over-idealize people, situations, and the future, and then become disappointed when their idealized vision is not met. Inevitably they find something missing in the other (boss, employee, job): "You're not who I thought you were." This can lead to moodiness, anger, or rejection of the other and a longing for something or someone else that meets their ideal.

SYNERGISTIC POTENTIAL

Type 4s have a need to be seen and understood, and also can see deeply into others. They are able to feel accepted and understood by one another. They both appreciate aesthetics and creativity and will be glad to have a kindred spirit who shares that.

In the midst of stormy weather, keeping a firm hand on the tiller will serve Type 4s with other Type 4s. Calm and steady is the best approach to take when Type 4s become temperamental and moody. They want to trust that you have the capacity to stay with them and can hang in when it get tough. They desperately want to feel seen, understood, and appreciated for their depth, sensitivity, and authenticity. This builds trust and will bring out the best in Type 4s.

If one is the boss, the employee can feel accepted and seen. A Type 4 boss can be a good mentor and will offer creative freedom to their employee. If the employee is given some free rein and can bring their authentic and creative expression to their work (they abhor the mundane), they will work hard and produce.

TYPE 5, THE DETACHED OBSERVER, AND TYPE 5, THE DETACHED OBSERVER

Emotional health: Average healthy Type 5s can be arrogant, be emotionally and physically distant, resemble the absent-minded professor, and be judgmental and rejecting. They wall themselves off from others and share little of themselves, their energy, or their ideas. They are more comfortable relating to their ideas than to people. People are abstractions, and their knowledge comes not from experience but from acquiring information, so it is also an abstraction—a thought about an idea. Working virtually would reinforce their tendencies.

Healthier Type 5s engage, experience, and take an interest in others and the world around them. They come out of their ivory tower and interact with the organization, boss, team, and so on. They are more generous with their time, energy, and information, and contribute actively and collaboratively. Others' needs are taken into account, and they become more expressive of their needs, wants, and feelings.

Instincts: One-to-one Type 5s can be the most intense of the three instinctual Types, and they have a greater need to make connections with others. They may also be more confrontational (8ish) than the other Type 5s. The social Type 5s are more aware of the group and have a greater need to fit in, albeit from a safe distance, where they maintain the observer role. Self-preservation 5s are the most 5ish of the 5s. They have more need than the others to maintain their boundaries and have private time. Self-preservation 5s share very little of themselves with others.

AREAS FOR INTERPERSONAL CONFLICT

Type 5s are, more often than not, individual contributors, happy to work on their own and offer up their ideas and innovations. If these two are on a team together, they will have a tough time collaborating. Both like to be in control and are not particularly communicative or likely to share information with each other. Their communication style, whether interpersonal or across team boundaries, is likely to be impersonal in content and medium, to the point, and sparse.

SYNERGISTIC POTENTIAL

These two will enjoy intellectual sparring, will recognize each other's needs for space and distance, will respect and be stimulated by each other's intellect and innovative thinking, and are likely to be accepting of the other in all of their *quirkiness*. They are highly self-reliant and dispassionate and have a live-and-let-live attitude that they appreciate about each other.

If one is the boss and the other an employee, this situation can work well. The boss will be happy to leave the Type 5 employee alone to get the job accomplished. The employee will go to the boss for help only when absolutely necessary, which will suit the Type 5 boss just fine. There will be a mutual respect and understanding of the other's needs.

TYPE 6, THE LOYAL SKEPTIC, AND TYPE 6, THE LOYAL SKEPTIC

Emotional health: Average healthy Type 6s act skeptical, play devil's advocate, search for hidden motives and agendas, have difficulty trusting others, and have self-doubt. They are indecisive and waffle when they have made decisions. To overcome their insecurities, they can overly self-promote and show off. Worry and anxiety about *what could happen* can paralyze them. Often, they can take an apparently benign situation and blow it up into a worst-case scenario. They have a felt need to be responsible, and at the same time this creates pressure for them to deliver.

Healthier Type 6s trust their instincts and intuition, trust others more easily, ask directly rather than assuming that the motives they've attributed to others are the truth, and are self-confident. They are thoughtful analyzers and gifted at research and planning. They are loyal, dedicated, and often warm, and can be your biggest champion.

Instincts: One-to-one Type 6s are more likely to test the loyalty of others. You may think you've earned their trust, but you can count on them to test your loyalty over and over. They are also more competitive than the others, looking to prove their desirability. Social Type 6s are more conscious of where they fit in with the group and have a need for strong alliances. Self-preservation Type 6s are the most focused on security—money, health, home … and turn to important alliances for safety, whether to a group of like-minded individuals, to organizations, or by forming alliances with important others.

AREAS FOR INTERPERSONAL CONFLICT

If both focus on what could go wrong, nothing may get accomplished. These two could get mired in worrying about potential negative consequences and miss out on creative ideation and solutioning. Their hyper-alert stance can trigger suspicion and misinterpretation of motives in the other, making it difficult to build trust. Accusations may start to fly and power/authority issues surface. The tone can become mean and retaliatory.

Any boss-to-subordinate relationship can bring out Type 6s' authority issues, and Type 6 can easily move into the role of devil's advocate as the subordinate. It will also bring out the boss's ambivalence toward being the authority.

The best tack for Type 6s is to make their thinking transparent—to ask when they have worries or concerns rather than making up their own story and then believing it to be the truth.

SYNERGISTIC POTENTIAL

These two will innately understand the other's need to be able to trust, and they know how to forge these bonds of trust. They can function well in a team environment, both having a natural inclination to be a team player. They will enjoy being able to count on the other to take responsibility for follow-through, and they will appreciate each other's analytical rigor and need for thorough planning and preparation.

If they share the same side of an issue, they can forge a strong bond and take on tough challenges together.

TYPE 7, THE ENTHUSIAST, AND TYPE 7, THE ENTHUSIAST

Emotional health: Average healthy 7s have difficulty making and/or honoring commitments; or they over-commit and then have time-management challenges, are impatient, are distractible, and have a short attention span. Type 7s like to keep their options wide open, are indecisive, and change their priorities. They can lack follow-through, and can be perfectionistic, critical, and sharp-edged.

Healthy Type 7s slow down, focus, develop expertise, synthesize, empathize, become grounded and wise. They are joyful, visionary, and inspirational.

Instincts: One-to-one Type 7s are more intense than the social and self-preservation 7s, and their focus is on their inner world and strong individual connections. Social 7s are probably the most active and busy of the three, bordering on frenetic. They are more community minded than the others as well. Self-preservation 7s' focus is on the *many:* friends, physical pleasures such as entertaining, food, their environment, and so on.

AREAS FOR INTERPERSONAL CONFLICT

As with all same-Type interactions, they can easily trigger in each other things they don't like about themselves. In the case of Type 7s, on a project together (whether teammates or boss and subordinate), for example, they may get frustrated with each other's difficulty closing down options, shifting priorities, and problems with project completion. They will both happily leap into the beginning of a project or plan with great enthusiasm and miss some of the potential downsides of implementing their plan. When things start unraveling, they get stressed, or worse—bored; this kind of situation brings out the critical, judgmental, sharp-edged impatience of Type 7. Neither wants to hurt their work relationship, so they avoid confrontation. Or if they do confront, the critical, sharp-edged tone can take on the authoritative voice of judgment (the downside of Type 1).

SYNERGISTIC POTENTIAL

In a boss–subordinate relationship, this combination can work well. Type 7 doesn't like to micromanage and doesn't like to be micromanaged. They are independent workers and leaders. They share a common positive outlook, are both visionary, and contribute a lot of energy and enthusiasm to their common cause. They will enjoy each other's free-spirited nature and quick mind. They will enjoy a playful, light banter and can create an upbeat work environment.

The openness of Type 7 means anything is possible, and they would rather look to the future than at how things have been done in the past or not worked in the past. Type 7s' resiliency and optimism for the future will help them get through tough times.

TYPE 8, THE BOSS, AND TYPE 8, THE BOSS

Emotional health: Average healthy Type 8s like to be in control and call the shots; are impulsive, impatient, confrontational, direct, condemning, demanding, unaware of consequences, insensitive, and overbearing; can dominate a conversation or meeting; and can take revenge for acts of disloyalty.

Healthy Type 8s are generous, protective, supportive, empathic, persistent, determined, and capable of greatness; believe in themselves; can be warm and caring and show vulnerability; and can be inclusive, be decisive, and take time to make good decisions.

Instincts: Type 8 is an Instinctual Type, and these are simply three variations of how Type 8s act out their instincts. One-to-one Type 8s are probably the most *lusty*. They have a lust for life or whatever/whomever they focus their attention on. Social 8s have more group and social awareness than the others. They are inclined to focus on their cause and put energy there. These are the *justice* seekers. Relationships and physical well-being take a backseat. Self-preservation 8s put their focus on their inner circle—their literal or figurative *family*. They appear more introverted and no-nonsense than the others—almost 5ish at times.

AREAS FOR INTERPERSONAL CONFLICT

Who's the boss? Type 8s don't take orders, commands, or direction easily. These two will challenge one another, each believing they know the path forward. This can trigger Type 8s' core issue—fear of others' having power or control over them. A good approach is to offer plenty of encouragement, freedom, and support to a Type 8 subordinate, and to give them free rein with boundaries clearly outlined.

Type 8s want to win and are highly competitive. In a team situation, in a boss–subordinate situation, or on cross-teams where there is a need for collaboration, this could be explosive. On a sales team, their competitive spirit can work to everyone's advantage.

SYNERGISTIC POTENTIAL

What a powerhouse duo! If the two are on the same team, taking on the same challenge, they will have a tremendous capacity to move heaven and earth to realize their vision. A critical ingredient for their success is for each to have a very clearly defined territory so that they are not butting heads. Each needs his or her own, jointly agreed-upon range of control. They share the stage and respect each other's strength. I have seen two Type 8 leaders working together in this kind of situation, and what they managed to accomplish was extraordinary.

Both will appreciate each other's clear, direct, no-nonsense manner of communication. Loyalty is the other special ingredient that makes this partnership work. If one of them does anything that smacks of disloyalty or tries to undermine the other's authority, all bets are off.

TYPE 9, THE PEACEMAKER, AND TYPE 9, THE PEACEMAKER

Instincts: One-to-one Type 9s are a warmer, more assertive version of this Type. They are drawn to intense connection episodically. Social 9s get along well with everybody and may use charm to maintain connection with the group. Self-preservation Type 9s are probably the most withdrawn of the 9s. They are often focused on home and practical matters.

AREAS FOR INTERPERSONAL CONFLICT

Given that average healthy Type 9s choose harmony over conflict creates an interesting conundrum for two 9s working together. Anger is suppressed and builds over time in deference to peace and comfort. They can be darned stubborn and resistant. How will differences be resolved? Someone will have to move out of their comfort zone to initiate contact and face their fear of loss of the relationship in order to resolve issues.

Type 9s are not known as change seekers—it is more comfortable to maintain the status quo than to rock the boat. They are less inclined than other Types to take decisive action or initiative or to provide direction. They are more comfortable deferring to others, and then they complain, blame, or act in a passive-aggressive way when things don't work out. Type 9s can find each other boring and miss the stimulation of the other Types. Because they suppress strong feelings, they can appear rather flat and low energy. Whether boss and employee or team members, all of this can be problematic. The ship needs fuel, a rudder, and direction. Who will take the helm?

SYNERGISTIC POTENTIAL

On the high side, Type 9s are able to see multiple viewpoints, are often empathic and kind, and assert when needed. They are known to have strong opinions, which, when expressed, can provide guidance and direction. Their self-accepting nature will serve each other and the team. Together they will be able to integrate multiple viewpoints and come up with a balanced, thoughtful, integrated approach to whatever situation arises. Their calm steadiness offers ballast when navigating turbulent seas and can help bring ease to an organization or team. As long as they let go of the need to appease all stakeholder groups and take decisive action on their instincts and intuition, they will offer great leadership and team cohesion.

 STOP AND REFLECT

EXERCISE FOR TYPE DYNAMICS—TO BETTER UNDERSTAND AND IMPROVE INTERACTIONS

This exercise is an effective way to take a look at difficult interactions you have with others. When you go through this process, you'll have a better idea of what is going on with both of you and between you (the third person in the interaction).

The best place to start is to take a position that the other person's words and actions are not directed at you. People are often harder on themselves than they are on you. The same judgments, criticisms, lies, and so on are being enacted at them.

As a general rule, people who annoy you do not intend to do so. They are acting from their interpretation of events based on their worldview (beliefs, motivations, history) and their self-identity.

When you get *hooked*, this exercise will help give you insight into your dynamic.

Instructions: This is a good process to work on with your coach or to work through in your journal. Take a moment to contemplate the dynamic. Imagine observing yourself and the other person sitting in chairs facing each other.

Describe the situation as you observe it. See how objective you can be. Name your characters. Write a story about them. Imagine what is going on in the interior world of each of them. See if you can put yourself in their shoes.

What assumptions do you have about each of them? How do you know they are true?

Is this interaction familiar? When has it shown up in your life? What circumstances trigger it?

How is each person feeling about the other? What might they be thinking about each other?

How do you benefit when you react in this way? How does it harm you and others?

How is each person getting hooked by the other?

If you could reenact the situation, what might you say or do differently to get a better result (both short and long term)?

What need is each person trying to get met (such as safety, freedom, connection)? What are they trying to avoid (such as vulnerability, failure, loss of control, conflict)?

AN INSIDEOUT LEADER'S STORY: **HOW WILL LARS NAVIGATE?**

In parallel, Chris coaches Lars on up-leveling his own interpersonal skills. They have weekly coaching sessions in addition to email and phone communication and use a variety of methods to get underneath some of Lars's longstanding patterns that have become obstacles to his success. While they make progress, Lars wants something to jolt him out of his comfort zone.

There is a storm brewing on the horizon, and Lars wants to be equipped to weather it. How is he going to take care of himself? He has a desire to stay centered, no matter what happens. Chris suggests that they do some immersion coaching. This requires them to get away for a few days together and do some in-depth work. Lars agrees that this could be just what he needs.

Both Chris and Lars are looking forward to going deeper and getting Lars prepared for the rough seas ahead. They work out some clearly defined learning goals for his immersion coaching, and Chris focuses the agenda on working with the core issues of Lars's Enneagram Type. Chris spends a lot of time preparing the content and setting up a supportive context for their time together.

The day finally arrives as they board the airplane. Both feel a tinge of excitement and anxiety. Lars knows this is what he really needs, but he is also aware of the time and financial commitment he is making. It's a leap of faith. The success of this intensive coaching session depends on him. He has to go all out, drop his defenses, and approach this time with curiosity, openness, and willingness. Does he have the courage to do it?

➜ Lars's story continues on p. 376

PART 5

HOW DO WE CHANGE FROM THE INSIDEOUT?

Now that you have found your Enneagram Type, so what? This is the most frequently asked question I get—So what? Now what? At the end of each of the Enneagram Type descriptions in Chapter 5 are practices to help you work with your Enneagram Type's traps and ways you can use to get a grip before your subconscious has its grip on you. Chapter 10, "InsideOut—Leaders' Tool Kit," offers useful tips and practices for everyone. But before you jump ahead, take a moment to get an overview of the brain basics and how our brains change—and therefore we change.

AN INSIDEOUT LEADER'S STORY: **IMMERSION COACHING BEGINS**

Chris and Lars launch their four days together with dinner and a conversation to set the context for the next few days. There is plenty of time built into the agenda for self-reflection, something that Lars ordinarily makes little time for, given his busy schedule. Reflection will be like giving his brain a chance to breathe again. He has been running at such a fast pace, traveling the globe, and has had little time to reflect on what has happened or to make meaning of it. He knows that his creative ideas are often sparked when he has space in his life to write and let his mind meander. But there has been little of this since he signed on for his executive position.

Lars arrives with a brand new journal so that he can capture his insights. The room is set up with markers, a flip chart, paints, music, and so on. This serves to heighten his curiosity and anticipation. Because he has developed a lot of trust with Chris, he is willing to go along with the program. In truth, it feels wonderful having a workshop designed especially for him.

Over the course of the next few days, Chris and Lars hike and talk, and they do a variety of activities to tap into some of the subconscious triggers that spark Lars's reactions. They use different modalities (art, music, movement, journal writing, provocative questions, metaphor and other exercises) to unearth some of Lars's subconscious material and bring it to light. They explore Lars's Enneagram Type and map it to some of the reactive patterns that he knows cause him problems.

One significant pattern they have been working with is brought further into the light: When Lars is in a very stressful situation or going through periods of extended anxiety, he can become defensive and flare up in order to get people to back off (which they generally do). To others, his reactions seem disproportionate to the situation and irrational. After the outburst, Lars retreats and buries his head in the sand, hoping the problem will go away and things magically resolve. Type 6 retreats to Type 9. He doesn't like himself very much when this happens; however, he continues to build a case against the other person if he or she retreats in kind.

The sleeping Type 6 gets a wake-up call. His avoidance behavior creates just the disaster he tries to avoid. He leaves Type 9 in a panic and takes the highway to Type 3, desperate to ward off danger. Lars covers up his fear, exhibits false bravado, dons his mask of success, and begins to embellish his stories to avoid failure. Types 9 and 3 reinforce each other in an unhealthy loop, while the core issue for Type 6—fear and anxiety—precipitates this movement around the Enneagram.

Now that they've identified a core pattern, how will Chris help Lars to unravel it?

➜ Lars's story continues on p. 379

CHAPTER 9

OUR BRAIN—THE BASICS

Let's take a look at the fundamental structure of the brain.

THE TRIUNE BRAIN

Our brain has an onionlike structure consisting of three layers, or three brains contained one inside the other. It actually illustrates our evolution. We can divide the brain into three highly interconnected parts: the reptilian brain, the mammalian or limbic brain, and the neocortex. These three parts of the brain do not operate independently of one another. They have established numerous interconnections through which they influence one another.

The reptilian brain is our survival brain, the center of our instincts, and the oldest of the three. It controls the body's vital functions, such as heart rate, breathing, body temperature, balance, sex drive, autonomic functions, and hormones. It is the seat of the fear response (flight, fight, freeze) and includes the main structures found in a reptile's brain: the brainstem and the cerebellum.

The reptilian brain is reliable but tends to be somewhat rigid and compulsive. When fear arises, it reacts quickly without thinking and subverts the rest of the brain.

The mammalian (limbic) brain emerged with the first mammals and controls emotion and memory. It can record memories of behavior that produced happy/pleasant or disagreeable experiences, and it is responsible for what are called *emotions* in human beings.

The amygdala is part of the limbic system and performs a primary role in the memory of emotional reactions. Just as the reptilian brain reacts quickly and can subvert the neocortex, the limbic brain operates and feels danger 80,000 times faster than the neocortex can think about what is happening, and can trigger a fear response. While we like to think of ourselves as responding *rationally*, often we are making emotional decisions and having emotional reactions masked as rationality.

The limbic brain is the seat of the value judgments we make, often unconsciously, that exert such a strong influence on our behavior.

The last and newest part of the human brain to evolve is the neocortex. This is our *executive brain*. It is most evolved in primates and is the last area of the brain to mature—at about age 25! The neocortex is the rational, objective part of the brain and has the capacity for foresight, insight, and self-awareness. The neocortex does not produce emotions, but rather it modulates and integrates feelings and speaks about our feelings. It is the part of us responsible for the development of human language, abstract thought, imagination, and consciousness.

All three areas of the brain are linked to each other, but when we have reactions such as fear (fight, flight, freeze) and strong emotions, often the connections sever temporarily and our brain is flooded with hormones. Remember being told to count to 10 before reacting? There is a good reason for that. This *pause* allows the chemicals to subside and the brain areas to reconnect.

AN INSIDEOUT LEADER'S STORY: **CHRIS WORKS WITH LARS TO UNRAVEL HIS PATTERNS**

One of the things that Chris asks of Lars is to start using the practice called Fresh Start, which you'll find in InsideOut—Leaders' Tool Kit. The goal of this practice is for Lars to learn to be an observer of his inner critic, in order to lessen its power over him. He knows that this is his fear voice and it keeps him stuck. If he is really going to make some leaps, he has to break free. Lars commits to doing Fresh Start for at least the next six months.

The inner critic is partly responsible for Lars's lack of executive presence. He feels insecure and lacks confidence. He hesitates to offer opinions, and people see the tentative way he enters the fray and his sometimes-awkward assertions. These are reflected in his body language. Lars knows he has to befriend this inner voice that for too long has had a hold on him.

Lars starts a meditation practice. The intent is to cultivate his inner observer—to notice his internal reactions rather than acting on them. He also sees that meditation helps him to start his day feeling calm and centered.

One of Lars's most important goals for this work is to improve his ability to stay centered and on course, no matter what happens and no matter what others say or do. Chris uses some of Wendy Palmer's somatic exercises and emphasizes her Basic Centering Practice (InsideOut Leaders' Tool Kit). He gives Lars this tool to use so that in any situation, Lars can immediately access his center, lower his anxiety and fear, and trust that he will be able to respond effectively to whatever comes his way.

Another significant element of their work together is for Lars to learn how to access, listen to, and act upon his intuition and inner guidance. This is pivotal for Lars because he so often ignores or doesn't trust it in deference to his inner critic. Lars admits that he is afraid to listen to his intuition because he is a slave to his inner critic, the voice that tells him what he should or shouldn't do. He is used to either obeying it or reacting against it, but either way, his intuition is largely ignored except in very low risk situations.

His inner critic is familiar, and it has so many manifestations with so many different voices shouting for his attention that he can hardly hear his intuitive voice. Lars is afraid to trust a relatively untested internal voice—his intuition. Chris and Lars do some considerable work in this area. Lars knows he has to let go of the familiar and try something new if he is going to make a breakthrough.

There are many other exercises they use, and you'll find some of them in the section on the Journey of Type 6.

Lars and Chris take a beautiful hike through olive terraces, past farms, and into the mountains. For the first time in recent memory, Lars feels joy. Not just joy but elation! His playful and mischievous side is alive and visible (7 Wing), and he experiences the transformational nature of these sensations. He feels absolutely vibrant.

Lars and Chris part company after a celebratory dinner and a full and transformative few days together. Lars feels replenished, excited to practice his new skills, and he wants to continue diving for pearls of wisdom. He is grateful for this time with Chris and believes that it has been truly life changing.

Chris and Lars agree to continue the coaching to help Lars sustain the gains he's made and to further his leadership development. Although Lars is going back to face some rough times ahead, he feels confident that he is prepared to weather the storms ahead.

➔ Lars's story continues on p. 387

OUR NEUROBIOLOGY AND CHANGE

The Enneagram is a rich and compelling system that can help you fairly quickly and accurately identify and focus in on your own habitual patterns of thinking, feeling, and acting, and to see yourself more clearly. Once you home in on patterns you want to shift, what do you do? Can you really change? If so, how do your internal systems work to create new patterns?

First the good news: New behaviors can be learned throughout life. The brain is what the neuroscientists call *plastic* and continues to grow throughout our lifetime. It is constantly being altered with every experience, encounter, and interaction we have.

This concept is not new. In 1949, Donald O. Hebb, a Canadian behavioral psychologist, proposed that learning links neurons in new ways, and that when two neurons fire at the same time repeatedly (or when one fires, causing another to fire), chemical changes occur in both, so that the two neurons tend to connect more strongly. This was actually proposed by Freud 60 years before and has been summarized by neuroscientist Carla Shats: neurons that fire together wire together.[32]

Just a bit about how this works. The basic cell in the brain is the neuron, and new neurons can grow in the brain throughout life. Neurons are connected by something called a *synapse* (try recalling your high school biology class). On average, ten thousand synaptic connections are made between neurons—influencing what they do. How many synaptic connections are there in the brain? Between one hundred trillion and one quadrillion!

When synapses fire due to repetition of new thoughts, reactions, behaviors, and actions, new neural connections form. This leads to gene activation, which leads to protein production, which leads to alterations in the synapses, which means the brain is changing.

This is called *neural plasticity*. "We have more possible firing patterns in the brain than known atoms in the universe—it's nearly infinite," writes Dr. Norman Doidge in *The Brain That Changes Itself*. "The brain is the most complex thing in the universe. The brain is so complicated it staggers its own imagination."[33]

To take it a step further, Dr. Daniel Siegel coined the phrase *interpersonal neurobiology* to describe how the brain changes through interactions among the brain, the mind (defined, in part, as a process that regulates the flow of energy and information), and our relationships.[34]

We often hear people say, "I am the way I am, and I am too old to change," or we may say to ourselves, "Why bother, they'll never change." Yet what we are learning about the human brain flies in the face of those beliefs. Our neural pathways (habits, impulses, and patterns) seem pretty hard-wired, and it is true—they influence what we do and don't do. Our thoughts and feelings ride the neural pathways like the rails on a roller-coaster.

However, we can create new neural pathways throughout life, and our unused ones eventually atrophy. If we choose to, we can rid ourselves of patterns or habits that are self-limiting; and we can create new ones that bring more ease, harmony, and pleasure into our lives and that transform the way we lead.

WHAT HAPPENS WHEN THE BRAIN IS FACED WITH CHANGE?

THE DEVIL YOU KNOW IS BETTER THAN THE DEVIL YOU DON'T KNOW.

Once you identify your Enneagram Type and become aware of some of your subconscious drivers and reactive patterns, you may just decide that you want to make some changes in your behavior and expand your repertoire of responses to people and situations. Earlier I wrote about integrating your three Centers of Intelligence and your shadow. How do we do this, and how does this integration work in your neurobiology?

The prefrontal cortex (PFC) is key in your ability to integrate and have more harmony in your life. If you could see an image of your brain, the PFC, the key area for emotional regulation, is the part that would light up to show the locus of your ability to have a considered response rather than a habitual reaction. For instance, if you are the type who reacts when you perceive that someone is telling you what to do, rather than responding defensively, you can press the pause button, take a breath, and choose to respond rather than react.

The PFC is one of the most integrative areas of the brain, integration being the linkage of differentiated parts of the brain—the right and left hemispheres of the cortex, the reptilian brain, the mammalian brain, and so on. *Harmony* both within us and with others emerges from this integration. **This is key.** The brain is open to influence from other brains. Our ability to be calm and feel a sense of peace and harmony can spread to others.

The PFC has another function. It acts like working memory (RAM) in a computer, and it takes a lot of energy and burns a lot of glucose. It can deal comfortably with only a few concepts before we start feeling some discomfort in the form of fatigue and perhaps anger. When you hear people say they are out of bandwidth, they aren't kidding. We start feeling overloaded, our stress increases, and our ability to manage our reactivity is reduced. When you notice people who are not acting their best in a stressful situation, it's no wonder.

In these kinds of situations, when the prefrontal cortex is overloaded, we lose the capacity to manage our fear response, and our backup system takes over the controls—the *basal ganglia*. This is the part of the brain that stores our unconscious memories and habits and allows us to act on autopilot. We might call this the *subconscious mind* (below conscious awareness). Now, how we *show up* is being driven by our subconscious.

According to biologist Bruce Lipton, our subconscious mind is where our habits, patterns, and beliefs live. Our conscious mind, where our thoughts are formed, occupies only 5 percent of our attention and is busy dealing with the day-to-day demands of life. Ninety-five percent of what we do is run by the subconscious mind. If you are using your mind for thinking, your subconscious mind is running the show.

Studies have shown that 70 percent of our inner dialog is both negative and repetitive/redundant.[35] The repetitive nature of these thoughts is what I call our *blah, blah, blah* inner radio station. This is our patterned thinking that is part of our subconscious and is driving our behavior and attitudes toward others and life.

Do we really want to continue feeding ourselves a steady diet of negative thoughts? Are we even aware that we have this inner dialog? Even though there may be a more effective way to do things that can lead us to a better result and more ease in our lives, it takes much less energy and effort to behave habitually, it is more predictable (the devil we know), and therefore it is more comforting.

Change takes attention to our inner world as well as intention. It is easier to let our subconscious manage our lives. Unfortunately, there are consequences—many negative—for continuing in this vein.

Back to the PFC as an integrator: when we react or act on habitual impulse, we lose the integrative capacity of the PFC and we experience a sense of disharmony both within us and with others. However, if we pause rather than react and take a more considered response, then we get brain integration. When the PFC links differentiated parts of the brain and the nervous system (the body, brainstem, limbic system, and cortex) and maps our mind with other people's minds, there is a sense of attunement—feeling at one and in harmony with others.

WHY DO WE RESIST CHANGING OUR PATTERNS AND BELIEFS?

Because it means that instead of changing others, I have to change *me*! That means there's something *wrong* with me. I don't want to hear that the beliefs on which I have based much of my life and decisions may be inaccurate or subject to further exploration. I don't want to believe that I have participated in creating many of the problems in my life. **Answer:** There's nothing *wrong* with you, but our tried-and-true coping strategies become overused, and what once may have been a functional response is no longer the best approach—you may have outgrown your success formula.

Because it's hard. It takes focused attention and effort to create new patterns. Relate this to improving your golf swing, the way you weight your body and hold the grip when you swing your club. First, an instructor shows you a way to slightly adjust your swing. When you try it, it feels awkward, as if you are a beginner again—it's uncomfortable and unnatural. Then the ball flies in an unpredictable way, and, frustrated, you feel like a fool and are ready to go back to your old swing. However, you are motivated to improve your game and know that to take your game to the next level, you have to do something different, and you have to keep practicing until it becomes your *new normal*. You are laying down new neural pathways in your brain, and it takes a while to become a superhighway.

Because we are often rewarded for doing what it is we do. What do I mean by this? There are several ways we get rewarded. If our culture and our Enneagram Type are compatible, our culture will reward our behavior because it is seen as desirable. Often, others will reinforce our behavior because it serves them in some way. For instance, if we are the People Pleaser (Type 2), others benefit greatly from our doing things for them, rescuing them, and being there for them, often at our own expense. While we may become exhausted and depleted from putting our attention on others, both at work and at home, the rewards are great.

We are getting some of our needs met—such as appreciation—and it makes us feel lovable because we believe that people need us and because our ego rewards us. It tells us "Job well done"—we are supposed to help and we did. We are such good people. Bravo! It can be intoxicating when we are rewarded. Can you see how addictive these patterns are and why it would be difficult to change—to have the will to change?

SO WHY CHANGE?

Because to get these rewards, we need to keep feeding our ego, and each of us pays a great price for this. We are not getting our real needs met because they are our ego needs—these rewards are not filling the needs of our spirit and true inner longing. This type of ego need is a bottomless pit.

What happens for Type 2s when the appreciation doesn't come or people don't want their help and the flattery isn't working? When they aren't seen as indispensable? When they get pushed away? The ego has a field day. Type 2s become upset, feel unlovable, feel taken for granted, and may become demanding. Their sense of self-worth plummets. In the case of Type 2s, they have created or tried to create a codependency, and have confused this with being loved and lovable. No one can make us feel truly lovable; we have to *know* and feel it on the inside. Over time, you can see that this is a zero sum game.

Earlier in this section, you learned that taking the high road that leads to brain integration has its own rewards, but they are rewards of calm, contentedness, solidity, being relaxed, and being more in harmony with ourselves and with others. By choosing not to react, we are able to avoid interpersonal disasters and self-destructive behaviors. These are not the rewards that the ego is looking for, but they are the rewards of a life filled with meaningful relationships and healthy interactions with others—a life of purpose and joy.

HOW DO WE CHANGE OUR PATTERNS?

To change, we have to change the subconscious mind. How? With practice and by creating and having new experiences, the subconscious mind can learn. Brain areas increase and shrink depending on input. Brain wiring strengthens or weakens based on our real and imagined actions. But not just our brains! Our biology is changing at the same time. When we are stressed, we flood our body with hormones that affect our cells. When we bring more harmony into our lives (both inside and out), we affect our biology in a positive way.

SEEM EASY?

The neural pathways that we create by repeating a behavior become speedy and efficient, and these emerge as our habits, both good and bad. Once these habits are ingrained, it is increasingly difficult, but not impossible, to change them. You have to have sufficient motivation, intention, focused attention (read, no multitasking), and practice to create new neural pathways.

Fortunately, an "inner observer" is built into our brain functioning to help us awaken to our patterns. Our inner observer is like a fair witness that doesn't judge what it observes; it just notices. Once we become conscious of our habits, worldviews, and beliefs and their motivators, we can make use of our plasticity despite our age. Humans are the only species that has this capability. If we pause before acting or reacting out of habit, we can engage more of our brain. The self-awareness we develop through cultivating our inner observer enables choice, and choice opens up the possibility for change.

SELF-INSIGHT—THE OPEN DOOR

Humans have the capacity to integrate, to take the high road rather than reverting to our habitual impulses (the low road) and reacting in a patterned way. How? Through self-insight. The first step is to have the desire, motivation, and intent to tune in to our inner dialog. We activate our inner observer or fair witness to awaken to our habits and patterns as if we are tuning in to our own radio station.

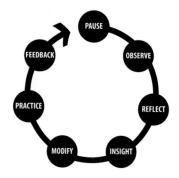

Meditation is one very effective method for cultivating our inner observer. Another is to practice bringing ourselves back to the present moment, observing and reflecting on our reactions rather than acting on them. We can press the pause button before acting on our negative thought patterns and then choose a different thought.

The next step is to stop and reflect on our observations. By creating this space, we often get insights about ourselves. Having insights creates a pleasurable response in the brain, *and this is when change can happen.*

EXAMPLE

Let's look at a *reactive pattern* for Type 1: They are prone to criticize, judge, and offer corrective behavior to better or improve others. Situation—manager and employee. Manager: "I am about to level some sharp criticism at one of my employees."

Pause: Internal feeling is impatience. I can feel my heart speeding up. I don't want to lose control, but I am about to snap. Message to self: Move away from the situation before reacting. Take a moment to regroup. Take a deep belly breath.

Observe: (Notice my inner dialog.) "How could he make a mistake like this? Doesn't he know that he has to follow the procedures exactly? He is so incompetent. I can see that I am going to have an ongoing problem with him, and I just can't afford any more mistakes." I call this the radio station of the internal critic. The first step is to notice, and the next is to choose something else—not to criticize the inner voice but just notice it is there.

Reflect: (Curiosity) "I am really having a strong reaction to that person; I wonder what's really bothering me. I don't like feeling this way."

"I get so impatient. Do I need to be so rigid about this? What am I really worried about? Is it how it will reflect on me? It's not doing me any good, and losing my temper is not going to improve the situation."

Insight: (Curiosity and wonder.) "I want to fix everything (and everyone) and make things perfect. Is that really possible? Is that really desirable? I know I have been like this since I was a kid. I got really frustrated when things weren't the way I thought they should be." Much more could be written here, but this is an avenue for exploration that opens up the opportunity for insight. "What if I could just let it go—do my best? What would that be like? What would it be like if my attention were focused on seeing the best in situations and others—and even myself—rather than looking for flaws?

"Perhaps there was a good reason for why he did what he did. I guess I didn't take the time to ask him about what he was intending." Good feelings about this new insight. The new behavior to try on could be a shift of focus: look for the best in others, processes, or situations and amplify that. Focus on what is working.

Modify: Whatever comes from your insight, try the new behavior. It will seem awkward at first, like trying a new golf or tennis swing.

When the next instance of your reactive pattern arises, and it inevitably will, pause and remember the goal (new behavior).

Practice: Keep at it, and eventually you will be able to do it without thinking about it.

Feedback: Notice how you feel. Does your self-perception shift in any way? Notice your body—tense, relaxed, where? Are you getting any kind of feedback from others—directly or indirectly (by the way they are responding to you)?

Catching yourself in the act and pressing the pause button is a critical first step. Cultivating your *fair witness* will be key so that you can observe rather than criticize yourself. The most important thing to remember is to invite curiosity into your life. Be curious about your reactions, your inner dialog, and the behavior of others. I guarantee that you will be surprised at what you learn!

 AN INSIDEOUT LEADER'S STORY: **LARS'S RETURN TO THE OFFICE**

As predicted, shortly upon Lars's return, a restructuring is announced along with layoffs. NHH is in turmoil. Productivity plummets while everyone is preoccupied with the rumor mill and saving their jobs. Lars has a hard time getting the attention of his LT. One of the rumors is that a division reporting to Lars will be sold off. Lars puts his strategic plan on hold.

They have their next off-site meeting, but it is tough for Lars to get engagement. They get through the meeting, but it is unclear how to forward their work in light of the uncertainty.

Within two months, Caitlin is removed from her position and replaced by Markus. Unlike Caitlin, Markus is very traditional and intent on maintaining the status quo. He has been with NHH for his entire professional life and faces retirement in the next couple of years. He is unsupportive of the changes that Lars is implementing and, in fact, cuts Lars's budget for leadership development, team development, consulting, and coaching to zero! In addition, Lars must run all his purchase orders through Markus. Lars is being cut off at the knees. His new skills are tested.

The big question for Lars is whether NHH is backing off the change agenda and is recommitting to the status quo. The signs could certainly be interpreted that way.

Chris has a couple more months left in his contract with Lars, so they use it well. While Lars is upset at what is happening to him and his organization, he stays calm and centered. He does not react outwardly. He passes each test with flying colors. With each success, his confidence grows and his willingness to trust himself and his intuition mounts.

➜ Lars's story continues on p. 388

CHAPTER 10

INSIDEOUT— LEADERS' TOOL KIT

Enlightenment is an accident. Practice makes us accident-prone.

—Attributed to Shunryu Suzuki Roshi

Discovering your Enneagram Type and understanding it cognitively is not enough to take you from *drift* to *shift*. What it does do is expand your self-understanding and your worldview, and it opens up the door to new insights. However, shifting your patterns takes focused attention and practice.

This section contains some suggested practices to help you build your emotional intelligence. I have personally used all of the following practices, and more. Different ones have been helpful at different times along my journey. I have also used many of these with clients, successfully. Most of them are now incorporated into my daily life.

To start with, try one and stay with it. Practices are just that, practices. To build a muscle or learn a new skill, you have to practice. Most of these are simple and can be enjoyable. Start anywhere. Just start somewhere. Track your progress in your journal (see Part 6)—especially your insights. Enjoy!

 AN INSIDEOUT LEADER'S STORY: **WHAT HAPPENS NEXT?**

You'll have to wait for another book to learn how the story ends. It is still unfolding. What I can tell you is that Tony uses Lars's weakened status in the organization. He files a complaint that he assuredly feels is justified, and this ensures Tony's own survival at NHH.

However, despite the action taken by Tony and the cascade of unsettling events surrounding it, Lars is holding steady. He uses the uncertainty and the many challenges being thrown his way as grist for the mill. Lars practices his skills, continues to learn and grow, and is proud of the quantum leaps he has made. He is confounding his new boss, who doesn't know what to make of it all. People he wouldn't have expected to are seeking out Lars as a beacon of light and a source of calm in the rough seas.

→ Lars's story continues on p. 392

CURIOSITY IS YOUR GUIDE

The most important travel companion you can have with you is your curiosity. When you invite curiosity on your journey, your defenses drop, and your "I know" or "I should know" will not be at your side. Instead, you will feel drawn further and further along by your openness to what is around the next bend, and you will begin to ask yourself, "Why do I believe that?" "Why do I do that?" "When did I stop doing that?" "Do I really act like that?" "How do other people experience me?" "What would I be like if I weren't … ?" "What if I could … ?" "What do you think of that?" "Tell me more … ," "When did you notice?" "Who are you?" "What can I learn from … ?"

These are some of the undefended questions that curiosity asks. Curiosity doesn't judge, criticize, critique, or have answers. Curiosity is living the questions until the insights appear. Curiosity notices, is awake and aware. Curiosity takes an interest in what and who is around it and asks, "What can I learn?" Curiosity moves toward, not away from. Curiosity is a bridge to the unknown.

Curiosity asks a question of clarification before reacting or responding—and generally finds out that it is reacting to something that was projected onto the other person rather than what was really there. Curiosity invites connection, ideas, innovation, intuition. If you are a leader, it is one of your most trusted allies. It will take you far.

Curiosity becomes interested in subtlety. It is the doorway to being present with yourself and with others. It will guide you to your insights, your deepest longings, and back to yourself.

 STOP AND REFLECT

PRACTICES

▸ When you are about to react, remember: *Get curious, not furious!*

▸ If you are feeling a wall around your heart, take a deep belly breath and ask yourself, "What if I had a little more generosity in my heart right now? What would that feel like?"

▸ If you are feeling tense, take a deep belly breath and ask yourself, "What would it feel like if I felt a little more relaxed in my jaw, shoulders, hands, legs right now?

▸ If you are feeling sad or depressed, take some space. Relax your mind and allow yourself to wonder what is going on with you. Be curious about your feelings and what they are trying to tell you. Ask, "How am I not taking care of myself right now?"

▸ When you have a decision to make, ask your gut what it wants to do, ask your heart how it feels about the decision and what it wants, and ask your head what it thinks. Make sure to involve all three. They each have a perspective and a voice.

▸ When you are about to react to someone, ask a question for clarification.

▸ If you are feeling anxious, take a little break and sit down and write about your anxiety. Be curious about what it wants to tell you, what it is protecting.

▸ When someone points out something about you that you don't like, inquire. Find out more about it. Begin to get curious and notice when you are doing it. Don't judge; just notice the circumstances that evoke this part of you.

▸ If you have a dream that sticks with you, be curious about what your subconscious might be trying to communicate. Write about the dream—the symbols, your feelings—and see what unfolds.

▸ When people hold a different opinion or point of view, rather than expressing your own position, inquire. Be curious about what they think and why. You might learn something. Remember, understanding doesn't mean agreement.

THE POWER OF PRESENCE

This is one of the most important, if not the most important, practices. When we are present both to ourselves and to others, we can interrupt our habitual patterns and effectively respond to what is called for in the moment. Our awareness expands, and our ability to see reality more clearly is greatly heightened.

The body is the only part of us that is in the present moment. Our mind is in the past and future, we have feelings about past and future pleasures and pains, but our bodily sensations are in the here and now. Tune in to your senses, to your sensations. What do you feel, and where do you feel it? Be curious about what is going on—with you and with others. Listen deeply, and stay open to what can unfold.

Curiosity is the doorway to presence. People experience presence in different ways and at different times. When we are in conversation, our ability to remain curious and open to learning drops us into a profound experience of being present. As a consequence, we gain access to our intuition or inner knowing.

Our true home is in the present moment. To live in the present moment is a miracle. ... Once we learn to touch this peace, we will be healed and transformed. It is not a matter of faith; it is a matter of practice.
—Thich Nhat Hanh, *Touching Peace*[36]

PRACTICE: Bring your attention into your body. Breathe into your belly—into your center. How far can you place your attention—behind you, in front of you, to the left of you, to the right of you, above you, below you? Can you expand your field of attention? Breathe into your belly.

When you feel the impulse to say something, stay quiet and bring yourself back to curiosity—to the desire to learn rather than to be the one with the answer, the clever thing to say, the judgment or opinion. Feel the force of gravity on your body. When you feel quiet inside—as if a space has opened up inside—you will find a clear, grounded, inclusive, and wise voice, almost as if it is coming through you, rather than from you.

PRACTICE: It is a practice to just *be with* someone, particularly when they need to speak or be heard. The solid presence you provide helps them to feel heard and accepted. It is truly one of the greatest gifts we can give someone (and ourselves). Try it. Just deeply listen and stay curious without the need to contribute. Allow for the silence when they pause.

NOTICE: Begin to notice your repeating thought patterns. What are you telling yourself inside your head, day after day? Write them in your journal.

NOTICE: Does your inner dialogue turn against you?

 Write in your journal: If you could shift your inner dialogue, what would it say?

 How does your inner dialogue increase your ability to spread positive feelings toward others?

AN INSIDEOUT LEADER'S STORY: **WHAT DID LARS LEARN?**

If he could do it again, he would go slower and take time to develop trust with the team. He would meet them where they were, listen to them and acknowledge their fears and concerns. He would have recognized the signals and not been so intent on his own agenda. Lars realizes that he had a very aggressive change agenda and high expectations for where he thought his LT should be, in terms of skill and trust.

He used the wrong style for this team at the early stage of their change process. What they required was involving, coaching, asking, explaining, and teaching. Lars needed to take the time, focus his energy, and be patient.

Lars didn't take time to assess their readiness level. They did not have the experience, skill, education, or training to deliver what he asked of them.

WHAT KIND OF LEADERSHIP WAS CALLED FOR AT THAT STAGE OF THEIR TEAM DEVELOPMENT AND CHANGE PROCESS?

It would have been important for Lars to step out of his own comfort zone, flex his style, and take the time to build one-to-one relationships with each member of his LT. It would have served Lars and his team if he had led by walking around—being out and about, asking questions, having conversations, and making small talk. He needed to get them to open up through the channel of relationship.

Lars realized that he should have been more patient and expressed less frustration and judgment. In hindsight, the team would have been well served had he taken the time to build relationships with each of his team members and provided needed clarity about the vision he was asking them to step into. He would have put in place different methods for them to develop the skills they needed to up-level. He would have made his expectations clear up front.

They needed a high degree of specificity, structure, clarity, and vision that Lars did not provide early enough in his new role. He also needed to express a high degree of relational behavior with conversations that included, "What do you think? Let me explain …" They needed Lars to coach them, to help them develop new skills and new ways of behaving. There were blind spots and skill gaps—they didn't know what they didn't know.

At the early stages, Lars needed to let the team know that he would still make decisions but would engage their thinking and give them direction at a high level until they were ready to step into their roles as leaders and team players.

HOW DID LARS'S ENNEAGRAM TYPE INFLUENCE HIS STYLE?

Lars got tripped up because he was brought into a bigger job than he had ever undertaken before and wanted to be successful. The voices of self-doubt (Type 6) reared their heads: "Am I up to this? Can I succeed? Can I build a team that will influence change in the larger organization?"

Lars was angry with himself, and the team thought he was angry with them. Lars was also impatient with himself and he worried about how he appeared to others. He acted overconfident when he was scared. He was afraid to fail (Type 3).

Lars inappropriately abdicated authority (Type 6) and hid out (Type 9) instead of reaching out and building trust with the individual team members and helping them to develop their skills and confidence.

Finally, Lars needed to lead with his own vulnerability. He was asking his LT to do things that he was unwilling to do himself. He asked the team to be learners, to make mistakes, to challenge their peers, to say what was on their minds, but he didn't model these behaviors. That was the most powerful thing he could have done.

Lars needed to have asked himself, "How do I contribute to this dynamic? Does this reflect what I mirror to them?" With the help of Chris, Lars eventually did ask himself this question and that is when he was able to harness the power of the Enneagram.

FRESH START

This practice was inspired by the morning pages in the *Artist's Way*, by Julia Cameron. Fresh Start is designed to surface your intuitive voice and your creativity, and to dim the voice of your inner critic. Your commitment to yourself is to spend a few minutes every morning over a period of at least three consecutive months. Your reward will be a fresh start to your day, an ability to clearly distinguish your intuitive voice from your critical voice and an opening into your creativity, and perhaps even the diminishment of the fears that hold you back.

WHAT IS FRESH START?

When you roll out of bed in the morning, write three to five pages of stream-of-consciousness thoughts in a notebook or journal. Feel free to write whatever is on the tip of your mind—for example, "I'm so excited because I'm having coffee with … ," "I am exhausted and the kids are about to descend on me," "Sigh, another day. I have a ton to do today and I didn't even get through yesterday's to-do list." And so on. Or "I don't know what to say." Write it. Fresh Start is a way to clear your mind and start your day fresh.

Most important, there is no wrong way to do this. Just write down whatever is on your mind. You can scribble, draw … there are no rules. Don't try to sound intelligent, although you can. Feel free to complain, feel sorry for yourself, write angry thoughts, write whatever judgments you have, get out your frustration, admit your envy, be humorous, be playful. No one will read these entries except you. And don't read them for at least three months after writing them.

Just write in your notebook or journal every day upon awaking.

All that stuff you write down helps clear the decks, allowing you to access your more creative, innovative self and your passion. The stuff you write contains all the gunk that clogs up your pipes and limits the more free-flowing you. Write about it!

Important: Remember that your inner critic's negative opinions are not the truth! Don't let your inner critic inhibit your writing. See if you can turn the volume down on that channel; send the critic on a spaceship; or just notice that the inner critic is there, thank it, and refocus on your writing. This takes practice. Because there is no wrong way to do your Fresh Start, your inner critic's opinion doesn't count.

WHY DO FRESH START?

Because it will help you to start your day in a good way so that you can focus on what's important. It will help you to disempower your fears and, most important, your inner critic. The point is to stop taking the inner critic as *the truth*. Realize that the voice of the inner critic stands between you and your best self, your centered self, and your integrated self.

Once you manage to quiet the voice of your inner critic, you can find the still point within you. This is your center, where you gain access to your source of wisdom and unimagined solutions. You can even pose questions to your journal and ask for guidance. In fact, try that. You'll be surprised what you learn.

So put your worries, concerns, anger, and anything else that comes to mind in your journal. Just be sure to write three to five pages of it every day.

GRATITUDE ALPHABET

Along with Fresh Start and meditation, you can use the Gratitude Alphabet every day, as time allows. This is something I developed spontaneously many years ago when I was going through a difficult time in my life. Starting your day feeling grateful for the important things in your life keeps you focused on them. It will help you to let go of fear and lack, and will kick-start your day with feelings of abundance and self-worth.

Each of us has the seeds of greatness within us, and the Gratitude Alphabet is a way of watering and fertilizing these seeds so that we grow into the person we can be. When I start my day with this practice, I feel such a sense of joy and good fortune.

My capacity to give to others grows, too. Giving makes me feel happy, and the whole process begins to feed on itself. Practice thanking others. Let others know how they have had a positive effect on you, inspired you, touched you, and challenged you. It's the cheapest and most valuable gift you can give.

Your team longs to have positive feedback from you that is specific and meaningful. When you offer this to people you work with, it spreads. Most of us just think it or think about it. Say it! It feels good. It evokes that *flow* among people, and it lifts the spirit. It costs nothing, but the payback is enormous.

How does it work? The practice is simple, and it goes like this:

For each letter of the alphabet, think of at least one thing you are grateful for, and speak it aloud, and *say it as if it were true 100 percent of the time*. For example, I am grateful for the following:

A—for the Abundance in my life

B—for my inner and outer Beauty, for my Body that is carrying me through this life

C—for my Courage and Compassion

D—for the spark of the Divine within me

E—for my Energy and Enthusiasm

F—for my Family, who loves and cares about me, for my Friends, who support me

G—for my Goodness, for my Groundedness, and for the Gratitude
  I feel

H—for my Health, Humor, Humility, Home, Happiness

And so on ...

As I go through my Gratitude Alphabet, with each letter I feel my sense of gratitude growing and my joy increasing. When it really comes down to it, we have so much, and it is so easy to forget what we have and to focus on what's not working. Some days, when I am really low, it is difficult to put much energy into my practice, but I manage, and with each letter I feel better and better.

THEN I BEGIN LIVING
INTO THAT FOR WHICH
I AM GRATEFUL.

CENTERING BASIC PRACTICE,
BY WENDY PALMER

Wendy Palmer is the founder of Conscious Embodiment, and she is a sixth-degree black belt in aikido. Through her workshops, she offers simple yet deep techniques that help you to recognize how your mind and body habitually react to pressure, and to access more skillful responses.

This is a practice you can do many times a day. It can be quite useful when you enter a meeting, go to a gathering, are about to have a difficult encounter, or are upset and need to come back to your center. It is simple and takes just a few moments. The payoff is great.

This can be done standing or sitting.

Choose a quality associated with your vision of what you want to embody (such as softness, acceptance, power, grounding, generosity, strength, courage).

Start by working with your breath and posture:

▸ Inhaling, uplift your posture and lengthen your spine; exhale downward toward the earth, softening your chest and settling into the earth.

▸ Focus on the space (presence) behind and in front, to the left and the right. This is your field, your personal space.

▸ Expand your field (presence) to fill the room.

▸ Let gravity soften your shoulders and your jaw.

▸ Invite your quality by asking, "What if there were a little more_____(your quality) in my being?" Take a few moments.

Expanding your personal space cultivates inclusiveness. Continued focus on your expanded field of presence creates an environment that welcomes other people—family, team, or organization—into your personal space. You give the nonverbal message "We are in this together."

The more you practice, the more familiar it becomes to be in your center. Center can become a place of refuge. You can take refuge from obsessive thoughts of the future and of the past and be able to rest in your center. You will learn how to become a stable presence.

THE ROLE OF INTUITION

As a leader, you get a ton of inputs and don't often have much time for a lot of analysis and research. Whether in meetings or in day-to-day situations, you're asked to make many decisions—hiring, firing, product enhancements, media damage control, shareholder concerns, whom to trust, budgets, and so on. Intuition is the voice you can hear when you are able to quiet the inner committee of voices:

I should, there's not enough, you're not enough, where would they be without me? I need to know, I'm losing control, he is making me look bad, I think they are trying to sabotage me, I need to plan, I need to prepare, I don't trust myself, I know what's best, they're idiots, they're smarter, they're better, I'm nobody special, I'm a fraud, just a little bit more, I should have his position …

With all this internal noise pollution, how can we hear the voice of intuition, which is wise, trusts, and acts from an awake, aware, conscious place?

On the Leader's Journey, the role of intuition is critical. How will you know which path to take? In a change or transformation process, you'll come to many choice points. There will be times when you feel like nothing is happening—when, in fact, everything is happening. When you're poised between two trapeze grabs in midair, you have to be able to trust something. Can you trust your own inner guidance system— your intuition, the voice that is constantly trying to be heard and has your best interests at heart?

Practice in risk-free situations. If the phone rings, without looking, see if you can guess who it is. Who is the first person that comes to mind? When someone is about to tell you their birth date, see if you can guess before they say it; what month or day immediately comes to mind? Guess what time it is before looking at your watch. It is something you have to practice and develop; it's a voice you have to learn to recognize. The more you practice, the more you'll be on target and you'll surprise yourself how often you are on target.

HOW DO YOU RECOGNIZE THE VOICE OF INTUITION?

Have you ever heard a little voice inside you say, "Don't do that" or "Don't say that" or "Choose this" or "This person is going to try to do you harm" or "Go here"? Did you listen to it, or did you listen to the voice of fear, doubt, the inner critic, and *should*; the voice of the part of you who needed to say or do something in order to be seen or at the center of attention; or the voice that willed you on because you didn't trust the quieter, more subtle voice inside you among the chorus?

Sometimes the voice of impulse, the one that often gets you into trouble, is the one that gets the airtime and is acted upon. Others of us feed the voice of the inner critic that tells us what's right, what's best, what's required, what's nice, what's not nice, what not to be like, what we're not good enough for … or the *should* voice, the fear voice that we feed with gourmet meals—at the expense of ourselves. Analyzing and optimizing decisions, weighing all the different angles of a decision, is another barrier to hearing our intuitive voice. Anxiety, wanting to just *get it over with*, or our greed and gluttony can get in the way.

Speaking from personal experience, when I have ignored that little voice, it has gotten me in some kind of trouble. When I have trusted and listened to it, my choices have been divinely guided. Perhaps they may not have seemed so at first, but time and again my inner guide has shown itself to be looking out for me and having my best interests at heart.

In one case, I was driving in the fast lane on the freeway in San Francisco and feeling that rush to get ahead. There came a little voice inside of me that said, "Why are you in such a hurry? Move over to the next lane." So I did move over. Within 15 seconds, the cars that had been in front of me crashed, and I would have been among them had I not listened to my inner guidance.

One of the benefits you'll experience as a result of working with the Enneagram is that you'll have more access to your intuition. Our personality is habitual and reactive. When you become aware of your deeply embedded patterns and relax around them, you are freed up to begin acting from your center.

Intuition may be just one of the voices in the chorus when we are operating from our personality. Often we can't recognize our intuitive voice or hear it. If we do hear it, the personality tends to get deferential treatment. However, from center you'll have greater access to your intuition because you'll be able to give airtime to your intuitive voice by turning up the volume on your *intuitive channel* and lowering the volume on your well-rehearsed, more reactive *personality channel*.

When have you heard this voice? Felt the sensation of this quiet knowing, heard it, and then acted upon it? What happened as a result of acting on your intuitive voice?

Remember a time when you ignored this voice. What was the message? Why did you ignore it? Was there another voice you listened to instead? Name that voice. What happened?

What are your internal signals? How do you know it is your voice of intuition? What are your sensations and images? What are your personal signs?

What are some of the messages your inner critic gives you? Do you listen?

WHAT IS INTUITION, AND WHERE DOES IT COME FROM?

Often people use the words *intuition* and *instinct* to describe the same thing. It is hard to tease the two apart because they seem so similar. Yet they are two distinct voices. Instinct is more of an impulse to act. It comes from the gut or *belly brain* and is often referred to as the *hara* in the world of martial arts. We have sexual instincts (pro-creative) and survival instincts (flight, fight, fear, and forming social connections). Instincts are unlearned responses to stimuli and can be an inner warning system that directs your attention to danger or action. You can choose to act on them or not, but they are incredibly fast at grabbing your attention and can save your life.

Many years ago, I was on a bus coming home from work in San Francisco's financial district. It was holiday shopping season and I was carrying some purchases, my purse, and a duffle bag. One man on that bus caught my attention, and I had an instant fear reaction. When I exited the bus, I noticed that he left as well. I stopped to see which direction he was going in and was relieved that he headed in the opposite direction. A few minutes later and 25 feet from the front door of my apartment building, I heard footsteps behind me. I stopped in my entryway—cars were racing by in rush-hour traffic—and turned to see who was behind me. Sure enough, it was the same man. I watched him pass, somewhat relieved, and thought perhaps I was being over-concerned.

It is always with excitement that I wake up in the morning wondering what my intuition will toss up to me, like gifts from the sea. I work with it and rely on it. It's my partner.

—Jonas Salk

The previous week, I read a magazine article that warned not to get caught in your entryway with your back to the street. Remembering that, I turned to face the street, dropped my bags, crouched down with my purse in my lap, and was rooting around in my purse in search of my apartment keys. Some movement caught my attention just in time for me to look up and see the same man lunging at me. Without thought, I let out the most blood-curdling scream I have ever heard. He froze and I screamed again. He ran. I was shaking.

The point of relating this story is to demonstrate how our instincts work and that there are occasions when acting instead of analyzing or rationalizing is the best response. Your instincts are there to keep you safe, alive, and able to perpetuate the species.

On another similar occasion, I let my rational mind override my instincts, and I was not so lucky. My purse was ripped from my wrist and I was punched in the face. In these types of situations, it is best to trust your instincts.

The following story demonstrates how our intuition works in concert with our head, heart, and gut:

I had finished my coursework in graduate school, and it was time to choose a thesis topic. It was important for me to research and write about something that mattered and that evoked my passion. I wanted the process to be fun and enjoyable too. Holding that intention, I went about my life believing that my thesis topic would soon be revealed.

In short order, I was at a community meeting to discuss the increasing conflicts on the hiking trails among the mountain bikers, hikers, and equestrians. I sat there quietly listening to the impassioned pleas from each of the interest groups. There was blaming, judging, and righteousness in the air. I wanted to contribute to the conversation but didn't quite know what to say that would be useful. Angeles Arrien had taught me well to track my reason and motivation for speaking before opening my mouth:

Is it right speech?

It is right action?

Is it the right place?

Is it the right time?

I was riveted to my chair, taking in all of the different points of view. Everyone had a case, and the meeting was polarized. What could I possibly contribute to the conversation? I felt a growing quiet inside of me. Curiosity took over. There was a growing sense of excitement in my belly. I had come to know myself well enough by then that when this sensation took hold, I knew it was time to act and time to speak. Yet I didn't know what I wanted to say. Before I could plan anything, I found myself standing up and opening my mouth.

Words flowed effortlessly. Then I stopped. I had stunned myself. I was brought out of my stupor by the room erupting in applause. At the end of the meeting, people approached me and thanked me. I then knew what I would write my thesis about, and I had met the key people I ended up interviewing for my research.

Our instincts, our heart, and our rational mind guide our intuition. It cannot be accessed when we are in a reactive state. We must invite it in. It's a quiet knowing that forms inside of us—the part of us that knows just what to say or do, at the right time, the right place, and with the right words. It is our sixth sense, our inner knowing.

Intuition is generally not an impulsive feeling, but we may want to act impulsively on our intuition, as demonstrated in my story, when I impulsively stood up to speak. These are our lightbulb moments of clarity.

CULTIVATE AND DEVELOP YOUR INTUITION

Intuition can arise when we stop willing the moment to be something other than it is. It requires radical acceptance—acceptance of ourselves and whatever is happening in the moment—and a willingness to see reality as it is.

You will recognize your intuitive state as the creative and spontaneous aspect of yourself, undistorted by fear, as you are grounded in your body, fully present in the moment. It comes through expanded awareness. Connecting with our intuitive voice requires that we expand our peripheral vision and relax our mind.

If you are having trouble hearing your intuitive voice when you are making a decision, Freud suggested that one flip a coin and then see if one is disappointed by the answer!

CULTIVATING YOUR INTUITION

Here are some suggestions to get you going: Start small. One step. Pick one of these things and integrate it into your life. Pay attention to the different ways and forms your intuition uses to speak to you— through dreams, symbols, sensations, animals crossing your path. Notice any changes. Keep track in your journal. Slowly, after you have brought one new practice fully into your life, try another. You will start seeing some subtle shifts. Notice. Jot it down in your journal. With time, you will begin to hear and act on that little voice inside of you that has been trying to get your attention for your whole life. Trust it. It is your friend.

 STOP AND REFLECT

HUNCHES: Follow your hunches. See where they lead. Over time, you will become more adept at following them and seeing how they open up possibilities for you. When was the last time you followed a hunch? What happened?

Jump to the practice Fresh Start

FRESH START: A key block to hearing and acting on our intuitive voice and being able access our creativity is the often-commanding voice of our inner critic. It is known to have its way with us and diminish the voice of our inner guidance.

Fresh Start helps us to tune in to our inner critic in a more direct and conscious way and loosen its grip on us. Many of us don't easily distinguish the voice of our inner critic from that of our *true self*. We say and do things that we often resent or don't like because we act as if we *are* our inner critic—the voice of should, must, right, wrong, judgment, the slave driver. When we make conscious contact with our inner critic, we can gently shift to our center and open to a more integrative voice within us—our intuitive voice.

DREAMS: Pay attention to your dreams. Keep a dream journal on your nightstand and write down as much as you can remember about your dreams as soon as you wake up. Capture the images, symbols, words, and feelings you had during the dream. Don't try to analyze it or make sense of it. Just write down as much as you can remember.

Over time, look for recurring themes, images, and symbols—in your night dreams, daydreams, and life dreams. What do these mean to you? How do they relate to your life story—the one you have lived and the one you want to live into?

NATURE: Take time in nature—every day if possible. Being in nature connects us with our own inner nature. Walk alone. Gently shift your focus to the here and now, the present moment. Tune in to your sensations. What are you feeling inside? Relaxed, tight in the chest, warm in the heart? Do you feel the sun, wind, rain, or cold on your skin? Notice the smells, sights, and sounds of the leaves and earth beneath your feet. Listen to the birdcalls and bird songs, the crickets, the cicadas.

Use all of your senses to experience life right in this precious moment: colors, forms, a leaf floating through the sky, flowers and the details of its shape and form, mountains, shades of colors. Watch the bees gathering pollen, the birds looking for bugs, the seagulls returning to land at the end of the day. Watch a cat hunt. Let in the impressions of your surroundings, and then tune in to your body again. Can you feel the elation in your heart and the wonders of Mother Nature?

Your mind will begin to relax, and invariably, unexpected insights, patterns, and perhaps the resolution of a question you have will come to you. Pose a question as you embark on your walk, and then just let it go and pay attention to the miracle of life all around you.

Nature's symbols: Shift your focus. Do you want to have greater access to your heart, your feelings, and your heart's desire? Look for hearts in nature: rocks, mountainsides, flowers, clouds, leaves, a carving in a wall. How did you fail to notice before? They are everywhere. All we have to do is shift our focus of attention.

What animals cross your path? Do these same animals show up in your dreams too? Is it possible that their crossing your path or coming to you in dreams is not just a coincidence? Many things that happen can seem like random events. Notice. *Animal-Speak: Understanding Animal Messengers, Totems, and Signs*, by Ted Andrews, is a wonderful book for looking up the cross-cultural meanings and significance of animals and what they may be trying to communicate.

PEOPLE / THE IMPORTANT STRANGER

Notice what people show up in your life—an unexpected meeting, call, or introduction. Are you open to seeing past your initial perception of them? Do you dismiss them out of hand, or do you take time to open to what they might have to teach you, offer you, or share with you?

I have lost count of the many times in my life when it would have been so easy to dismiss someone out of hand because of their look, my rush to be somewhere else, or not being present. The amazing conversations, heart connections, learning, and gifts that have come from an openness and willingness have been innumerable.

Who are the important strangers that have graced your life? Whom did you ignore? What made the difference? Write about the important strangers that you encounter this week or month.

COINCIDENCE? SYNCHRONICITY?

Were you just thinking about someone, and the phone rang and they were on the other end of the line; or did you bump into them or get mail from them? See if you can cultivate this. Think about some-one or notice when you do and see what happens. You could even contact this person to find out if they were thinking about you. Track these things. Cultivate this inner knowing.

WANDERING AND WONDERING / FOCUS OF ATTENTION

Take time out to let your mind wander and wonder. Did you lie in the grass and watch clouds float by as a child? Did the cloud shapes form and re-form into characters? Remember the simple joys when your mind was fully relaxed. Take in impressions.

Begin to notice what grabs your attention. Where is your focus of at-tention? Look at the nine Enneagram Types, and see where they are likely to place their attention. Notice whether your attention gravi-tates to this place, and then gently return to your body sensations—the present moment. Again, let your mind wander and wonder with-out an agenda. When you relax and take in impressions, insights and answers will begin forming.

FOCUS OF ATTENTION BY ENNEAGRAM TYPE

TYPE 1   Needing to improve something, being right, evaluating, creating structure and organization

TYPE 2   Love, relationships, seeking approval, wanting to help and please

TYPE 3   Accomplishing goals, success, performing, seeking admiration

TYPE 4   Longing for what could be, what is missing, past upsets and hurts, finding yourself, being special

TYPE 5   Problem solving, being the expert, figuring things out, ideas, being self-sufficient

TYPE 6   How to feel safe and secure, what could go wrong, what if? preparing / planning, needing to know

TYPE 7   Possibilities, anticipation, future plans, change, diversions

TYPE 8   Being in power and control, wanting justice, blame, righting a wrong

TYPE 9   Comfort and peace, stability, fantasy, fitting in, avoiding conflict, accommodating others

WRITE A POEM

You can try a modified (Japanese) haiku: three lines of five syllables, seven syllables, and five syllables, to include an aspect of nature.

OTHER DOORWAYS

There are many ways of accessing our subconscious mind; there are many ways of knowing:

▸ Play—find time to play just for pure enjoyment. Give yourself permission to be a kid again.

▸ Read poetry—reflect about it, write about it, draw it, feel it.

▸ Listen to a variety of music to cultivate different mood states.

▸ All types of movement help us to put our focus in the present moment—martial arts, mountain biking, hiking, yoga, walking, dance, kayaking, swimming, badminton …

▸ Prayer and meditation—answers come during times of self-reflection. Listen to the subtle messages.

▸ Journal writing—ask questions of your journal. Pose a question and then let your pen move across the page without editing. See what comes. Don't judge it—just move with it.

▸ Art—draw, paint, scribble. Form / no form. Just let the unedited version of you come through in living color.

RECLAIM YOUR PASSION

Do what you love. Leaders show the way; they light the path for others to follow. If you aren't able to tap into your passion, how can you inspire others to follow you? The following suggestions for your journal writing are to help you tap into your well of passion and inspiration.

There are so many things that bring us joy. Try doing something every day that brings you joy. The more joy in you, the more capacity you have to give to others. Connecting to your passion can help you unearth buried dreams.

What do you do to continually replenish and refresh yourself? How do you take care of yourself so that your light can shine brightly for others? Spend time every day doing something you love. Is it painting, dancing, singing, or playing an instrument; spending time with your spouse, partner, friends, dog, or cat; hiking, playing tennis, doing volunteer work; spending time with wise elderly folk?

What are you passionate about?

What did you love to do as a child?

Was there a path not taken for practical reasons? Is there a way to rejoin that path?

When did you notice your passion waning?

Remember when Tinker Bell's light went out? She lost her energy, and it took the support of all the children of the world clapping for her to revive her. Do you have a support network of people who can clap for you?

On one of your walks, pose the following questions to yourself. See what arises. Write about it: Remember a time when you were young and absolutely engrossed in what you were doing; you were passionate and joyful. What was it? What were you doing? How were you feeling? Write the story of this time in your life. See how you can weave these loose threads back into the fabric of your life.

Let the beauty we love, be what we do.

—Rumi[37]

MINDFULNESS MEDITATION

Meditating is an important doorway through which to develop your leadership presence. Understanding with the mind is not enough. Meditation has a powerfully positive effect on us, and current brain research scientifically proves what many have experienced for thousands of years. When we meditate, we are taking a look at our mind and seeing how it works. Just looking. Normally we are engaged in *to do's*, results, replaying the past, planning the future … Thoughts arise and dissolve. Meditation gives us a chance to examine those thoughts.

"One thing that meditation does for those who practise it a lot is that it cultivates attentional skills," Dr. [Zoran] Josipovic says, adding that those harnessed skills can help lead to a more tranquil and happier way of being.

—Matt Danzico, "Brains of Buddhist Monks Scanned in Meditation Study," BBC News[38]

Some people find it very valuable to join a meditation group. It can also provide you with structure and a community of practice. Most communities around the world have meditation centers. Searching the Internet for "insight meditation" is a good starting place. There are many different meditation communities: Zen meditation, vipassana meditation, Tibetan meditation, and so on. Find one that is right for you.

Meanwhile, starting with five minutes a day will do you wonders! You can also stop many times during the day and just take a moment to breathe into your belly and focus on your breath.

BENEFITS: There are many, and these are just a few:

▸ If you start your day with meditation, you will likely feel more grounded and centered as you enter your day.

▸ You will be developing your nonjudging mind.

▸ You will be able to start interrupting your patterns because you are more able to self-observe and become your own *fair witness.*

▸ Over time, you will find yourself less reactive and more present.

▸ Meditation reduces stress and improves immune system function.

HOW TO QUIET THE MIND:

▸ Find a comfortable place to sit.

▸ Intentionally relax each body part; start with your feet and move upward toward your head.

▸ Begin to focus on your breathing, and track your breath from your belly until you breathe out your nostrils and in again.

▸ Stay focused on following your breath. As with most of us, you may not even finish the first breath before being distracted by a thought.

▸ Without judging, notice the thought and let it go. Don't force it away or resist it. Just see it as a thought floating through your awareness, and then gently bring your attention back to your breath.

PART 6

YOUR JOURNAL OF SELF-DISCOVERY

WHAT'S YOUR NARRATIVE? A LITTLE STORY OF YOUR LIFE.

Your journal is a significant part of your self-discovery and pattern-shifting process. Through guided self-reflection, the insights you have will give you the opportunity to be the author of your own unfolding life story. You can also visit your past and re-story it in a way that reveals a new truth.

INSTRUCTIONS

It is unlikely that you will go through this entire exercise in one sitting. Chances are, you will return to it many times in the coming days, weeks, or months. That's OK. In between your writing days, begin to notice how your Enneagram Type plays out in day-to-day life. Reflect on your day at the end of it or in the middle of it. See what you notice. Keep this book or your journal handy to jot down ideas.

SETTING

Find a quiet place without distraction. I often find that going to a special place in nature—sitting under a tree, on a hill, in my garden, at the edge of the sea—allows me to be quiet inside so that I can connect more deeply with myself.

PREPARATION

Take a few moments to meditate, to quiet your mind and connect with your heart. Set your intention for the time you're going to spend with your journal. Be open to what is revealed. Don't edit your comments. Allow a free flow of words to move through you, and forget about grammar, spelling, saying the right thing, making sense. This activity isn't for anyone else's review. It's only for you.

FOCUS / YOUR LENS

Read the description of your Enneagram Type. Look back on your life—your earliest memories. Can you see life patterns related to your Enneagram Type woven into the tapestry of your story?

WRITE

Write about what you see and feel, and write down memories of events that shaped your personal narrative.

REFLECT

What do you notice in your narrative that is related to your Enneagram Type?

- Patterns of relationship interactions
- Consistent feedback (three or more people have said something similar to you)
- Patterns of thinking
- Patterns of feeling
- Patterns of acting

How have these patterns helped you? They may have been important coping strategies when you were young.

How have they gotten in your way?

What have they cost you?

WRITE

Write your reflections.

STOP AND REFLECT

REFLECT/WRITE

What are the beliefs you hold about yourself?

How do your beliefs restrict you? How do they expand you?

PLOT

When you look back over your life story, you may notice a *plot*—events that originally appeared random or coincidental may form a central theme in your narrative. What is the plot of your story?

RED THREAD

What are the themes that run through your story—the red threads you see in your narrative tapestry?

TITLE IT

What is the title of your story?

OTHER INPUTS

Do you have a journal or diary from years past? Take a look. Are you surprised to see what you knew early on? Compare it with the story you just wrote.

• Examine the elements of loneliness and belonging. What is your relationship to being alone? What is your relationship to belonging? Do you want both and experience tension?

• Each Type has a special strategy for staying away from the present moment. What is your strategy? What makes the present moment difficult for you?

THE REST IS STILL UNWRITTEN

What is your narrative—the big story of your life that is waiting to be written?

 WHAT IS YOUR PERSONAL MYTH?

NOTE

Freud and Jung believed that "myth is grounded in the un-conscious."[39]

... along the way we learn to trust our hearts, read the seemingly inconspicuous signs, and understand that as we look to fulfill a dream, it looks to find us just the same, if we let it.

—Paulo Coehlo, *The Alchemist*[40]

REFLECT

Describe your personal mythology—symbols, storylines, and arche-types that surface in your dreams—for example, water, elevators, falling, running. Consider your daydreams, night dreams, and life dreams. Is there a common theme that runs through them, or are there recurring symbols that show up?

WRITE

Your *red threads* are made up of elements or themes that run through the tapestry of your life. These are your beliefs, patterns, consistent feedback, recurring events, and repetitive interactions.

What are your *golden threads*—symbols, dreams, unusual occurrences, people or animals that consistently cross your path (coincidences and serendipities)?

What symbols and stories speak to you? Ask them what they are trying to tell you.

What hasn't fully come into being in your life yet? You may have a wish, a dream, a desire—something that you have wanted to bring into tangible form but haven't yet done. It could also be a quality that you want to develop (to be more dynamic, quiet, gentle, powerful, assertive).

What has become too small for you—what have you outgrown? Are you playing small? What keeps you in a place you have outgrown?

If you were being authentically you, with no mask or pretense, who would you be? Describe yourself.

If you could express the inner beauty of who you are, who would you create yourself to be?

What are your core assets—the aspects of parts of your history that you choose to bring forward and that you will use as a foundation for the next part of your life?

If you were to take one courageous step toward your destiny, what would that be?

When you wake up two years from now and you are living fully and joyfully, what are you doing? How are you feeling? What is your life like, and how did you create it?

ACKNOWLEDGMENTS

This book has been evolving over my entire life, and many events and circumstances have conspired to bring it into tangible form. Many people have shared my journey over the last few decades and have helped to plant the seeds for this book to grow.

First, I must thank my family for believing in me, wanting me to grow and evolve into the best person I could be. Each member of my family has been a source of inspiration, a font of love, and a container of support. Although my father and sister are no longer alive, they have been very much with me on this journey, cheering me on every step of the way. My Aunt Jennifer and Uncle Donn have given their time, support, insights, and love throughout this process. Mom and brother Bill have given nothing but encouragement. They are my biggest fans.

I am grateful to Shayna and Bear, my canine companions. They taught me what it means to love fearlessly, with total abandon. They taught me what it means to be committed, present, and selfless. Their inner and outer beauty makes me sing and ache with love. They are my teachers.

Angeles Arrien showed up in my life in October 1992, and my path took a left-hand turn toward an unimagined future. An announcement arrived about a weekend event at Mills College featuring Michael Meade and Angeles Arrien. I jumped at the chance to attend, never having heard of Angeles. I was immediately drawn to and enchanted by her. She spoke words that resonated in me. Before the weekend came to a close, I signed up for a six-day workshop in Arizona, and that was the beginning of a long association with a woman who has been a source of inspiration and a font of wisdom for me.

Angeles has been my teacher, mentor, and a mirror to let me see the very best of who I was—and am. Her wisdom is timeless, and I have been blessed to receive her generosity of spirit and love. Through my early work with Angie, I reclaimed my love of anthropology from my early childhood years and left a successful career to go to graduate school.

I enrolled in California Institute of Integral Studies (CIIS) to get my master's degree in social and cultural anthropology, and it opened new worlds I never could have imagined. It was just at this time that the Enneagram came to my attention. Never did I guess what a wild ride I was taking when I pulled that first book off the shelf.

Don Riso and Russ Hudson entered my story in the late '90s. Since I had read quite a bit about the Enneagram and attended other workshops, the ground was fertile and I was ready—I needed to hear what they had to say. They teach the Enneagram with compassion and a desire to help human consciousness evolve. I am grateful for their tireless work to bring the Enneagram into greater public awareness, as I am for Helen Palmer, who wrote the first book on the Enneagram. We are all beneficiaries of their early trailblazing.

Dr. Roxanne Howe-Murphy, Pam Fox Rollin, Samantha Schoenfeld were my Enneagram colleagues in the early years. I am grateful to them for our collaborations and their continued friendship, support, encouragement and inspiration.

Dr. Daniel Siegel piqued my interest in neurobiology when I met him at an Enneagram conference early in 2000. I was taken by the hopefulness of the ideas he shared. He has a special perspective on human behavior, combining neurobiological and interpersonal tools in language accessible to the layperson. He is committed to transforming teaching methods in order to create more well-adjusted, happier children—and therefore a healthier planet.

I thank the members of my women's group, started in the early '90s, who continue to be an extraordinary support not only to me but to one another. I am grateful for the many friends who cheered me on with each step I took: Helen Crothers, Carole Henmi, Joan Gallagher, Janet Crawford, Julia Young, Annie Nisson, Patty Lynn Thorndike, Judith Forrest, Elise Giancola, Pia Glavind, Ingeborg Vestergaard, Marlita Kahn, Catherine Stearns, Katja Wittenstein, Lynn White, Graham Dixon, Andrew Merrett, Martin McDonnell, Walther Albrecher, Kerstin Unger, Fredric Cederlund, Elisabet Sahtouris, Windy Goodale, Wendy Zito, Vera Middelhauve, Florian Reithner, Alyssa Levy, Paula Love, Bev Crawford.

Special thanks go to those dear friends and colleagues who took time to read my manuscript, help me with my book title, and give me much-needed feedback—Pam Fox Rollin, Drew Dougherty, Christine Cavanaugh-Simmons, David Frigstad, Jos Nietsen, Mary Bast, Mario Sikora, Michael J. Goldberg, Christy Anderson, Jeff Jackson, Maurice Monnett, Dr. Liz Alexander, Karen Seriguchi, Lynne Sedgmore. Bea Chestnut helped inform my understanding of the Instincts (subtypes) and has been a wonderful support.

Sandra Shelley, my friend who happens to be a brilliant therapist, was gracious enough to author her understanding of Carl Jung's journey of individuation for my book.

Having experienced the work of Wendy Palmer, I was compelled to include a sample of her work. The somatic coaching she offers is a beautiful complement to the Enneagram. She works to help her clients balance the three Centers of Intelligence.

I couldn't have done this without my brilliant editors. Elissa Rabellino, my copy editor, does the work of saints. Her attention to detail is astounding. Ann Matranga is a gifted writer and developmental editor. She was generous with her time and consistently showed her commitment to make this book a standout. Between the two, the book was polished, and they brought out its shine. Special thanks to my book designer, Ceci Sorochin, who is not only delightful to work with but incredibly talented. Here's to Jennifer Keith and her wonderful illustrations on my Enneagram Typing Cards.

Susan Furness is an amazing woman and businesswoman, and, happily, my publicist. We have easily been able to bridge our friendship and business relationship. With Susan at my side, anything seems possible.

Special helpers showed up along the way to guide me on my journey, people who briefly touched my life and made a big difference—Jim, David, Tahlecion, Lynton, Nina, Judy.

Finally, I thank my colleagues and clients. Through our work together, I gained both a deeper understanding of the Enneagram and the inspiration to write this book.

Without my incredible community, I can't imagine where I would be right now. It does take a village.

To the Enneagram community, I continue to learn from and be inspired by all the many ways you bring new insights about this ancient symbol and system. Thank you all for your many contributions.

Thank you to the Enneagram, my friend, my companion and my teacher.

To my birth family and my global family: Family is the soil in which we are planted, and each one of us is a seed. Sometimes family gives us just the perfect challenges—just the right soil and nutrients in order to grow and become the person we were born to be. We must push up and through the soil, like pushing through the birth canal, toward the light. People seem to grow through adversity; through the challenges each of us faces in life. We are born of and through resistance toward the pull of the possible and the infinite.

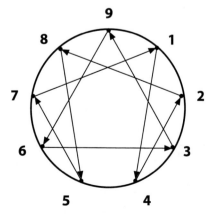

APPENDIX Type Comparison Chart[41]

ENNEATYPE	EMOTIONAL COMPULSION	THINKING COMPULSION	WANT TO AVOID	WANT/DESIRE	HOW I SEE MYSELF	RED FLAG	ANTIDOTES
8 Boss	Lust	Vengeance	Being controlled or violated; feeling weak.	Protect myself, feel strong and powerful, highly self-sufficient.	Strong	Feeling that I must push and struggle to make things happen. Use more force than necessary. Being highly self-sufficient.	Slow down. Feel. Express caring. Ask for and receive help. Use a feather rather than a hammer.
9 Peacemaker	Sloth	Indolence	Loss of connection and separation.	Have peace of mind, wholeness, to be connected.	Peaceful	Outwardly accommodating myself to others. Stuck. Don't know what I want. Resistant to change. Lack of vitality.	Stay engaged. Allow yourself to feel uncomfortable. Connect with your anger. Prioritize.
1 Perfectionist	Anger	Resentment	Being bad, corrupt, or defective, imperfect.	To be perfect; be good, integrity.	Reasonable	Feeling a sense of personal obligation to fix everything myself. Everything and everyone needs improvement, including me.	Enjoy life and others without needing to improve or fix. Learn what is good enough both for you and for others.
2 People Pleaser	Pride	Flattery	Being unworthy, not being loved.	Feel loved for myself.	Loving	Believing I must win others over by "people pleasing" and seducing.	Attend to your own needs first. Accept help. Learn to love yourself and know others appreciate and love you for who you are, not what you do for them.
3 Achiever	Deceit	Vanity	Being worthless, without value.	Feel valuable and worthwhile; recognizing	Outstanding	Striving for recognition, admiration, status, and attention. The image I project is more important than who I really am.	Enjoy what you are doing without focusing on what you'll achieve. Make contact with your heart's desire.
4 Individualist	Envy	Melancholy	Being without identity, personal significance.	Find and express unique identity and personal significance.	Unique	Holding on to and intensifying my feelings through my imagination and fantasy. Focusing on what is missing or what I don't have in my life that I perceive others have.	Take specific steps toward a tangible outcome. Focus on being more objective. Extend your sensitivity toward others.
5 Detached Observer	Avarice	Stinginess	Being useless, incompetent, incapable.	Be capable and competent.	Perceptive	Withdrawing from reality into concepts and mental worlds, and removed from the immediacy of life.	Make contact with your heart and body. Have lived experiences. Feel your power. Engage others.
6 Loyal Skeptic	Fear/worry	Cowardice	Being without support or guidance.	Find support and guidance.	Reliable	Self-doubting. Becoming dependent on something or someone outside myself for guidance and/or security.	Connect with your own inner guidance and trust your instincts. Meditate. Quiet your mind. Trust more, prepare less.
7 Enthusiast	Gluttony	Planning and anticipating	Being trapped in emotional pain; deprivation.	Be satisfied and fulfilled.	Enthusiastic	Feeling that something better is available somewhere else. "The grass is greener." When my attention is on future possibilities and not in the "here and now." Terrified to close down options.	Fully experience and appreciate the now. Fully digest each experience. Create more space and less activity in your life. Allow yourself to feel deeply.

DEEPLY HELD BELIEFS OF THE NINE TYPES

These beliefs make up a key element of the core dynamics of each of the Enneagram Types and set up their life patterns. They are key drivers of the behavior for each Type. We are often unaware that we even hold these beliefs, and if we are aware of them, we rarely question their validity. In fact, we have strategies to selectively pay attention to information that confirms and therefore reinforces our beliefs.

For example, if you believe you are nobody special and don't matter, you might not bother sharing your opinion or making your needs known. You might also try to blend in and avoid drawing attention to yourself. You might notice that people don't seem to pay attention to you, which serves to reinforce your self-assessment. If people do solicit your opinion or try to draw you out, you might discount it and think they just want something from you.

Further, you might try to maintain this belief by choosing a relationship (work or personal) with someone who stands out, gets the attention, and has strong opinions. As a result, you shrink in proportion, while resenting that person. You may try to dampen his or her energy either directly or behind the scenes.

Again, we selectively pay attention to the data that confirms and reinforces our beliefs. The following breaks them out into the nine Types:

Type 1: I'm bad, corrupt, and imperfect. I need to improve myself, everyone, and my environment. I must project an image of perfection; of a good person; and of being right, just, and fair. If I follow the rules and do what is expected of me, I earn my autonomy.

Type 2: I'm not lovable. I need to earn love. If I am a good person and help people, I will be loved. I must project an image of warmth, likability, and helpfulness. I must make myself indispensable to others to earn the approval and appreciation I desire.

Type 3: I'm not worthwhile / I am without value. I must project an image of success and achieve my goals, and then I will earn others' admiration. This will mean that I am valuable and worthwhile.

Type 4: I don't feel seen or understood. I must be flawed. There is something missing. Others have something I don't have, and I want it, but I don't want to be like them. I am sensitive and deep. I must express my uniqueness. I need to stand out and be special.

Type 5: I'm afraid of not being competent or capable. I must become an expert and project an image of intellect and competence. This will be my source of power and safety. It is important to keep others at a distance. I don't have the energy to deal with people's demands on me. I have to minimize my needs. I don't want to rely on other people. There is no support for me.

Type 6: I'm not good enough. I have to earn other people's trust by being responsible. The world is an unsafe place. Everyone acts out of self–interest. Other people are not trustworthy. I can't trust.

Type 7: I will be deprived and trapped in pain. I will never be able to escape. There's not enough _____. I don't want my freedom limited. Life is a buffet and I need to taste it all.

Type 8: I'm afraid of being weak and vulnerable. I must project an image of power, strength, and control. I won't let others control me, so I need to take control and power. There's only room for one top dog.

Type 9: I'm nobody special. I am easygoing. I am without opinion, and if I have an opinion or create conflict, I will lose my connection to others. I must be seen as kind and giving. I must accommodate others' needs to get along. It is better to tamp down my anger and passion and to forget my own needs in order to keep the peace and stay peaceful.

UNDERLYING MOTIVATIONS

Another way to view the driving motivations for each type is to frame them in terms of what each Type wants and what each Type wants to avoid:

Type 1 wants to be perfect and right, and to seek perfection in others and the world.
Type 1 wants to avoid feeling bad, wrong, imperfect.

Type 2 wants to feel worthy of love, needed, and appreciated.
Type 2 wants to avoid rejection, feeling unworthy, and feeling unwanted.

Type 3 wants to be admired, recognized, and therefore feel valuable.
Type 3 wants to avoid failure and feeling worthless.

Type 4 wants to feel special and unique, and to find themselves.
Type 4 wants to avoid feeling insignificant, without personal identity.

Type 5 wants to be the expert and competent.
Type 5 wants to avoid having needs and feeling incapable.

Type 6 wants security and predictability (*to know*).
Type 6 wants to avoid being without support and guidance.

Type 7 wants freedom, options, to be stimulated, and to feel satisfied.
Type 7 wants to avoid feeling trapped, stuck in emotional pain, and being deprived.

Type 8 wants to be in control and to be powerful.
Type 8 wants to avoid feeling weak and vulnerable.

Type 9 wants to be comfortable and peaceful.
Type 9 wants to avoid conflict and loss of connection/love.

ESSENTIAL GIFTS OF THE NINE ENNEAGRAM TYPES

Although this list is not exhaustive, it offers some of the special gifts of each Type and what we can learn from them.

Type 1: Integrity, discipline, completion, structure, responsibility

Type 2: Empathy, giving, warmth, relationship

Type 3: Ambition, sustained focus on goals, mentorship, accomplishment

Type 4: Authenticity, listening to the heart's desire, creative expression, sensitivity

Type 5: Innovation, intellectual depth, inner knowing, non-attachment

Type 6: Preparation, research, loyalty, social connection, your champion

Type 7: Joy, playfulness, spontaneity, vision, optimism, synthesis

Type 8: Strength, self-worth, grounded realism, connection to personal power

Type 9: Acceptance, kindness, holistic perspective, mediation

ORIGINS OF THE ENNEAGRAM

The term *Enneagram* finds its roots in two Greek words, *ennea* (nine) and *grammos* (something written or drawn).

Some say the Enneagram originated with the Sufis, although this seems to have been disproved, and many trace the Enneagram symbol back to Plato and Pythagoras.

In his book *The 9 Ways of Working*, Michael J. Goldberg writes, "The Enneagram styles are very old. Homer (ca. 750 B.C.E.) knew the basic themes as they are today. Odysseus travels through each of the Enneagram domains in *exact reverse numerical order.*"[42]

He continues,

> **Homer must have known something of the relationships among the Enneagram Types as well, because he knew the critical order. He was likely associated with long-established civilizations to the east, the Chaldeans and the Persians, who had developed elaborate cosmologies. Indeed, Proclus (410–485 C.E.), head of the Athenian Academy, and other commentators believed Homer to be part of an ancient wisdom tradition that was later represented in a distinct form in Pythagoras and Plato and their followers.**[43]

Over many years of study, I collected bits and pieces of Enneagram history through those who are part of its lineage, its growth and development, and its transition from an oral tradition to a written and more mainstream tradition. It would take a family tree to identify all those who have contributed to the Enneagram's travels through time and space.

My own coincidental (or was it?) connection to Enneagram history came about in 2006. I was on holiday with a friend in Mallorca, Spain—an island in the Mediterranean. We were touring the north

coast by car when I saw a sign for a monastery. Spontaneously, I turned in to the driveway and found myself on a spectacular piece of land beside cliffs and, below them, the sea. The parking lot was deserted, but in short order an elderly man appeared to take our entrance fee. We began wandering the grounds and arrived at the monastery itself.

As we entered, on a wall full of symbols I saw a series of posters. One caught my eye, a nine-pointed star made of three intersecting triangles, called an *enneagon*. Where was I? What was the nature of this monastery? There were alchemical symbols, astrological symbols, and writings in Latin and Catalán. I began to take photos.

We entered the simple, small living quarters of a monk who had resided there in the 13th century, Ramón Llull. On the wall of his cell, I saw another poster, of an enneagon in three colors—red, yellow, and green. My curiosity was growing and my intuition was sounding. Who was this man, Ramón Llull? Did he have anything to do with the Enneagram?

We left the monastery and continued wandering around the grounds until we came to a beautiful space surrounded by trees. Embedded in the ground, inside the tree border, were two large versions of the colored enneagons. I was astounded. What went on here? Turning to my right, I saw a reflecting pool. The meaning was not lost on me. This place was designed for self-reflection and inner alchemy.

I sat there for a while, hoping the pieces of a puzzle would fall into place and the land would speak to me. Nothing occurred, even though I knew I had stumbled upon something important.

Roll the tape forward a few years, and I am living on Mallorca. The reasons for that are another story. I will just note that I had felt an immediate resonance with the island when I arrived on my first visit.

As a result of that first visit to Mallorca, you are reading this book. When I began research on the genesis and evolution of the Enneagram, I discovered that Ramón Llull had played a part. Michael J. Goldberg wrote the following in his book *The 9 Ways of Working*, and noted that it was transmitted to him via a conversation with Oscar Ichazo:

> **Ramón Llull of Majorca (d. 1315) was a Neo-Platonist and kabbalist, whose grand attempt to synthesize Islamic and Christian thought—the Great**

**Art—is a most important precursor to the Ennea-
gram of personality. Llull arrayed the nine "Digni-
ties of God"—the principles which superintend
the world—around the figure of the Enneagram:
basic themes of the Enneagram—including the
interaction of a formal series of polarized forces as
a pathway to development—came to a full flower
in Kabbalah. The Jesuit Athanasius Kircher (1601–
80), a Llullian, wrote that the Tree of Life, the basic
symbol of Kabbalist practice, and the Enneagram
were equivalent systems.[44]**

Others have also tied the Enneagram's foundation to Ramón Llull.

Continuing my search for the origins of the Enneagram and the
difference between the two different symbols (Ennegram and enneagon: both nine-pointed stars), I came upon an article coauthored
by Virginia Wiltse and Helen Palmer. Their research reaches back to
Evagrius of Pontus, a fourth-century Christian monk who was a Py-
thagorean and a classical scholar who wrote, among other works,
Chapters on Prayer. Evagrius was considered one of the Desert Fa-
thers and wrote about human strengths and weaknesses. He focused
on human temptations and their remedies. Wiltse and Palmer wrote:

> **The Prologue to the Chapters on Prayer directs
> attention to another side of Evagrius.**
>
> **He reveals himself to be a contemplative who rec-
> ognized that the spiritual life could be advanced
> by looking to the heavens and considered the
> very structure of God's creation a symbolic macro-
> cosm that is mirrored in the microcosm of human
> dynamics and the human aspiration for spiritual
> advancement. In the prologue to the Chapters
> on Prayer, Evagrius used numbers to express "the
> decipherable orderliness of creation," and as a
> metaphor through which he could share the sacred
> secrets of the heavens.**

They assert that the three intersecting triangles (the enneagon) represents the harmony and balance that humans can attain, and that the

Enneagram know today represents a "dynamic map of interactions among archetypal forces," that can lead us to "spiritual maturity."[45]

While there is no agreement among historians on a single narrative about the history and evolution of the Enneagram, there does seem to be agreement that its early history and wisdom came together in the work of George Ivanovich Gurdjieff (1866–1949), a teacher from the Caucasus. His sources remain subject to speculation, but we know that his travels through Asia and Africa influenced the development of his work and his teachings.

Gurdjieff's work was first published by one of his students, P. D. Ouspensky, in a 1947 book, *In Search of the Miraculous*. Although Gurdjieff used the Enneagram figure to describe possibilities of human development, he believed that the symbol was alchemical and used it for symbolic communication. His teachings framed it as a personality system. Gurdjieff called the Enneagram "a universal symbol" and "a fundamental hieroglyph of a universal language."

The next sighting of the Enneagram was in 1968, in Santiago, Chile, where Bolivian-born philosopher Oscar Ichazo began a wisdom school called Arica (it was started in Arica, Chile—hence the name). Ichazo is considered the father of the Enneagram of personality. He took the nine-pointed symbol and mapped to it what he described as nine distinct "ego fixations."

This, along with several other dimensions of personality, formed the basis for the Enneagram of personality. Ichazo understood that all Enneagram Types are available to each of us, and he understood each of their paths for development. It stands to reason that Ichazo's work was influenced by Ramón Llull.

Claudio Naranjo, a Chilean psychiatrist and student in the Arica school, brought Ichazo's teachings to Berkeley, California, where he started a self-development program based on his own understanding of the Enneagram. He merged it with modern personality theory, which is largely the way the Enneagram is taught today, and influenced the work of Don Riso and Helen Palmer—two prominent teachers who popularized the Enneagram through their writings and teachings.

Several published teachers of the Enneagram continued to evolve our modern understanding of the nine-pointed symbol and what it has to teach us about self-understanding and transformation.

Among these teachers are Helen Palmer, David Daniels, Don Riso and Russ Hudson, Richard Rohr and Elizabeth Wagele, Sandra Maitri, A. H. Almaas, Michael J. Goldberg, Jerome Wagner, and Kathy Hurley and Theodorre Donson. For additional Enneagram resources, please see the Selected Bibliography.

CONCLUSION

There is no one narrative that tells the whole history. My experience has taught me that the Enneagram is not a fixed entity. I have seen that the Enneagram continues to reveal itself and is always in a state of becoming, as we learn more about human nature. Each Enneagram teacher stands on the shoulders of others who shed light on this dynamic, living system.

If you have the desire and you're ready, the Enneagram can be a road map for your journey of self-transformation—a map of your inner landscape, where you journey deeper and deeper over time. It can take you to places you may not have known existed. It brings unconscious material to light. There are exercises in this book that provide ways for you to begin working with your Enneagram Type in order to start shifting your patterns.

If you are trying to decide whether to explore the Enneagram for your own development, the most important questions to ask yourself are, "Is this relevant? Do I recognize myself and others in these nine Types? Does this material help me to see myself more clearly? Does it help me to understand others better? Am I ready to start dismantling some of my defenses? Am I ready to pull back the curtain on my personality and see who's there?" If you can answer yes to these questions, then the Enneagram will be a worthwhile pursuit.

THE HISTORY OF ITS LINEAGE IS LESS IMPORTANT THAN ITS CURRENT-DAY RELEVANCE FOR YOUR LIFE.

NOTES

1. Joseph Campbell with Bill Moyers, *The Power of Myth* (New York: Doubleday, 1988), 206.

2. Robert Frost and Louis Untermeyer, *Robert Frost's Poems* (New York: St. Martin's Paperbacks, 2002).

3. Chris Argyris, "Teaching Smart People How to Learn," Harvard Business School, *Reflections* 4, no. 2, orig. pub. in *Harvard Business Review* (May 1991).

4. Robert Cooper, "A New Neuroscience of Leadership: Bringing Out More of the Best in People," © Copyright by Robert K. Cooper and Advanced Excellence Systems LLC, *Strategy & Leadership Journal* (January 2001).

5. Julia Glass, *I See You Everywhere* (New York: Anchor Books, 2008), 17.

6. Paul Vitello, "Ray Anderson, Businessman Turned Environmentalist, Dies at 77," *New York Times*, August 10, 2011, http://www.nytimes.com.

7. The Johari Window was created by Joseph Luft and Harry Ingham in 1955 in the United States to help people better understand their interpersonal communication and relationships.

8. Campbell and Moyers, *The Power of Myth*, 149.

9. Don Riso and Russ Hudson, *The Wisdom of the Enneagram: The Complete Guide to Psychological and Spiritual Growth for the Nine Personality Types* (New York: Bantam Books, 1999).

10. Joseph Campbell, *Reflections on the Art of Living: A Joseph Campbell Companion*, ed. Diane K. Osbon (New York: HarperCollins, 1991).

11. Carl Jung, *Memories, Dreams, Reflections*, ed., Aniela Jaffé (New York: Vintage Books, 1989), 326.

12. Campbell and Moyers, *The Power of Myth*, 124.

13. I have condensed some of the 17 stages of the hero's journey for purposes of this book. The entire journey can be read, with examples from cultures around the world, in *The Hero with a Thousand Faces*, listed in the bibliography.

14. T. S. Eliot, *Four Quarte*ts (New York: Harcourt, 1943).

15. Paulo Coelho and Alan R. Clarke, *The Alchemis*t (New York: HarperCollins, 1993), 178.

16. John Moyne and Coleman Barks, *Open Secret: Versions of Rumi* (Putney, VT: Threshold Books, 1984), 7.

17. Coelho and Clarke, *The Alchemist*, xiii.

18. Joseph Campbell, *The Hero with a Thousand Faces* (Novato, CA: New World Library, 2008), 74.

19. Joseph Campbell, *Pathways to Bliss: Mythology and Personal Transformation* (Novato, CA: New World Library, 2004), 116.

20. Jash Raj Subba, *Mythology of the People of Sikkim* (New Delhi: Gyan Publishing House, 2009), 135.

21. Robert Bly, *A Little Book on the Human Shadow* (San Francisco: HarperCollins Publishers, 1988), 17.

22. Ibid., 20.

23. Antonio Machado, *Times Alone: Selected Poems of Antonio Machado*, tr. Robert Bly (Middletown, CT: Wesleyan University Press, 1983).

24. Kahlil Gibran, *The Prophet* (New York: Knopf, 1973).

25. Kahlil Gibran, *Jesus the Son of Man* (New York: Knopf, 2000), 92.

26. Gibran, *The Prophet*.

27. M. Esther Harding, *The Way of All Women* (Boston: Shambhala, 1970), 5.

28. Cooper, "A New Neuroscience of Leadership," 11–15.

29. Riso and Hudson identified the underlying feelings and "concerned with" (what I call "focus") for each of the Triads. This information can be found in the chapter "The Triadic Self" in *The Wisdom of the Enneagram*, pp. 49–59. I have added envy as the underlying feeling for the Heart Center, as other teachers find this to be more accurate.

30. Alyce Parsons, Kathy Hurley, and Theodorre Donson, *Essential Self, Essential Style* (Lakewood, CO: Wind-Walker Press, 2002).

31. Riso and Hudson, *The Wisdom of the Enneagram*.

32. Norman Doidge, MD, *The Brain That Changes Itself: Stories of Personal Triumph from the Frontiers of Brain Science* (New York: Viking, 2007), 63.

33. Ibid., 63.

34. Chautauqua Institution, "Dan Siegel: The Brain and the Developing Mind," 2009, http://fora.tv/2009/06/30/Dan_Siegel_The_Brain_and_the_Developing_Mind. Also see Daniel J. Siegel, MD, TEDxBlue, October 18, 2009, http://www.youtube.com/watch?v=Nu7wEr8AnHw&feature=player_embedded.

35. Bruce Lipton, interview by Iain McNay, "The Power of Consciousness," Conscious TV, YouTube, August 15, 2010, http://www.conscious.tv/programme.php.

36. Thich Nhat Hanh, *Touching Peace: Practicing the Art of Mindful Living*, rev. ed. (Berkeley, CA: Parallax Press, 2009), 1.

37. Moyne and Barks, *Open Secret*, 7.

38. Matt Danzico, "Brains of Buddhist Monks Scanned in Meditation Study," BBC News, April 23, 2011, http://www.bbc.co.uk/news/world-us-canada-12661646.

39. Campbell and Moyers, *The Power of Myth*, 58.

40. Coelho and Clark, *The Alchemist*, 178.

41. Type Names, Basic Fear/Desire, Sense of Self, and Wake-up Call were developed by Don Riso and Russ Hudson of the Enneagram Institute.

42. Michael J. Goldberg, *The 9 Ways of Working: How to Use the Enneagram to Discover Your Natural Strengths and Work More Effectively* (New York: Marlowe and Company, 1996), 340.

43. Ibid., 341.

44. Ibid.

45. Virginia Wiltse and Helen Palmer, "Hidden in Plain Sight: Observations on the Origins of the Enneagram," first published in the *Enneagram Journal of the International Enneagram Association*, excerpted from revised 2011 edition, http://www.enneagram-worldwide.com/enneagram-teachers/helen-palmer/enneagram-origins.php.

SELECTED BIBLIOGRAPHY

Almaas, A. H. *Facets of Unity: The Enneagram of Holy Ideas*. Boston: Shambhala Publications, Inc., 1998.

Altman, Y, M. Özbilgin, and E. Wilson. *A study on organisational effectiveness and well-being at work: CEL as a case-study*. Barcelona: ESADE: Institute of Labor Studies, 2007.

Argryis, Chris. "Teaching Smart People How to Learn." *Reflections* 4, no. 2. Orig. pub. in *Harvard Business Review*, May 1991.

Arrien, Angeles, PhD. *The Four-Fold Way: Walking the Paths of the Warrior, Teacher, Healer, and Visionary*. San Francisco: HarpersCollins Publishers, 1993.

———. *Second Half of Life: Opening the Eight Gates of Wisdom*. Boulder, CO: Sounds True, Inc., 2007.

Bast, Mary, and Clarence Thompson. *Out of the Box: Coaching with the Enneagram*. Louisberg, KS: Ninestar Publishing, 2005.

Berry, Ian. *Changing What's Normal*: Adelaide, Australia: Customer Centred Consulting Pty Ltd, 2011.

Bly, Robert. *A Little Book on the Human Shadow*. San Francisco: HarperCollins Publishers, 1988.

Campbell, Joseph. *The Hero with a Thousand Faces*. Novato, CA: New World Library, 2008.

———. *Pathways to Bliss: Mythology and Personal Transformation*. Novato, CA: New World Library, 2004.

Campbell, Joseph, with Bill Moyers. *The Power of Myth*. New York: Broadway Books, 2001.

Cannino, Sylviane. *Communiquer avec authenticité: et rester vrai*. Paris: Eyrolles, 2009.

Centre for Excellence in Leadership. *Living Spirituality in the Workplace—the CEL Way*. Produced by Howardsgate. © CEL January 2008.

Chödrön, Pema. *When Things Fall Apart: Heart Advice for Difficult Times*. Boston: Shambhala, 1997.

Csikszentmihalyi, Mihaly. *Finding Flow: The Psychology of Engagement with Everyday Life*. New York: Basic Books, 1997.

Doidge, Norman, MD. *The Brain That Changes Itself: Stories of Personal Triumph from the Frontiers of Brain Science*. New York: Viking, 2007.

Franck, Frederick. *To Be Human Against All Odds*. Berkeley, CA: Asian Humanities Press, 1991.

Goldberg, Michael J. *Travels with Odysseus: Uncommon Wisdom from Homer's Odyssey*. Tempe, AZ: Circe's Island Press, 2006.

———. *The 9 Ways of Working: How to Use the Enneagram to Discover Your Natural Strengths and Work More Effectively*. New York: Marlowe and Company, 1999.

Goleman, Daniel. *Emotional Intelligence: Why It Can Matter More Than IQ*. New York: Bantam Books, 1995.

Gurdjieff, G. I. *Beelzebub's Tales to His Grandson*. New York: Viking Arkana, 1992.

Hanh, Thich Nhat. *The Miracle of Mindfulness: An Introduction to the Practice of Meditation*. Boston: Beacon Press, 1975.

Howe-Murphy, Roxanne, with a foreword by Don Riso and Russ Hudson. *Deep Coaching: Using the Enneagram as a Catalyst for Profound Change*. El Granada, CA: Enneagram Press, 2007.

Jaworski, Joseph, and Peter Senge. *Synchronicity*. San Francisco: Berrett-Koehler Publishers, Inc., 2011.

Kornfield, Jack. *A Path with Heart: A Guide Through the Perils and Promises of Spiritual Life*. New York: Bantam Books, 1993.

Kouzes, J. M., and Barry Pozner. *The Leadership Challenge Workbook*. San Francisco: Jossey-Bass, 2003.

Leider, Richard J. *The Power of Purpose: Creating Meaning in Your Life and Work*. San Francisco: Berrett-Koehler Publishers, Inc., 1997.

Lipton, Bruce H. *The Biology of Belief: Unleashing the Power of Consciousness, Matter, and Miracles*. Carlsbad, CA: Hay House, Inc., 2005.

Lipton, Bruce H., and Steve Bhaerman. *Spontaneous Evolution: Our Positive Future (and a Way to Get There from Here)*. Carlsbad, CA: Hay House, Inc., 2009.

Maitri, Sandra. *The Spiritual Dimension of the Enneagram: Nine Faces of the Soul*. New York: Jeremy P. Tarcher / Putnam, 2001.

Marshall, Lisa J. *Speak the Truth and Point to Hope: The Leader's Journey to Maturity*. Dubuque, Iowa: Kendall/Hunt Publishing Co., 2004.

Moyne, John, and Coleman Barks. *Open Secret: Versions of Rumi*. Putney, VT: Threshold Books, 1984.

Neal, Judi. *Edgewalkers: People and Organizations That Take Risks, Build Bridges, and Break New Ground*. Westport, CT: Praeger Publishers, 2006.

Naranjo, Claudio, MD. *Character and Neurosis: An Integrative View*. Nevada City, CA: Gateways/IDHHB, Inc., 2001.

Oriah Mountain Dreamer. *The Call: Discovering Why You Are Here*. San Francisco: HarperSanFrancisco, 2003.

Ouspensky, P. D. *In Search of the Miraculous: Fragments of an Unknown Teaching*. New York: Harcourt, Brace & World, 1949.

Palmer, Wendy. *The Intuitive Body: Discovering the Wisdom of Conscious Embodiment and Aikido*. Berkeley, CA: Blue Snake Books, 2008.

Parsons, A., Kathy Hurley, and Theodorre Donson. *Essential Self, Essential Style*. Lakewood: WindWalker Press, 2002.

Renesch, John. *The Great Growing Up: Being Responsible for Humanity's Future*. Prescott, AZ: Hohm Press, 2011.

Riso, Don Richard, and Russ Hudson. *The Wisdom of the Enneagram: The Complete Guide to Psychological and Spiritual Growth for the Nine Personality Types*. New York: Bantam, 1999.

———. *Understanding the Enneagram: The Practical Guide to Personality Types*. Boston: Houghton Mifflin, 1993.

Ryckman, Richard. *Theories of Personality*. Belmont, CA: Thomson/Wadsworth, 2004.

Sahtouris, Elisabet, and James E. Lovelock. *Earth Dance: Living Systems in Evolution.* Lincoln, NB: iUniverse Press, 2000.

Satir, Virginia. *Making Contact.* Berkeley, CA: Celestial Arts, 1976.

Siegel, Daniel J., MD. *The Developing Mind: Toward a Neurobiology of Interpersonal Experience.* New York: Guilford Press, 1999.

———. *Mindsight: The New Science of Personal Transformation.* New York: Bantam, 2010.

Stone, Douglas, Bruce Patton, and Sheila Heen. *Difficult Conversations: How to Discuss What Matters Most.* New York: Penguin, 2000.

Tallon, Robert, and Mario Sikora. *Awareness to Action: The Enneagram, Emotional Intelligence, and Change.* Scranton, PA: University of Scranton Press, 2006.

Tart, Charles T. *Waking Up: Overcoming the Obstacles to Human Potential.* Boston: Shambhala, 1986.

Tolle, Ekhart. *A New Earth: Awakening to Your Life's Purpose.* New York: Penguin, 2005.

Whyte, David. *Crossing the Unknown Sea: Work as a Pilgrimage of Identity.* New York: Riverhead Books, 2001.

———. *The Heart Aroused: Poetry and the Preservation of the Soul in Corporate America.* New York: Bantam, 1994.

———. Midlife and the Great Unknown: Finding Courage and Clarity Through Poetry. Boulder, CO: Sounds True, 2003.

Yochanan, Altman. "In Search of Spiritual Leadership: Making a Connection with Transcendence." *Journal of Human Resource Management International Digest* 18, no. 6 (2010): 35–38.

Zander, Rosamund Stone, and Benjamin Zander. *The Art of Possibility: Transforming Professional and Personal Life.* New York: Penguin, 2002.

ABOUT THE AUTHOR

Wendy Appel lives in Sóller on Mallorca's northwest coast. Her stone house is at the base of the majestic Tramuntana Mountain range, nestled within an eclectic orchard complete with a citrus grove. In this setting, Wendy found a source of alchemy to transform her consulting experience and intellectual insight into a framework for leadership. As she sifted through three decades of professional success and two decades of work with the Enneagram, she wrote her first book, *InsideOut*.

Wendy's work as a coach, consultant, and writer is grounded in her own leadership. Through professional experience, self-reflection, and extensive study, she came to understand the ways of a leader inside and out. She was an early adopter of e-publishing, e-learning, and multimedia before she left the high-tech world to study cultural anthropology. She added a master of arts degree in cultural anthropology to her undergraduate degree in Spanish.

Since that time, she remains committed to her own learning, and at the same time she has opened self-development channels for others. Descriptive titles for her work include consultant, facilitator, change leader, coach for teams and their leaders, thought partner, public speaker, and workshop leader. She has worked in many industries, including health care sectors such as health care delivery and insurance, biotech, pharma, and medical devices.

Transformation—alchemy to turn managerial skills into leadership—is at the heart of Wendy's first book and is the focus of her work. She penned her book surrounded by lemons, a fruit she appreciates for its ability to add a zesty twist to almost any dish or drink. Today she serves up *InsideOut*.